SpringBoard®

English Language Arts
California Edition

Grade
9

CollegeBoard

ABOUT THE COLLEGE BOARD

The College Board is a mission-driven not-for-profit organization that connects students to college success and opportunity. Founded in 1900, the College Board was created to expand access to higher education. Today, the membership association is made up of more than 6,000 of the world's leading educational institutions and is dedicated to promoting excellence and equity in education. Each year, the College Board helps more than seven million students prepare for a successful transition to college through programs and services in college readiness and college success—including the SAT® and the Advanced Placement Program®. The organization also serves the education community through research and advocacy on behalf of students, educators and schools. For further information, visit www.collegeboard.com.

ISBN: 978-1-4573-0465-1

2 3 4 5 6 7 8   19 20 21 22
Printed in the United States of America

ACKNOWLEDGMENTS

The College Board gratefully acknowledges the outstanding work of the classroom teachers and writers who have been integral to the development of this revised program. The end product is testimony to their expertise, understanding of student learning needs, and dedication to rigorous and accessible English Language Arts instruction.

Colleen Ancrile
English Teacher
Los Angeles Unified School District
Sun Valley, California

Alli Bennett
Assistant Principal
Bethel School District 403
Spanaway, Washington

Kirstin A. Daniels
English Teacher
Sunnyside Unified School District
Tucson, Arizona

Paul DeMaret
SpringBoard/AP English Teacher
Poudre School District
Fort Collins, Colorado

Allison Fonseca
English Teacher
Hillsborough County Public Schools
Tampa, Florida

Karen Fullam
Advanced Academics Coordinator
Hillsborough County Public Schools
Tampa, Florida

Ron Lybarger
English Teacher/Department Head
Decatur Public School District #61
Decatur, Illinois

Glenn Morgan
English Teacher
San Diego Unified School District
San Diego, California

Michelle Nellon
English Teacher
Los Angeles Unified School District
Sun Valley, California

Carmen P. Padilla, M.Ed.
English Teacher
Los Angeles Unified School District
Los Angeles, California

Stephanie Sharpe
English Teacher
Hillsborough County Public Schools
Tampa, Florida

Susan Van Doren
English/AP English Language/AP
Computer Science Teacher
Douglas County School District
Zephyr Cove, Nevada

Rebecca Wenrich
English Teacher
Peninsula School District 401
Gig Harbor, Washington

Tom Wilkins
English Teacher
Fayette County Public Schools
Lexington, Kentucky

SPRINGBOARD ENGLISH LANGUAGE ARTS

Lori O'Dea
Executive Director
Content Development

Doug Waugh
Executive Director
Product Management

Joely Negedly
Senior Director
Humanities Curriculum and Instruction

JoEllen Victoreen
Senior Product Manager
English Language Arts

Julie Manley
Senior Director
Professional Learning

Sarah Balistreri
Director
ELA Content Development

Eden Orlando
SpringBoard District Coach

Jennifer Duva
English Language Arts Editor

Rebecca Grudzina
English Language Arts Editor

Spencer Gonçalves
Assistant ELA Editor

Jessica Pippin
Assistant ELA Editor

RESEARCH AND PLANNING ADVISORS

We also wish to thank the members of our SpringBoard Advisory Council and the many educators who gave generously of their time and their ideas as we conducted research for both the print and online programs. Your suggestions and reactions to ideas helped immeasurably as we planned the revisions. We gratefully acknowledge the teachers and administrators in the following districts.

ABC Unified School District
Cerritos, California

Bellevue School District 405
Bellevue, Washington

Charleston County School District
Charleston, South Carolina

Clark County School District
Las Vegas, Nevada

Denver Public Schools
Denver, Colorado

Hillsborough County Public Schools
Tampa, Florida

Kenton County School District
Fort Wright, Kentucky

Los Angeles Unified School District
Los Angeles, California

Milwaukee Public Schools
Milwaukee, Wisconsin

Newton County Schools
Covington, Georgia

Noblesville Schools
Noblesville, Indiana

Oakland Unified School District
Oakland, California

Orange County Public Schools
Orlando, Florida

Peninsula School District
Gig Harbor, Washington

Quakertown Community School District
Quakertown, Pennsylvania

St. Vrain School District
Longmont, Colorado

Scottsdale Public Schools
Phoenix, Arizona

Seminole County Public Schools
Sanford, Florida

Spokane Public Schools
Spokane, Washington

Contents

Unit 1 Coming of Age

Activities

Unit 2 Defining Style

Activities

Unit 3 Coming of Age in Changing Times

Activities

Unit 4 Exploring Poetic Voices

Activities

Unit 5 Coming of Age on Stage

Activities

To the Student

WELCOME TO SPRINGBOARD!

Dear Student,

Welcome to the SpringBoard program! This program has been created with you in mind: it contains the English Language Arts content you need to learn, the tools to help you learn, and tasks to strengthen the critical thinking skills that will help you succeed in high school and beyond.

In SpringBoard, you will explore compelling themes through reading, writing, discussions, performances, and research. You will closely read short stories, novels, poems, historical texts, and articles. You'll also view and interpret films, plays, and audio texts while comparing them to their related print versions. With frequent opportunities to write creatively and analytically throughout the program, you will develop fluency, research skills, and an understanding of how to craft your writing based on audience and purpose. Through collaborative discussions, presentations, performances, and debates with your peers, you will deepen your understanding of the texts you've read and viewed and learn how to convey your ideas with clarity and voice.

Tools to help you learn are built into every lesson. At the beginning of each activity, you will see suggested learning strategies, each of which is explained in full in the Resources section of your book. These strategies will help you deeply analyze text, collect evidence for your writing, and critically think about and discuss issues and ideas. Within the activities, you'll also notice explanations about essential vocabulary and grammar concepts that will enrich your ability to read and write effectively.

High school is the time to challenge yourself to develop skills and habits you need to be successful throughout your academic life and career. The SpringBoard program provides you with meaningful and engaging activities built on the rigorous standards that lead to college and career success. Your participation in SpringBoard will help you advance your reading, writing, language, and speaking and listening skills, all while helping you build confidence in your ability to succeed academically.

We hope you enjoy learning with the SpringBoard program. It will give you many opportunities to explore ideas and issues collaboratively and independently and to cultivate new skills as you prepare for your future.

Sincerely,

SpringBoard

AP CONNECTIONS

When you reach high school, you may have an opportunity to take Advanced Placement (AP) classes or other rigorous courses. When the time comes to make that decision, we want you to be equipped with the kind of higher-order thinking skills, knowledge, and behaviors necessary to be successful in AP classes and beyond. You will see connections to AP in the texts that you read, the strategies you use, and the writing tasks you encounter throughout the course.

Connections to AP Language and Literature will help you

- Read closely and analyze both literary and nonfiction texts

- Analyze relationships among author's purpose, literary/stylistic devices, rhetorical appeals, and desired effects for intended audiences

- Write with attention to selecting textual evidence and organizational patterns according to purpose and audience

- Write to interpret and evaluate multiple perspectives in literature

- Develop the control of language and command of conventions required for academic writing

THE SPRINGBOARD DIFFERENCE

SpringBoard is different because it provides instruction with hands-on participation that involves you and your classmates in daily discussions and analysis of what you're reading and learning. You will have an opportunity to

- Discuss and collaborate with your peers to explore and express your ideas

- Explore multiple perspectives by reading a variety of texts—both fiction and nonfiction—that introduce you to different ways of thinking, writing, and communicating

- Examine writing from the perspective of a reader and writer and learn techniques that good writers use to communicate their message effectively

- Gain a deep understanding of topics, enabling you to apply your learning to new and varied situations

- Take ownership of your learning by practicing and selecting strategies that work for you

- Reflect on your growth and showcase your best work as a reader, writer, speaker, and listener in a working Portfolio

HIGH SCHOOL AT A GLANCE
Grade 9

Investigating the thematic concept of **coming of age**, you will read Harper Lee's novel *To Kill a Mockingbird*; informational articles about college; short stories by Poe and Collier; historical articles about segregation; poetry by Wordsworth, Neruda, Lorde, and Silko; and Shakespeare's *Romeo and Juliet*. From your reading, you will gather evidence from texts and incorporate it in written and oral responses, including a presentation using multiple forms of media.

You will encounter more varied and complex writing in this grade as you write in a variety of modes including argumentative, explanatory, and narrative writing. Film texts are a large part of Grade 9 activities. In Unit 2, you will study a film director's style and analyze how style is evident in the transformation of print texts to films. In Unit 5, you will study *Romeo and Juliet* and analyze how key scenes are represented in multiple film versions as well as the print text.

Grade 10

In this grade, you will explore the thematic concept of culture. Texts include Chinua Achebe's *Things Fall Apart*, Sophocles' *Antigone*, Susan B. Anthony's "On Women's Right to Vote," and the Nobel Prize acceptance speeches of Alexander Solzhenitsyn and Elie Wiesel. You will be challenged to use evidence from these texts in both your written and oral responses. For example, you will study the extent to which one's culture influences one's worldview, and incorporate textual evidence in a written argument. Research plays a role as you investigate the Ibo culture represented in *Things Fall Apart* and present your findings in a collaborative presentation using digital media.

Film texts play a role when you analyze the degree of objectivity and subjectivity present in documentary films while also gathering evidence about environmental issues.

Grade 11

In this grade, you will explore concepts that have shaped American thought and discourse since its revolution through the study of American literature and rhetoric. You will read foundational U.S. documents such as Lincoln's Second Inaugural Address and The Declaration of Independence, essays by Ralph Waldo Emerson and Henry David Thoreau, and poetry by Langston Hughes and Walt Whitman. You will also read full-length works from the 20th century: Arthur Miller's drama *The Crucible*, Jon Krakauer's *Into the Wild*, and Zora Neale Hurston's *Their Eyes Were Watching God*. These texts will help you gather evidence to incorporate in writing, speeches, performances, and presentations about the American Dream, what it means to be an American, the freedom of speech, the role of media in a democracy, and literary movements like Transcendentalism and the Harlem Renaissance.

You will compare print and film versions of *Their Eyes Were Watching God*, and study various features of news outlets while working collaboratively to create your own news collection of news pieces.

Grade 12

Your SpringBoard journey culminates in Grade 12 with a year-long focus on using literary theory to analyze complex texts through multiple perspectives. You will encounter James Baldwin's "Stranger in the Village," George Orwell's "Shooting an Elephant," Shakespeare's *Othello*, and George Bernard Shaw's *Pygmalion*. Throughout the level, you will learn about and apply Archetypal, Cultural, Feminist, Historical, Marxist, and Reader Response Criticism to both literary and informational texts. You will also use your knowledge of these theories to shed new light on film, photography, and media coverage of newsworthy events, including Hurricane Katrina.

Senior English offers many opportunities for you to synthesize your learning through rigorous writing and speaking tasks. Independent research, film study, and presentations go hand in hand with your study of print texts, and allow you to develop complex and nuanced understandings of the texts, films, and issues in the course.

CLASSROOM TOOLS

As you move through each SpringBoard unit, your teacher will guide you to use tools that will help you develop strong study habits, keep your work organized, and track your learning progress.

Reader/Writer Notebook

Your **Reader/Writer Notebook** is a place to record and keep track of vocabulary words, grammar practice, notes and reflections on readings, some writing assignments, brainstorms, and other items as determined by your teacher. You will use your Reader/Writer Notebook often, so think of it as an extension of the main SpringBoard book.

Word Wall

Your teacher will regularly add new vocabulary words to the class **Word Wall**. The Word Wall gives you and your classmates a visual reminder of the words you are learning throughout the unit of study. Also, you can use the Word Wall to easily check the spelling of new words.

Performance Portfolio

Your **Performance Portfolio** is a place to keep your assignments organized so that you can see your growth and learning across the school year. Keeping a portfolio will make it easier to share your work with others, reflect on what you are learning, revise certain pieces of work, and set goals for future learning.

Your teacher will guide you to include items in your portfolio that illustrate a wide range of work, such as first drafts, final drafts, quickwrites, notes, reading logs, graphic organizers, audio and video examples, and graphics that represent a variety of genres, forms, and media created for a multitude of purposes. As you progress through the course, you will have opportunities to revisit prior work, revise it based on new learning, and reflect on the learning strategies and activities that help you be successful.

Independent Reading

Based on your personal interests and preferences, you will be encouraged to select books, articles, and other texts to read independently. Reading independently not only reinforces the learning you're doing in class, but it also gives you a chance to expand your knowledge about topics that fascinate you.

You can find **Independent Reading Lists** in the Resources section at the back of your book. The lists provide ideas for texts that complement the reading you're doing in each SpringBoard unit. These are suggestions to get you started, but you may also choose other readings with input from your teacher, family, and peers.

While you work your way through each SpringBoard unit, your teacher will give you time to read independently. You can record general thoughts or reactions to your independent reading in the **Independent Reading Log** in the Resources section of your book. You may also use the Independent Reading Log to respond to the occasional **Independent Reading Links** that you'll encounter in each SpringBoard unit. These links prompt you to think about your independent reading by responding to questions, doing research, making connections between texts and themes, discussing ideas in book groups, and recommending titles to your classmates.

We hope you enjoy exploring the texts, topics, and themes in SpringBoard and that you feel inspired to deepen your reading, writing, speaking, and analytic skills through the program.

California Common Core State Standards

Reading Standards for Literature

Key Ideas and Details	RL.9–10.1	Cite strong and thorough textual evidence to support analysis of what the text says explicitly as well as inferences drawn from the text.
	RL.9–10.2	Determine a theme or central idea of a text and analyze in detail its development over the course of the text, including how it emerges and is shaped and refined by specific details; provide an objective summary of the text.
	RL.9–10.3	Analyze how complex characters (e.g., those with multiple or conflicting motivations) develop over the course of a text, interact with other characters, and advance the plot or develop the theme.
Craft and Structure	RL.9–10.4	Determine the meaning of words and phrases as they are used in the text, including figurative and connotative meanings; analyze the cumulative impact of specific word choices on meaning and tone (e.g., how the language evokes a sense of time and place; how it sets a formal or informal tone). **(See grade 9–10 Language standards 4–6 for additional expectations.) CA**
	RL.9–10.5	Analyze how an author's choices concerning how to structure a text, order events within it (e.g., parallel plots), and manipulate time (e.g., pacing, flashbacks) create such effects as mystery, tension, or surprise.
	RL.9–10.6	Analyze a particular point of view or cultural experience reflected in a work of literature from outside the United States, drawing on a wide reading of world literature.
Integration of Knowledge and Ideas	RL.9–10.7	Analyze the representation of a subject or a key scene in two different artistic mediums, including what is emphasized or absent in each treatment (e.g., Auden's "Musée des Beaux Arts" and Breughel's *Landscape with the Fall of Icarus*).
	RL.9–10.8	(Not applicable to literature)
	RL.9–10.9	Analyze how an author draws on and transforms source material in a specific work (e.g., how Shakespeare treats a theme or topic from Ovid or the Bible or how a later author draws on a play by Shakespeare).
Range of Reading and Level of Text Complexity	RL.9–10.10	By the end of grade 9, read and comprehend literature, including stories, dramas, and poems, in the grades 9–10 text complexity band proficiently, with scaffolding as needed at the high end of the range. By the end of grade 10, read and comprehend literature, including stories, dramas, and poems, at the high end of the grades 9–10 text complexity band independently and proficiently.

Reading Standards for Informational Text

Key Ideas and Details	RI.9–10.1	Cite strong and thorough textual evidence to support analysis of what the text says explicitly as well as inferences drawn from the text.
	RI.9–10.2	Determine a central idea of a text and analyze its development over the course of the text, including how it emerges and is shaped and refined by specific details; provide an objective summary of the text.
	RI.9–10.3	Analyze how the author unfolds an analysis or series of ideas or events, including the order in which the points are made, how they are introduced and developed, and the connections that are drawn between them.
Craft and Structure	RI.9–10.4	Determine the meaning of words and phrases as they are used in a text, including figurative, connotative, and technical meanings; analyze the cumulative impact of specific word choices on meaning and tone (e.g., how the language of a court opinion differs from that of a newspaper). **(See grade 9–10 Language standards 4–6 for additional expectations.) CA**
	RI.9–10.5	Analyze in detail how an author's ideas or claims are developed and refined by particular sentences, paragraphs, or larger portions of a text (e.g., a section or chapter).
	RI.9–10.5a	**Analyze the use of text features (e.g., graphics, headers, captions) in functional workplace documents. CA**
	RI.9–10.6	Determine an author's point of view or purpose in a text and analyze how an author uses rhetoric to advance that point of view or purpose.
Integration of Knowledge and Ideas	RI.9–10.7	Analyze various accounts of a subject told in different mediums (e.g., a person's life story in both print and multimedia), determining which details are emphasized in each account.
	RI.9–10.8	Delineate and evaluate the argument and specific claims in a text, assessing whether the reasoning is valid and the evidence is relevant and sufficient; identify false statements and fallacious reasoning.
	RI.9–10.9	Analyze seminal U.S. documents of historical and literary significance (e.g., Washington's Farewell Address, the Gettysburg Address, Roosevelt's Four Freedoms speech, King's "Letter from Birmingham Jail"), including how they address related themes and concepts.
Range of Reading and Level of Text Complexity	RI.9–10.10	By the end of grade 9, read and comprehend literary nonfiction in the grades 9–10 text complexity band proficiently, with scaffolding as needed at the high end of the range. By the end of grade 10, read and comprehend literary nonfiction at the high end of the grades 9–10 text complexity band independently and proficiently.

Writing Standards

Text Types and Purposes	W.9–10.1	Write arguments to support claims in an analysis of substantive topics or texts, using valid reasoning and relevant and sufficient evidence.
	W.9–10.1a	Introduce precise claim(s), distinguish the claim(s) from alternate or opposing claims, and create an organization that establishes clear relationships among claim(s), counterclaims, reasons, and evidence.
	W.9–10.1b	Develop claim(s) and counterclaims fairly, supplying evidence for each while pointing out the strengths and limitations of both in a manner that anticipates the audience's knowledge level and concerns.
	W.9–10.1c	Use words, phrases, and clauses to link the major sections of the text, create cohesion, and clarify the relationships between claim(s) and reasons, between reasons and evidence, and between claim(s) and counterclaims.
	W.9–10.1d	Establish and maintain a formal style and objective tone while attending to the norms and conventions of the discipline in which they are writing.
	W.9–10.1e	Provide a concluding statement or section that follows from and supports the argument presented.
	W.9–10.2	Write informative/explanatory texts to examine and convey complex ideas, concepts, and information clearly and accurately through the effective selection, organization, and analysis of content.
	W.9–10.2a	Introduce a topic **or thesis statement**; organize complex ideas, concepts, and information to make important connections and distinctions; include formatting (e.g., headings), graphics (e.g., figures, tables), and multimedia when useful to aiding comprehension. **CA**
	W.9–10.2b	Develop the topic with well-chosen, relevant, and sufficient facts, extended definitions, concrete details, quotations, or other information and examples appropriate to the audience's knowledge of the topic.
	W.9–10.2c	Use appropriate and varied transitions to link the major sections of the text, create cohesion, and clarify the relationships among complex ideas and concepts.
	W.9–10.2d	Use precise language and domain-specific vocabulary to manage the complexity of the topic.
	W.9–10.2e	Establish and maintain a formal style and objective tone while attending to the norms and conventions of the discipline in which they are writing.

Writing Standards

Text Types and Purposes	W.9–10.2f	Provide a concluding statement or section that follows from and supports the information or explanation presented (e.g., articulating implications or the significance of the topic).
	W.9–10.3	Write narratives to develop real or imagined experiences or events using effective technique, well-chosen details, and well-structured event sequences.
	W.9–10.3a	Engage and orient the reader by setting out a problem, situation, or observation, establishing one or multiple point(s) of view, and introducing a narrator and/or characters; create a smooth progression of experiences or events.
	W.9–10.3b	Use narrative techniques, such as dialogue, pacing, description, reflection, and multiple plot lines, to develop experiences, events, and/or characters.
	W.9–10.3c	Use a variety of techniques to sequence events so that they build on one another to create a coherent whole.
	W.9–10.3d	Use precise words and phrases, telling details, and sensory language to convey a vivid picture of the experiences, events, setting, and/or characters.
	W.9–10.3e	Provide a conclusion that follows from and reflects on what is experienced, observed, or resolved over the course of the narrative.
Production and Distribution of Writing	W.9–10.4	Produce clear and coherent writing in which the development, organization, and style are appropriate to task, purpose, and audience. (Grade-specific expectations for writing types are defined in standards 1–3 above.)
	W.9–10.5	Develop and strengthen writing as needed by planning, revising, editing, rewriting, or trying a new approach, focusing on addressing what is most significant for a specific purpose and audience. (Editing for conventions should demonstrate command of Language standards 1–3 up to and including grades 9–10.)
	W.9–10.6	Use technology, including the Internet, to produce, publish, and update individual or shared writing products, taking advantage of technology's capacity to link to other information and to display information flexibly and dynamically.
Research to Build and Present Knowledge	W.9–10.7	Conduct short as well as more sustained research projects to answer a question (including a self-generated question) or solve a problem; narrow or broaden the inquiry when appropriate; synthesize multiple sources on the subject, demonstrating understanding of the subject under investigation.

Writing Standards

Research to Build and Present Knowledge	W.9–10.8	Gather relevant information from multiple authoritative print and digital sources, using advanced searches effectively; assess the usefulness of each source in answering the research question; integrate information into the text selectively to maintain the flow of ideas, avoiding plagiarism and following a standard format for citation **including footnotes and endnotes. CA**
	W.9–10.9	Draw evidence from literary or informational texts to support analysis, reflection, and research.
	W.9–10.9a	Apply *grades 9–10 Reading standards* to literature (e.g., "Analyze how an author draws on and transforms source material in a specific work [e.g., how Shakespeare treats a theme or topic from Ovid or the Bible or how a later author draws on a play by Shakespeare]").
	W.9–10.9b	Apply *grades 9–10 Reading standards* to literary nonfiction (e.g., "Delineate and evaluate the argument and specific claims in a text, assessing whether the reasoning is valid and the evidence is relevant and sufficient; identify false statements and fallacious reasoning").
Range of Writing	W.9–10.10	Write routinely over extended time frames (time for research, reflection, and revision) and shorter time frames (a single sitting or a day or two) for a range of tasks, purposes, and audiences.

Speaking and Listening Standards

Comprehension and Collaboration	SL.9–10.1	Initiate and participate effectively in a range of collaborative discussions (one-on-one, in groups, and teacher-led) with diverse partners on *grades 9–10 topics, texts, and issues*, building on others' ideas and expressing their own clearly and persuasively.
	SL.9–10.1a	Come to discussions prepared, having read and researched material under study; explicitly draw on that preparation by referring to evidence from texts and other research on the topic or issue to stimulate a thoughtful, well-reasoned exchange of ideas.
	SL.9–10.1b	Work with peers to set rules for collegial discussions and decision-making (e.g., informal consensus, taking votes on key issues, presentation of alternate views), clear goals and deadlines, and individual roles as needed.
	SL.9–10.1c	Propel conversations by posing and responding to questions that relate the current discussion to broader themes or larger ideas; actively incorporate others into the discussion; and clarify, verify, or challenge ideas and conclusions.
	SL.9–10.1d	Respond thoughtfully to diverse perspectives, summarize points of agreement and disagreement, and, when warranted, qualify or justify their own views and understanding and make new connections in light of the evidence and reasoning presented.
	SL.9–10.2	Integrate multiple sources of information presented in diverse media or formats (e.g., visually, quantitatively, orally) evaluating the credibility and accuracy of each source.
	SL.9–10.3	Evaluate a speaker's point of view, reasoning, and use of evidence and rhetoric, identifying any fallacious reasoning or exaggerated or distorted evidence.
Presentation of Knowledge and Ideas	SL.9–10.4	Present information, findings, and supporting evidence clearly, concisely, and logically **(using appropriate eye contact, adequate volume, and clear pronunciation)** such that listeners can follow the line of reasoning and the organization, development, substance, and style are appropriate to purpose **(e.g., argument, narrative, informative, response to literature presentations)**, audience, and task. **CA**
	SL.9–10.4a	**Plan and deliver an informative/explanatory presentation that: presents evidence in support of a thesis, conveys information from primary and secondary sources coherently, uses domain specific vocabulary, and provides a conclusion that summarizes the main points. (9th or 10th grade) CA**
	SL.9–10.4b	**Plan, memorize, and present a recitation (e.g., poem, selection from a speech or dramatic soliloquy) that: conveys the meaning of the selection and includes appropriate performance techniques (e.g., tone, rate, voice modulation) to achieve the desired aesthetic effect. (9th or 10th grade) CA**
	SL.9–10.5	Make strategic use of digital media (e.g., textual, graphical, audio, visual, and interactive elements) in presentations to enhance understanding of findings, reasoning, and evidence and to add interest.
	SL.9–10.6	Adapt speech to a variety of contexts and tasks, demonstrating command of formal English when indicated or appropriate. (See grades 9–10 Language standards 1 and 3 for specific expectations.)

Language Standards

Conventions of Standard English	L.9–10.1	Demonstrate command of the conventions of standard English grammar and usage when writing or speaking.
	L.9–10.1a	Use parallel structure.*
	L.9–10.1b	Use various types of phrases (noun, verb, adjectival, adverbial, participial, prepositional, absolute) and clauses (independent, dependent; noun, relative, adverbial) to convey specific meanings and add variety and interest to writing or presentations.
	L.9–10.2	Demonstrate command of the conventions of standard English capitalization, punctuation, and spelling when writing.
	L.9–10.2a	Use a semicolon (and perhaps a conjunctive adverb) to link two or more closely related independent clauses.
	L.9–10.2b	Use a colon to introduce a list or quotation.
	L.9–10.2c	Spell correctly.
Knowledge of Language	L.9–10.3	Apply knowledge of language to understand how language functions in different contexts, to make effective choices for meaning or style, and to comprehend more fully when reading or listening.
	L.9–10.3a	Write and edit work so that it conforms to the guidelines in a style manual (e.g., *MLA Handbook*, Turabian's *Manual for Writers*) appropriate for the discipline and writing type.
Vocabulary Acquisition and Use	L.9–10.4	Determine or clarify the meaning of unknown and multiple-meaning words and phrases based on *grades 9–10 reading and content*, choosing flexibly from a range of strategies.
	L.9–10.4a	Use context (e.g., the overall meaning of a sentence, paragraph, or text; a word's position or function in a sentence) as a clue to the meaning of a word or phrase.
	L.9–10.4b	Identify and correctly use patterns of word changes that indicate different meanings or parts of speech (e.g., *analyze, analysis, analytical; advocate, advocacy*) and **continue to apply knowledge of Greek and Latin roots and affixes. CA**
	L.9–10.4c	Consult general and specialized reference materials (e.g., **college-level** dictionaries, **rhyming dictionaries, bilingual dictionaries**, glossaries, thesauruses), both print and digital, to find the pronunciation of a word or determine or clarify its precise meaning, its part of speech, or its etymology. **CA**
	L.9–10.4d	Verify the preliminary determination of the meaning of a word or phrase (e.g., by checking the inferred meaning in context or in a dictionary).

Language Standards

Vocabulary Acquisition and Use	L.9–10.5	Demonstrate understanding of figurative language, word relationships, and nuances in word meanings.
	L.9–10.5a	Interpret figures of speech (e.g., euphemism, oxymoron) in context and analyze their role in the text.
	L.9–10.5b	Analyze nuances in the meaning of words with similar denotations.
	L.9–10.6	Acquire and use accurately general academic and domain-specific words and phrases, sufficient for reading, writing, speaking, and listening at the college and career readiness level; demonstrate independence in gathering vocabulary knowledge when considering a word or phrase important to comprehension or expression.

California English Language Development Standard

Part I: Interacting in Meaningful Ways

Communicative Modes	Standard Code	Emerging	Expanding	Bridging
Collaborative	PI.9–10.1	**Exchanging information/ideas** Engage in conversational exchanges and express ideas on familiar current events and academic topics by asking and answering *yes-no* questions and *wh-* questions and responding using phrases and short sentences.	**Exchanging information/ideas** Contribute to class, group, and partner discussions, sustaining conversations on a variety of age and grade-appropriate academic topics by following turn-taking rules, asking and answering relevant, on-topic questions, affirming others, providing additional, relevant information, and paraphrasing key ideas.	**Exchanging information/ideas** Contribute to class, group, and partner discussions, sustaining conversations on a variety of age and grade-appropriate academic topics by following turn-taking rules, asking and answering relevant, on-topic questions, affirming others, and providing coherent and well-articulated comments and additional information.
	PI.9–10.2	**Interacting via written English** Collaborate with peers to engage in short, grade-appropriate written exchanges and writing projects, using technology as appropriate.	**Interacting via written English** Collaborate with peers to engage in increasingly complex grade-appropriate written exchanges and writing projects, using technology as appropriate.	**Interacting via written English** Collaborate with peers to engage in a variety of extended written exchanges and complex grade-appropriate writing projects, using technology as appropriate.
	PI.9–10.3	**Supporting opinions and persuading others** Negotiate with or persuade others in conversations using learned phrases (e.g., *Would you say that again? I think … *), as well as open responses to express and defend opinions.	**Supporting opinions and persuading others** Negotiate with or persuade others in conversations (e.g., to provide counter-arguments) using a growing number of learned phrases (*I see your point, but …*) and open responses to express and defend nuanced opinions.	**Supporting opinions and persuading others** Negotiate with or persuade others in conversations in appropriate registers (e.g., to acknowledge new information in an academic conversation but then politely offer a counterpoint) using a variety of learned phrases, indirect reported speech (e.g., *I heard you say X, and I haven't thought about that before. However …*), and open responses to express and defend nuanced opinions.
	PI.9–10.4	**Adapting language choices** Adjust language choices according to the context (e.g., classroom, community) and audience (e.g., peers, teachers).	**Adapting language choices** Adjust language choices according to the context (e.g., classroom, community), purpose (e.g., to persuade, to provide arguments or counterarguments), task, and audience (e.g., peers, teachers, guest lecturer).	**Adapting language choices** Adjust language choices according to the task (e.g., group presentation of research project), context (e.g., classroom, community), purpose (e.g., to persuade, to provide arguments or counterarguments), and audience (e.g., peers, teachers, college recruiter).

Communicative Modes	Standard Code	Emerging	Expanding	Bridging
Interpretive	PI.9–10.5	**Listening actively** Demonstrate comprehension of oral presentations and discussions on familiar social and academic topics by asking and answering questions, with prompting and substantial support.	**Listening actively** Demonstrate comprehension of oral presentations and discussions on a variety of social and academic topics by asking and answering questions that show thoughtful consideration of the ideas or arguments, with moderate support.	**Listening actively** Demonstrate comprehension of oral presentations and discussions on a variety of social and academic topics by asking and answering detailed and complex questions that show thoughtful consideration of the ideas or arguments, with light support.
	PI.9–10.6a	**Reading/viewing closely** Explain ideas, phenomena, processes, and text relationships (e.g., compare/contrast, cause/effect, evidence-based argument) based on close reading of a variety of grade-appropriate texts, presented in various print and multimedia formats, using short sentences and a select set of general academic and domain-specific words.	**Reading/viewing closely** Explain ideas, phenomena, processes, and relationships within and across texts (e.g., compare/contrast, cause/effect, themes, evidence-based argument) based on close reading of a variety of grade-appropriate texts, presented in various print and multimedia formats, using increasingly detailed sentences, and an increasing variety of general academic and domain-specific words.	**Reading/viewing closely** Explain ideas, phenomena, processes, and relationships within and across texts (e.g., compare/contrast, cause/effect, themes, evidence-based argument) based on close reading of a variety of grade-level texts, presented in various print and multimedia formats, using a variety of detailed sentences and a range of general academic and domain-specific words.
	PI.9–10.6b	**Reading/viewing closely** Explain inferences and conclusions drawn from close reading of grade-appropriate texts and viewing of multimedia using familiar verbs (e.g., *seems that*).	**Reading/viewing closely** Explain inferences and conclusions drawn from close reading of grade-appropriate texts and viewing of multimedia using an increasing variety of verbs and adverbials (e.g., *indicates that, suggests, as a result*).	**Reading/viewing closely** Explain inferences and conclusions drawn from close reading of grade-level texts and viewing of multimedia using a variety of verbs and adverbials (e.g., *creates the impression that, consequently*).
	PI.9–10.6c	**Reading/viewing closely** Use knowledge of morphology (e.g., common prefixes and suffixes), context, reference materials, and visual cues to determine the meaning of unknown and multiple-meaning words on familiar topics.	**Reading/viewing closely** Use knowledge of morphology (e.g., affixes, Greek and Latin roots), context, reference materials, and visual cues to determine the meaning of unknown and multiple-meaning words on familiar and new topics.	**Reading/viewing closely** Use knowledge of morphology (e.g., derivational suffixes), context, reference materials, and visual cues to determine the meaning, including figurative and connotative meanings, of unknown and multiple-meaning words on a variety of new topics.

Communicative Modes	Standard Code	Emerging	Expanding	Bridging
Interpretive	PI.9–10.7	**Evaluating language choices** Explain how successfully writers and speakers structure texts and use language (e.g., specific word or phrasing choices) to persuade the reader (e.g., by providing evidence to support claims or connecting points in an argument) or create other specific effects, with substantial support.	**Evaluating language choices** Explain how successfully writers and speakers structure texts and use language (e.g., specific word or phrasing choices) to persuade the reader (e.g., by providing well-worded evidence to support claims or connecting points in an argument in specific ways) or create other specific effects, with moderate support.	**Evaluating language choices** Explain how successfully writers and speakers structure texts and use language (e.g., specific word or phrasing choices) to persuade the reader (e.g., by providing well-worded evidence to support claims or connecting points in an argument in specific ways) or create other specific effects, with light support.
	PI.9–10.8	**Analyzing language choices** Explain how a writer's or speaker's choice of phrasing or specific words (e.g., describing a character or action as *aggressive* versus *bold*) produces nuances and different effects on the audience.	**Analyzing language choices** Explain how a writer's or speaker's choice of phrasing or specific words (e.g., using figurative language or words with multiple meanings to describe an event or character) produces nuances and different effects on the audience.	**Analyzing language choices** Explain how a writer's or speaker's choice of a variety of different types of phrasing or words (e.g., hyperbole, varying connotations, the cumulative impact of word choices) produces nuances and different effects on the audience.
Productive	PI.9–10.9	**Presenting** Plan and deliver brief oral presentations and reports on grade-appropriate topics that present evidence and facts to support ideas.	**Presenting** Plan and deliver a variety of oral presentations and reports on grade-appropriate topics that present evidence and facts to support ideas by using growing understanding of register.	**Presenting** Plan and deliver a variety of oral presentations and reports on grade-appropriate topics that express complex and abstract ideas well supported by evidence and sound reasoning, and are delivered using an appropriate level of formality and understanding of register.
	PI.9–10.10a	**Writing** Write short literary and informational texts (e.g., an argument about water rights) collaboratively (e.g., with peers) and independently.	**Writing** Write longer literary and informational texts (e.g., an argument about water rights) collaboratively (e.g., with peers) and independently by using appropriate text organization and growing understanding of register.	**Writing** Write longer and more detailed literary and informational texts (e.g., an argument about water rights) collaboratively (e.g., with peers) and independently using appropriate text organization and register.

Communicative Modes	Standard Code	Emerging	Expanding	Bridging
Productive	PI.9–10.10b	**Writing** Write brief summaries of texts and experiences by using complete sentences and key words (e.g., from notes or graphic organizers).	**Writing** Write increasingly concise summaries of texts and experiences by using complete sentences and key words (e.g., from notes or graphic organizers).	**Writing** Write clear and coherent summaries of texts and experiences by using complete and concise sentences and key words (e.g., from notes or graphic organizers).
	PI.9–10.11a	**Justifying/arguing** Justify opinions by articulating some relevant textual evidence or background knowledge, with visual support.	**Justifying/arguing** Justify opinions and positions or persuade others by making connections between ideas and articulating relevant textual evidence or background knowledge.	**Justifying/arguing** Justify opinions or persuade others by making connections and distinctions between ideas and texts and articulating sufficient, detailed, and relevant textual evidence or background knowledge, using appropriate register.
	PI.9–10.11b	**Justifying/arguing** Express attitude and opinions or temper statements with familiar modal expressions (e.g., *can, may*).	**Justifying/arguing** Express attitude and opinions or temper statements with a variety of familiar modal expressions (e.g., *possibly/likely, could/would*).	**Justifying/arguing** Express attitude and opinions or temper statements with nuanced modal expressions (e.g., *possibly/potentially/certainly/absolutely, should/might*).
	PI.9–10.12a	**Selecting language resources** Use familiar general academic (e.g., *temperature, document*) and domain-specific (e.g., *characterization, photosynthesis, society, quadratic functions*) words to create clear spoken and written texts.	**Selecting language resources** Use an increasing variety of grade-appropriate general academic (e.g., *dominate, environment*) and domain-specific (e.g., *characterization, photosynthesis, society, quadratic functions*) academic words accurately and appropriately when producing increasingly complex written and spoken texts.	**Selecting language resources** Use a variety of grade-appropriate general (e.g., *anticipate, transaction*) and domain-specific (e.g., *characterization, photosynthesis, society, quadratic functions*) academic words and phrases, including persuasive language, accurately and appropriately when producing complex written and spoken texts.
	PI.9–10.12b	**Selecting language resources** Use knowledge of morphology to appropriately select basic affixes (e.g., The skull protects the brain).	**Selecting language resources** Use knowledge of morphology to appropriately select affixes in a growing number of ways to manipulate language (e.g., diplomatic, stems are branch*ed* or unbranch*ed*).	**Selecting language resources** Use knowledge of morphology to appropriately select affixes in a variety of ways to manipulate language (e.g., changing *humiliate* to *humiliation* or *incredible* to *incredibly*).

Part II: Learning About How English Works

Language Processes	Standard Code	Emerging	Expanding	Bridging
Structuring Cohesive Texts	PII.9–10.1	**Understanding text structure** Apply analysis of the organizational structure of different text types (e.g., how arguments are organized by establishing clear relationships among claims, counterclaims, reasons, and evidence) to comprehending texts and to writing brief arguments, informative/explanatory texts and narratives.	**Understanding text structure** Apply analysis of the organizational structure of different text types (e.g., how arguments are organized by establishing clear relationships among claims, counterclaims, reasons, and evidence) to comprehending texts and to writing increasingly clear and cohesive arguments, informative/explanatory texts and narratives.	**Understanding text structure** Apply analysis of the organizational structure of different text types (e.g., how arguments are organized by establishing clear relationships among claims, counterclaims, reasons, and evidence) to comprehending texts and to writing clear and cohesive arguments, informative/explanatory texts and narratives.
	PII.9–10.2a	**Understanding cohesion** Apply knowledge of familiar language resources for referring to make texts more cohesive (e.g., using pronouns to refer back to nouns in text) to comprehending and writing brief texts.	**Understanding cohesion** Apply knowledge of a growing number of language resources for referring to make texts more cohesive (e.g., using nominalizations to refer back to an action or activity described earlier) to comprehending texts and to writing increasingly cohesive texts for specific purposes and audiences.	**Understanding cohesion** Apply knowledge of a variety of language resources for referring to make texts more cohesive (e.g., using nominalization, paraphrasing, or summaries to reference or recap an idea or explanation provided earlier) to comprehending grade-level texts and to writing clear and cohesive grade-level texts for specific purposes and audiences.
	PII.9–10.2b	**Understanding cohesion** Apply knowledge of familiar language resources for linking ideas, events, or reasons throughout a text (e.g., using connecting/transition words and phrases, such as *first, second, third*) to comprehending and writing brief texts.	**Understanding cohesion** Apply knowledge of familiar language resources for linking ideas, events, or reasons throughout a text (e.g., using connecting/transition words and phrases, such as *meanwhile, however, on the other hand*) to comprehending texts and to writing increasingly cohesive texts for specific purposes and audiences.	**Understanding cohesion** Apply knowledge of familiar language resources for linking ideas, events, or reasons throughout a text (e.g., using connecting/transition words and phrases, such as *on the contrary, in addition, moreover*) to comprehending grade-level texts and to writing cohesive texts for specific purposes and audiences.

Language Processes	Standard Code	Emerging	Expanding	Bridging
Expanding and Enriching Ideas	PII.9–10.3	**Using verbs and verb phrases** Use a variety of verbs in different tenses (e.g., past, present, future, simple, progressive) appropriate to the text type and discipline to create short texts on familiar academic topics.	**Using verbs and verb phrases** Use a variety of verbs in different tenses (e.g., past, present, future, simple, progressive, perfect) appropriate to the text type and discipline to create a variety of texts that explain, describe, and summarize concrete and abstract thoughts and ideas.	**Using verbs and verb phrases** Use a variety of verbs in different tenses (e.g., past, present, future, simple, progressive, perfect), and mood (e.g., subjunctive) appropriate to the text type and discipline to create a variety of texts that describe concrete and abstract ideas, explain procedures and sequences, summarize texts and ideas, and present and critique points of view.
	PII.9–10.4	**Using nouns and noun phrases** Expand noun phrases to create increasingly detailed sentences (e.g., adding adjectives for precision) about personal and familiar academic topics.	**Using nouns and noun phrases** Expand noun phrases in a growing number of ways (e.g., adding adjectives to nouns; simple clause embedding) to create detailed sentences that accurately describe, explain, and summarize information and ideas on a variety of personal and academic topics.	**Using nouns and noun phrases** Expand noun phrases in a variety of ways (e.g., more complex clause embedding) to create detailed sentences that accurately describe concrete and abstract ideas, explain procedures and sequences, summarize texts and ideas, and present and critique points of view on a variety of academic topics.
	PII.9–10.5	**Modifying to add details** Expand sentences with simple adverbials (e.g., adverbs, adverb phrases, prepositional phrases) to provide details (e.g., time, manner, place, cause) about familiar activities or processes.	**Modifying to add details** Expand sentences with a growing variety of adverbials (e.g., adverbs, adverb phrases, prepositional phrases) to provide details (e.g., time, manner, place, cause) about familiar or new activities or processes.	**Modifying to add details** Expand sentences with a variety of adverbials (e.g., adverbs, adverb phrases and clauses, prepositional phrases) to provide details (e.g., time, manner, place, cause) about a variety of familiar and new activities and processes.

Language Processes	Standard Code	Emerging	Expanding	Bridging
Connecting and Condensing Ideas	PII.9–10.6	**Connecting ideas** Combine clauses in a few basic ways (e.g., creating compound sentences using *and, but, so;* creating complex sentences using *because*) to make connections between and to join ideas (e.g., *I want to read this book because it describes the solar system*).	**Connecting ideas** Combine clauses in a growing number of ways to create compound and complex sentences that make connections between and link concrete and abstract ideas, for example, to express a reason (e.g., *He stayed at home on Sunday in order to study for Monday's exam*) or to make a concession (e.g., *She studied all night even though she wasn't feeling well*).	**Connecting ideas** Combine clauses in a variety of ways to create compound and complex sentences that make connections between and link concrete and abstract ideas, for example, to make a concession (e.g., *While both characters strive for success, they each take different approaches through which to reach their goals.*), or to establish cause (e.g., *Women's lives were changed forever after World War II as a result of joining the workforce*).
	PII.9–10.7	**Condensing ideas** Condense ideas in a few basic ways (e.g., by compounding verb or prepositional phrases) to create precise and detailed simple, compound, and complex sentences (e.g., *The students asked survey questions and recorded the responses*).	**Condensing ideas** Condense ideas in a growing number of ways (e.g., through embedded clauses or by compounding verbs or prepositional phrases) to create more precise and detailed simple, compound, and complex sentences (e.g., *Species that could not adapt to the changing climate eventually disappeared*).	**Condensing ideas** Condense ideas in a variety of ways (e.g., through a variety of embedded clauses, or by compounding verbs or prepositional phrases, nominalization) to create precise simple, compound, and complex sentences that condense concrete and abstract ideas (e.g., *Another issue that people may be concerned with is the amount of money that it will cost to construct the new building*).
Foundational Literacy Skills: Literacy in an Alphabetic Writing System • Print concepts • Phonological awareness • Phonics and word recognition • Fluency	PIII.9–10	**See Chapter 6 [of the California ELD Standards] for information on teaching reading foundational skills to English learners of various profiles based on age, native language, native language writing system, schooling experience, and literacy experience and proficiency. Some considerations are as follows:** • Native language and literacy (e.g., phoneme awareness or print concept skills in native language) should be assessed for potential transference to English language and literacy. • Similarities between the native language and English should be highlighted (e.g., phonemes or letters that are the same in both languages). • Differences between native language and English should be highlighted (e.g., some phonemes in English may not exist in the student's native language; native language syntax may be different from English syntax).		

Coming of Age

Visual Prompt: What comes to mind when you hear the phrase "coming of age"?

Unit Overview

Ninth grade marks the beginning of many important transitions, including the experience of becoming an adult. In this unit, you will explore the theme of coming of age and examine how writers in a variety of texts use stylistic choices to create the voices of characters who are going through life-changing experiences. Along the way, you will study texts independently, conduct interviews, analyze arguments regarding the value of postsecondary education, and examine the complex relationship between an author's purpose, his or her audience, and the ways in which he or she appeals to readers. By the end of the unit, your academic coming of age will be marked by a heightened understanding of voice, appeals, and persuasive techniques.

Coming of Age

Contents

Activities

Language and Writer's Craft
- Verb Mood (1.5)
- Parallel Structure (1.15)

MY INDEPENDENT
READING LIST

_____
_____
_____
_____
_____
_____
_____
_____
_____
_____
_____
_____
_____
_____
_____
_____
_____
_____
_____
_____
_____

Previewing the Unit

My Notes

Learning Targets

- Preview the big ideas and the vocabulary for the unit.
- Identify and anaylze the skills and knowledge needed to successfully complete Embedded Assessment 1.
- Develop strategies for completing Embedded Assessment 1.

Making Connections

As you read about coming of age, you will learn about voice and style, the characteristics that make a writer's or speaker's work distinctive. You will evaluate texts and make inferences based on textual evidence. Then you will conduct an interview and write an interview narrative in which you capture the voice of the interviewee.

Essential Questions

Based on your current knowledge, write answers to these questions in the My Notes space.

1. What does it mean to "come of age"?
2. How do authors and speakers persuade and influence an audience?

Developing Vocabulary

Go back to the Contents page and use a QHT strategy to analyze and evaluate your knowledge of the Academic Vocabulary and Literary Terms for the unit. As a reminder, use the "Q" to identify words you do not know, an "H" for words you have heard and might be able to identify, and a "T" for words you know well enough to teach to someone else.

Unpacking Embedded Assessment 1

Read the following assignment for Embedded Assessment 1, and summarize the major elements in your Reader/Writer Notebook.

> Your assignment is to interview a person who has attended a postsecondary institution (i.e., a two- or four-year college, a training or vocational school, the military). From that interview, you will write a narrative that effectively portrays the voice of the interviewee while revealing how the experience contributed to his or her coming of age.

Summarize in your own words what you will need to know for this assessment. With your class, create a graphic organizer that represents the skills and knowledge you will need to accomplish this task and **strategize** how you will complete the assignment. To help you complete your graphic organizer, be sure to review the criteria in the Scoring Guide on page 55.

Independent Reading Plan

Reading independently gives you a chance to expand your knowledge about topics that fascinate you while also reinforcing and deepening the learning you are doing in class. Each of the texts you will read and study in this course can help you analyze and understand your independent reading texts in new and enlightening ways.

Discuss your independent reading plan with a partner by responding to these questions:

- How do you go about choosing what to read independently? Where can you find advice on which books or articles to read?

- What genre of texts do you most enjoy reading outside of class?

- How can you make time in your schedule to read independently?

- How do you think literary theory might change your perspective of the texts you read independently?

- Look at the Independent Reading Link on this page and think about which text or author you plan on reading during the first half of Unit 1.

My Notes

INDEPENDENT READING LINK

Read and Respond

For independent reading during this unit, you may want to include biographies or autobiographies about people who interest you. Look for life-changing experiences they had as young adults. Note these experiences in your Reader/ Writer Notebook.

Talking About Voice

Learning Targets

- Identify and analyze how a writer's use of language creates a distinct voice.
- Cite textual evidence of voice to support inferences about a speaker.

Creating Voice

1. **Quickwrite:** When you think of pizza, what comes to mind? Write a paragraph describing pizza and showing your attitude toward it. You will come back to this later.

Literary Terms

Voice is a writer's (or speaker's) distinctive use of language to express ideas as well as his or her persona.
Tone is a writer's (or speaker's) attitude toward the subject. Tone is conveyed through the person's choice of words and detail.
Diction refers to a writer's word choices, which often convey voice and tone.

ACADEMIC VOCABULARY

To **infer** or to make an **inference** is to come to a conclusion about ideas or information not directly stated. You infer something based on reasoning and evidence (details).

WORD CONNECTIONS

Roots and Affixes

The word *syntax* refers to rules for the construction of a sentence. The Greek prefix *syn-* means "together." The root *-tax* means "order" or "arrangement." The prefix *syn-* is found in words like *synthesis*, *synonym*, and *synchronize*. The root *-tax* occurs in *taxonomy* and *taxidermy*.

If several different people were asked to describe pizza, you might expect to get a variety of responses. Even though the subject would be the same, the descriptions might be quite different because each person uses a different **tone** and **voice**. Tone is a writer's (or speaker's) attitude toward a subject, and it is created through specific word choice, or **diction**. Voice is a result of a writer's (or speaker's) use of language, and it may be so unique that it's almost like a fingerprint: a sign of the writer's or speaker's identity. This fingerprint results from three central aspects of how language is used in the text.

- **Diction**—Word choice intended to convey a certain effect
- **Syntax**—Sentence structure; the arrangement of words and the order of grammatical elements in a sentence
- **Imagery**—The words or phrases, including specific details and figurative language, that a writer uses to represent persons, objects, actions, feelings, and ideas descriptively by appealing to the senses

Experienced writers choose language carefully knowing that readers draw conclusions or **inferences** based on their diction, imagery, and syntax.

2. Following is one person's description of pizza. What inferences can you draw about Speaker 1 based upon the speaker's voice? Write your inferences in the graphic organizer that follows. Cite details of the speaker's voice that led you to that conclusion.

Speaker 1: Eating pizza is rather like embarking on a transcontinental excursion. You embark on the journey without being quite certain of what you will encounter. A well-made pizza contains the aromatic essence of fresh basil, oregano, and garlic that beckon invitingly. Once you bite into a perfectly sliced piece of pizza, your taste buds awaken and celebrate. When properly prepared, pizza is an extraordinary culinary creation.

Speakers	Inferences About the Speaker (What might you infer about the speaker's age, status, and preferences?)	Diction (What word choices does the speaker make—formal or informal?)	Syntax (Are the sentences short, long, simple, or complex?)	Imagery (What words and phrases include sensory details to create images?)	Tone (What can you conclude about the speaker's attitude toward the subject?)
Speaker 1					
Speaker 2					
Speaker 3					
Speaker 4					

3. Inferences are justifiable only if they can be supported by textual evidence. Discuss your conclusions about Speaker 1 with a neighbor, comparing the annotations and the inferences you have drawn based upon them. Evaluate how supportable the inferences are based on the evidence you provide to support your inferences. Rank each of your inferences from "strongly supported by evidence" to "somewhat supported by evidence."

Be prepared to justify your inferences—and your rankings—by explaining how the textual evidence supports your conclusions.

My Notes

_____

_____

_____

_____

Talking About Voice

4. Now read the remaining speakers' descriptions with a partner, highlighting and annotating each passage for the diction, syntax, and imagery that contribute to the voice and tone. Write your annotations in the graphic organizer on the previous page to capture your responses.

Speaker 2: It's yummy. I like it when the cheese is really gooey. My mom makes it for dinner on the weekends. When it's too hot, I have to wait for it to cool. Mom says if I don't wait, I will burn my tongue. I like the way pizza smells. When I smell pizza cooking it always makes me want to eat it right up!

Inference about the speaker: _____

Speaker 3: As long as not one speck of gross disgusting animal flesh comes anywhere near my pizza, I can eat it. I prefer pizza with mushrooms, tomatoes, and spinach. Goat cheese is especially nice, too. A thin whole-wheat crust topped with imported cheese and organic vegetables makes a satisfying meal.

Inference about the speaker: _____

Speaker 4: Pizza is, like, one of the basic food groups, right? I mean, dude, who doesn't eat pizza? Me and my friends order it, like, every day. We usually get pepperoni, and it's great when they are, like, covering the whole top! Dude, hot steamy pizza dripping with cheese and loaded with pepperoni is awesome.

Inference about the speaker: _____

Group Discussion Norms

During this course, you will participate in discussions with partners and in groups. All members of a group need to communicate effectively as speakers and listeners. To make collaborative discussions productive:

- Prepare for discussions. This preparation may mean doing research, reading assigned texts, or completing analyses of texts so that you are ready to share ideas.

- Organize your thoughts and speak clearly. Listen with an open mind to the viewpoints of others, posing and responding to questions to help broaden discussions and make new connections based on evidence and reasoning shared within the group.

- Establish rules for collegial discussions, including hearing the views of all group members and deciding how to settle disagreements on next steps. To foster meaningful discussion, ask questions to clarify understanding and listen attentively to other group members' responses.

- If your group is charged with creating a group project, establish clear goals for the project, responsibilities for individual roles for project tasks, and deadlines for each part of the project.

- Be aware of nonverbal communication such as eye contact, body posture, head nods, hand gestures, and vocal cues.

Narrative Voices

Learning Targets

- Apply a strategy for active reading and note-taking.
- Provide textual evidence to analyze and interpret writers' choices that create voice, engage readers, and suggest meanings.

Introducing the Strategy: Double-Entry Journal

A **double-entry journal** is a note-taking strategy for actively reading a text. In your journal, you can connect your own experiences to those of the characters, share your opinions about what is happening, trace the development of the characters, and comment on the writer's choices that create the voice of the narrator.

A double-entry journal can be used with any reading. In this unit, you will be reading texts written in a **narrative** structure. As you read these narratives, use the format below as a model for recording notes in a double-entry journal. In the left column ("Vivid Text"), copy or summarize passages that spark your thoughts in some way, citing the page number with the quotation. In the right column, write your thoughts about the passage or some element of the narrative (character, plot, theme).

If you are having trouble thinking of what to write, try using these stems:

- I really like/dislike this part because ...
- I wonder why ... ?
- The diction/imagery creates a tone of ...
- This quote shows the narrator's/character's voice by ...
- I predict that ...
- This reminds me of the time when I ...
- If it was me, I would ...

My Notes

Literary Terms

A **narrative** is a story about a series of events that includes character development, plot structure, and theme. A narrative can be a work of fiction or nonfiction.
A **narrator** is the person telling the story and is often the protagonist or main character of the story.

Vivid Text (The book says ...)	Analysis/Question/Opinion (I say ...)

Preview

In this activity, you will read a narrative and highlight quotes that give you pause, or stand out to you.

Setting a Purpose for Reading

- Underline words, phrases, or sentences that stand out to you.
- Circle unknown words and phrases. Try to determine the meaning of the words by using context clues, word parts, or a dictionary.

INDEPENDENT READING LINK

Read and Respond

As you study the first part of this unit, apply the strategies and information you learn to your independent reading. For example, be aware of your reactions to what you read. Then use a double-entry journal strategy to cite the text and note your thoughts, such as a personal experience, a question, or a prediction.

My Notes

_____

_____

_____

_____

_____

_____

_____

GRAMMAR & USAGE
Dashes

Writers use **dashes** to indicate a break in thought or speech. Dashes provide a sharper break than commas, and emphasize certain content. Dashes can also be used to indicate an unfinished statement or question. Notice how Anderson uses dashes in paragraph 2 to call attention to the different types of lunch bags. Notice the dashes in paragraph 4. Think about what the dashes emphasize.

Find other sentences with dashes and consider how dashes are used to create voice and tone.

testament: evidence that something is true

terminal: extreme, severe

inconspicuous: not easy to see or notice

reconstituted: to change something by adding water to it

Morse code: a system of signals developed in the 1830s to send messages

ABOUT THE AUTHOR
Born in 1961, Laurie Halse Anderson always loved reading and writing. Even as a child, she made up stories and wrote for fun. As an adult, she did freelance reporting until she began publishing her work. Her novel *Speak*, which won numerous awards and was a best seller, was made into a movie. In 2009, she won the Margaret A. Edwards Award for *Catalyst, Fever 1793*, and *Speak*. She continues to write historical fiction, like *Chains*, and young adult novels, like *Wintergirls*. She says she is inspired by her readers, who write to her with comments or attend her readings.

Novel

From
Speak

by Laurie Halse Anderson

Spotlight

1   I find my locker after social studies. The lock sticks a little, but I open it. I dive into the stream of fourth-period lunch students and swim down the hall to the cafeteria.

2   I know enough not to bring lunch on the first day of high school. There is no way of telling what the acceptable fashion will be. Brown bags—humble **testament** to suburbia, or **terminal** geek gear? Insulated lunch bags—hip way to save the planet, or sign of an over involved mother? Buying is the only solution. And it gives me time to scan the cafeteria for a friendly face or an **inconspicuous** corner.

3   The hot lunch is turkey with **reconstituted** dried mashed potatoes and gravy, a damp green vegetable, and a cookie. I'm not sure how to order anything else, so I just slide my tray along and let the lunch drones fill it. This eight-foot senior in front of me somehow gets three cheeseburgers, French fries, and two Ho-Hos without saying a word. Some sort of **Morse code** with his eyes, maybe. Must study this further. I follow the Basketball Pole into the cafeteria.

4   I see a few friends—people I used to think were my friends—but they look away. Think fast, think fast. There's that new girl, Heather, reading by the window. I could sit across from her. Or I could crawl behind a trash can. Or maybe I could dump my lunch straight into the trash and keep moving right on out the door.

5   The Basketball Pole waves to a table of friends. Of course. The basketball team. They all swear at him—a bizarre greeting practiced by athletic boys with zits. He smiles and throws a Ho-Ho. I try to scoot around him.

6 Thwap! A lump of potatoes and gravy hits me square in the center of my chest. All conversation stops as the entire lunchroom gawks, my face burning into their retinas. I will be forever known as "that girl who got nailed by potatoes the first day." The Basketball Pole apologizes and says something else, but four hundred people explode in laughter and I can't read lips. I ditch my tray and bolt for the door.

7 I motor so fast out of the lunchroom the track coach would draft me for varsity if he were around. But no, Mr. Neck has cafeteria duty. And Mr. Neck has no use for girls who can run the one hundred in under ten seconds, unless they're willing to do it while holding on to a football.

8 Mr. Neck: "We meet again."

9 Me:

10 Would he listen to "I need to go home and change," or "Did you see what that bozo did"? Not a chance. I keep my mouth shut.

11 Mr. Neck: "Where do you think you're going?"

12 Me:

13 It is easier not to say anything. Shut your trap, button your lip, can it. All that crap you hear on TV about communication and expressing feelings is a lie. Nobody really wants to hear what you have to say.

14 Mr. Neck makes a note in his book. "I knew you were trouble the first time I saw you. I've taught here for twenty-four years and I can tell what's going on in a kid's head just by looking in their eyes. No more warnings. You just earned a demerit for wandering the halls without a pass."

Second Read

- Reread the narrative to answer these text-dependent questions.
- Write any additional questions you have about the text in your Reader/Writer Notebook.

1. **Key Idea and Details:** Who is narrating the story? What textual evidence supports your answer?

2. **Key Ideas and Details:** The narrator's observations are sarcastic and humorous. Do they reflect her true feelings about others? What evidence in the text supports your answer?

3. **Craft and Structure:** What effect does the use of dashes in paragraph 4 have?

WORD CONNECTIONS

Etymology

The word *bizarre* comes from a French word meaning "odd." However, it may have originally meant "handsome or brave." An alternate origin is the Italian word *bizarro*, meaning "angry and fierce."

GRAMMAR & USAGE
Compound Sentences

A **compound sentence** is two or more simple sentences joined by a comma and a coordinating conjunction—*and, or, but, so,* or *yet.* The parts of a compound sentence—called independent clauses—can also be joined by a semicolon.

The lock sticks a little, but I open it.

The lock sticks a little; I open it.

Reread paragraph 6. Find the compound sentence formed from three independent clauses.

My Notes

_____

_____

_____

_____

_____

_____

_____

_____

_____

_____

Narrative Voices

My Notes

_____
_____
_____
_____
_____
_____
_____
_____

4. **Key Ideas and Details:** Melinda (the protagonist) has a vivid inner voice. What is significant, then, about the fact that she never actually speaks in this passage?

Working from the Text

Choose four examples from the text that stood out to you, making sure you choose a variety of types. Record them below. Exchange with a partner and write responses to each other's comments, explaining your own reaction to the vivid text or how you feel about your partner's response. Did you see things the same way or differently? Why?

Vivid Text (The book says ...)	Analysis/Question/Opinion (I say ...)	Responses to Comments

Check Your Understanding

Anderson was 38 years old when *Speak* was published, yet she captures a teen girl's voice through her diction, syntax, and imagery. To explore how, choose two quotes you think sound particularly authentic, and write a response in a double-entry journal that explains how the quotes contribute to the narrator's teen voice. What inferences can you draw about the character of Melinda based on these quotes?

Parallel Structure

Learning Targets
- Analyze syntax and identify parallel structure among words, phrases, and clauses.
- Use understanding of parallel structure to improve sentences.
- Use parallel structure for clarity in writing.

Syntax and Parallel Structure

In her book *Artful Sentences*, Virginia Tufte explains that, "Parallelism is saying like things in like ways." A sentence has parallel structure when related ideas are expressed in the same grammatical form. By using **parallel structure**, writers can create sentences that communicate even complex ideas very clearly. Some writers use parallel structure deliberately, thinking about the **syntax**, or arrangement of words and grammatical elements, in their sentences. Parallel structure can also occur naturally in sentences, when a writer puts words together in a way that sounds clear, balanced, and even powerful. As you will see in the examples that follow, the parallelism in a sentence can be found among words, phrases, or clauses. You will also see examples of parallelism among sentences.

Parallel Words: nouns, pronouns, adjectives, adverbs, gerunds

> **Nouns:** On Fridays, the cafeteria serves *roasted vegetables*, *turkey burgers*, and *fruit salad*.

> **Pronouns:** Neither *Sara* nor *her brother* understood why people wanted *them* to run for Student Council.

> **Adjectives:** Hailey was not only *creative* and *smart*, but she was also *hardworking*.

> **Adverbs:** During group projects, they work together *quickly* and *effectively*.

> **Gerunds:** He enjoys *playing* soccer, *reading* comics, and *lifting* weights.

Parallel Phrases: prepositional phrases (prepositions followed by nouns)

> When I got home from school, my cat raced *down* the stairs, *over* the railing, and *into* the front hall.

Parallel Clauses: parallel subject and verb

> To prepare for opening night, *we swept the stage floor*, *we dusted the props*, and *we fixed the lights*.

Faulty Parallelism

To identify and correct faulty parallelism:
1. look for the parts of the sentence that are parallel
2. find any elements that are not parallel
3. revise them to match.

Identify and correct the faulty parallelism in each of these examples.

Faulty parallelism: The high school offers psychology and human geography, and you can take computer science, too.

Correct parallelism:

LEARNING STRATEGIES:
Marking the Text

GRAMMAR & USAGE
Compound Sentences

Correlative conjunctions are used in pairs to join sentence parts. Some common correlative conjunctions are *either/or, both/and, whether/or,* and *not only/but also*. The sentence parts joined by correlative conjunctions should be grammatically parallel.

The following sentence is not parallel because the correlative conjunctions link an adjective (*inspiring*) with a noun phrase (*source of information*).

Not Parallel: *The speech was not only inspiring, but also a source of information.*

To make the sentence parallel, an adjective can be substituted for the noun phrase. Alternatively, a noun phrase can be substituted for the adjective.

Parallel (adjectives): *The speech was not only inspiring but also informative.*

Parallel (noun phrases): *The speech was not only an inspiration, but also a source of information.*

My Notes

Parallel Structure

Faulty parallelism: Javier spends all of his time either working on his music or he updates his social media page.

Correct parallelism:

Faulty parallelism: A skillful computer coder must have a logical mind, debugging skills, and he or she must be able to solve problems.

Correct parallelism:

Power of the Parallel

Parallel structure can be a deliberate and convincing rhetorical technique in speeches or dramatic, powerful writing. It provides balance and repetition, allowing the audience to easily concentrate and quickly comprehend what the speaker says.

1. Read the opening paragraph from *A Tale of Two Cities* by Charles Dickens and underline the parallel structure.

   "It was the best of times, it was the worst of times, it was the age of wisdom, it was the age of foolishness, it was the epoch of belief, it was the epoch of incredulity, it was the season of Light, it was the season of Darkness, it was the spring of hope, it was the winter of despair, we had everything before us, we had nothing before us, we were all going direct to Heaven, we were all going direct the other way— in short, the period was so far like the present period, that some of its noisiest authorities insisted on its being received, for good or for evil, in the superlative degree of comparison only."

2. Read these sentences from Franklin D. Roosevelt's first Inaugural Address and underline the parallel structure. Try to identify the grammatical forms that are parallel.

   "So, first of all, let me assert my firm belief that the only thing we have to fear is fear itself – nameless, unreasoning, unjustified terror which paralyzes needed efforts to convert retreat into advance."

   "It can be helped by insistence that the Federal, the State, and the local governments act forthwith on the demand that their cost be drastically reduced. It can be helped by the unifying of relief activities which today are often scattered, uneconomical, [and] unequal."

3. Read these sentences from the Gettysburg Address by Abraham Lincoln and underline the parallel structure.

   "But, in a larger sense, we cannot dedicate, we cannot consecrate, we cannot hallow this ground."

   "… government of the people, by the people, for the people, shall not perish from the earth."

4. Read these sentences from Abraham Lincoln's second Inaugural Address and underline the parallel structure.

"To strengthen, perpetuate, and extend this interest [slavery] was the object for which the insurgents would rend the Union, even by war ..."

"With malice toward none; with charity for all; with firmness in the right, as God gives us to see the right, let us strive on to finish the work we are in ..."

5. Underline the parallel clauses in these sentences from John F. Kennedy's Inaugural Address.

"The torch has been passed to a new generation of Americans—born in this century, tempered by war, disciplined by a hard and bitter peace, proud of our ancient heritage. ..."

"Let every nation know, whether it wishes us well or ill, that we shall pay any price, bear any burden, meet any hardship, support any friend, oppose any foe, to assure the survival and the success of liberty."

6. Martin Luther King Jr., in his "I Have a Dream" speech, takes parallelism one step further to create a memorable form of repetition called **anaphora**. Read the sentences below. How would you describe this form of parallelism? Discuss with a partner what effect this parallelism has.

"Now is the time to make real the promises of democracy. Now is the time to rise from the dark and desolate valley of segregation to the sunlit path of racial justice. Now is the time to lift our nation from the quicksands of racial injustice to the solid rock of brotherhood. Now is the time to make justice a reality for all of God's children."

Check Your Understanding

Rewrite the following sentences to correct the faulty parallelism. Use the My Notes space or separate paper.

1. Maria likes hiking, to swim, and to ride a bicycle.

2. Ms. Shapiro said that Anthony would get a good grade because he was a good student, he took good notes, he studied for tests early, and his labs were completed carefully.

3. Coach Taylor told the players that they should get a lot of sleep, eat a good breakfast, arrive early, and to do warm-up exercises before the game.

4. The dictionary can be used for these purposes: to find word meanings, pronunciations, correct spellings, and looking up irregular verbs.

My Notes

Literary Terms
Anaphora is the repetition of the same word or group of words at the beginnings of two or more clauses or lines.

Defining Experiences

LEARNING STRATEGIES:
Guided Reading, Close Reading, Marking the Text, Note-taking, Visualizing, Word Map

My Notes

Learning Targets

- Explain how a writer creates effects through the connotations of words and images.
- Use textual details to support interpretive claims.

Preview

In this activity, you will read a short story and note any words or phrases that create imagery and voice.

Setting a Purpose for Reading

- Write an exclamation point (!) next to words or phrases that create interesting imagery.
- Highlight words or phrases that create the narrator's voice.
- Circle unknown words and phrases. Try to determine the meaning of the words by using context clues, word parts, or a dictionary.

Literary Terms

Juxtaposition is the arrangement of two or more things for the purpose of comparison.
A **flashback** is an interruption or transition to a time before the current events in a narrative.

ABOUT THE AUTHOR

Eugenia Collier (b. 1928) grew up and continues to live in Baltimore. Retired now, she taught English at several universities. She has published two collections of short stories, a play, and many scholarly works. Her noteworthy and award-winning story "Marigolds" powerfully captures the moment of the narrator's coming of age.

Short Story

by Eugenia Collier

shantytown: a run-down town in which most of the people are poor

1   When I think of the home town of my youth, all that I seem to remember is dust—the brown, crumbly dust of late summer—arid, sterile dust that gets into the eyes and makes them water, gets into the throat and between the toes of bare brown feet. I don't know why I should remember only the dust. Surely there must have been lush green lawns and paved streets under leafy shade trees somewhere in town; but memory is an abstract painting—it does not present things as they are, but rather as they *feel*. And so, when I think of that time and that place, I remember only the dry September of the dirt roads and grassless yards of the **shantytown** where I lived. And one other thing I remember, another incongruency of memory—a brilliant splash of sunny yellow against the dust—Miss Lottie's marigolds.

2   Whenever the memory of those marigolds flashes across my mind, a strange nostalgia comes with it and remains long after the picture has faded. I feel again the

chaotic emotions of adolescence, illusive as smoke, yet as real as the potted geranium before me now. Joy and rage and wild animal gladness and shame become tangled together in the multicolored skein of fourteen-going-on-fifteen as I recall that devastating moment when I was suddenly more woman than child, years ago in Miss Lottie's yard. I think of those marigolds at the strangest times; I remember them vividly now as I desperately pass away the time. ...

3 I suppose that futile waiting was the sorrowful background music of our impoverished little community when I was young. The Depression that gripped the nation was no new thing to us, for the black workers of rural Maryland had always been depressed. I don't know what it was that we were waiting for; certainly not for the prosperity that was "just around the corner," for those were white folks' words, which we never believed. Nor did we wait for hard work and thrift to pay off in shining success, as the American Dream promised, for we knew better than that, too.

4 Perhaps we waited for a miracle, amorphous in concept but necessary if one were to have the **grit** to rise before dawn each day and labor in the white man's vineyard until after dark, or to wander about in the September dust offering some meager share of bread. But God was **chary** with miracles in those days, and so we waited—and waited.

5 We children, of course, were only vaguely aware of the extent of our poverty. Having no radios, few newspapers, and no magazines, we were somewhat unaware of the world outside our community. Nowadays we would be called culturally deprived and people would write books and hold conferences about us. In those days everybody we knew was just as hungry and ill clad as we were. Poverty was the cage in which we all were trapped, and our hatred of it was still the vague, undirected restlessness of the zoo-bred flamingo who knows that nature created him to fly free.

6 As I think of those days I feel most poignantly the tag end of summer, the bright, dry times when we began to have a sense of shortening days and the imminence of the cold.

7 By the time I was fourteen, my brother Joey and I were the only children left at our house, the older ones having left home for early marriage or the lure of the city, and the two babies having been sent to relatives who might care for them better than we. Joey was three years younger than I, and a boy, and therefore vastly inferior. Each morning our mother and father trudged wearily down the dirt road and around the bend, she to her domestic job, he to his daily unsuccessful quest for work. After our few chores around the tumbledown shanty, Joey and I were free to run wild in the sun with other children similarly situated.

8 For the most part, those days are ill-defined in my memory, running together and combining like a fresh watercolor painting left out in the rain. I remember squatting in the road drawing a picture in the dust, a picture which Joey gleefully erased with one sweep of his dirty foot. I remember fishing for minnows in a muddy creek and watching sadly as they eluded my cupped hands, while Joey laughed uproariously. And I remember, that year, a strange restlessness of body and of spirit, a feeling that something old and familiar was ending, and something unknown and therefore terrifying was beginning.

9 One day returns to me with special clarity for some reason, perhaps because it was the beginning of the experience that in some **inexplicable** way marked the end of innocence. I was loafing under the great oak tree in our yard, deep in some reverie which I have now forgotten, except that it involved some secret, secret thoughts of one of the Harris boys across the yard. Joey and a bunch of kids were bored now with the old tire suspended from an oak limb, which had kept them entertained for a while.

My Notes

grit: toughness, determination

chary: ungenerous, wary

WORD CONNECTIONS

Etymology

The name *marigold* comes from Middle English, around the 1300s, and is a conflation, or blend, of the name "Mary" and the word "gold." Gold refers to the brilliant yellow-gold bloom that is most characteristic of the plant. In some cultures, the marigold's strong, musty scent is believed to attract the spirits of the dead. The bright yellow-orange blooms are prominently used during the November Day of the Dead celebrations in Mexico.

inexplicable: unable to be explained or understood

idleness: not being active
prospect: possibility or chance of happening

GRAMMAR & USAGE
Subjunctive Verbs
Formal diction sometimes requires the use of verbs in the **subjunctive mood**. In English, the only common use of the subjunctive mood is to express a doubt, a wish, a possibility, or a situation contrary to fact. In these cases, the verb *were*, not *was*, is used with a singular subject; for example:

Right: If I were born in the 1800s ...

Wrong: If I was born in the 1800s ...

The narrator of "Marigolds" uses the subjunctive verb *were* in a sentence in paragraph 3. Think about why the author would choose to use the subjunctive.

10 "Hey, Lizabeth," Joey yelled. He never talked when he could yell. "Hey, Lizabeth, let's go somewhere."

11 I came reluctantly from my private world. "Where you want to go? What you want to do?"

12 The truth was that we were becoming tired of the formlessness of our summer days. The **idleness** whose **prospect** had seemed so beautiful during the busy days of spring now had degenerated to an almost desperate effort to fill up the empty midday hours.

13 "Let's go see can we find some locusts on the hill," someone suggested.

14 Joey was scornful. "Ain't no more locusts there. Y'all got 'em all while they was still green."

15 The argument that followed was brief and not really worth the effort. Hunting locust trees wasn't fun anymore by now.

16 "Tell you what," said Joey finally, his eyes sparkling. "Let's us go over to Miss Lottie's."

17 The idea caught on at once, for annoying Miss Lottie was always fun. I was still child enough to scamper along with the group over rickety fences and through bushes that tore our already raggedy clothes, back to where Miss Lottie lived. I think now that we must have made a tragicomic spectacle, five or six kids of different ages, each of us clad in only one garment—the girls in faded dresses that were too long or too short, the boys in patchy pants, their sweaty brown chests gleaming in the hot sun. A little cloud of dust followed our thin legs and bare feet as we tramped over the barren land.

My Notes

18 When Miss Lottie's house came into view we stopped, **ostensibly** to plan our strategy, but actually to reinforce our courage. Miss Lottie's house was the most ramshackle of all our ramshackle homes. The sun and rain had long since faded its rickety frame siding from white to a sullen gray. The boards themselves seemed to remain upright not from being nailed together but rather from leaning together, like a house that a child might have constructed from cards. A brisk wind might have blown it down, and the fact that it was still standing implied a kind of enchantment that was stronger than the elements. There it stood and as far as I know is standing yet—a gray, rotting thing with no porch, no shutters, no steps, set on a cramped lot with no grass, not even any weeds—a monument to decay.

19 In front of the house in a squeaky rocking chair sat Miss Lottie's son, John Burke, completing the impression of decay. John Burke was what was known as queer-headed. Black and ageless, he sat rocking day in and day out in a mindless stupor, lulled by the monotonous squeak-squawk of the chair. A battered hat atop his shaggy head shaded him from the sun. Usually John Burke was totally unaware of everything outside his quiet dream world. But if you disturbed him, if you intruded upon his fantasies, he would become enraged, strike out at you, and curse at you in some strange enchanted language which only he could understand. We children made a game of thinking of ways to disturb John Burke and then to elude his violent retribution.

20 But our real fun and our real fear lay in Miss Lottie herself. Miss Lottie seemed to be at least a hundred years old. Her big frame still held traces of the tall, powerful woman she must have been in youth, although it was now bent and drawn. Her smooth skin was a dark reddish brown, and her face had Indian-like features and the stern stoicism that one associates with Indian faces. Miss Lottie didn't like intruders either, especially children. She never left her yard, and nobody ever visited her. We never knew how she managed those necessities which depend on human interaction— how she ate, for example, or even whether she ate. When we were tiny children, we thought Miss Lottie was a witch and we made up tales that we half believed ourselves about her **exploits**. We were far too sophisticated now, of course, to believe the witch nonsense. But old fears have a way of clinging like cobwebs, and so when we sighted the tumbledown shack, we had to stop to reinforce our nerves.

21 "Look, there she is," I whispered, forgetting that Miss Lottie could not possibly have heard me from that distance. "She's fooling with them crazy flowers."

22 "Yeh, look at 'er."

23 Miss Lottie's marigolds were perhaps the strangest part of the picture. Certainly they did not fit in with the crumbling decay of the rest of her yard. Beyond the dusty brown yard, in front of the sorry gray house, rose suddenly and shockingly a dazzling strip of bright blossoms, clumped together in enormous mounds, warm and passionate and sun-golden. The old black witch-woman worked on them all summer, every summer, down on her creaky knees, weeding and cultivating and arranging, while the house crumbled and John Burke rocked. For some perverse reason, we children hated those marigolds. They interfered with the perfect ugliness of the place; they were too beautiful; they said too much that we could not understand; they did not make sense. There was something in the vigor with which the old woman destroyed the weeds that intimidated us. It should have been a comical sight—the old woman with the man's hat on her cropped white head, leaning over the bright mounds, her big backside in the air—but it wasn't comical, it was something we could not name. We had to annoy her by whizzing a pebble into her flowers or by yelling a dirty word, then dancing away from her rage, reveling in our youth and mocking her age. Actually, I think it was the flowers we wanted to destroy, but nobody had the nerve to try it, not even Joey, who was usually fool enough to try anything.

ostensibly: for a pretended reason

My Notes

exploits: actions

Defining Experiences

24   "Y'all git some stones," commanded Joey now and was met with instant giggling obedience as everyone except me began to gather pebbles from the dusty ground. "Come on, Lizabeth."

25   I just stood there peering through the bushes, torn between wanting to join the fun and feeling that it was all a bit silly.

26   "You scared, Lizabeth?"

27   I cursed and spat on the ground—my favorite gesture of phony bravado. "Y'all children get the stones, I'll show you how to use 'em."

28   I said before that we children were not consciously aware of how thick were the bars of our cage. I wonder now, though, whether we were not more aware of it than I thought. Perhaps we had some dim notion of what we were, and how little chance we had of being anything else. Otherwise, why would we have been so preoccupied with destruction? Anyway, the pebbles were collected quickly, and everybody looked at me to begin the fun.

29   "Come on, y'all."

30   We crept to the edge of the bushes that bordered the narrow road in front of Miss Lottie's place. She was working placidly, kneeling over the flowers, her dark hand plunged into the golden mound. Suddenly zing—an expertly aimed stone cut the head off one of the blossoms.

31   "Who out there?" Miss Lottie's backside came down and her head came up as her sharp eyes searched the bushes. "You better git!"

32   We had crouched down out of sight in the bushes, where we stifled the giggles that insisted on coming. Miss Lottie gazed warily across the road for a moment, then cautiously returned to her weeding. Zing—Joey sent a pebble into the blooms, and another marigold was beheaded.

33   Miss Lottie was enraged now. She began struggling to her feet, leaning on a rickety cane and shouting. "Y'all git! Go on home!" Then the rest of the kids let loose with their pebbles, storming the flowers and laughing wildly and senselessly at Miss Lottie's impotent rage. She shook her stick at us and started shakily toward the road crying, "Git 'long! John Burke! John Burke, come help!"

34   Then I lost my head entirely, mad with the power of inciting such rage, and ran out of the bushes in the storm of pebbles, straight toward Miss Lottie, chanting madly, "Old witch, fell in a ditch, picked up a penny and thought she was rich!" The children screamed with delight, dropped their pebbles, and joined the crazy dance, swarming around Miss Lottie like bees and chanting, "Old lady witch!" while she screamed curses at us. The madness lasted only a moment, for John Burke, startled at last, lurched out of his chair, and we dashed for the bushes just as Miss Lottie's cane went whizzing at my head.

35   I did not join the merriment when the kids gathered again under the oak in our bare yard. Suddenly I was ashamed, and I did not like being ashamed. The child in me sulked and said it was all in fun, but the woman in me flinched at the thought of the malicious attack that I had led. The mood lasted all afternoon. When we ate the beans and rice that was supper that night, I did not notice my father's silence, for he was always silent these days, nor did I notice my mother's absence, for she always worked until well into evening. Joey and I had a particularly bitter argument after supper; his **exuberance** got on my nerves. Finally I stretched out upon the pallet in the room we shared and fell into a fitful doze. When I awoke, somewhere in the middle of the night,

exuberance: extreme good cheer or high spirits

my mother had returned, and I vaguely listened to the conversation that was audible through the thin walls that separated our rooms. At first I heard no words, only voices. My mother's voice was like a cool, dark room in summer—peaceful, soothing, quiet. I loved to listen to it; it made things seem all right somehow. But my father's voice cut through hers, shattering the peace.

36 "Twenty-two years, Maybelle, twenty-two years," he was saying, "and I got nothing for you, nothing, nothing."

37 "It's all right, honey, you'll get something. Everybody out of work now, you know that."

38 "It ain't right. Ain't no man ought to eat his woman's food year in and year out, and see his children running wild. Ain't nothing right about that."

39 "Honey, you took good care of us when you had it. Ain't nobody got nothing nowadays."

40 "I ain't talking about nobody else, I'm talking about *me*. God knows I try." My mother said something I could not hear, and my father cried out louder, "What must a man do, tell me that?"

41 "Look, we ain't starving. I get paid every week, and Mrs. Ellis is real nice about giving me things. She gonna let me have Mr. Ellis's old coat for you this winter—"

42 "Damn Mr. Ellis's coat! And damn his money! You think I want white folks' leavings? Damn, Maybelle"—and suddenly he sobbed, loudly and painfully, and cried helplessly and hopelessly in the dark night. I had never heard a man cry before. I did not know men ever cried. I covered my ears with my hand but could not cut off the sound of my father's harsh, painful, despairing sobs. My father was a strong man who could whisk a child upon his shoulders and go singing through the house. My father **whittled** toys for us, and laughed so loud that the great oak seemed to laugh with him, and taught us how to fish and hunt rabbits. How could it be that my father was crying? But the sobs went on, unstifled, finally quieting until I could hear my mother's voice, deep and rich, humming softly as she used to hum to a frightened child.

43 The world had lost its boundary lines. My mother, who was small and soft, was now the strength of the family; my father, who was the rock on which the family had been built, was sobbing like the tiniest child. Everything was suddenly out of tune, like a broken accordion. Where did I fit into this crazy picture? I do not now remember my thoughts, only a feeling of great bewilderment and fear.

44 Long after the sobbing and humming had stopped, I lay on the pallet, still as stone with my hands over my ears, wishing that I too could cry and be comforted. The night was silent now except for the sound of the crickets and of Joey's soft breathing. But the room was too crowded with fear to allow me to sleep, and finally, feeling the terrible aloneness of 4 A.M., I decided to awaken Joey.

45 "Ouch! What's the matter with you? What you want?" he demanded disagreeably when I had pinched and slapped him awake.

46 "Come on, wake up."

47 "What for? Go 'way."

48 I was lost for a reasonable reply. I could not say, "I'm scared and I don't want to be alone," so I merely said, "I'm going out. If you want to come, come on."

49 The promise of adventure awoke him. "Going out now? Where to, Lizabeth? What you going to do?"

My Notes

whittled: cut and shaped from wood

Defining Experiences

Furies: in classical mythology, three spirits of revenge who pursued and punished wrongdoers

My Notes

squalor: bad or dirty conditions

50 I was pulling my dress over my head. Until now I had not thought of going out. "Just come on," I replied tersely

51 I was out the window and halfway down the road before Joey caught up with me.

52 "Wait, Lizabeth, where you going?"

53 I was running as if the **Furies** were after me, as perhaps they were—running silently and furiously until I came to where I had half known I was headed: to Miss Lottie's yard.

54 The half-dawn light was more eerie than complete darkness, and in it the old house was like the ruin that my world had become—foul and crumbling, a grotesque caricature. It looked haunted, but I was not afraid, because I was haunted too.

55 "Lizabeth, you lost your mind?" panted Joey.

56 I had indeed lost my mind, for all the smoldering emotions of that summer swelled in me and burst—the great need for my mother who was never there, the hopelessness of our poverty and degradation, the bewilderment of being neither child nor woman and yet both at once, the fear unleashed by my father's tears. And these feelings combined in one great impulse toward destruction.

57 "Lizabeth!"

58 I leaped furiously into the mounds of marigolds and pulled madly, trampling and pulling and destroying the perfect yellow blooms. The fresh smell of early morning and of dew-soaked marigolds spurred me on as I went tearing and mangling and sobbing while Joey tugged my dress or my waist crying, "Lizabeth, stop, please stop!"

59 And then I was sitting in the ruined little garden among the uprooted and ruined flowers, crying and crying, and it was too late to undo what I had done. Joey was sitting beside me, silent and frightened, not knowing what to say. Then, "Lizabeth, look."

60 I opened my swollen eyes and saw in front of me a pair of large, calloused feet; my gaze lifted to the swollen legs, the age-distorted body clad in a tight cotton nightdress, and then the shadowed Indian face surrounded by stubby white hair. And there was no rage in the face now, now that the garden was destroyed and there was nothing any longer to be protected.

61 "M-miss Lottie!" I scrambled to my feet and just stood there and stared at her, and that was the moment when childhood faded and womanhood began. That violent, crazy act was the last act of childhood. For as I gazed at the immobile face with the sad, weary eyes, I gazed upon a kind of reality which is hidden to childhood. The witch was no longer a witch but only a broken old woman who had dared to create beauty in the midst of ugliness and sterility. She had been born in **squalor** and lived in it all her life. Now at the end of that life she had nothing except a falling-down hut, a wrecked body, and John Burke, the mindless son of her passion. Whatever verve there was left in her, whatever was of love and beauty and joy that had not been squeezed out by life, had been there in the marigolds she had so tenderly cared for.

62 Of course I could not express the things that I knew about Miss Lottie as I stood there awkward and ashamed. The years have put words to the things I knew in that moment, and as I look back upon it, I know that that moment marked the end of innocence. Innocence involves an unseeing acceptance of things at face value, an ignorance of the area below the surface. In that humiliating moment I had looked beyond myself and into the depths of another person. This was the beginning of compassion, and one cannot have both compassion and innocence.

63 The years have taken me worlds away from that time and that place, from the dust and squalor of our lives, and from the bright thing that I destroyed in a blind, childish striking out at God knows what. Miss Lottie died long ago and many years have passed since I last saw her hut, completely barren at last, for despite my wild **contrition** she never planted marigolds again. Yet, there are times when the image of those passionate yellow mounds returns with a painful **poignancy**. For one does not have to be ignorant and poor to find that his life is as barren as the dusty yards of our town. And I too have planted marigolds.

contrition: sorrow or remorse for one's wrongs
poignancy: a strong, sad feeling

Second Read

- Reread the short story to answer these text-dependent questions.
- Write any additional questions you have about the text in your Reader/Writer Notebook.

1. **Craft and Structure:** In the first paragraph, what two images does the narrator juxtapose for contrast? What are the connotations of these juxtaposed images?

2. **Craft and Structure:** What is the meaning of *amorphous* in paragraph 4?

3. **Craft and Structure:** What do you learn about the narrator through the author's use of flashback? Cite text evidence to support your answer.

4. **Craft and Structure:** Notice that in paragraph 9, the narrator uses foreshadowing. What is the effect of this hinting at events to come? Highlight other hints or foreshadowing provided by the narrator.

5. **Key Ideas and Details:** Why are the marigolds so important to Miss Lottie, and why do the children hate them?

My Notes

Defining Experiences

6. **Key Ideas and Details:** What can you infer from the text as to Lizabeth's reasons for her final act of destruction?

7. **Craft and Structure:** How does the author use juxtaposition to show how Lizabeth has changed through her experience?

Working from the Text

Language and Writer's Craft: Verb Mood

Writers use verb mood to express an attitude. Verbs may be in one of three moods: **indicative**, **imperative**, or **conditional**. Almost all verbs we use are indicative, which is used to state a fact or describe something. The imperative mood is used to give a command or make a request. The conditional form of a verb expresses something that has not happened or something that could happen hypothetically. In the below example, the author shares an image with us that should have evoked humor but did not.

> "It should have been a comical sight—the old woman with the man's hat on her cropped white head, leaning over the bright mounds, her big backside in the air—but it wasn't comical, it was something we could not name."

The subjunctive form of the verb is used to express doubt or describe a wish, a doubt, or a situation contrary to fact. When using the verb "to be" in the subjunctive, use *were* rather than *was*. The subjunctive form is often used in a clause beginning with *if*.

PRACTICE Which mood is demonstrated in each of the examples below? How does the narrator's use of verb moods help create her voice in the story?

Example 1: "Perhaps we waited for a miracle, amorphous in concept but necessary if one were to have the grit to rise before dawn each day and labor in the white man's vineyard until after dark, or to wander about in the September dust offering some meager share of bread.

Example 2: "Y'all git some stones," commanded Joey now and was met with instant giggling obedience as everyone except me began to gather pebbles from the dusty ground. "Come on, Lizabeth."

Example 3: "We had crouched down out of sight in the bushes, where we stifled the giggles that insisted on coming."

Word Choice: Diction and Imagery

Writers choose words both for their literal meanings (their dictionary definitions, or **denotations**) and for their implied meanings (their emotional associations, or **connotations**).

Writers create their intended effects through particular connotations—the associations or images readers connect with certain words. Some words provoke strong positive or negative associations. These reactions are central to how we, as readers, draw inferences about the tone, the characters, and the meaning of a text.

8. Consider the following sentence from the chapter of *Speak* that you read in Activity 1.3, "Spotlight": "I dive into the stream of fourth-period lunch students and swim down the hall to the cafeteria." What connotations do the images of diving into and swimming through other students have here?

9. Rewrite the sentence, trying to keep the same denotative meaning but changing the connotations to make them neutral.

10. Now consider what is conveyed by Anderson's diction (particularly the verbs) in this sentence.

    "I ditch my tray and bolt for the door."

    Based on the verbs, what inferences might you draw about the speaker's feelings in this moment?

11. Now revise Anderson's sentence to be more neutral.

12. Find examples of diction and imagery that convey Lizabeth's distinctive voice in "Marigolds." Use the graphic organizer that follows to record your examples.

My Notes

Literary Terms

It is always important to know the **denotation**, or precise meaning, of a word, but often the **connotations**, or associations and emotional overtones attached, help the reader make important inferences about meaning.

Defining Experiences

Diction and Imagery That Convey Voice:	
Opening	"dry September of the dirt roads" "arid, sterile dust"
First encounter with Miss Lottie	
Overheard conversation	
Final act of destruction	
Closing	

Check Your Understanding

Read this sentence from "Marigolds."

Each morning our mother and father trudged wearily down the dirt road and around the bend, she to her domestic job, he to his daily unsuccessful quest for work.

Circle words that you think have negative connotations. Replace them with words that have positive connotations. With a partner, take turns reading your sentences aloud. Discuss how the sentences have changed.

Writing to Sources: Explanatory Text

Explain how the author uses diction, imagery, and other literary devices such as juxtaposition and flashback to create the narrator's voice and present a particular point of view. In your writing, be sure to:

- Begin with a clear thesis that states your position.
- Include multiple direct quotations from the text to support your claims. Introduce and punctuate all quotations correctly.
- Include transitions between points and a statement that provides a conclusion.

Learning How to Interview

GRAMMAR & USAGE
Direct and Indirect
Quotations

A **direct quotation** states a speaker's exact words. These words are enclosed in quotation marks.

Example: *Mr. Neck asked, "Where do you think you're going?"*

An **indirect quotation** restates what was said but does not give the speaker's exact words. Quotation marks are not used with indirect quotations.

Example: *I was about to bolt through the door when Mr. Neck asked me where I was going.*

Think about why an author would choose to use either a direct or indirect quotation. What are the advantages and disadvantages of each?

My Notes

_____

_____

_____

_____

_____

_____

_____

_____

_____

Learning Targets
- Develop effective open-ended interview questions.
- Reproduce another person's voice through direct and indirect quotations in writing.

Interviewing: First Steps

For Embedded Assessment 1, you will be writing an interview narrative. To prepare for the interview, you will first practice your interview skills by interviewing a partner. You will then draft an introduction and present your partner to your classmates.

1. The first (and very important piece) of information you need is your partner's name: _____

2. Write four questions that you could ask to learn important information about your partner.

   •

   •

   •

   •

3. When you interview someone, it is important to ask open-ended questions. Open-ended questions or statements require more than a simple "yes" or "no" response. They give your interviewee an opportunity to provide insight and explanation. In the question pairs below, circle the open-ended question or statement.

   a. Explain some of the best parts of playing soccer.

      Do you like playing soccer?

   b. As the youngest child in your family, do you think you get your own way?

      What are the advantages and disadvantages of being the youngest child in your family?

4. Revise each of the following to be an open-ended question.

   Is it fun to be in the band?

   Revision:

   Have you always lived in this town?

   Revision:

5. Look back at the four questions you wrote. Make sure they are open-ended questions or statements. If they are not, revise them as you write them in the question boxes below. Leave the answer boxes empty for now.

Question 1:	Answer:
Question 2:	Answer:
Question 3:	Answer:
Question 4:	Answer:

6. Now interview your partner. While your partner is answering, take notes in the answer boxes above. Try to write down some parts of the answer exactly, using quotation marks to show you are quoting your partner word for word (a direct quotation), as opposed to paraphrasing him or her (an indirect quotation).

Learning How to Interview

7. Prepare to introduce your partner to the class. Look back over your interview notes, and highlight the parts that best capture your partner's voice and convey a sense of who she or he is. Be sure to include **direct** and **indirect quotations** in your introduction.

The hardest part of any presentation can be the beginning. Here are some ways you might begin your introduction (your partner's name goes in the blank):

- I would like to introduce _____.

- I would like you all to meet _____.

- This is my new friend _____.

Write the opening of your introduction:

8. The other challenging part of any presentation is the closing. Sometimes people do not know how to end the introduction, so they say "That's it," or "I'm done." Don't end your introduction that way! You want to end your introduction on a strong note that encourages the rest of your class to get to know your partner.

You might end your introduction like this:

- I enjoyed getting to talk to _____ because

_____.

- _____ is an interesting person, and I'm glad I got the

chance to meet my partner because _____.

Write the ending of your introduction:

9. Introductions are a natural situation in which to use parallel structure. For example, a person might say, "He likes listening to hip-hop, watching football, and playing video games." Review your introduction, and find a place where you can revise it to incorporate an example of parallel structure. Then, write your introduction on a separate sheet of paper. Use the opener you already wrote, include the information from your notes that you highlighted, and then finish with the closing you wrote. Be sure your introduction shows respect for your partner.

Introducing Your Partner

10. Practice introducing your partner by reading your introduction aloud while standing next to your partner. When you introduce your partner, you may use your written introduction, but try not to rely on it the whole time. Avoid hiding behind your paper.

As you practice, make sure your introduction:

- has a clear opening and an effective conclusion.
- includes a mixture of direct and indirect quotations.
- features at least one effective example of parallel structure.
- effectively captures your partner's voice and conveys his or her personality to your classmates.

Check Your Understanding

In two different colors, highlight the direct and indirect quotations you used in your introduction. Then annotate your interview narrative to explain why you chose to use the direct quotations you included—and not the ones you only cited indirectly. Also annotate the sentence where you used parallel structure and explain what makes it parallel.

My Notes

Conversations with Characters

My Notes

Learning Targets

- Analyze the diction, syntax, and imagery by which an author creates the voice of a narrator.
- Write open-ended questions to prepare for an interview.

Exploring Coming of Age

1. What does it mean to come of age? Use the web organizer below or create one to explore different aspects of what coming of age involves. Consider the different texts you have read in class and your independent reading: What did the characters learn about the world? About themselves? How did they grow as a result of their experiences?

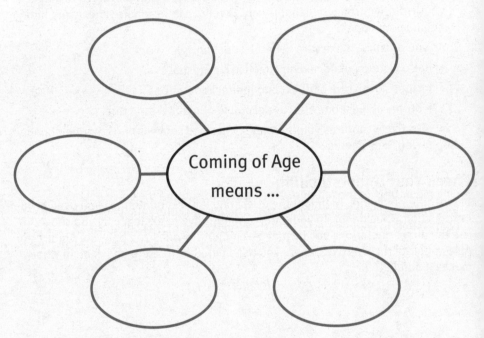

Coming of Age means ...

2. Now imagine that you are interviewing a character from "Marigolds." You could choose Miss Lottie and tell about the destruction of her flowers from her point of view. Another option is to have the narrator tell the story of the overheard conversation between her parents and explain its significance.

On the next page, write five open-ended questions you would ask either of these characters. These questions should push the character to reflect on the significance of key events revealed in the narrative—what he or she learned about himself or herself or about the world.

INDEPENDENT READING LINK

Read and Connect

Identify the coming-of-age elements in the text you are reading independently. Make a list of the key events that contribute to the main character's coming of age. As practice for the upcoming interview narrative, write a brief interview with the main character.

Interview Questions

1.

2.

3.

4.

5.

My Notes

3. One major goal of the interview narrative is to capture the voice of your interviewee. Use the graphic organizer below to analyze the style that contributes to your character's (rather than the author's) voice.

How would you describe the voice of your character?	What features of language (diction, syntax, imagery, etc.) characterize her voice?	What kinds of things does the character usually talk about? With what tone?

Conversations with Characters

4. Now, use the space below to draft an interview with the character. Answer the questions from the character's perspective and voice, using details from the text to develop your answers. Try to integrate direct and indirect quotations in your interview narrative. If you do not have enough space here, use your Reader/Writer Notebook to write your interview narrative.

Interview with _____

Check Your Understanding

With your partner, annotate at least five of the choices you have made that help to recreate the voice of your interviewee. Explain why you made these choices.

Two Versions of One Narrative

Learning Targets
- Compare and contrast language and content in two texts in different genres.
- Explain how a writer's choices regarding language and content construct the meaning of a text.
- Construct interview questions appropriate to a particular audience and topic.
- Draft an account of an interview narrative.

Preview

In this activity, you will read two texts about the same incident by the same author, Luis J. Rodriquez. One version is a **poem**; the other is **prose**.

Setting a Purpose for Reading

- Underline words, phrases, or sentences that help create the voice of the narrator.
- Circle unknown words or phrases. Try to determine the meaning of words by using context clues, word parts, or a dictionary.

Literary Terms
Prose is ordinary written or spoken language using sentences and paragraphs without deliberate or regular meter or rhyme; in contrast, **poetry** is written in lines and stanzas.

My Notes

ABOUT THE AUTHOR
Award-winning author Luis J. Rodriguez was born near the U.S.-Mexico border. He is a leading Chicano writer and is best known for his memoir of gang life in Los Angeles, *Always Running*. Rodriguez left the gang life in his late teens and has since worked in many jobs, from bus driver to newspaper reporter and community activist. He has developed many outreach programs to assist teens throughout the country. He continues to write both poetry and narrative works and is a co-organizer of the Chicago Poetry Festival.

Memoir

from ***Always Running***

by Luis J. Rodriguez

1   One day, my mother asked Rano and me to go to the grocery store. We decided to go across the railroad tracks into South Gate. In those days, South Gate was an Anglo neighborhood, filled with the families of workers from the auto plant and other nearby industry. Like Lynnwood or Huntington Park, it was forbidden territory for the people of Watts.

Two Versions of One Narrative

ceremony: a formal act

My Notes

2 My brother insisted we go. I don't know what possessed him, but then I never did. It was useless to argue; he'd force me anyway. He was nine then, I was six. So without **ceremony,** we started over the tracks, climbing over discarded market carts and tore-up sofas, across Alameda Street, into South Gate: all-white, all-American.

3 We entered the first small corner grocery store we found. Everything was cool at first. We bought some bread, milk, soup cans and candy. We each walked out with a bag filled with food. We barely got a few feet, though, when five teenagers on bikes approached. We tried not to pay any attention and proceeded to our side of the tracks. But the youths pulled up in front of us. While two of them stood nearby on their bikes, three of them jumped off theirs and walked over to us.

4 "What do we got here?" one of the boys said. "Spics to order—maybe with some beans?"

5 He pushed me to the ground; the groceries splattered onto the asphalt. I felt melted gum and chips of broken beer bottle on my lips and cheek. Then somebody picked me up and held me while the two others seized my brother, tossed his groceries out, and pounded on him. They punched him in the face, in the stomach, then his face again, cutting his lip, causing him to vomit.

shrill: high pitched and sharp

6 I remember the **shrill**, maddening laughter of one of the kids on a bike, this laughing like a raven's wail, a harsh wind's shriek, a laugh that I would hear in countless beatings thereafter. I watched the others take turns on my brother, this terror of a brother, and he doubled over, had blood and spew on his shirt, and tears down his face. I wanted to do something, but they held me and I just looked on, as every strike against Rano opened me up inside.

7 They finally let my brother go and he slid to the ground, like a rotten banana squeezed out of its peeling. They threw us back over the tracks. In the sunset I could see the Watts Towers, shimmers of 70,000 pieces of broken bottles, sea shells, ceramic and metal on spiraling points puncturing the heavens, which reflected back the rays of a falling sun. My brother and I then picked ourselves up, saw the teenagers take off, still laughing, still talking about those stupid greasers who dared to cross over to South Gate.

disdain: strong dislike or disapproval

8 Up until then my brother had never shown any emotion to me other than **disdain**. He had never asked me anything, unless it was a demand, an expectation, an obligation to be his throwaway boy-doll. But for this once he looked at me, tears welled in his eyes, blood streamed from several cuts—lips and cheeks swollen.

9 "Swear—you got to swear—you'll never tell anybody how I cried," he said.

10 I suppose I did promise. It was his one last thing to hold onto, his rep as someone who could take a belt whipping, who could take a beating in the neighborhood and still go back risking more— it was this pathetic plea from the pavement I remember. I must have promised.

Poetry

'Race' POLITICS

by Luis J. Rodriguez

My brother and I
—shopping for *la jefita*—
decided to get the "good food"
over on the other side
5   of the tracks.

We dared each other.
Laughed a little.
Thought about it.
Said, what's the big deal.
10   Thought about that.
Decided we were men,
not boys.
Decided we should go wherever
we damn wanted to.

15   Oh, my brother—now he was bad.
Tough dude. Afraid of nothing.
I was afraid of him.

So there we go,
climbing over
20   the iron and wood ties,
over discarded sofas
     and bent-up market carts,
over a weed-and-dirt road,
into a place called South Gate
25   —all white. All American.

We entered the forbidden
narrow line of hate,
imposed,
transposed,
30   supposed,
a line of power/powerlessness
full of meaning,
meaning nothing—
those lines that crisscross

My Notes

la jefita: slang for mother

GRAMMAR & USAGE
Reciprocal Pronouns
In line 6 of the poem, Luis J. Rodriguez uses the **reciprocal pronoun** "each other" to speak of himself and his brother. Use "each other" when each of two subjects is doing the same thing or acting in the same way toward the other. The only other reciprocal pronoun is "one another." This pronoun is generally used when three or more subjects are doing the same thing.

imposed: made in a forceful way

abdomen: stomach and organs

35   the **abdomen** of this land,
that strangle you
in your days, in your nights.
When you dream.

There we were, two Mexicans,
40   six and nine—from Watts no less.
Oh, this was plenty reason
to hate us.

Plenty reason to run up behind us.
Five teenagers on bikes.
45   Plenty reason to knock
the groceries out from our arms—
a splattering heap of soup
cans, bread and candy.

Plenty reason to hold me down
50   on the hot asphalt; melted gum,
and chips of broken
beer bottle on my lips
and cheek.
Plenty reason to get my brother
55   by the throat, taking turns
punching him in the face,
cutting his lower lip,
punching, him vomiting.
Punching until swollen and dark blue
60   he slid from their grasp
like a rotten banana from its peeling.

When they had enough, they threw us back,
dirty and lacerated;
back to Watts, its towers shiny
65   across the orange-red sky.

My brother then forced me
to promise not to tell anybody
how he cried.
He forced me to swear to God,
70   to Jesus Christ, to our long-dead
Indian Grandmother—
keepers of our **meddling** souls.

meddling: interfering

Second Read

- Reread the memoir and the poem to answer these text-dependent questions.
- Write any additional questions you have about the text in your Reader/Writer Notebook.

Always Running

1. **Key Ideas and Details:** Like most narratives, this text immediately introduces the setting, characters, and conflict. Based on details in the first four paragraphs, what connects all three of these elements?

2. **Craft and Structure:** Choose a word that could replace *discarded* in paragraph 2 without changing the meaning or tone.

3. **Key Ideas and Details:** How does the description in paragraphs 4-7 of the bullies, their words, and their actions shape your perceptions of them? Of Rano?

4. **Craft and Structure:** What is the meaning of *obligation* as used in paragraph 8?

5. **Key Ideas and Details:** How does the description in paragraphs 8-10 shape your perception of the narrator's relationship to his brother? What does it help you infer about his decision to write this piece?

6. **Craft and Structure:** Find an example of foreshadowing. What does this suggest about the narrator's later life?

My Notes

Two Versions of One Narrative

"'Race' Politics"

7. **Key Ideas and Details:** Point out several fragments in the poem. What different effects do they create?

8. **Key Ideas and Details:** How does Rodriguez's use of repetition affect the tone? How do specific sensory details contribute to the effect of the repetition?

9. **Craft and Structure:** In line 27, what does the "narrow line of hate" refer to?

10. **Integration of Knowledge and Ideas:** The excerpt from *Always Running* and the poem "'Race' Politics" describe the same central incident. How is the focus in the two versions different?

Working from the Text

11. Use the graphic organizer on the following page to collect details from *Always Running* that indicate differences in the way the prose story is told compared to the poetic version in "'Race' Politics." Then discuss which components of coming of age are present in the two texts. Which voice do you think is more effective? Which is easier to visualize and understand? Why? Which version do you think is more powerful? Why?

Additions	What details or language have been added?	What is the effect of these changes?
Deletions	What details or language have been removed?	What is the effect of these changes?
Alterations	What is the effect of these changes?	What is the effect of these changes?

Identifying Parallel Structure

12. Rodriguez uses parallel structure in his poem. He uses prepositional phrases in lines 20–24 ("climbing over/the iron and wood ties/over discarded sofas/and bent-up market carts,/over a weed-and-dirt road ..."), and again to end the poem ("to God/to Jesus Christ, to our long-dead Indian Grandmother ..."). Use the My Notes space to describe the effect he creates with his use of parallel structure.

Two Versions of One Narrative

Introducing the Strategy: RAFT

RAFT is commonly considered a writing strategy. The letters stand for Role, Audience, Format, and Topic. Although RAFT can be used as a tool to analyze texts, it is most often used to generate and create ideas by asking writers to think about the role, audience, format, and topic of a text they want to write.

13. Now imagine the story is being told by a different narrator. Use the RAFT strategy to come up with different possible voices you could use to describe the same incident. Working with your discussion group members, brainstorm some possibilities in each category of the chart.

Role	Audience
Format	**Topic**

14. **Group Discussion:** With your group, review the group discussion norms in Activity 2. Then choose several combinations from the preceding graphic organizer and discuss how the writer's or speaker's diction, syntax, and imagery would likely change based on a different audience, situation, and purpose. What sorts of details would be added, deleted, or altered?

15. Next, choose the voice of one of the characters and practice answering interview questions. With a partner, role-play how the interview might sound. First, one of you can ask questions while the other answers in the voice of one of the characters. The interviewee should try to maintain the voice of the character by keeping word choice, language, and culture in mind. Then, switch roles.

Here are some possible questions to help you get started. Ask additional follow-up questions. Remember that good interview questions are open ended—they cannot be answered with a simple "yes" or "no."

Q: Can you tell me what happened today outside the grocery store?
A:

Q: Who would you say is mostly to blame for the incident and why?
A:

Q: If you could go back and change the incident, what would you do differently and why?
A:

Q: What is one way this incident could possibly end up having a positive outcome?
A:

Q: What did you learn from this incident?
A:

Check Your Understanding

How does changing the speaker, audience, or format influence the telling of an incident?

Narrative Writing Prompt

Write a brief narrative that relates the event Rodriguez tells in his memoir and poem. Choose one of the individuals you identified in the RAFT strategy and retell the story from that person's point of view. Be sure to:

- Find an appropriate voice for that individual and identify his or her context—that is, his or her knowledge of the situation and perspective on it.
- Begin with a statement that identifies the individual and that context.
- Incorporate some direct quotations from your responses to your partner's interview questions.

My Notes

Reading an Interview Narrative

Learning Targets
- Analyze how the relationship between a writer, the target audience, and the writer's purpose informs a writer's choices.
- Analyze the intended effect of a descriptive narrative on readers' perspectives.

Preview
In this activity, you will read an article about Chuck Liddell and analyze how the author incorporates narrative elements into his writing.

Setting a Purpose for Reading
- Annotate any instances of character and setting.
- Circle unknown words and phrases. Try to determine the meaning of the words by using context clues, word parts, or a dictionary.

My Notes

Nonfiction

WMDs

by Brian O'Connor, *Men's Fitness*

mosh pit: an area at a concert where people dance wildly and dangerously

1   WHO IS THE NEW AMERICAN FIGHTER? For starters, he resembles Chuck Liddell: With a thick coil of a neck and a close-cropped Mohawk, the Ultimate Fighting Championship's (UFC) light-heavyweight title-holder looks like a Marine who'd take great delight in clearing a **mosh pit**. And that Chinese calligraphy tattooed on the side of his head? Obviously his threshold for pain far surpasses that of the average Joe—and Jim, Bill, and Bob combined.

2   And that's helpful when you work inside an octagonal cage for a living. As a mixed martial artist (the technical term for Ultimate Fighting Championship competitors), Liddell, aka "The Iceman," combines fisticuffs, kickboxing, wrestling, and choke holds to either knock out his opponent or force him to "tap out," indicating a **submission**. In any other **context**, of course, this behavior would pass for felonious assault, so being within arm's length of Liddell for a day imparts a clarifying effect. Here's a man not only capable of kneeing you in the ribs until you're coughing blood, but who'd enjoy doing it. Or he could deliver a flying kick to your face that floors you, or land a haymaker with such ferocity that your brain trickles out your nose. Yes, the clarity is unmistakable: You are not a fighter, and Chuck Liddell is.

submission: an act of accepting that someone else has control over you

context: situation

3   But then you start talking with Chuck Liddell, and that clarity becomes clouded. You discover he grew up in sunny, sleepy Santa Barbara, Calif., and he has a degree

in accounting with a minor in business from Cal Poly San Luis Obispo. And then you learn that nearly 80% of the Ultimate Fighters have at least some college education, if not degrees. Many are communications grads, engineers, and computer programmers who come from farms and middle-class suburbs. In that respect, they are just like you. "If I weren't fighting, I'd be in the business world," says the 37-year-old Liddell. "I did well in school, was the captain of the wrestling team and the football team, and always got along well with people, so I'm sure I would have gotten a job in the real world. I probably wouldn't have liked that, though."

4 And then it becomes clear that Liddell, like most professional fighters, has made a decision: to reject the life of the suit and the cubicle and revert to the most primal of instincts. And somewhere in the balance, he's maximizing his youthful exuberance and finding his own sense of manhood.

5 "After the Spike TV show began airing, my career and the sport and the fan base changed," says Liddell, whose $1 million purses have bought him a mansion and a Ferrari. "People accepted us and became more educated about what we do. I get noticed everywhere now, and it's surprising who recognizes me—like this one 50-year-old lady who had a tattoo of my face on her shoulder. It's gotten a lot crazier."

6 During the hour we linger in Muggs, dozens of men drift into the bar, all somehow not working on a Wednesday at 1 p.m., and none of them drinking. Liddell politely tries to step toward the front door, but that's not going to happen. The owner would like to snap a few photos; one guy has his buddy Sean on the phone—"Chuck, can you talk to him?" "Hey, can you sign this for me?" Liddell diplomatically obliges. The sound of backslapping and the hushed murmur of awe and **deference** fill the air.

deference: respectfulness

7 Eventually we escape in a hired SUV that takes us to Manhattan's Peninsula Hotel before shuttling us to a taping of *Late Night With Conan O'Brien* and then The *Wiseguy Show* on Sirius Satellite Radio ...

8 The SUV stops and **Liddell** exits toward the **gilded** entrance ... where a small pack of fans congregate. He calmly signs autographs, gloves, and posters ... It occurs to me that the Chinese calligraphy tattooed on his head, which **Liddell** translates as "place of peace and prosperity" is a self-fulfilling prophecy. He is living in the moment.

gilded: coated with gold

9 In a few weeks, he'll return to his grueling training schedule, walking a wheelbarrow filled with 150 pounds of concrete up and down a steep San Luis Obispo driveway. And when he returns to the octagon to do battle with his next opponent, a college degree might seem inconsequential, but it's not. He's defending against multiple disciplines from competitors who have grown up on MMA—from Japan, Britain, Eastern Europe, and Canada—guys who are helping the sport evolve and adding new martial-arts disciplines into the mix. And they're **gunning** for him. "Fighting is like chess, and boxing is like checkers" says **Liddell**. "You have to defend against guys who are coming at you with all sorts of new tactics, new martial arts. You must be aware on different levels."

gunning: to go after with determination

10 In many ways, then, **Liddell's** job isn't unlike yours. You're competing in a global economy against younger guys looking to supplant you. As the world changes, so change is what a man must do to survive. **Chuck Liddell** has made his choice ...

My Notes

Reading an Interview Narrative

My Notes

Second Read

- Reread the article to answer these text-dependent questions.
- Write any additional questions you have about the text in your Reader/Writer Notebook.

1. **Key Ideas and Details:** In both fiction and nonfiction, characters are brought to life through details about their appearance, actions, and speech. Mark the descriptions in the interview that help you get a clear picture of Liddell. What can you infer about Liddell based on these details?

2. **Craft and Structure:** Where does O'Connor shift from explanatory text to narrative text in his interview write-up? Why is this shift in writing types effective?

3. **Craft and Structure:** What is the effect of describing Liddell in the future tense in paragraph 9?

Working from the Text

You have written an interview in a Q and A transcript format, but an interview narrative does more: it tells a story. An interview narrative contains certain elements that are common to all narratives:

- It has a **plot**—a sequence of events with a beginning, a middle, and an end.
- It features **characters** who are developed using various techniques of characterization (appearance, words, and actions).
- It has a **setting**.
- There is a central **conflict**, if not several, that may or may not be resolved.
- It is told from a particular **point of view**, or several, which affects how readers think and feel about the story.
- It has a **theme** or themes—a main message about life.

Introducing the Strategy: SOAPSTone

SOAPSTone stands for Speaker, Occasion, Audience, Purpose, Subject, and Tone. It is both a reading and a writing tool for analyzing the relationship between a writer, his or her purpose, and the target audience of the text. SOAPSTone guides you in asking questions to analyze a text or to plan for writing a composition. The questions are as follows:

- Who is the speaker? The speaker (or writer) is the voice that tells the story.
- What is the occasion? The occasion is the time and place of the story; it is the context that prompted the writing.
- Who is the audience? The audience is the person or persons to whom the piece is directed.
- What is the purpose? The purpose is the reason behind the text or what the writer wants the audience to think as a result of reading the text.
- What is the subject? The subject is the focus of the text.
- What is the tone? The tone is the speaker's (or writer's) attitude toward the topic.

4. Once you have read and marked the interview narrative, conduct a SOAPSTone analysis of the article using the graphic organizer on the following page.

My Notes

Reading an Interview Narrative

SOAPSTone	Analysis	Textual Support
Speaker: What does the reader know about the writer?		
Occasion: What are the circumstances surrounding this text?		
Audience: Who is the target audience?		
Purpose: Why did the author write this text?		
Subject: What is the topic?		
Tone: What is the author's tone, or attitude, toward the subject?		

My Notes

Check Your Understanding

How does O'Connor use details and his voice as a writer to appeal to his target audience?

Writing to Sources: Explanatory Text

Explain how the writer uses the elements of the interview to create a narrative. Use the SOAPSTone notes to provide examples of the elements of narrative that the writer incorporates. In your writing, be sure to:

- Begin with a clear thesis that states your position.
- Include direct quotations from the text to support each specific claim you make. Introduce and punctuate all quotations correctly.
- Include transitions between points and a concluding statement.

Examining the Art of Questioning

Learning Targets
- Transform an interview transcript into a narrative.
- Develop criteria for carefully crafting questions, including follow-up questions.
- Sequence questions to improve logical flow in an interview.

LEARNING STRATEGIES:
SOAPSTone, Manipulatives,
Rearranging

Preview
You have just read an article about Chuck Liddell, who was interviewed by the writer of the article. On the next page, you will read a **transcript** by a different writer of an interview with Chuck Liddell. While you are reading, think about how a transcript is different from an article.

Setting a Purpose for Reading
- Annotate any differences you notice between this transcript and the article you previously read.
- Circle unknown words and phrases. Try to determine the meaning of the words by using context clues, word parts, or a dictionary.

> **ACADEMIC VOCABULARY**
> A **transcript** is a written copy or record of a conversation that takes place between two or more people. It can be used as the basis for creating an interview narrative.

My Notes

Interview Transcript

Chuck Liddell

by Steven Yaccino

Chuck "the Iceman" Liddell still lives in the town of his **alma mater**. That's right: This trained lethal weapon earned a B.A. in accounting at Cal Poly before claiming the Ultimate Fighting Championship light heavyweight title in 2005. He's since become a mixed martial arts superstar, appearing on an episode of HBO's *Entourage* and authoring the memoir *Iceman: My Fighting Life*. Here, Liddell revisits his Cal Poly days, back when he juggled priorities and drank a lot of caffeine.

alma mater: the school from which a person graduated

Occupation: UFC fighter

Grew up: Santa Barbara, Calif.

College attended: California Polytechnic State University, San Luis Obispo

Major: Accounting

Graduation year: 1995

Nickname: The Iceman. My trainer called me that because I don't get nervous before fights.

Favorite drink / midnight snack: Mountain Dew was my favorite drink through college; it kept me up studying for a lot of tests. Also, any kind of candy.

INDEPENDENT READING LINK

Read and Connect
Create a SOAPSTone analysis of a section of your independent reading book. Then determine how effectively the author appeals to his or her audience based on tone and purpose.

Examining the Art of Questioning

How and why did you choose your major?

I was just good at it. Numbers have always come easy to me. When you came in as a freshman at Cal Poly, you had to declare a major. After about three years, I thought about changing it to construction management, because I was doing construction over the summers, or to PE. Originally, PE was the major I wanted, but my grandparents didn't see it as a real major. They saw it as I was going to be a PE teacher: They didn't realize that at Cal Poly, it was only two classes away from being pre-med. They didn't see that as looking for a real job. I think being a PE coach is a real job, but that's just me.

Were you a part of any activities like sports, music, clubs, or theater?

I played football my first year, and I wrestled for all five. You start football before school starts, and when you're done with football, wrestling has already started. Then when you're done with wrestling, there are three or four weeks and you're back into spring ball. And then you have a half of a summer and you're back into summer football.

It was just a little much. Plus, I was trying to cut weight for wrestling and trying to put on weight for football. It got to the point where I had to make a decision about where I wanted to be. I think I made the right decision with what I ended up doing.

Do you keep in touch with any of your college friends?

Yeah, a bunch of them. I still live in San Luis Obispo, so there's a bunch of us still here. Up until a couple years ago, my best friend in college lived a block away from me.

Were you a bookworm or a slacker?

I was the guy that would cram for everything, so I guess I was a bit of a slacker. I was a procrastinator. I spent a lot of all-nighters getting ready for tests.

Did you have a role model when you were in college?

Not really. I just kind of learned stuff on my own.

What was the biggest obstacle you overcame in college?

The biggest thing was balancing working out, competing, and academics to graduate. And also working in the summers to try and save money.

What did you like most and least about your school?

I love the town. It's a small town; it's beautiful here. I like visiting big cities, but I don't do well there for long periods of time.

Tell us one way in which college changed you.

I grew up while I was in college. I learned how to take care of myself. I learned how to prioritize things. I learned how to get things done.

If you could go back, what about college would you do differently?

I might have cared a little more about my grades. I ended up with a 3.1, but I could have easily done a lot better. I just didn't care too much.

I had a class where I was actually tutoring two kids from the wrestling team, but I got a C because I didn't do any of the homework. The teacher said if I turned in my homework on the day of the final, she'd give me my A or else she was going to give me a C. The guys I was tutoring gave me the homework to copy, and I copied four of them and said forget it: I'll take the C. Stuff like that. Not that it matters too much. I mean, I graduated.

What was your favorite hangout spot?

I used to bar-tend in college at a cool place. It was called Brubeck's. I worked probably six or seven days a week. We'd get a lot of different people there; it was a lot of fun.

Which schools did you apply to?

U of C-Berkeley, Cal Poly, and other West Coast schools. I went with Cal Poly because I wanted to wrestle and play football.

Did you get into all of them?

I got into all the schools I applied to except Cal Poly. I guess they lost my application. I never got a rejection or an acceptance. I either messed up on the application or it just didn't get through. My coach had to get me in. They have a way for a lot of teams to get you into the school. I don't know how it worked exactly, but I had the grades and SATs to get into my major.

Second Read

- Reread the interview to answer these text-dependent questions.
- Write any additional questions you have about the text in your Reader/Writer Notebook.

1. **Craft and Structure:** Explain the connection between Liddell's nickname, "The Iceman," and his demeanor before a fight.

2. **Key Ideas and Details:** Reorder the interviewer's questions to create a clear sense of progression and to form stronger connections between the questions and responses.

My Notes

Examining the Art of Questioning

3. **Craft and Structure:** Where do you find examples of parallel structure in Liddell's responses? Why do you think he uses parallel structure in each instance?

4. **Key Ideas and Details:** After reading this interview, what inferences can you make about Liddell's character traits?

Working from the Text

Reread each question from the transcript and annotate the text as follows:

- Label each question as an open-ended or a closed question. Focus on the question itself, rather than on the answer. Not every interviewee will generously answer a closed question with an extended response.

- Evaluate each question on a scale of 1–3 in terms of its effectiveness. Keep in mind the goals of the interview you will soon be conducting (to explore the significance of the person's college experience—how it contributed to his or her coming of age and becoming successful).
  1 = I learned a lot about the person from the answer elicited by this question.
  2 = I learned something about the person, but I wanted to learn more.
  3 = I did not learn very much about the person from the answer elicited by this question.

5. Now write down the five questions you thought were least effective (you probably gave them a 3) in the left-hand column of the graphic organizer. With a partner, revise the questions to make them more open and effective. You might add a follow-up question to do so. **Follow-up questions** do exactly what the name implies: They follow up on something the interviewee has said. For example:

Q: What was the best thing that happened to you in college?

A: I guess when I got a "D" in my physics class.

Follow-up Q: That doesn't sound like a very good thing. Why was it the best thing that happened to you?

You might not have anticipated the answer to that question, but pursuing the topic could lead to some interesting information about your interviewee. You should be flexible about your planned questions and allow for follow-up questions. Here are a few ways you could follow up on an answer:

- Why do you think that?
- That sounds interesting. Could you tell me more about it?
- What happened next?
- How has that influenced your life?

Original Question	Revision or Follow-up Question	My Notes

Examining the Art of Questioning

My Notes

6. Now that you have finished reading the interview transcript, look carefully at the order of the questions. Does the sequence of questions create a logical flow? If not, what order would flow better? Be prepared to justify your choices.

Check Your Understanding

For Embedded Assessment 1, you will write your own interview narrative. You will create interview questions, conduct an interview, and record answers to draft a transcript much like the one you have just analyzed. Write a brief reflection on strategies you can use to plan for your interview and ask effective questions.

Transforming the Transcript

Learning Targets

- Examine an interview transcript and transform it into a narrative.
- Compare and evaluate two approaches to establishing point of view and focus in an interview narrative, and choose which best fits purpose and audience.

Preview

In this activity, you will read excerpts from two student essays and identify each point of view.

Setting a Purpose for Reading

- Circle personal pronouns.
- Highlight the sentences that integrate quotes and speaker tags such as "she says" or "she explains" to describe the speaker's voice.
- Underline any descriptive information.

LEARNING STRATEGIES:
Marking the Text, Drafting

My Notes

Excerpt 1

As we begin the interview, Mrs. Gamer appears stressed, but includes her enthusiastic commentary and gesticulations nonetheless. It seems almost as if she's performing a play as she constructs her answers, and after all, she originally planned to pursue film studies. Upon questioning about her friend group, this vivacious pseudo-actress begins rambling off an extensive list of names, describing her old group in a dramatic whisper as "low drama, high impact." She continues on to outline her favorite classes, revealing a pattern: "A class on Chaucer with Dr. Ganim; Baroque Art with Dr. Pelzel; American Art and Architecture with Dr. Carrott…," she tells me. Her explanation for her favorite teacher is "because he loved Pedro Almodóvar just as much as I did." It is from these statements that the picture of a budding librarian emerges. But there is another trend accompanying the conversation: Mrs. Gamer was not the A student she makes herself out to be. On being asked what her study habits were like, she stares at me with a bewildered, gaping expression. "Study habits?" she intones gently.

Excerpt 2

Before she graduated from high school, Ruth took many steps to prepare herself for college. She remembers, "I always studied and worked hard; I had an after-school job and saved earnings to travel and go to college." A step she took to prepare herself was taking the PSAT and SAT exams. Ruth knew she wanted to study abroad and go far away for college. She applied to CU Boulder, University of Northern Colorado, Wittenberg University, Ithaca College, and Gettysburg College. She was accepted into all of these colleges, except for Gettysburg, and chose to attend Wittenberg. After considering the schools she chose, she recalled, "My main reason for attending Wittenberg was to please my dad. He really wanted me to attend a small Lutheran school, and because he was paying for my tuition, I thought it was the right thing to do." While at Wittenberg, Ruth played on the school's varsity lacrosse team, met her future husband, and studied hard. "I was a very balanced student," she recalls. "I knew I had to keep my priorities straight—and that's what I did." But she was restless, despite being well prepared. "I always felt that there was something bigger and better waiting ahead for me," she explains.

Transforming the Transcript

Working from the Text

1. Identify the point of view in each excerpt.

2. With your group members, discuss the strengths and weaknesses of these two approaches.

   How is the pacing different in the two excerpts?

   As readers, which do you prefer? Why?

   Which best allows the writer to capture the voice of the interviewee? How?

Check Your Understanding

Explain which point of view is stronger and why.

Narrative Writing Prompt

Write a narrative using the "Chuck Liddell" interview transcript from Activity 1.10 and incorporate your chosen point of view, narrative approach, and quotations from the transcript. Be sure to:

- Include the three descriptive techniques (appearance, speech, and actions) to describe Liddell and focus on a key incident.
- Craft your narrative into a logical or chronological organization.
- Use varied approaches to incorporate direct quotations into your narrative.

Planning an Interview

Learning Target
• Plan and prepare to conduct an effective interview.

Planning an Interview

For Embedded Assessment 1, you will conduct an interview and write a narrative in which you present that interview. You have probably noticed that conducting an interview takes a good deal of planning. You need to begin planning now for the interview you will conduct.

The focus of your interview will be to find out about a person's overall postsecondary education experience and to discover at least one important incident during that time that influenced the interviewee's coming of age.

Step One

Make a list of people you might be able to interview. Include only people with whom you could have a face-to-face meeting before the assignment is due.

Name of Person I Might Be Able to Interview	Why I Would Like to Interview This Person About His or Her Postsecondary Experience

Step Two

Contact the people on your list to schedule your interview with one of them. Let the person know why you are conducting the interview and that some portions of it may be shared with your classmates.

Step Three

Write the details of your appointment:

• I have arranged to interview:

• Date the interview is scheduled:

• Time:

• Place:

LEARNING STRATEGIES:
Brainstorming, Generating Questions, Writer's Checklist

My Notes

Planning an Interview

Step Four

Brainstorm a list of questions and possible follow-up questions you might ask during the interview. Keep in mind the focus of your interview as you think of potential questions.

1.

2.

3.

4.

5.

6.

Step Five

Now exchange questions with a classmate. Have your classmate evaluate your questions. As you read your classmate's questions, suggest revisions, follow-up questions, or shifts in order.

Remember, you probably will not ask all these questions. Once your conversation begins to flow, you will ask follow-up questions. It is important, though, to walk into your interview with a list of questions to start the interview and to keep it going.

Step Six

With your group members, preview the "Writer's Checklist" in the Embedded Assessment for the interview narrative. Identify those skills you have specifically addressed in this unit.

Independent Reading Checkpoint

Choose one of the readings from the first half of this unit. Compare author's voice and tone with the author's voice and tone in your independent reading text as they described a coming-of-age experience.

Writing and Presenting an Interview Narrative

ASSIGNMENT

Your assignment is to interview a person who has attended a postsecondary institution (i.e., a two- or four-year college, a training or vocational school, the military) and to write an interview narrative that effectively portrays the voice of the interviewee while revealing how the experience contributed to his or her coming of age.

Planning: Plan and conduct the interview.	▪ Have you arranged a time and place to meet with your interviewee? ▪ Are you satisfied with the list of questions you might ask? If not, revise them. ▪ Have you considered recording the interview? Or will you simply take hand-written notes, or both? Have you asked permission to record the interview? ▪ How will you set up the interview as a conversation rather than an interrogation? ▪ What will you do to remind yourself to ask good follow-up questions rather than simply sticking to the questions on your list? ▪ What question(s) will you ask to get your interviewee to describe in depth at least one specific coming-of-age incident from his or her college or postsecondary institution experience? ▪ When you feel that you have adequate information, you can begin to draw the interview to a close. Remember to take good notes and to thank the interviewee.
Prewriting: Prepare to write the interview narrative.	▪ How will you make time to read over your notes and add to, delete, or refine them as the basis for your interview narrative? ▪ What quotes or descriptions of the person will you use to give a vivid picture and create an authentic voice?
Drafting: Decide how to structure your interview narrative.	▪ What will you include in the introduction? ▪ Have you included information about the person's experiences in general and those related to attending college or a postsecondary institution in particular? ▪ Have you used vivid and precise imagery, carefully chosen diction, and a mix of direct and indirect quotations to convey a sense of the interviewee's voice?
Revising and Editing for Publication: Review and revise to make your work the best it can be.	▪ Have you carefully transformed your questions and answers into a narrative? ▪ Have you arranged to share your draft with a partner or with your writing group? ▪ Have you consulted the Scoring Guide and the activities to prepare for revising your draft? ▪ Did you use your available resources (e.g., spell check, dictionaries, Writer's Checklist) to edit for conventions and prepare your narrative for publication?

Reflection

A successful interview can be a rewarding experience for both the interviewer and the interviewee. What did you learn that you did not expect to learn, and how would you evaluate the experience for both you and your interviewee?

Writing and Presenting an Interview Narrative

SCORING GUIDE

Scoring Criteria	Exemplary	Proficient	Emerging	Incomplete
Ideas	The narrative • insightfully describes one or more postsecondary education incidents that influenced the interviewee's coming of age • uses vivid examples of character description • develops an engaging and authentic character and presents that person's unique perspective.	The narrative • describes one or more incidents from the interviewer's postsecondary education experience • includes examples of character description • develops the character and presents the person's perspective.	The narrative • begins to describe an incident about the interviewee's postsecondary education experience • includes limited examples of character description • develops some aspects of character but does not provide a clear perspective.	The narrative • does not describe an incident from the interviewee's postsecondary education experience • does not contain examples of character description • does not develop the character or the person's perspective.
Structure	The narrative • follows the structure of the genre with well-sequenced events • clearly orients the reader and uses effective transitions for coherence • demonstrates a consistent point of view.	The narrative • follows the structure of the genre with a sequence of events • orients the reader and uses transitions for coherence • uses a mostly consistent point of view.	The narrative • follows some structure of the genre • somewhat orients the reader with limited coherence • uses an inconsistent point of view.	The narrative • does not follow the structure of the genre • fails to orient the reader and has no coherence • uses confusing points of view.
Use of Language	The narrative • purposefully uses quotations with telling details, and vivid imagery to convey a strong sense of the inteviewee's voice • smoothly embeds direct and indirect quotations • demonstrates strong command of conventions and spelling.	The narrative • uses quotations and telling details to portray the interviewee's voice • embeds some direct and/or indirect quotations • demonstrates general command of conventions and spelling; minor errors do not interfere with meaning.	The narrative • uses limited quotations to portray the voice of the interviewee • contains one or no embedded quotations • demonstrates limited command of conventions and spelling; errors begin to interfere with meaning.	The narrative • uses no quotations to portray the voice of the interviewee • contains no embedded quotations • contains frequent errors in grammar and conventions that interfere with meaning.

Previewing Embedded Assessment 2 and Preparing to Write an Argument

Learning Targets

- Identify the knowledge and skills needed to successfully complete Embedded Assessment 2 and reflect on prior learning that supports the knowledge and skills needed.
- Examine the essential elements of an argument.

Making Connections

In the first part of this unit, you studied voice in coming-of-age narratives in both fictional and nonfictional forms. For independent reading, you have been reading biographical texts. Now, you will shift your focus from narrative texts to persuasive texts. You will review the rhetorical appeals of ethos, pathos, and logos and how they work together with evidence to support the claim in an argument.

Essential Questions

Now that you have read texts and explored the concept of coming of age, how would you change your answer to the first essential question that asks, "What does it mean to 'come of age'?"

To prepare for the second half of this unit, think about the second essential question: How do authors and speakers persuade and influence an audience?

Developing Vocabulary

Look back at the vocabulary you have studied in the first part of this unit. Which terms do you know well and can use effectively in class discussions and in your writing? Which terms do you need to learn more about or practice using more frequently?

Unpacking Embedded Assessment 2

Read the assignment for Embedded Assessment 2: Writing an Argumentative Essay. What knowledge must you have (what do you need to know) to succeed on Embedded Assessment 2? What skills must you have (what must you be able to do)?

> Your assignment is to write an essay of argumentation about the value of a college education. Your essay must be organized as an argument in which you assert a precise claim, support it with reasons and evidence, and acknowledge and refute counterclaims fairly.

In your own words, summarize what you will need to know to complete this assessment successfully. With your class, create a graphic organizer to represent the skills and knowledge you will need to complete the tasks identified in the Embedded Assessment.

LEARNING STRATEGIES:
Close Reading, Summarizing, Marking the Text, Discussion Groups

My Notes

INDEPENDENT READING LINK

Read and Respond
To help you choose which side of the argument for your essay, select articles and other essays about the topic for independent reading. As you read, write in your Reader/Writer Notebook the points of the argument that seem most convincing.

Previewing Embedded Assessment 2 and Preparing to Write an Argument

My Notes

Essential Elements of an Argument

In Embedded Assessment 2, you will write an argumentative essay. An **argument** is a discussion in which reasons are put forward in support of and against a claim. A written argument must meet several conditions in order to be a valid argument and not merely an effort to persuade.

1. The central claim needs to be debatable.
2. The claim must be supported by evidence.
3. The writer needs to address the opposition by acknowledging counterclaims and the evidence supporting them.

With these conditions in mind, consider the following elements of an effective argument:

- **Introduction and claim:** an opening that grabs the reader's attention while informing the reader of the claim, which is a clear and straightforward statement of the writer's belief about the topic of the argument.
- **Supporting paragraphs:** the reasons offered in support of a claim, supported by different types of evidence.
- **Concession and/or refutation:** restatements of valid counterclaims made by the opposing side (concessions), or the writer's arguments against those opposing viewpoints (refutations), explaining why the writer's position is more valid.
- **Conclusion/call to action:** closing statements restating the major arguments in defense of a thesis (the claim) with a final challenge to the reader to take action.

An argument has three major purposes:

- To change a reader's or listener's point of view
- To ask the reader or listener to take an action
- To gain acceptance for the writer's ideas about a problem or issue

1. **Discussion Group:** Form a group of three or four students to share information. For Embedded Assessment 1, you wrote an interview narrative about a person who had attended a postsecondary institution. What did you learn about the advantages or disadvantages of postsecondary education from your interviewee? What claims did your interviewee make? Use the space below and the My Notes space to write 3–5 advantages or disadvantages about postsecondary education as described by each person you interviewed. Add a direct quotation from the interviewee to support your interviewee's claim.

2. You will next view a presentation called "Why Go?" produced by the College Board (youcango.collegeboard.org/why-go). As you view this presentation, take notes on the reasons given in support of the central claim. Be as specific as possible, and include quotes as you record evidence in support of each reason.

Reason	Support/Evidence
Greater Wealth	
More Security	
Better Health	
Close Family	
Stronger Community	

3. Which of these reasons is the most and least persuasive? Why?

Check Your Understanding

Write a paragraph in which you state the central claim of the presentation, "Why Go?". Include evidence from the graphic organizer that supports the claim.

Building an Argument

My Notes

Learning Targets
- Evaluate how reasons and evidence support a claim.
- Examine and select appropriate evidence to support a persuasive claim.

Preview
In this activity, you will read an informational text on the financial benefits of a college education and analyze the claim and supporting evidence.

Setting a Purpose for Reading
- As you read the informational text, identify the claim and highlight any supporting evidence.
- Circle unknown words and phrases. Try to determine the meaning of the words by using context clues, word parts, or a dictionary.

Informational Text

Education Still Pays

1   As the cost of higher education continues to climb, prospective students and their families might wonder: "Does it still pay to get an education?" According to the most recent data from the U.S. Bureau of Labor Statistics (BLS): Yes, it does.

2   For decades, BLS data have shown that workers with more education have lower unemployment and higher earnings than workers with less education. And 2013 data are no exception.

3   For example, as the chart shows, the unemployment rate drops with every additional level of education attained. Workers with less education than a high school diploma had the highest unemployment rate (11 percent), while those with a doctoral degree had the lowest rate (2.2 percent).

4   Earnings by educational attainment generally follow the opposite pattern, peaking for workers with a professional degree—a group that includes lawyers and dentists—and decreasing as education levels fall. The earnings data in the chart are medians; within each education level, half of workers earned more than the amount shown, and half earned less.

5   Keep in mind that education alone doesn't determine your success in the job market. Wages and employment vary based on a number of factors, including occupation, geographic location, and experience. Find out which occupations match your interests, skills, and career goals to determine the level of education that is likely to pay off for you.

6   These data come from the BLS Current Population Survey, a monthly survey of households that collects information about demographic and labor force characteristics.

www.bls.gov/CPS

Unemployment rates and earnings for full-time wage and salary workers ages 25 and older, by educational attainment, 2013

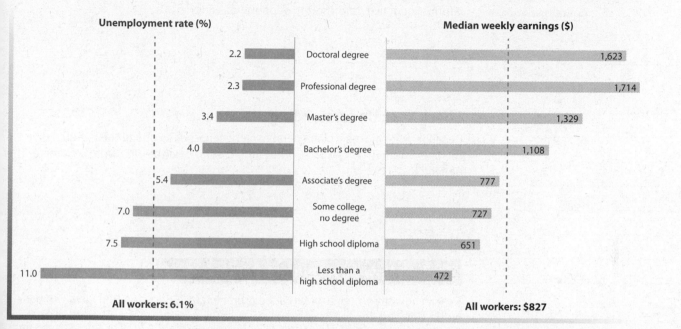

Unemployment rate (%)   **Median weekly earnings ($)**

Unemployment rate (%)	Degree	Median weekly earnings ($)
2.2	Doctoral degree	1,623
2.3	Professional degree	1,714
3.4	Master's degree	1,329
4.0	Bachelor's degree	1,108
5.4	Associate's degree	777
7.0	Some college, no degree	727
7.5	High school diploma	651
11.0	Less than a high school diploma	472

All workers: 6.1%   **All workers: $827**

Second Read

- Reread the informational text to answer these text-dependent questions.
- Write any additional questions you have about the text in your Reader/Writer Notebook.

1. **Key Ideas and Details:** What claim does this article make?

2. **Key Ideas and Details:** How does this article support the claim?

3. **Key Ideas and Details:** What is the source of this information? Is the data cited reliable? Why or why not?

4. **Key Ideas and Details:** How does the presentation of data in a chart aid the reader?

My Notes

Building an Argument

Working from the Text

In the presentation "Why Go?" greater wealth was given as one of the benefits of a college education. How would your career choices and potential earnings be affected by having a college degree? Use information from the presentation, informational text, and chart to support your answer.

Check Your Understanding

Describe what makes a claim persuasive. Then, choose one of the benefits given in the presentation "Why Go?"—other than greater wealth—and write a claim for that benefit.

Explain How an Argument Persuades

Explain how the writer structures the argument in "Education Still Pays." In your writing, be sure to:

- Identify the claim made by the writer and analyze how clear and direct it is.
- Explain what reasons and supporting evidence the writer uses and how counterclaims are addressed. Evaluate the effectiveness of the reasons, evidence, and refutations of counterclaims.
- Explain how the writer concludes the essay and how effective that ending is.

Using Rhetorical Appeals

Learning Targets
- Identify and analyze the effectiveness of the use of logos, ethos, and pathos in texts.
- Explain how a writer or speaker uses rhetoric to advance his or her purpose.

Elements of Rhetoric

Rhetoric is the use of words to persuade in writing or speech. Aristotle defined rhetoric as "the ability, in each particular case, to see the available means of persuasion." He described three main types of rhetoric: *logos, ethos,* and *pathos*. Authors and speakers use **rhetorical appeals** in their arguments to persuade the intended audience that their claims are right.

The Rhetorical Triangle

Together, these rhetorical appeals are central to understanding how writers and speakers appeal to their audiences and persuade them to accept their messages. It is helpful to think of them as three points of a triangle.

Logos: Text—What information, evidence, and logical reasoning are offered within the text?

Pathos: Audience—What values, beliefs, and emotions are appealed to within the text? How does the text evoke the audience's feelings?

Ethos: Speaker—What perception of the speaker is created within the text? How does the text evoke the audience's trust?

Literary Terms
Rhetorical appeals are emotional, ethical, and logical appeals used to persuade an audience to agree with the writer or speaker.
Logos is a rhetorical appeal to reason or logic.
Ethos is a rhetorical appeal that focuses on the character or qualifications of the speaker.
Pathos is a rhetorical appeal to the reader's or listener's senses or emotions.

My Notes

_____
_____
_____
_____
_____

INDEPENDENT READING LINK
Read and Respond
In your independent reading, look for elements of an effective argument that you have been studying in this unit, including claims, counterclaims, and supporting evidence. Note the most effective elements in your Reader/Writer Notebook.

Using Rhetorical Appeals

My Notes

Preview

In this activity, you will read a speech and analyze the use of rhetorical appeals.

Setting a Purpose for Reading

- As you read the speech, underline any examples of logos, ethos, and pathos.
- Circle unknown words and phrases. Try to determine the meaning of the words by using context clues, word parts, or a dictionary.

ABOUT THE AUTHOR

Barack Obama (b. 1961) became the 44th president of the United States in 2009. As a senator from Illinois, Obama rose to national prominence after giving a speech at the 2004 Democratic National Convention. He worked as a civil-rights lawyer and a teacher prior to entering politics. He was the first African American president of the United States.

Speech

REMARKS BY THE PRESIDENT IN A NATIONAL ADDRESS TO

AMERICA'S Schoolchildren

by President Barack Obama
Wakefield High School, Arlington, Virginia, September 8, 2009

1   … I know that for many of you, today is the first day of school. And for those of you in kindergarten, or starting middle or high school, it's your first day in a new school, so it's understandable if you're a little nervous. I imagine there are some seniors out there who are feeling pretty good right now with just one more year to go. And no matter what grade you're in, some of you are probably wishing it were still summer and you could've stayed in bed just a little bit longer this morning.

2   I know that feeling. When I was young, my family lived overseas. I lived in Indonesia for a few years. And my mother, she didn't have the money to send me where all the American kids went to school, but she thought it was important for me to keep up with an American education. So she decided to teach me extra lessons herself, Monday through Friday. But because she had to go to work, the only time she could do it was at 4:30 in the morning.

3   Now, as you might imagine, I wasn't too happy about getting up that early. And a lot of times, I'd fall asleep right there at the kitchen table. But whenever I'd complain, my mother would just give me one of those looks and she'd say, "This is no picnic for me either, buster."

4   So I know that some of you are still adjusting to being back at school. But I'm here today because I have something important to discuss with you. I'm here because I want to talk with you about your education and what's expected of all of you in this new school year.

5   Now, I've given a lot of speeches about education. And I've talked about responsibility a lot. I've talked about teachers' responsibility for inspiring students and pushing you to learn. I've talked about your parents' responsibility for making sure you stay on track, and you get your homework done, and don't spend every waking hour in front of the TV or with the Xbox. I've talked a lot about your government's responsibility for setting high standards, and supporting teachers and principals, and turning around schools that aren't working, where students aren't getting the opportunities that they deserve.

6   But at the end of the day, we can have the most dedicated teachers, the most supportive parents, the best schools in the world—and none of it will make a difference, none of it will matter unless all of you fulfill your responsibilities, unless you show up to those schools, unless you pay attention to those teachers, unless you listen to your parents and grandparents and other adults and put in the hard work it takes to succeed. That's what I want to focus on today: the responsibility each of you has for your education.

7   I want to start with the responsibility you have to yourself. Every single one of you has something that you're good at. Every single one of you has something to offer. And you have a responsibility to yourself to discover what that is. That's the opportunity an education can provide.

8   Maybe you could be a great writer—maybe even good enough to write a book or articles in a newspaper—but you might not know it until you write that English paper—that English class paper that's assigned to you. Maybe you could be an innovator or an inventor—maybe even good enough to come up with the next iPhone or the new medicine or vaccine—but you might not know it until you do your project for your science class. Maybe you could be a mayor or a senator or a Supreme Court justice—but you might not know that until you join student government or the debate team.

9   And no matter what you want to do with your life, I guarantee that you'll need an education to do it. You want to be a doctor, or a teacher, or a police officer? You want to be a nurse or an architect, a lawyer or a member of our military? You're going to need a good education for every single one of those careers. You cannot drop out of school and just drop into a good job. You've got to train for it and work for it and learn for it.

10   And this isn't just important for your own life and your own future. What you make of your education will decide nothing less than the future of this country. The future of America depends on you. What you're learning in school today will determine whether we as a nation can meet our greatest challenges in the future.

11   You'll need the knowledge and problem-solving skills you learn in science and math to cure diseases like cancer and AIDS, and to develop new energy technologies and protect our environment. You'll need the insights and critical-thinking skills you gain in history and social studies to fight poverty and homelessness, crime and discrimination, and make our nation more fair and more free. You'll need the creativity and **ingenuity** you develop in all your classes to build new companies that will create new jobs and boost our economy.

12   We need every single one of you to develop your talents and your skills and your intellect so you can help us old folks solve our most difficult problems. If you don't do that—if you quit on school—you're not just quitting on yourself, you're quitting on your country.

13   Now, I know it's not always easy to do well in school. I know a lot of you have challenges in your lives right now that can make it hard to focus on your schoolwork.

GRAMMAR & USAGE
Inappropriate Shifts in Voice
Multiple verbs within a sentence should have the same voice: either active or passive.

Active voice means the subject is doing the verb's action:

The girl attended the concert.

Passive voice means the subject is acted upon:

The concert was attended by the girl.

Inappropriate shifts can confuse an audience. Think about what effect President Obama creates by using active voice, rather than passive voice, in his speech.

My Notes

ingenuity: the skill or intelligence of being able to solve problems

Using Rhetorical Appeals

14 I get it. I know what it's like. My father left my family when I was two years old, and I was raised by a single mom who had to work and who struggled at times to pay the bills and wasn't always able to give us the things that other kids had. There were times when I missed having a father in my life. There were times when I was lonely and I felt like I didn't fit in.

15 So I wasn't always as focused as I should have been on school, and I did some things I'm not proud of, and I got in more trouble than I should have. And my life could have easily taken a turn for the worse.

16 But I was—I was lucky. I got a lot of second chances, and I had the opportunity to go to college and law school and follow my dreams. My wife, our First Lady Michelle Obama, she has a similar story. Neither of her parents had gone to college, and they didn't have a lot of money. But they worked hard, and she worked hard, so that she could go to the best schools in this country.

17 Some of you might not have those advantages. Maybe you don't have adults in your life who give you the support that you need. Maybe someone in your family has lost their job and there's not enough money to go around. Maybe you live in a neighborhood where you don't feel safe, or have friends who are pressuring you to do things you know aren't right.

18 But at the end of the day, the circumstances of your life—what you look like, where you come from, how much money you have, what you've got going on at home—none of that is an excuse for neglecting your homework or having a bad attitude in school. That's no excuse for talking back to your teacher, or cutting class, or dropping out of school. There is no excuse for not trying. Where you are right now doesn't have to determine where you'll end up. No one's written your destiny for you, because here in America, you write your own destiny. You make your own future.

19 That's what young people like you are doing every day, all across America.

20 Young people like Jazmin Perez, from Roma, Texas. Jazmin didn't speak English when she first started school. Neither of her parents had gone to college. But she worked hard, earned good grades, and got a scholarship to Brown University—is now in graduate school, studying public health, on her way to becoming Dr. Jazmin Perez.

21 I'm thinking about Andoni Schultz, from Los Altos, California, who's fought brain cancer since he was three. He's had to endure all sorts of treatments and surgeries, one of which affected his memory, so it took him much longer—hundreds of extra hours—to do his schoolwork. But he never fell behind. He's headed to college this fall.

22 And then there's Shantell Steve, from my hometown of Chicago, Illinois. Even when bouncing from foster home to foster home in the toughest neighborhoods in the city, she managed to get a job at a local health care center, start a program to keep young people out of gangs, and she's on track to graduate high school with honors and go on to college.

23 And Jazmin, Andoni, and Shantell aren't any different from any of you. They face challenges in their lives just like you do. In some cases they've got it a lot worse off than many of you. But they refused to give up. They chose to take responsibility for their lives, for their education, and set goals for themselves. And I expect all of you to do the same.

24 That's why today I'm calling on each of you to set your own goals for your education—and do everything you can to meet them. Your goal can be something as simple as doing all your homework, paying attention in class, or spending some time each day reading a book. Maybe you'll decide to get involved in an extracurricular

activity, or volunteer in your community. Maybe you'll decide to stand up for kids who are being teased or bullied because of who they are or how they look, because you believe, like I do, that all young people deserve a safe environment to study and learn. Maybe you'll decide to take better care of yourself so you can be more ready to learn. And along those lines, by the way, I hope all of you are washing your hands a lot, and that you stay home from school when you don't feel well, so we can keep people from getting the flu this fall and winter.

25 But whatever you resolve to do, I want you to commit to it. I want you to really work at it.

26 I know that sometimes you get that sense from TV that you can be rich and successful without any hard work—that your ticket to success is through rapping or basketball or being a reality TV star. Chances are you're not going to be any of those things.

27 The truth is, being successful is hard. You won't love every subject that you study. You won't click with every teacher that you have. Not every homework assignment will seem completely relevant to your life right at this minute. And you won't necessarily succeed at everything the first time you try.

28 That's okay. Some of the most successful people in the world are the ones who've had the most failures. J.K. Rowling's—who wrote Harry Potter—her first Harry Potter book was rejected 12 times before it was finally published. Michael Jordan was cut from his high school basketball team. He lost hundreds of games and missed thousands of shots during his career. But he once said, "I have failed over and over and over again in my life. And that's why I succeed."

29 These people succeeded because they understood that you can't let your failures define you—you have to let your failures teach you. You have to let them show you what to do differently the next time. So if you get into trouble, that doesn't mean you're a troublemaker, it means you need to try harder to act right. If you get a bad grade, that doesn't mean you're stupid, it just means you need to spend more time studying.

30 No one's born being good at all things. You become good at things through hard work. You're not a varsity athlete the first time you play a new sport. You don't hit every note the first time you sing a song. You've got to practice. The same principle applies to your schoolwork. You might have to do a math problem a few times before you get it right. You might have to read something a few times before you understand it. You definitely have to do a few drafts of a paper before it's good enough to hand in.

31 Don't be afraid to ask questions. Don't be afraid to ask for help when you need it. I do that every day. Asking for help isn't a sign of weakness, it's a sign of strength because it shows you have the courage to admit when you don't know something, and that then allows you to learn something new. So find an adult that you trust—a parent, a grandparent or teacher, a coach or a counselor—and ask them to help you stay on track to meet your goals.

32 And even when you're struggling, even when you're discouraged, and you feel like other people have given up on you, don't ever give up on yourself, because when you give up on yourself, you give up on your country.

33 The story of America isn't about people who quit when things got tough. It's about people who kept going, who tried harder, who loved their country too much to do anything less than their best. It's the story of students who sat where you sit 250 years ago, and went on to wage a revolution and they founded this nation. Young people. Students who sat where you sit 75 years ago who overcame a Depression and won a world

My Notes

Using Rhetorical Appeals

war; who fought for civil rights and put a man on the moon. Students who sat where you sit 20 years ago who founded Google and Twitter and Facebook and changed the way we communicate with each other.

34   So today, I want to ask all of you, what's your contribution going to be? What problems are you going to solve? What discoveries will you make? What will a President who comes here in 20 or 50 or 100 years say about what all of you did for this country?

35   Now, your families, your teachers, and I are doing everything we can to make sure you have the education you need to answer these questions. I'm working hard to fix up your classrooms and get you the books and the equipment and the computers you need to learn. But you've got to do your part, too. So I expect all of you to get serious this year. I expect you to put your best effort into everything you do. I expect great things from each of you. So don't let us down. Don't let your family down or your country down. Most of all, don't let yourself down. Make us all proud.

36   Thank you very much, everybody. God bless you. God bless America. Thank you.

Second Read

- Reread the speech to answer these text-dependent questions.
- Write any additional questions you have about the text in your Reader/Writer Notebook.

1. **Key Ideas and Details:** The president begins his speech with statements about the audience's feelings and then a story about his own childhood. Why does he begin his speech in this way?

2. **Key Ideas and Details:** What is the main idea of this speech?

3. **Craft and Structure:** What rhetorical appeal (logos, ethos, or pathos) is represented by the hypothetical situations in paragraph 9?

4. **Craft and Structure:** What type of appeal is most prominent in paragraphs 13–16? Why might the speaker choose to include his own personal story here?

5. **Craft and Structure:** In paragraph 17, what is the effect of the president's repeated use of the word *maybe*?

6. **Craft and Structure:** In paragraphs 18–24, what does the president do to overcome potential resistance by his audience? Does this approach rely more on logos or on pathos? Explain.

7. **Craft and Structure:** What is the purpose of the questions the president asks in paragraph 34?

Working from the Text

8. Review the rhetorical appeals definitions at the beginning of the activity. Find one example of each appeal from President Obama's speech and write the quote in the appropriate box of the rhetorical triangle below.

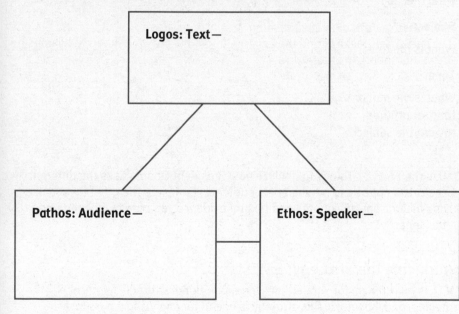

Logos: Text—

Pathos: Audience—

Ethos: Speaker—

Using Rhetorical Appeals

9. In your group, conduct a brief SOAPSTone analysis of the speech. Be prepared to discuss your analysis with the class.

SOAPSTone	Analysis	Textual Support
Speaker: What does the reader know about the writer?		
Occasion: What are the circumstances surrounding this text?		
Audience: Who is the target audience?		
Purpose: Why did the author write this text?		
Subject: What is the topic?		
Tone: What is the author's tone, or attitude, toward the subject?		

10. Use the SMELL strategy to analyze how President Obama uses the different rhetorical appeals to persuade his audience. Complete the graphic organizer and include specific quotes and textual evidence you noted while reading the speech.

Introducing the Strategy: SMELL

SMELL is an acronym for sender, message, emotional strategies, logical strategies, and language. This strategy is useful for analyzing a persuasive speech or essay by asking five essential questions:

- What is the sender-receiver relationship? Who are the images and language meant to attract? Describe the speaker (or writer) of the text.
- What is the message? Summarize the thesis of the text.
- What is the desired effect of the emotional strategies?
- What logic is being used? How does it (or its absence) affect the message? Consider the logic of images as well as words.
- What does the language of the text describe? How does it affect the meaning and effectiveness of the writing? Consider the language of images as well as words.

Sender-Receiver Relationship: Who are the senders (speaker/writer) and receivers (audience) of the message, and what is their relationship (consider what different audiences the text may be addressing)? How does the sender attempt to establish his/her *ethos*?

Message: What is a literal summary of the content? What is the meaning/significance of this information?

Emotional Strategies: What emotional appeals (*pathos*) are included? What seems to be their desired effect?

Logical Strategies: What logical arguments/appeals (*logos*) are included? What is their effect?

Language: What specific language supports the message? How does it affect the text's effectiveness? Consider both images (if appropriate) and actual words. What is the speaker's voice in the text?

Using Rhetorical Appeals

Language and Writer's Craft: Parallel Structure

You have learned that **parallel structure** consists of a series of words, phrases, or clauses that are similar in grammatical form. Parallelism is one way writers use syntax, or sentence structure, to create powerful sentences for effect and to show that two or more ideas have the same level of importance. Parallelism enhances the rhetorical appeal of a writer or speaker and is frequently used in speeches. In the excerpt below, President Obama's use of repetitive sentence structure tells us that all parties who hold responsibility in education hold equal responsibility.

Example: "Now, I've given a lot of speeches about education. And I've talked about responsibility a lot. I've talked about teachers' responsibility for inspiring students and pushing you to learn. I've talked about your parents' responsibility for making sure you stay on track, and you get your homework done, and don't spend every waking hour in front of the TV or with the Xbox. I've talked a lot about your government's responsibility for setting high standards, and supporting teachers and principals, and turning around schools that aren't working, where students aren't getting the opportunities that they deserve."

PRACTICE Read the passage below and underline the instances of parallel structure that have the most persuasive impact on the reader or listener. Explain and defend your choice.

"But at the end of the day, we can have the most dedicated teachers, the most supportive parents, the best schools in the world—and none of it will make a difference, none of it will matter unless all of you fulfill your responsibilities, unless you show up to those schools, unless you pay attention to those teachers, unless you listen to your parents and grandparents and other adults and put in the hard work it takes to succeed. That's what I want to focus on today: the responsibility each of you has for your education."

Check Your Understanding

How does President Obama's use of parallel structure and rhetorical appeals persuade the audience?

Writing to Sources: Argument

Analyze the effectiveness of President Obama's argument in his speech. Evaluate his claim, supporting evidence, concession, and conclusion. In your writing, be sure to:

- Begin with a thesis that identifies the claim made by Obama and states your position on how effectively he argues for that claim.
- Explain what reasons and supporting evidence Obama uses and evaluate the effectiveness of his reasons and evidence.
- Include multiple direct quotations from the text to support your own claims. Introduce and punctuate all quotations correctly.

Targeting Your Audience

Learning Targets
- Identify different types of evidence and their purposes.
- Select evidence, appeals, and techniques specifically to reach a target audience.

LEARNING STRATEGIES:
Discussion Groups,
Brainstorming, Graphic
Organizer, KWHL Chart

Connecting with an Audience

To make an argument compelling, writers and speakers use a variety of reasons and evidence that they think will convince their audience to agree with them. Knowing the audience helps the writer or speaker decide what reasons and evidence to use.

My Notes

_____

_____

_____

1. With your group members, review the informational text, speech, and presentation you have encountered in this half of the unit and identify examples of the different types of evidence used. Then explain the purpose of each as a tool of persuasion.

A. Type of Evidence/Support	B. Example from Class Readings/Presentation	C. Used to ... (logos, ethos, pathos? In what way?)
Facts and Statistics: Numbers drawn from surveys, studies, or observations, as well as pieces of commonly accepted information about the world		
Personal Experience/Anecdote: A true story that describes a person's experience relative to the topic		
Illustrative Example (brief or extended): Description of a specific experience or example to support the validity of a generalization		

_____

_____

_____

_____

Targeting Your Audience

A. Type of Evidence/Support	B. Example from Class Readings/Presentation	C. Used to ... (logos, ethos, pathos? In what way?)
Expert/Personal Testimony: The use of a person's words or conclusions to support a claim, whether the person is like the audience or is distinguished by his or her expertise		
Hypothetical Case: Use of a "what if" or possible scenario in order to challenge the audience to consider its implications		

My Notes

2. List each resource you cited, and then describe the target audience.

Resource 1:

Resource 2:

Resource 3:

Preview

In this activity, you will read an editorial and identify how an author crafts an argument to connect with the audience.

Setting a Purpose for Reading

- Highlight any information that helps you figure out who the audience is in this article.
- Circle unknown words and phrases. Try to determine the meaning of the words by using context clues, word parts, or a dictionary.

Editorial

An *Early Start* on College

More Minnesota teens should use dual-credit enrollment

January 14, 2012, *StarTribune*

1 Taking advanced, **dual**-enrollment classes made a big difference in Paj Ntaub Lee's life.

2 Her Hmong immigrant parents didn't encourage her to go to college; they thought graduating from high school, then getting married or finding a job would be enough for their child.

3 But her exposure to college and higher-level courses while at Johnson High School in St. Paul set her on a path to graduate from St. Olaf College in Northfield.

4 Her experience should be shared by more Minnesota students, and the **Legislature** should expand the programs that make that possible.

5 Participating in any of the state's dual-credit programs can prepare more students for college work, save money and increase postsecondary graduation rates. Taking more-challenging classes can also open educational doors for not only the highest-performing students, but for kids across the academic spectrum.

6 Those are the conclusions of a recent study conducted by the Center for School Change (CSC) at Macalester College. Minnesota students can participate in one of five dual-credit options—Advanced Placement or International **Baccalaureate** classes, postsecondary options, concurrent enrollment programs or Project Lead the Way, which allows students to take courses in technical and scientific areas.

7 Each program allows students to earn college credit while still in high school.

8 The study showed that the programs are increasing in popularity— between 2001 and 2006, about 38,000 state students took AP or IB exams, and an average of about 5,500 students a year participated in postsecondary options during those years. Concurrent enrollment increased from 17,581 to 21,184 between 2008 and 2010.

9 A 2010 Minnesota State Colleges and Universities report showed that 53 percent of those who enrolled in a Minnesota public college within two years of graduation had to take at least one **remedial** course.

10 But if more students take advantage of dual-credit options, more will be prepared for college and other postsecondary level work. That will reduce the need for remedial courses and save money for students, families and taxpayers.

11 To expand the options to include more students, the CSC report rightly recommends that the Legislature change the **statutes** to allow ninth and tenth graders to participate and to allow colleges and universities to advertise about the savings.

12 Paj Ntaub Lee now works for the CSC and helped do the research for the center's report. She's a supporter—and a good example of why more Minnesota students should take advantage of dual-credit options.

My Notes

dual: having two of something

legislature: a body of persons with the authority to make or change laws

Baccalaureate: a degree of bachelor given by a university or college

remedial: concerned with providing extra academic help for students

statute: a law or written rule that the government has made

Targeting Your Audience

Second Read

3. **Key Ideas and Details:** What is the central claim in this editorial? How does the writer introduce it?

4. **Craft and Structure:** What claim does the author use the CSC study to support?

5. **Craft and Structure:** What claim does the author make in paragraph 10?

6. **Craft and Structure:** Which rhetorical appeal is the most effective in this article and why?

Working from the Text

The *StarTribune* editorial addresses multiple audiences. In the space below, identify each audience. Use quotes you highlighted to show how each audience is referenced or directly addressed in the text.

Check Your Understanding

How do audiences shape the argument of an author?

Writing to Sources: Argument

Return to the speech in Activity 1.15 and reread it in light of what you have learned about targeting the audience and rhetorical appeals, thinking about the audience that Obama was addressing. Then revise the analysis of Obama's argument that you wrote taking these issues into account. In your writing, be sure to:

- Revise your thesis to include your idea of Obama's audience and how effective his speech is in supporting his claim for that audience.
- Explain what techniques and rhetorical appeals he used to reach that audience and explain why you think those techniques and appeals were effective or not for that audience.
- Include direct quotations from the text to support each specific claim you make. Introduce and punctuate all quotations correctly.

Learning Targets

- Identify counterclaims and refutations in an argument.
- Analyze conclusions to an argument.
- Describe counterclaims and refutations in writing.

Preview

In this activity, you will read two editorials and analyze the elements of an argument, including the central claims, counterclaims, and supporting evidence.

Setting a Purpose for Reading

- Draw a star next to elements of an argument.
- Highlight the different types of evidence (facts, personal experience, illustrative, personal testimony, and hypothetical case) used in each editorial.
- Circle unknown words and phrases. Try to determine the meaning of the words by using context clues, word parts, or a dictionary.

ABOUT THE AUTHOR

Robert Reich is the Chancellor's Professor of Public Policy at the University of California, Berkeley, as well as an author, political commentator, and political economist. Reich was the 22nd United States Secretary of Labor under President Clinton from 1993 to 1997, and served in the administrations of Presidents Ford and Carter. He has published over 12 books and is featured in the recent documentary, *Inequality for All*.

Opinion

Why College Isn't (And Shouldn't Have to Be) For Everyone

by Robert Reich, March 22, 2015, The Huffington Post

1 I know a high school senior who's so worried about whether she'll be accepted at the college of her choice she can't sleep.

2 The parent of another senior tells me he stands at the mailbox for an hour every day waiting for a hoped-for acceptance letter to arrive.

3 Parents are also uptight. I've heard of some who have stopped socializing with other parents of children competing for admission to the same university.

4 Competition for places top-brand colleges is absurdly intense.

5 With inequality at record levels and almost all the economic gains going to the top, there's more pressure than ever to get the golden ring.

My Notes

prestigious: respected and admired

grotesque: unnatural, odd, or ugly

My Notes

burnish: to polish or make smooth

6 A degree from a **prestigious** university can open doors to elite business schools and law schools — and to jobs paying hundreds of thousands, if not millions, a year.

7 So parents who can afford it are paying **grotesque** sums to give their kids an edge.

8 They "enhance" their kid's resumes with such things as bassoon lessons, trips to preserve the wildlife in Botswana, internships at the Atlantic Monthly.

9 They hire test preparation coaches. They arrange for consultants to help their children write compelling essays on college applications.

10 They make generous contributions to the elite colleges they once attended, to which their kids are applying — colleges that give extra points to "legacies" and even more to those from wealthy families that donate tons of money.

11 You might call this affirmative action for the rich.

12 The same intensifying competition is affecting mid-range colleges and universities that are doing everything they can to **burnish** their own brands — competing with other mid-range institutions to enlarge their applicant pools, attract good students, and inch upward on the U.S. News college rankings.

13 Every college president wants to increase the ratio of applications to admissions, thereby becoming more elite.

14 Excuse me, but this is nuts.

15 The biggest absurdity is that a four-year college degree has become the only gateway into the American middle class.

16 But not every young person is suited to four years of college. They may be bright and ambitious but they won't get much out of it. They'd rather be doing something else, like making money or painting murals.

17 They feel compelled to go to college because they've been told over and over that a college degree is necessary.

18 Yet if they start college and then drop out, they feel like total failures.

19 Even if they get the degree, they're stuck with a huge bill — and may be paying down their student debt for years.

20 And all too often the jobs they land after graduating don't pay enough to make the degree worthwhile.

21 Last year, according to the Federal Reserve Bank of New York, 46 percent of recent college graduates were in jobs that don't even require a college degree.

22 The biggest frauds are for-profit colleges that are raking in money even as their students drop out in droves, and whose diplomas are barely worth the ink-jets they're printed on.

23 America clings to the conceit that four years of college are necessary for everyone, and looks down its nose at people who don't have college degrees.

24 This has to stop. Young people need an alternative. That alternative should be a world-class system of vocational-technical education.

25 A four-year college degree isn't necessary for many of tomorrow's good jobs.

26 For example, the emerging economy will need **platoons** of technicians able to install, service, and repair all the high-tech machinery filling up hospitals, offices, and factories.

27 And people who can upgrade the software embedded in almost every gadget you buy.

28 Today it's even hard to find a skilled plumber or electrician.

29 Yet the vocational and technical education now available to young Americans is typically underfunded and inadequate. And too often denigrated as being for "losers."

30 These programs should be creating winners.

31 Germany — whose median wage (after taxes and transfers) is higher than ours -- gives many of its young people world-class technical skills that have made Germany a world leader in fields such as precision manufacturing.

32 A world-class technical education doesn't have to mean young people's fates are determined when they're fourteen.

33 Instead, rising high-school seniors could be given the option of entering a program that extends a year or two beyond high school and ends with a diploma acknowledging their technical expertise.

34 Community colleges — the under-appreciated crown jewels of America's feeble attempts at equal opportunity — could be developing these curricula. Businesses could be advising on the technical skills they'll need, and promising jobs to young people who complete their degrees with good grades.

35 Government could be investing enough money to make these programs thrive. (And raising taxes on top incomes enough to temper the wild competition for admission to elite colleges that grease the way to those top incomes.)

36 Instead, we continue to push most of our young people through a single funnel called a four-year college education — a funnel so narrow it's causing applicants and their parents excessive stress and worry about "getting in;" that's too often ill suited and unnecessary, and far too expensive; and that can cause college dropouts to feel like failures for the rest of their lives.

37 It's time to give up the idea that every young person has to go to college, and start offering high-school seniors an alternative route into the middle class.

platoons: a group of soldiers or people doing something together

My Notes

ABOUT THE AUTHOR

The former education columnist at *TIME*, Andrew J. Rotherham previously served as Special Assistant to the President for Domestic Policy during President Clinton's administration. He is also a former member of the Virginia Board of Education. Rotherham co-founded Bellwether Education, a non-profit educational organization, and is currently a contributing editor to *U.S. News & World Report*.

My Notes

Opinion

Actually, College Is Very Much Worth It

by Andrew J. Rotherham, May 19, 2011, *Time*

1   Lately it's become fashionable—especially among the highly credentialed—to question whether it's really "worth it" to go to college. A recent report from the Harvard Graduate School of Education proposed deemphasizing college as the primary goal of our education system in favor of "multiple pathways" for students. Earlier this month, *New York Magazine* devoted almost 4,000 words to profiling **venture capitalists** (and college graduates) James Altucher and Peter Thiel and their efforts to convince Americans that they'd be better off skipping college. Thiel is even creating a $100,000 fellowship for young people who agree to delay going to college in favor of an **internship**.

2   Make no mistake, there is widespread dissatisfaction with higher education. According to a new survey released by the Pew Research Center, only 40 percent of Americans felt that colleges provided an "excellent" or "good" value for the money. At the same time, 86 percent of college graduates still felt the investment was a good one for them.

3   To understand these competing views, you have to juggle a few different ideas at once. First, there are plenty of problems with higher education—poor quality, even at brand-name schools, and out-of-control costs are two of the biggest. College presidents themselves shared some of these concerns and others with the Pew researchers. Second, it's true: College isn't for everyone. There are plenty of rewarding and important jobs and careers that do not require college. And due to the sluggish economy, there may in fact be more graduates than the current job market needs, or a temporary "college bubble." Jobs for recent grads are harder to find, and salaries are lower, but that won't last forever. And in spite of all of this, the data make clear that getting a college education is still a good idea—college graduates earn more, and are more likely to have a job in the first place—and is especially important for some Americans.

4   Anti-college sentiment is nothing new. Mark Twain admonished us not to let schooling interfere with education, and we've always celebrated the maverick who blazes their own path. These days, it's Facebook founder Mark Zuckerberg, Microsoft's Bill Gates, or Apple's Steve Jobs—all college dropouts—who are held up as evidence of why all that time sitting in class is better spent elsewhere. Perhaps, but it's also worth remembering that their companies are bursting with college graduates. And what about all the people who didn't finish college and are not at the **helm** of a wildly successful venture?

venture capitalist: someone who takes a risk and invests money into something new or different

internship: a position in which a person works or is trained to learn a job without getting paid

helm: a position of authority or control

5 Nobody spends a lot of time highlighting their stories, but let's not lose sight of what happens to them. According to the Bureau of Labor Statistics, in 2010, the median weekly earnings for someone with some college but no degree were $712, compared to $1038 for a college graduate. That's almost $17,000 over the course of a year and there is an even bigger divide for those with less education. College graduates are also more likely to be in jobs with better benefits, further widening the divide. Meanwhile, in 2010, the unemployment rate was 9.2 percent for those with only some college and more than 10 percent for those with just a high school degree, but it was 5.4 percent for college graduates. The economic gaps between college completers and those with less education are getting larger, too.

6 It's also odd to talk down college—which is the most effective **social mobility** strategy we have—at the very time Americans are becoming concerned about income inequality. Ron Haskins of the Brookings Institution found that without a college degree, only 14 percent of Americans from the bottom fifth of parental income reach the top two-fifths. But if they complete college, 41 percent of this same group can then expect to make it to the top two-fifths. Haskins' data also shows the extent to which debates like this are a luxury of the privileged, because their children enjoy much more of a safety net and the risks are different for them. In other words, children from low-income families gain more by going to college than children of the wealthy lose by not going.

7 So here's the key takeaway: Education gives you choices. Assuming you don't pile up mountains of debt that constrain your career options (and that outcome is avoidable) or go to a school where just fogging a mirror is good enough to get a diploma, there are not a lot of downsides to going to college. The stories of entrepreneurs who **bootstrapped** themselves are exciting but most of us are not a Gates or Zuckerberg. So before heeding the advice of the college **naysayers**, make sure you understand the stakes and the odds. Or, here's a good rule of thumb instead: When people who worked hard to achieve something that has benefitted them start telling you that it's really not all that important or useful—beware.

8 Disclosure: I'm a member of the Visiting Committee for the Harvard Graduate School of Education.

Second Read

- Reread the opinion texts to answer these text-dependent questions.
- Write any additional questions you have about the text in your Reader/Writer Notebook.

"Why College Isn't (And Shouldn't Have to Be) For Everyone"

1. **Key Ideas and Details:** What is the claim of this argument? How does the writer set up the claim?

My Notes

social mobility: the movement of people or groups to different positions in society

bootstrap: to develop without help from others

naysayer: someone who denies or opposes something

Evaluating Claims and Reasoning

My Notes

2. **Key Ideas and Details:** Where does the writer bring up the counterclaim, and how does he develop it?

3. **Key Ideas and Details:** What is the connotation of the word *absurdity* as used in paragraph 15? Why did the author choose that word?

"Actually, College Is Very Much Worth It"

4. **Key Ideas and Details:** The writer of this opinion piece begins by laying out the arguments against his central claim. How does this affect the appeal of his argument?

5. **Key Ideas and Details:** How does the author's use of the word *bursting* in paragraph 4 contribute to his argument?

6. **Key Ideas and Details:** What evidence does the writer present to support his opinion that a college education is a good idea?

Working from the Text

7. Compare the claims made by each of these two writers. Evaluate the reasons and evidence used by each writer. What is relevant and convincing?

For each text, write the claim and its supporting evidence in the chart.

"Why College Isn't (And Shouldn't Have to Be) For Everyone"	"Actually, College Is Very Much Worth It"
Claim:	Claim:
Evidence:	Evidence:
Counterclaims:	Counterclaims:
Evidence:	Evidence:

Evaluating Claims and Reasoning

My Notes

8. What elements, if any, do you think are missing from either of these pieces? Explain.

9. Why do you think Andrew J. Rotherham disclosed at the end of his article that he is a member of an educational group? How does this disclosure affect your perception of his argument?

Conclusion/Call to Action

An argument contains a conclusion that often restates the primary claim and tries to convince the reader to take an action.

10. What is the call to action in each of these pieces?

Check Your Understanding

Which writer presents the more convincing argument? Why? Cite evidence to support your conclusion.

Writing to Sources: Argument

Go back to the speech in Activity 1.15 and reread it in light of what you have learned about counterclaims and refutations and conclusions or calls to action. Then revise your analysis of Obama's argument to include this aspect of constructing an effective argument. In your writing, be sure to:

- Revise your thesis to address these new elements of constructing an argument.
- Explain how Obama addresses counterclaims. Evaluate the effectiveness of his refutations, taking into account his overall argument and his audience.
- Explain how Obama concludes the essay and how effective that ending is.
- Include direct quotations from the text to support each specific claim you make. Introduce and punctuate all quotations correctly.

Independent Reading Checkpoint

Meet with a partner or small group to discuss the evidence you plan to use from your independent reading to support your argument in your essay. Explain why your selections are effective.

Writing an Argumentative Essay

ASSIGNMENT

Your assignment is to write an argumentative essay about the value of a college education. Your essay must be organized as an argument in which you assert a precise claim, support it with reasons and evidence, and acknowledge and refute counterclaims fairly.

Planning: Make a plan for researching your topic and collecting evidence.	▪ What is your claim? Is it clear? What information do you need to support it? ▪ How will you use in your essay the articles you have been reading independently? ▪ How will you expand upon the articles in this unit by doing further research? ▪ How will you evaluate whether you have enough information to write your draft? ▪ How will you consider your audience and determine the reasons and evidence that will best convince them to support your argument?
Prewriting: Prepare to write the essay draft.	▪ How will you make time to read your notes and add to, delete, or refine them as the basis for your argument? ▪ What quotations will you use as evidence? ▪ What information do you have to address counterclaims?
Drafting: Decide how to structure your essay.	▪ What will you include in the introduction? How will you describe your claim? ▪ Have you used vivid and precise language, carefully chosen diction, and formal style? ▪ Have you acknowledged and addressed counterclaims? ▪ Have you written a strong conclusion with a call to action?
Revising and Editing for Publication: Review and revise to make your work the best it can be.	▪ Have you arranged to share your draft with a partner or with your writing group? ▪ Have you consulted the Scoring Guide and the activities to prepare for revising your draft? ▪ Did you use your available resources (e.g., spell check, dictionaries, Writer's Checklist) to edit for conventions and prepare your narrative for publication?

Reflection

Write an honest evaluation of your argument. Describe how you think it was effective (or not). What would you do differently next time to improve your argument?

📶 Technology Tip

After writing and revising your argument, you might consider presenting it in a different medium. For example, could you use technology to transform your argument into a video? Or could you support your written argument with illustrations or charts?

Writing an Argumentative Essay

SCORING GUIDE

Scoring Criteria	Exemplary	Proficient	Emerging	Incomplete
Ideas	The essay • includes a well-developed explanation of the issue, a claim, and a thesis statement • presents strong support or the central claim with relevant details and commentary • presents counterclaims and clearly refutes them with relevant reasoning and evidence • concludes by summarizing the main points and providing an effective call to action.	The essay • includes an explanation of the issue, a claim, and a thesis statement • presents support for the central claim but may not fully develop all evidence • presents and acknowledges counterclaims and offers some evidence to refute them • concludes by summarizing the main points and offering a call to action.	The essay • states the thesis but does not adequately explain the problem • includes some, support for the claim, but it is not developed and does not provide relevant evidence or commentary • describes some counterclaims, but they are vague and are not clearly refuted • concludes by repeating main topics rather and ends without a suggestion for change.	The essay • states a vague or unclear thesis • contains ideas that are poorly developed or not developed at all • provides vague or no descriptions of counterclaims and refutations • concludes without summarizing main points or suggesting change.
Structure	The essay • follows a clear multi-paragraph argumentative essay structure with a logical progression of ideas • showcases central points and uses effective transitions.	The essay • follows a multi-paragraph argumentative structure but may not have a clearly logical progression of ideas • develops central points and uses transitions.	The essay • demonstrates an awkward, unstructured progression of ideas • spends too much time on some irrelevant details and uses few transitions.	The essay • does not follow the organization of an argumentative essay • includes some details, but the writing lacks clear direction and uses no transitions.
Use of Language	The essay • uses a formal writing style • smoothly integrates credible source material into the text (with accurate citations) • demonstrates correct spelling and excellent command of standard English conventions.	The essay • uses a formal writing style • integrates credible source material into the text (with accurate citations) • demonstrates correct spelling and general command of standard English conventions.	The essay • mixes informal and formal writing styles • integrates some source material (citations may be missing or inaccurate) • includes some incorrect spelling and grammatical weaknesses that interfere with meaning.	The essay • uses inappropriate informal style • does not include source material citations • includes several errors in spelling and grammatical weaknesses that interfere with meaning.

Defining Style

Visual Prompt: What kind of story might this photograph inspire?

Unit Overview

Through the ages, stories were passed from generation to generation, sometimes orally and sometimes in writing. Sometime between 1830 and 1835, Edgar Allan Poe began to write structured stories for magazines. His stories fascinated and terrified readers. Poe's suspenseful writing style and distinct voice set his stories apart from other writers of his time. His works continue to influence artists today, including filmmaker Tim Burton. Burton's grotesque yet charming films are examples of unique style. In this unit, you will study how authors and a filmmaker develop their style using specific techniques.

Defining Style

GOALS:
- To identify specific elements of an author's style
- To review and analyze elements of fiction and write a short story
- To analyze syntactical structure and use clauses to achieve specific effects
- To develop close reading skills
- To identify cinematic techniques and analyze their effects

ACADEMIC VOCABULARY
commentary
textual commentary

Literary Terms
style
symbol
figurative language
literal language
tone
irony
allusions
dramatic irony
verbal irony
cinematic techniques
biography
autobiography
main idea
theme
mood

Contents

Activities

*Texts not included in these materials.

Language and Writer's Craft
- Clauses (2.6)
- Combining Sentences (2.13)
- Transitions (2.19)

MY INDEPENDENT READING LIST

_____
_____
_____
_____
_____
_____
_____
_____
_____
_____
_____
_____
_____
_____
_____
_____
_____
_____
_____
_____
_____
_____
_____
_____
_____
_____

Previewing the Unit

My Notes

Learning Targets

- Connect prior knowledge to the genre of short story.
- Analyze the skills and knowledge needed to complete Embedded Assessment 1 successfully.
- Make a plan for independent reading during this unit.

Making Connections

In this unit, you will build on your experiences reading and writing short stories. You will study elements of short stories not only to write your own original stories, but also to understand how to analyze and write about literature. As you study poetry, short stories, and film, you will analyze the elements that make up a writer's or director's style. You will also examine the ways in which directors of visual media manipulate their audience's reactions through the unique stylistic choices they make in creating their products.

Essential Questions

Based on your current knowledge, write your answers to these questions.

1. What makes a good story?

2. How does an artist define his or her style?

Developing Vocabulary

Look at the list of Academic Vocabulary and Literary Terms on the Contents page. Use a QHT or other strategy to analyze and evaluate your knowledge of those words. Use your Reader/Writer Notebook to make notes about meanings you know already. Add to your notes as you study this unit and gain greater understanding of each of these words.

Unpacking Embedded Assessment 1

Read the following assignment for Embedded Assessment 1:

> Your assignment is to write an original narrative from real or imagined experiences or events. Your story must include a variety of narrative techniques—such as foreshadowing, point of view, figurative language, imagery, symbolism, and/or irony—as well as effective details and a well-structured sequence of events.

With your class, create a graphic organizer to identify the skills and knowledge you will need to accomplish this task and plan how you will acquire them to complete the assignment. To help you complete your graphic organizer, be sure to review the criteria in the Scoring Guide.

INDEPENDENT READING LINK

Read and Discuss

The focus of this unit is on short stories. As you begin your study of the unit, discuss with peers effective ways to locate and select short stories. Browsing short story anthologies or reviewing collected works of short story authors are two examples of ways to find short stories. Choose three to four short stories to read independently. Make a plan for reading in which you decide which authors and kinds of stories you like, as well as a regular time you will set aside for reading.

Reviewing the Elements of a Story

Learning Targets

- Identify the elements of a short story and place them on a plot diagram.
- Create characters, conflicts, and choose a point of view for an original short story.
- Identify and discuss the effect of the point of view from which a story is told.

Elements of a Short Story/Narrative

A short story is a form of **narrative**. Narratives include made-up stories—fiction—as well as real-life stories—nonfiction. A short story is a work of fiction, and this genre includes certain literary elements.

Work with a partner and brainstorm in the My Notes section a list of elements of a plot. As a class, you will create a complete list of the literary terms associated with creating and analyzing the plot of any narrative.

Elements of Plot

After discussing the meanings of terms about plot, place the elements of plot that you identified in the appropriate place on the plot diagram below.

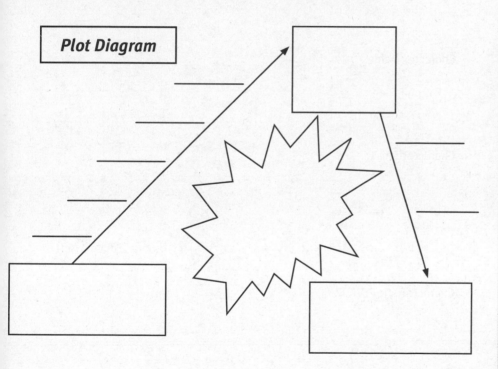

Plot Diagram

LEARNING STRATEGIES:
Graphic Organizer, Marking the Text, Rereading

My Notes

Reviewing the Elements of a Story

Planning a Story

In preparation for writing your own short story, brainstorm what you might include in a short story. Your ideas could become the basis of your short story for Embedded Assessment 1.

1. An essential element of a short story's plot is conflict. Think about possible conflicts that you could use to develop a plot, and use the following prompts to to think about both an internal and an external conflict for your character.

2. Think about a character for your short story. Create a name and two important characteristics of your character's personality.

External conflict: _____ versus _____

Internal conflict: _____

Character Name:

Characteristic 1:

Characteristic 2:

Comparing Points of View

The point of view is the position from which a story is being told. Authors consciously choose a point of view when writing a story. The point of view can be used in different ways and is a unique stylistic choice made by the author.

Read the following excerpts with different points of view:

First Person: From *The Great Gatsby* by F. Scott Fitzgerald

I decided to call to him. Miss Baker had mentioned him at dinner, and that would do for an introduction. But I didn't call to him, for he gave a sudden intimation that he was content to be alone — he stretched out his arms toward the dark water in a curious way, and, far as I was from him, I could have sworn he was trembling. Involuntarily I glanced seaward — and distinguished nothing except a single green light, minute and far away, that might have been the end of a dock. When I looked once more for Gatsby he had vanished, and I was alone again in the unquiet darkness.

Third-Person Limited: From *The Giver* by Lois Lowry

Usually, at the morning ritual when the family members told their dreams, Jonas didn't contribute much. He rarely dreamed. Sometimes he awoke with a feeling of fragments afloat in his sleep, but he couldn't seem to grasp them and put them together into something worthy of telling at the ritual.

But this morning was different. He had dreamed very vividly the night before.

His mind wandered while Lily, as usual, recounted a lengthy dream, this one a frightening one in which she had, against the rules, been riding her mother's bicycle and been caught by the Security Guards.

Third-Person Omniscient: From *Lord of the Flies* by William Golding

Signs of life were visible now on the beach. The sand, trembling beneath the heat haze, concealed many figures in its miles of length; boys were making their way toward the platform through the hot, dumb sand. Three small children, no older than Johnny, appeared from startlingly close at hand, where they had been gorging fruit in the forest. A dark little boy, not much younger than Piggy, parted a tangle of undergrowth, walked on to the platform, and smiled cheerfully at everybody. More and more of them came. Taking their cue from the innocent Johnny, they sat down on the fallen palm trunks and waited.

3. Reread the excerpts and underline the words or sentences that helped you determine point of view. What are the characteristics of each point of view?

a. First Person

b. Third-Person Limited

c. Third-Person Omniscient

My Notes

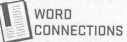

WORD CONNECTIONS

Roots and Affixes

The word *omniscient* has two Latin roots: *omni*, meaning "all" or "everything," and *sci*, meaning "knowing" or "knowledge." The root *omni* also occurs in *omnivorous* and *omnipotent*. The root *sci* occurs in *science*, *conscious*, *conscience*, and *conscientious*.

Reviewing the Elements of a Story

4. What are the advantages and disadvantages of each? Work in pairs to create a list.

   a. First Person

   b. Third-Person Limited

   c. Third-Person Omniscient

5. Examine and discuss the differences among the three points of view.

6. Think about what point of view you might use in your short story. Briefly explain why you chose that point of view.

Check Your Understanding

Why would an author choose to tell a story in the first person, third-person limited, or third-person omniscient point of view?

Narrative Writing Prompt

Return to the conflicts and characters that you created earlier in Activity 2.2. Write an opening to a story that presents the character, the conflict(s), and/or the setting using the point of view that you think would be best to narrate the story. Be sure to:

- Provide an introduction to the main character through description of appearance, actions, and voice.
- Include a central conflict that will drive the events of the story and develop the character.
- Include an internal or external conflict for the main character.
- Use a consistent point of view.

Analyzing Writer's Style

Learning Targets

- Make inferences about the effect a writer achieves by using specific sentence types and patterns.
- Emulate an author's style by writing a story opener in that style.

Writer's Style

You learned in Unit 1 that a writer's **style** or voice is created by elements such as *diction, syntax,* and *imagery,* as well as *point of view.* Review these elements to be sure you understand and can define them.

Certain stories grab the reader's attention and never let go until the story ends. Read the opening paragraph of "The Gift of the Magi" by O. Henry which you will read in this unit.

- Circle the **images** that stand out in the passage.
- Underline the **sentence fragments**, and annotate the text to describe what effect the author creates with these fragments.

"One dollar and eighty-seven cents. That was all. And sixty cents of it was in pennies.

Pennies saved one and two at a time by bulldozing the grocer and the vegetable man

and the butcher until one's cheeks burned with the silent imputation of parsimony

that such close dealing implied. Three times Della counted it. One dollar and

eighty-seven cents. And the next day would be Christmas."

In contrast, examine the opening of the short story "The Cask of Amontillado," by Edgar Allan Poe, which you will also be reading in this unit. After reading this passage, think about the effect of the **diction**, the **syntax**, and the **point of view**. What impression of the narrator does Poe create?

"The thousand injuries of Fortunato I had borne as I best could, but when he ventured

upon insult, I vowed revenge. You, who so well know the nature of my soul, will not

suppose, however, that I gave utterance to a threat. At length I would be avenged;

this was a point definitively settled—but the very definitiveness with which it was

resolved precluded the idea of risk."

Notice how the syntax affects the pacing of the action. Which story seems to set a faster pace or seems to set the action of the story in motion more quickly?

Poe uses long compound and complex sentences, while O. Henry uses sentence fragments for effect. A **sentence fragment** is a group of words that is grammatically incomplete and cannot stand alone. Writers change their sentence structure—their use of phrases, clauses, and different types of sentences—to create certain effects.

LEARNING STRATEGIES:
Marking the Text, Drafting

Literary Terms

Style refers to the distinctive way a writer uses language, characterized by elements of diction, syntax, imagery, organization, and so on.

GRAMMAR & USAGE
Semicolons

A **semicolon** joins two independent clauses that could be written as separate sentences. Writers often use a semicolon in this way to suggest a close relationship between the two clauses—a closer relationship than would be implied if they stood as separate sentences—and to create a longer sentence. Notice the semicolon in the third sentence of Poe's opening. The first independent clause is short and to the point, yet Poe allows his narrator to expand upon the point in a lengthy second clause. Think about how this longer sentence sets the pace of the narrator's voice.

My Notes

Analyzing Writer's Style

Emulating a Writer's Style

Every writer has a unique style. You will develop your own style as you develop your writing skills. One way to begin experimenting with style is to emulate another writer. To emulate a writer is to imitate the writer's style, including how he or she constructs sentences. For example, here is a sample paragraph written as an emulation of the opening of "The Cask of Amontillado":

> The deliberate rudeness of Lydia I had suffered silently, but when her actions bordered on bullying, I promised myself payback. You, who know my cautious, careful manner, do not think, however, that I indicated anything about my plans to Lydia. Eventually, I would get revenge, this I knew—but I would do so without any risk of blame.

Check Your Understanding

Choose one of the following style elements: diction, syntax, imagery, or point of view. Briefly describe how an author can use that element to create unique style and voice.

Narrative Writing Prompt

Choose one of the short story opening paragraphs in this activity and emulate that writer's style to write an original story opening. Be sure to:

- Emulate the style of the author you chose.
- Introduce a character, a setting, and/or a conflict in the opening.
- Vary your sentence types to create an effect (or to affect the pacing of the narrative).

INDEPENDENT READING LINK

Read and Connect

Compare the author's style in a short story you have read independently to the author's style in one of the opening paragraphs from this activity. Create a chart, Venn diagram, or other form of note taking to compare specific aspects of each author's style, such as sentence structure, syntax, and use of imagery.

The Meaning of Imagery and Symbols

Learning Targets
- Identify the imagery and symbols that writers use as a way to infer a writer's purpose and interpret meaning.
- Write an interpretive statement about meaning in a text by analyzing and synthesizing information.

Figurative and Literal Language
Think about imagery and **symbols** as you answer these questions.

1. When you see the words "fire" and "ice," what **literal** images come to mind? Brainstorm with your class a list of the ideas, objects, or events that you associate with these two words.

2. Now, with a partner, make meaning of the common **figurative** associations as presented in the sentences below:
   - "Her icy stare let me know just how she felt."
   - "He acted so cold to me that I knew he was still angry."
   - "His face was red and flushed with the heat of his anger."
   - "The fierce fire in her eyes made her attitude clear."

When images are used figuratively rather than literally, they are being used symbolically—that is, the image represents itself but also stands for something more abstract. What do the images of fire and ice represent or symbolize in the sentences above?

Preview
In this activity, you will read a poem and think about how the author uses symbols for effect.

Setting a Purpose for Reading
- Underline and annotate any examples of figurative and literal language.
- Circle unknown words and phrases. Try to determine the meaning of the words by using context clues, word parts, or a dictionary.

ABOUT THE AUTHOR
Robert Frost (1874–1963) was one of America's most popular twentieth-century poets. For much of his life, he lived on a farm in New Hampshire and wrote poems about farm life and the New England landscape. His apparently simple poems, however, have many layers of meaning.

LEARNING STRATEGIES:
Close Reading, Marking the Text, Oral Reading,

Literary Terms
A **symbol** is anything (any object, animal, event, person, or place) that represents itself but also stands for something else on a figurative level.

Literary Terms
Figurative language refers to the use of words to describe one thing in terms of another. In contrast to figurative language, **literal language** uses the exact meanings, or denotations, of words. For example, "ice" and "fire" have specific literal meanings, but Frost also uses these words figuratively, or *connotatively*.

My Notes

My Notes

Poetry

Fire and Ice

by Robert Frost

> Some say the world will end in fire,
> Some say in ice.
> From what I've tasted of desire
> I hold with those who favor fire.
>
> 5   But if it had to **perish** twice,
> I think I know enough of hate
> To know that for destruction ice
> Is also great
> And would **suffice**.

perish: die

suffice: be enough

Second Read

- Reread the poem to answer these text-dependent questions.
- Write any additional questions you have about the text in your Reader/Writer Notebook.

3. **Key Ideas and Details:** What is the central idea of the poem? Which details convey the central idea?

4. **Craft and Structure:** What human emotions does the author associate with the natural elements of fire and ice? What impact do these associations have on the poem's tone?

5. **Craft and Structure:** In line 3, the speaker says, "I've tasted of desire." Is this statement literal or figurative? Why?

Working from the Text

6. Read the poem again silently. Pay close attention to the punctuation marks that signal ends of sentences.

7. With a partner, take turns reading the poem aloud to each other. Read the poem so that you stop only at the end of each sentence, not each line.

8. As your partner reads the poem to you, circle the words associated with the two major images.

9. Using the words and phrases that you circled, discuss and analyze the purpose of the imagery and symbols in the poem with your partner. Annotate the text in the My Notes space.

Check Your Understanding

What is Robert Frost saying about human emotions in "Fire and Ice?" Use this sentence frame to write a response:

In _____, _____ suggests that _____.

    (*title of text*)   (*author*)   (*purpose/meaning/main idea*)

Writing to Sources: Explanatory Text

Explain how the author uses imagery and symbolism to convey purpose and meaning in his writing. Use the interpretative statement you wrote as a starting point. Be sure to:

- Begin with a clear thesis that states your position.
- Include direct quotations from the text to support your claims. Introduce and punctuate all quotations correctly.
- Include transitions between points and a statement that provides a conclusion.

Shared Gifts: Introducing Irony

LEARNING STRATEGIES:
Close Reading, Marking the Text, Predicting, Skimming/Scanning, SIFT, Drafting

Literary Terms

Tone is a writer's (or speaker's) attitude toward a subject, character, or audience. It can be serious, amused, sarcastic, indignant, objective, etc.
Irony occurs when something turns out to be quite different from what is expected.
Allusions are references that writers make to a well-known person, event, or place from history, music, art, or another literary work. Writers make these references to draw comparisons, create imagery, establish humor, or reinforce emotions. The three main categories of allusions are biblical, mythological, and historical/topical.

My Notes

_____

Learning Targets

- Explain how images signify the literal and symbolic importance of objects to the development of characters.
- Explain how situational irony contributes to the theme of "The Gift of the Magi."

Identifying Tone, Irony, and Allusions

1. Review all you know about the elements of short stories, including point of view, character, theme, imagery, and symbolism. You should already be familiar with these terms. Reflect on the following terms:
   - **Tone:** A writer's diction and imagery help create the tone. Irony is one common literary tone. To be able to recognize an author's tone, especially if the author is using an ironic tone, is a key factor in understanding an author's purpose or meaning. If you miss the irony, you miss the meaning.
   - **Irony:** This occurs when what is expected turns out to be quite different from what actually happens; one common form of irony is called **situational irony**. Writers use situational irony as a way to contradict the expectations of the characters or the reader.
   - **Allusions:** These are references an author makes to people, places, or events in the Bible, classical mythology, or history. Allusions are deliberate choices by the author and are often significant and important to understanding the story.

Preview

In this activity, you will read a short story and analyze how the author develops tone, creates irony, and uses allusions and symbols.

Setting a Purpose for Reading

- Underline references or allusions.
- Highlight words or phrases that create tone.
- Circle unknown words and phrases. Try to determine the meaning of the words by using context clues, word parts, or a dictionary.

ABOUT THE AUTHOR

William Sydney Porter (1862–1910), whose pen name was O. Henry, was born in Greensboro, North Carolina. Porter left school at the age of 15 and moved to Texas, where he wrote a humorous weekly paper. When that failed, he worked as a reporter and columnist for the *Houston Post*. He was later convicted of embezzling money (although there was some doubt about his guilt) and was sentenced to jail. While in jail, he started writing short stories. After serving his sentence, Porter moved to New York City, where he wrote under the pen name O. Henry for the magazine *New York World*. Porter became a prolific writer, publishing more than 600 short stories.

Short Story

The *Gift* of the Magi

by O. Henry

1 One dollar and eighty-seven cents. That was all. And sixty cents of it was in pennies. Pennies saved one and two at a time by bulldozing the grocer and the vegetable man and the butcher until one's cheeks burned with the silent **imputation** of **parsimony** that such close dealing implied. Three times Della counted it. One dollar and eighty-seven cents. And the next day would be Christmas.

2 There was clearly nothing to do but flop down on the shabby little couch and howl. So Della did it. Which instigates the moral reflection that life is made up of sobs, sniffles, and smiles, with sniffles predominating.

3 While the mistress of the home is gradually subsiding from the first stage to the second, take a look at the home. A furnished flat at $8 per week. It did not exactly beggar description, but it certainly had that word on the lookout for the **mendicancy squad**.

4 In the **vestibule** below was a letter-box into which no letter would go, and an electric button from which no mortal finger could coax a ring. Also appertaining thereunto was a card bearing the name "Mr. James Dillingham Young."

5 The "Dillingham" had been flung to the breeze during a former period of prosperity when its possessor was being paid $30 per week. Now, when the income was shrunk to 20, the letters of "Dillingham" looked blurred, as though they were thinking seriously of contracting to a modest and unassuming D. But whenever Mr. James Dillingham Young came home and reached his flat above he was called "Jim" and greatly hugged by Mrs. James Dillingham Young, already introduced to you as Della. Which is all very good.

6 Della finished her cry and attended to her cheeks with the powder rag. She stood by the window and looked out dully at a gray cat walking a gray fence in a gray backyard. Tomorrow would be Christmas Day, and she had only $1.87 with which to buy Jim a present. She had been saving every penny she could for months, with this result. Twenty dollars a week doesn't go far. Expenses had been greater than she had calculated. They always are. Only $1.87 to buy a present for Jim. Her Jim. Many a happy hour she had spent planning for something nice for him. Something fine and rare and sterling— something just a little bit near to being worthy of the honor of being owned by Jim.

7 There was a pier-glass between the windows of the room. Perhaps you have seen a pier-glass in an $8 flat. A very thin and very agile person may, by observing his reflection in a rapid sequence of longitudinal strips, obtain a fairly accurate conception of his looks. Della, being slender, had mastered the art.

imputation: accusation
parsimony: thriftiness

mendicancy squad: a group of police who picked up beggars and homeless people

vestibule: hallway

Shared Gifts: Introducing Irony

pic

My Notes

depreciate: lessen the value of

chaste: pure, simple
meretricious ornamentation: gaudy or flashy decoration

truant: absent from school

8 Suddenly she whirled from the window and stood before the glass. Her eyes were shining brilliantly, but her face had lost its color within twenty seconds. Rapidly she pulled down her hair and let it fall to its full length.

9 Now, there were two possessions of the James Dillingham Youngs in which they both took a mighty pride. One was Jim's gold watch that had been his father's and his grandfather's. The other was Della's hair. Had the Queen of Sheba lived in the flat across the airshaft, Della would have let her hair hang out the window some day to dry just to **depreciate** Her Majesty's jewels and gifts. Had King Solomon been the janitor, with all his treasures piled up in the basement, Jim would have pulled out his watch every time he passed, just to see him pluck at his beard from envy.

10 So now Della's beautiful hair fell about her rippling and shining like a cascade of brown waters. It reached below her knee and made itself almost a garment for her. And then she did it up again nervously and quickly. Once she faltered for a minute and stood still while a tear or two splashed on the worn red carpet.

11 On went her old brown jacket; on went her old brown hat. With a whirl of skirts and with the brilliant sparkle still in her eyes, she fluttered out the door and down the stairs to the street.

12 Where she stopped the sign read: "Mme. Sofronie. Hair Goods of All Kinds." One flight up Della ran, and collected herself, panting. Madame, large, too white, chilly, hardly looked the "Sofronie."

13 "Will you buy my hair?" asked Della.

14 "I buy hair," said Madame. "Take yer hat off and let's have a sight at the looks of it." Down rippled the brown cascade. "Twenty dollars," said Madame, lifting the mass with a practised hand.

15 "Give it to me quick," said Della.

16 Oh, and the next two hours tripped by on rosy wings. Forget the hashed metaphor. She was ransacking the stores for Jim's present.

17 She found it at last. It surely had been made for Jim and no one else. There was no other like it in any of the stores, and she had turned all of them inside out. It was a platinum fob chain simple and **chaste** in design, properly proclaiming its value by substance alone and not by **meretricious ornamentation**—as all good things should do. It was even worthy of The Watch. As soon as she saw it she knew that it must be Jim's. It was like him. Quietness and value—the description applied to both. Twenty-one dollars they took from her for it, and she hurried home with the 87 cents. With that chain on his watch Jim might be properly anxious about the time in any company. Grand as the watch was, he sometimes looked at it on the sly on account of the old leather strap that he used in place of a chain.

18 When Della reached home her intoxication gave way a little to prudence and reason. She got out her curling irons and lighted the gas and went to work repairing the ravages made by generosity added to love. Which is always a tremendous task, dear friends—a mammoth task.

19 Within forty minutes her head was covered with tiny, close-lying curls that made her look wonderfully like a **truant** schoolboy. She looked at her reflection in the mirror long, carefully, and critically.

20 "If Jim doesn't kill me," she said to herself, "before he takes a second look at me, he'll say I look like a Coney Island chorus girl. But what could I do—oh! what could I do with a dollar and eighty-seven cents?"

21 At 7 o'clock the coffee was made and the frying-pan was on the back of the stove hot and ready to cook the chops.

22 Jim was never late. Della doubled the fob chain in her hand and sat on the corner of the table near the door that he always entered. Then she heard his step on the stair away down on the first flight, and she turned white for just a moment. She had a habit of saying little silent prayers about the simplest everyday things, and now she whispered: "Please God, make him think I am still pretty."

23 The door opened and Jim stepped in and closed it. He looked thin and very serious. Poor fellow, he was only twenty-two—and to be burdened with a family! He needed a new overcoat and he was without gloves.

24 Jim stopped inside the door, as immovable as a **setter** at the scent of quail. His eyes were fixed upon Della, and there was an expression in them that she could not read, and it terrified her. It was not anger, nor surprise, nor disapproval, nor horror, nor any of the sentiments that she had been prepared for. He simply stared at her fixedly with that peculiar expression on his face.

25 Della wriggled off the table and went for him.

26 "Jim, darling," she cried, "don't look at me that way. I had my hair cut off and sold it because I couldn't have lived through Christmas without giving you a present. It'll grow out again—you won't mind, will you? I just had to do it. My hair grows awfully fast. Say 'Merry Christmas!' Jim, and let's be happy. You don't know what a nice—what a beautiful, nice gift I've got for you."

27 "You've cut off your hair?" asked Jim, **laboriously**, as if he had not arrived at that **patent** fact yet even after the hardest mental labor.

28 "Cut it off and sold it," said Della. "Don't you like me just as well, anyhow? I'm me without my hair, ain't I?"

29 Jim looked about the room curiously.

30 "You say your hair is gone?" he said, with an air almost of idiocy.

31 "You needn't look for it," said Della. "It's sold, I tell you—sold and gone, too. It's Christmas Eve, boy. Be good to me, for it went for you. Maybe the hairs of my head were numbered," she went on with a sudden serious sweetness, "but nobody could ever count my love for you. Shall I put the chops on, Jim?"

32 Out of his trance Jim seemed quickly to wake. He **enfolded** his Della. For ten seconds let us **regard with discreet scrutiny** some inconsequential object in the other direction. Eight dollars a week or a million a year—what is the difference? A mathematician or a wit would give you the wrong answer. The magi brought valuable gifts, but that was not among them. This dark **assertion** will be illuminated later on.

33 Jim drew a package from his overcoat pocket and threw it upon the table.

34 "Don't make any mistake, Dell," he said, "about me. I don't think there's anything in the way of a haircut or a shave or a shampoo that could make me like my girl any less. But if you'll unwrap that package you may see why you had me going a while at first."

35 White fingers and nimble tore at the string and paper. And then an ecstatic scream of joy; and then, alas! a quick feminine change to hysterical tears and wails, necessitating the immediate employment of all the comforting powers of the lord of the flat.

WORD CONNECTIONS

Content Connections

A *fob chain* is a short chain used to hold a pocket watch. Pocket watches were a popular style in the early 1900s and came in many different styles. Having a gold chain, however plain, would have elevated Jim above his impoverished social status, if only in appearance.

setter: a hunting dog

My Notes

laboriously: with difficulty
patent: obvious

enfolded: wrapped arms around
regard with discreet scrutiny: look at closely but not in an obvious way
assertion: a declaration or statement, often without proof

Shared Gifts: Introducing Irony

My Notes

36 For there lay The Combs—the set of combs, side and back, that Della had worshipped for long in a Broadway window. Beautiful combs, pure tortoise shell, with jeweled rims—just the shade to wear in the beautiful vanished hair. They were expensive combs, she knew, and her heart had simply craved and yearned over them without the least hope of possession. And now, they were hers, but the tresses that should have adorned the coveted adornments were gone.

37 But she hugged them to her bosom, and at length she was able to look up with dim eyes and a smile and say: "My hair grows so fast, Jim!"

38 And then Della leaped up like a little singed cat and cried, "Oh, oh!"

39 Jim had not yet seen his beautiful present. She held it out to him eagerly upon her open palm. The dull precious metal seemed to flash with a reflection of her bright and ardent spirit.

40 "Isn't it a dandy, Jim? I hunted all over town to find it. You'll have to look at the time a hundred times a day now. Give me your watch. I want to see how it looks on it."

41 Instead of obeying, Jim tumbled down on the couch and put his hands under the back of his head and smiled.

42 "Dell," said he, "let's put our Christmas presents away and keep 'em a while. They're too nice to use just at present. I sold the watch to get the money to buy your combs. And now suppose you put the chops on."

43 The magi, as you know, were wise men—wonderfully wise men—who brought gifts to the Babe in the manger. They invented the art of giving Christmas presents. Being wise, their gifts were no doubt wise ones, possibly bearing the privilege of exchange in case of duplication. And here I have lamely related to you the uneventful chronicle of two foolish children in a flat who most unwisely sacrificed for each other the greatest treasures of their house. But in a last word to the wise of these days let it be said that of all who give gifts these two were the wisest. Of all who give and receive gifts, such as they are wisest. Everywhere they are wisest. They are the magi.

Visual Prompt: The magi and their gifts were often the subject of fine art painters. Compare the symbolism in "The Gift of the Magi" to the symbolism in this painting.

Second Read

- Reread the story to answer these text-dependent questions.
- Write any additional questions you have about the text in your Reader/Writer Notebook.

2. **Key Ideas and Details:** What evidence has O. Henry provided in the text to support the inference that Della and Jim do not have a lot of money?

3. **Key Ideas and Details:** By the end of paragraph 6, the reader has met the two main characters—Della and Jim—and has a sense of their relationship. How does understanding their relationship underscore the story's central idea? What is the central idea?

4. **Craft and Structure:** O. Henry chooses specific words and phrases to point to the story's historical setting. Reread paragraphs 17–18. What language gives a sense of the story's time and place?

5. **Craft and Structure:** From what point of view is this story told? Read paragraph 32. What do you notice about the story's point of view in this paragraph?

6. **Integration of Knowledge and Ideas:** How does understanding the allusion to the magi help with understanding O. Henry's purpose in writing this story?

Shared Gifts: Introducing Irony

My Notes

7. **Craft and Structure:** How does the author use irony to create a surprise ending?

8. **Integration of Knowledge and Ideas:** How is the last paragraph different from the rest of the story in terms of its perspective or point of view?

Working from the Text

Introducing the Strategy: SIFT

The acronym SIFT stands for Symbol, Imagery, Figurative Language, and Tone or Theme. You can use this strategy to "sift" through the parts of a story in order to explore how a writer uses literary elements and stylistic techniques to convey meaning or theme. Identifying these elements is the key to helping you understand the author's purpose and **commentary** on life—the story's theme.

> **ACADEMIC VOCABULARY**
> **Commentary** refers to the expression of opinions or explanations about an event or situation. **Textual commentary** in an essay refers to explanations about the significance or importance of supporting details or examples in an analysis.

9. After reading the story, go back and scan for examples of symbols, imagery, figurative language, and tone/theme, and complete the SIFT graphic organizer. Record examples from "The Gift of the Magi" of each of the SIFT elements.

Literary Element	Text Details	Effects or Meanings of Details
Symbol:		
Imagery:		
Figurative Language:		
Tone/Theme:		

Shared Gifts: Introducing Irony

Determining Theme

To determine theme, you must consider how all elements work together within a story and what ideas about life these elements present. Also, keep these points in mind when writing the theme of a story:

A THEME IS NOT:

- A "topic" (such as love or sacrifice)
- A summary, such as "Two people sell their valuables to show their love for each other"
- A moral (e.g., "If you love someone, you will do anything for him or her")

A THEME IS:

- A general statement about life (e.g., "People show their love for each other by making sacrifices")

Based on these examples, why is the sentence above an appropriate general statement about, or theme of, "The Gift of the Magi"?

Check Your Understanding

O. Henry develops the theme in "The Gift of the Magi" by creating an ironic situation. Remember that writers use situational irony as a way to contradict the expectations of the characters or the reader. Think about how the situational irony in this story contradicts expectations of the characters. Write a thematic statement that shows how irony is used to reinforce the theme of the story.

Narrative Writing Prompt

Review paragraphs 12–15 of the short story, where Della goes to get her hair cut at Madame Sofronie's. Use this "unseen scene" as an inspiration to write your own scene in which you imagine what the two characters might be doing and saying as the haircutting progresses. Or you may want to imagine the scene in which Jim sells his watch to buy the combs for Della. Be sure to:

- Use description and details to create a setting and situation.
- Set up the conflict, and introduce any new characters and their perspectives for the reader.
- Use dialogue to create a vivid picture of the characters and to develop tension regarding the conflict.
- Provide a smooth transition to the next part of the narrative.

INDEPENDENT READING LINK

Read and Respond

Create a SIFT graphic organizer, similar to the one used in this activity, to identify the elements and techniques used in a short story you have read independently. Below the chart, write a few sentences to explain how the use of these elements contributes to the meaning and theme of the short story you read on your own.

Close Reading of a Short Story

Learning Targets
- Analyze the stylistic elements of foreshadowing, point of view, and imagery to interpret author's purpose.
- Apply the stylistic use of foreshadowing, point of view, and imagery in my own writing.

The Foreshadowing Technique

1. One technique that writers use to create suspense and anticipate the events of the story is foreshadowing. Writers use foreshadowing to give hints to the reader. As readers pay close attention to details and make connections to events and characters, they develop the ability to recognize these hints and how they create a sense of tension in the story. Sometimes, though, these hints are easy to spot only after reading the complete narrative and then rereading it.

Introducing the Strategy: Levels of Questions

Another complex skill that successful readers practice is asking questions about the text. Readers can actively involve themselves with the text by asking three levels of questions:

- **Level 1, Literal**—Literal questions can be answered by referring back to the text or consulting references.
  EXAMPLE: *What is "Coney Island"?*
- **Level 2, Interpretive**—Interpretive questions call for inferences; answers cannot be found directly in the text; however, textual evidence points to and supports your answers.
  EXAMPLE: *Why does the narrator call this young couple "the wisest"?*
- **Level 3, Universal**—Universal questions go beyond the text. What are the larger issues or ideas raised by the text?
- **EXAMPLE:** *Why are some people motivated to make sacrifices for others?*

Preview

In this activity, you will read a short story and interpret the author's purpose in using specific literary devices, such as foreshadowing and point of view.

Setting a Purpose for Reading

- As you read the story, use the My Notes space to write different levels of questions. Label your question as Level 1, Level 2, or Level 3.
- Circle unknown words and phrases. Try to determine the meaning of the words by using context clues, word parts, or a dictionary.

My Notes

My Notes

ABOUT THE AUTHOR
Liliana Heker (b. 1943) is an Argentine journalist and award-winning short-story writer. In Argentina, she edited the literary magazine *El Ornitorrinco*, which translates to "The Platypus." She has published multiple short story collections in Spanish, and some have been translated into English. In "The Stolen Party," Heker presents the events of a party through the eyes of a child.

Short Story

The Stolen Party

by Liliana Heker

Translated by Alberto Manguel

Chunk 1

1 As soon as she arrived she went straight to the kitchen to see if the monkey was there. It was: what a relief! She wouldn't have liked to admit that her mother had been right. Monkeys at a birthday? her mother had sneered. Get away with you, believing any nonsense you're told! She was cross, but not because of the monkey, the girl thought; it's just because of the party.

2 "I don't like you going," she told her. "It's a rich people's party."

3 "Rich people go to Heaven too," said the girl, who studied religion at school.

4 "Get away with Heaven," said the mother.

5 The girl didn't approve of the way her mother spoke. She was barely nine, and one of the best in her class.

6 "I'm going because I've been invited," she said. "And I've been invited because Luciana[1] is my friend. So there."

7 "Ah yes, your friend," her mother grumbled. She paused. "Listen, Rosaura,"[2] she said at last. "That one's not your friend. You know what you are to them? The maid's daughter, that's what."

8 Rosaura blinked hard: she wasn't going to cry. Then she yelled: "Shut up! You know nothing about being friends!"

9 Every afternoon she used to go to Luciana's house and they would both finish their homework while Rosaura's mother did the cleaning. They had their tea in the kitchen and they told each other secrets. Rosaura loved everything in the big house, and she also loved the people who lived there.

10 "I'm going because it will be the most lovely party in the whole world, Luciana told me it would. There will be a magician, and he will bring a monkey and everything."

---

[1] **Luciana** (Lū syə´nə)
[2] **Rosaura** (Rō sah´rə)

GRAMMAR &USAGE
Reciprocal Pronouns

Reciprocal pronouns are used to describe situations in which each individual in a pair or group performs the same action toward the other(s). The reciprocal pronoun *each other* is used to refer to two people, while *one another* is used to refer to three or more people. Heker uses *each other* in this sentence: "They had their tea in the kitchen and they told each other secrets." This indicates that each girl shares secrets with the other girl and reinforces Rosaura's sense that the friendship is mutual, rather than one-sided. As you read, look for other ways that the author leads readers to see events from Rosaura's perspective.

11 The mother swung around to take a good look at her child, and **pompously** put her hands on her hips.

12 *Monkeys at a birthday?* her mother had sneered. *Get away with you, believing any nonsense you're told!*

13 Rosaura was deeply offended. She thought it unfair of her mother to accuse other people of being liars simply because they were rich. Rosaura too wanted to be rich, of course. If one day she managed to live in a beautiful palace, would her mother stop loving her? She felt very sad. She wanted to go to that party more than anything else in the world.

14 "I'll die if I don't go," she whispered, almost without moving her lips.

Chunk 2

15 And she wasn't sure whether she had been heard, but on the morning of the party she discovered that her mother had starched her Christmas dress. And in the afternoon, after washing her hair, her mother rinsed it in apple vinegar so that it would be all nice and shiny. Before going out, Rosaura admired herself in the mirror, with her white dress and glossy hair, and thought she looked terribly pretty.

16 Senora Ines[3] also seemed to notice. As soon as she saw her, she said: "How lovely you look today, Rosaura."

17 Rosaura gave her starched skirt a light toss with her hands and walked into the party with a firm step. She said hello to Luciana and asked about the monkey. Luciana put on a secretive look and whispered into Rosaura's ear: "He's in the kitchen. But don't tell anyone, because it's a surprise."

18 Rosaura wanted to make sure. Carefully she entered the kitchen and there she saw it deep in thought, inside its cage. It looked so funny that the girl stood there for a while, watching it, and later, every so often, she would slip out of the party unseen and go and admire it. Rosaura was the only one allowed into the kitchen. Senora Ines had said: "You yes, but not the others, they're much too **boisterous**, they might break something." Rosaura had never broken anything. She even managed the jug of orange juice, carrying it from the kitchen into the dining room. She held it carefully and didn't spill a single drop. And Senora Ines had said: "Are you sure you can manage a jug as big as that?" Of course she could manage. She wasn't a **butterfingers**, like the others. Like that blonde girl with the bow in her hair. As soon as she saw Rosaura, the girl with the bow had said:

Chunk 3

19 "And you? Who are you?"

20 "I'm a friend of Luciana," said Rosaura.

21 "No," said the girl with the bow, "you are not a friend of Luciana because I'm her cousin and I know all her friends. And I don't know you."

22 "So what," said Rosaura. "I come here every afternoon with my mother and we do our homework together."

23 "You and your mother do your homework together?" asked the girl, laughing.

24 "I and Luciana do our homework together," said Rosaura, very seriously.

25 The girl with the bow shrugged her shoulders.

26 "That's not being friends," she said. "Do you go to school together?"

---

[3] **Señora Ines** (se nyōr´ā ē nes´)

pompously: in a self-important way

My Notes

boisterous: energetic; rowdy

butterfingers: a clumsy person

GRAMMAR & USAGE
Punctuating Dialogue

Both commas and colons can be used to introduce quotations. Typically, a comma is used to introduce a shorter quotation, and a colon is used for a longer quotation. A colon also signals a more definite break between the introductory clause and the quotation. Notice that, in paragraph 31, the author uses a colon to introduce the instructions given by Rosaura's mother. Think about how the longer pause provided by the colon affects the way you read her mother's words.

WORD CONNECTIONS

Content Connections/
Multiple Meaning Words

Charades is a parlor game that was invented in France in the 18th century. It became extremely popular with the middle and upper classes in Great Britain during the Victorian era. Given this history, it is especially fitting that the game should be played at a party, highlighting the differences between social classes. It is also worth noting that *charade*, used as a noun, can be defined as "a deception intended to create a pleasant appearance."

My Notes

27   "No."

28   "So where do you know her from?" said the girl, getting impatient.

29   Rosaura remembered her mother's words perfectly. She took a deep breath.

30   "I'm the daughter of the employee," she said.

31   Her mother had said very clearly: "If someone asks, you say you're the daughter of the employee; that's all." She also told her to add "And proud of it." But Rosaura thought that never in her life would she dare say something of the sort.

32   "What employee?" said the girl with the bow. "Employee in a shop?"

33   "No," said Rosaura angrily. "My mother doesn't sell anything in any shop, so there."

34   "So how come she's an employee?" said the girl with the bow.

35   Just then Señora Ines arrived saying shh shh, and asked Rosaura if she wouldn't mind helping serve out the hot dogs, as she knew the house so much better than the others.

36   "See?" said Rosaura to the girl with the bow, and when no one was looking she kicked her in the shin.

Chunk 4
37   Apart from the girl with the bow, all the others were delightful. The one she liked best was Luciana, with her golden birthday crown; and then the boys. Rosaura won the sack race, and nobody managed to catch her when they played tag. When they split into two teams to play charades, all the boys wanted her for their side. Rosaura felt she had never been so happy in all her life.

38   But the best was still to come. The best came after Luciana blew out the candles. First the cake. Señora Ines had asked her to help pass the cake around, and Rosaura had enjoyed the task immensely, because everyone called out to her, shouting "Me, me!" Rosaura remembered a story in which there was a queen who had the power of life or death over her subjects. She had always loved that, having the power of life or death. To Luciana and the boys she gave the largest pieces, and to the girl with the bow she gave a slice so thin one could see through it.

39   After the cake came the magician, tall and bony, with a fine red cape. A true magician: he could untie handkerchiefs by blowing on them and make a chain with links that had no openings. He could guess what cards were pulled out from a pack, and the monkey was his assistant. He called the monkey "partner."

40   "Let's see here, partner," he would say, "Turn over a card." And, "Don't run away, partner: time to work now."

41   The final trick was wonderful. One of the children had to hold the monkey in his **arms** and the magician said he would make him disappear.

42   "What, the boy?" they all shouted.

43   "No, the monkey!" shouted the magician.

44   Rosaura thought that this was truly the most amusing party in the whole world.

45   The magician asked a small fat boy to come and help, but the small fat boy got frightened almost at once and dropped the monkey on the floor. The magician picked him up carefully, whispered something in his ear, and the monkey nodded almost as if he understood.

46 "You mustn't be so unmanly, my friend," the magician said to the fat boy.

47 "What's unmanly?" said the fat boy.

48 The magician turned around as if to look for spies.

49 "A sissy," said the magician. "Go sit down."

50 Then he stared at all the faces, one by one. Rosaura felt her heart tremble.

51 "You, with the Spanish eyes," said the magician. And everyone saw that he was pointing at her.

52 She wasn't afraid. Neither holding the monkey, nor when the magician made him vanish; not even when, at the end the magician flung his red cape over Rosaura's head and **uttered** a few magic words ...and the monkey reappeared, chattering happily, in her arms. The children clapped furiously. And before Rosaura returned to her seat, the magician said:

53 "Thank you very much, my little countess."

54 She was so pleased with the compliment that a while later, when her mother came to fetch her, that was the first thing she told her.

Chunk 5

55 "I helped the magician and he said to me, 'Thank you very much, my little countess.'"

56 It was strange because up to then Rosaura had thought that she was angry with her mother. All along Rosaura had imagined that she would say to her: "See that the monkey wasn't a lie?" But instead she was so thrilled that she told her mother all about the wonderful magician.

57 Her mother tapped her on the head and said: "So now we're a countess!"

58 But one could see that she was beaming.

59 And now they both stood in the entrance, because a moment ago Señora Ines, smiling, had said: "Please wait here a second."

60 Her mother suddenly seemed worried.

61 "What is it?" she asked Rosaura.

62 "What is what?" said Rosaura. "It's nothing; she just wants to get the presents for those who are leaving, see?"

63 She pointed at the fat boy and at a girl with pigtails who were also waiting there, next to their mothers. And she explained about the presents. She knew, because she had been watching those who left before her. When one of the girls was about to leave, Señora Ines would give her a bracelet. When a boy left, Señora Ines gave him a yo-yo. Rosaura preferred the yo-yo because it sparkled, but she didn't mention that to her mother. Her mother might have said: "So why don't you ask for one, you blockhead?" That's what her mother was like. Rosaura didn't feel like explaining that she'd be horribly ashamed to be the odd one out. Instead she said:

64 "I was the best-behaved at the party."

65 And she said no more because Señora Ines came out into the hall with two bags, one pink and one blue.

My Notes

uttered: said

My Notes

marvelous: extraordinary

rummaged: searched thoroughly by moving things about

instinctively: naturally; from one's instincts

infinitely: extremely

66 First she went up to the fat boy, gave him a yo-yo out of the blue bag, and the fat boy left with his mother. Then she went up to the girl and gave her a bracelet out of the pink bag, and the girl with the pigtails left as well.

67 Finally she came up to Rosaura and her mother. She had a big smile on her face and Rosaura liked that. Señora Ines looked down at her, then looked up at her mother, and then said something that made Rosaura proud:

68 "What a **marvelous** daughter you have, Herminia."[4]

Chunk 6

69 For an instant, Rosaura thought that she'd give her two presents: the bracelet and the yo-yo. Señora Ines bent down as if about to look for something. Rosaura also leaned forward, stretching out her arm. But she never completed the movement.

70 Señora Ines didn't look in the pink bag. Nor did she look in the blue bag. Instead she **rummaged** in her purse. In her hand appeared two bills.

71 "You really and truly earned this," she said handing them over. "Thank you for all your help, my pet."

72 Rosaura felt her arms stiffen, stick close to her body, and then she noticed her mother's hand on her shoulder. **Instinctively** she pressed herself against her mother's body. That was all. Except her eyes. Rosaura's eyes had a cold, clear look that fixed itself on Señora Ines's face.

73 Señora Ines, motionless, stood there with her hand outstretched. As if she didn't dare draw it back. As if the slightest change might shatter an **infinitely** delicate balance.

Second Read

- Reread the story to answer these text-dependent questions.
- Write any additional questions you have about the text in your Reader/Writer Notebook.

2. **Key Ideas and Details:** What text evidence supports the idea that Rosaura's mother does not approve of her daughter attending the party? What inferences can you make about why the mother feels this way?

3. **Key Ideas and Details:** What is the story's theme? How does the text in Chunk 2 help shape and develop the theme?

---

[4] **Herminia** (er mē nyā´)

4. Key Ideas and Details: How does the interaction between Rosaura and Luciana's cousin in Chunk 3 develop the story's theme?

5. Craft and Structure: From what point of view is this story written? What effect does the chosen point of view have on the story?

6. Craft and Structure: At the end of the story, Señora Ines stands motionless with her hand outstretched, afraid she "might shatter an infinitely delicate balance." What do you think the phrase "infinitely delicate balance" means? Does this balance actually exist in the story?

7. Craft and Structure: How does the author use situational irony to create a surprise ending? How does the ironic tone in this story compare to the tone in "The Gift of the Magi?"

8. Craft and Structure: How does the author utilize foreshadowing to underscore Señora Ines's final action?

My Notes

Close Reading of a Short Story

Working from the Text

9. Reread each text-dependent question. Label the level of each question. Notice that these questions get at the meaning of the story.

10. Just as "The Gift of the Magi," has strong images of the comb and the watch, this story has a central image that may be used symbolically. Identify the image that is introduced at the beginning, appears in the middle, and ends the story.

11. How can this image be interpreted as symbolic?

Language and Writer's Craft: Clauses

A clause is a group of words that has a subject and a verb.

An **independent clause** is a complete thought that can function as a sentence. Read this example of an independent clause from "The Stolen Party."

> "The final trick was wonderful."

Two independent clauses can be joined by a comma and a **coordinating conjunction**, such as *and, but*, or *or*. Here is an example from the story.

> "He could guess what cards were pulled out from a pack, and the monkey was his assistant."

A **subordinate clause**, often called a **dependent clause**, does not express a complete thought and cannot function as a sentence. A subordinate clause is often introduced by a **subordinating conjunction** such as *after, when, while*, or *because*. Read this example from the story.

> "When one of the girls was about to leave, Señora Ines would give her a bracelet."

In this story, the author varies the order of clauses in sentences to create specific effects. Including a variety of clauses makes writing more interesting. Try to include a variety in your own writing.

PRACTICE Read the following sentences from the story. Then identify the independent clauses, the subordinate clauses, and any subordinating and coordinating conjunctions.

> "Rosaura won the sack race, and nobody managed to catch her when they played tag. When they split into two teams to play charades, all the boys wanted her for their side."

Check Your Understanding

Write a theme statement for this story. Share your statement with a group. After each group member reads his or her theme statement, give feedback to each group member by considering these points:

- Is the theme statement a complete statement?
- Does the statement avoid merely summarizing the story?
- Does the statement avoid making a moral out of the story?

Narrative Writing Prompt

Reread the final paragraphs of "The Stolen Party," when Señora Ines tries to hand Rosaura money instead of a gift like all the other children. This is a powerful moment as all three characters appear to be frozen in time and space. Think about how point of view has created the surprise and disappointment in both the reader and the main character.

Using the story starter that follows, write a continuation of the narrative that shows Rosaura's realizations, starting with Señora Ines's final words. Use dialogue, point of view, and imagery, as well as deliberate sentence structure, to emulate the author's style. You may want to devise an alternative resolution. Be sure to:

- Use dialogue to convey the experiences and attitudes of the characters.
- Include precise language, details, and imagery to engage the reader.
- Include clauses to add variety and interest to your writing.
- Maintain the limited point of view to show Rosaura's new perspective.

Rosaura glanced at the caged monkey as she and her mother turned from Señora Ines and walked out of the room. She gripped her money and, turning to her mother, said, "_____."

INDEPENDENT READING LINK

Read and Discuss

Using a short story you have read independently, plot the sequence of events by visualizing the events in a storyboard. Then compare the sequence of events with a peer. What similarities do you find? What differences?

Introducing a Story of Revenge

pick

LEARNING STRATEGIES:
Drafting, Graphic Organizer,
Sharing and Responding

Learning Targets

- Read and analyze a text to understand the historical context of a short story.
- Identify and cite textual evidence to support understanding of meaning.

Interpreting Meaning

1. Read the quotation assigned to your group. Discuss, and interpret the meaning of the quotation. What is this person's interpretation of revenge? For the remaining quotations, write each group's interpretation in the table.

My Notes

Quotation	Interpretation of Quotation
"An eye for an eye only ends up making the whole world blind." —Mahatma Gandhi	
"Don't get mad, get even." —Robert F. Kennedy	
"She got even in a way that was almost cruel. She forgave them." —Ralph McGill (about Eleanor Roosevelt)	
"Success is the sweetest revenge." —Vanessa Williams	
"Revenge is often like biting a dog because the dog bit you." —Austin O'Malley	

Preview

In this activity, you will read an informational text that will provide important historical information for an upcoming short story.

Setting a Purpose for Reading

- As you read the passage, underline any new information you learn or anything you find interesting.
- Circle unknown words and phrases. Try to determine the meaning of the words by using context clues, word parts, or a dictionary.

Informational Text

Catacombs
and Carnival

1   Centuries ago, in Italy, the early Christians buried their dead in *catacombs*, which are long, winding underground tunnels. Later, wealthy families built private catacombs beneath their *palazzos*, or palatial homes. *Nitre*, a crystalized salt growth, lined the dark, cool underground chambers, or *vaults*. In order to find their way in their underground tunnels, the owners would light torches or *flambeaux*.

2   These *crypts* were suitable not only for burial but also for storage of fine **vintage** wines such as *Amontillado, DeGrave*, and *Medoc*. A wine expert, or *connoisseur*, would store wine carefully in these underground vaults. Wine was stored in casks or *puncheons*, which held 72 to 100 gallons, or in *pipes*, which contained 126 gallons (also known as two hogsheads).

3   Edgar Allan Poe's story "The Cask of Amontillado" takes place in the catacombs during *Carnival*, a celebration that still takes place in many countries. The day before Ash Wednesday is celebrated as a holiday with carnivals, masquerade balls, and parades of costumed merrymakers. During Carnival, people celebrate by disguising themselves as fools, wearing *parti-striped dress or motley*, and capes, known as *roquelaires*. Women would celebrate wearing *conical caps*. Carnival is also called Mardi Gras, or Fat Tuesday, because of the feasting that takes place the day before Ash Wednesday. Starting on Ash Wednesday, which is the beginning of Lent, some Christians fast and do **penance** for their sins.

My Notes

vintage: representing the high quality of a past time

penance: punishment for a sin

WORD CONNECTIONS

Etymology

The term *Mardi Gras* literally translates to "Fat Tuesday," referencing the Catholic tradition of slaughtering and feasting upon a fattened calf on the last day of Carnival. In modern practice, Fat Tuesday is a day of gluttony, with party-goers feasting on food and drink before the Christian holy season of Lent/Easter begins.

Introducing a Story of Revenge

A lithograph of Carnival at the Theater (*teatro*) of S. Gallo and S. Benedetto (1856)

Second Read

- Reread the informational text to answer these text-dependent questions.
- Write any additional questions you have about the text in your Reader/Writer Notebook.

2. **Key Ideas and Details:** How does Carnival fit into the Christian religious calendar?

3. **Craft and Structure:** Based on what you learned in this text about catacombs and Carnival, why would a story set in the catacombs during Carnival be interesting?

4. **Craft and Structure:** In the first paragraph, five words appear in italics and are followed/preceded by the definition of the word. Why does the author of this text choose to do this?

Check Your Understanding

Review the image of Carnival. Write a brief interpretation of what is happening in that image using textual evidence and vocabulary from the passage.

Narrative Writing Prompt

Imagine that you are setting a story in a catacomb. Write a story starter describing the setting and introduce a character. Be sure to:

- Use figurative language and imagery to create a mood of suspense, fear, or terror.
- Use sentence structures effectively to create the mood you want.
- Use specific details to describe the setting and the character.

My Notes

Irony in the Vaults

LEARNING STRATEGIES:
Quickwrite, Graphic Organizer,
Rereading, Diffusing, Predicting,
Marking the Text, Think-Pair-
Share, Drafting

My Notes

Literary Terms

Dramatic irony occurs when the reader or audience knows more about the circumstances or future events than the characters in the scene.
Verbal irony occurs when a speaker or narrator says one thing while meaning the opposite.

Learning Targets

- Identify how irony is conveyed through the words, actions, and situations in a story.
- Acquire an understanding of challenging vocabulary by diffusing unknown words.
- Analyze how an author effectively uses syntax to create a distinct style.

Reviewing Irony

1. Think about the situational irony in the two short stories by O. Henry and Heker. This situational irony leads to an understanding of the theme or major idea of each story. What was ironic about the situation in each of the stories?

Introducing the Strategy: Diffusing

To diffuse a text means to read a passage, note unfamiliar words, and then use context clues, dictionaries, or other resources to discover meaning for the unfamiliar words.

Preview

In this activity, you will read a short story and analyze how the author conveys irony through words, actions, and situations.

Setting a Purpose for Reading

- Read the definitions for **dramatic** and **verbal irony**. As you read the story, highlight any examples of irony.
- Use the Diffusing strategy to circle unknown words and phrases. Try to determine the meaning of the words by using context clues, word parts, or a dictionary.

ABOUT THE AUTHOR

Born in Boston, Edgar Allan Poe (1809–1849) was orphaned as a young child and taken in by the Allan family of Richmond, Virginia. Poe and the Allans eventually had a falling out because of Poe's irresponsible behavior. This situation was characteristic of Poe's short and tragic life. Despite his personal difficulties and an unstable temperament, Poe was a literary genius, writing short stories, poetry, and literary criticism, for which he became internationally famous. His dark imagination produced stories that are known for their atmosphere of horror.

Short Story

The Cask of Amontillado

by Edgar Allan Poe

WORD CONNECTIONS

Roots and Affixes
The word *impunity* has a Latin root (from *poena*) that means "penalty" or "punishment." The prefix *in-* (spelled *im-* here) means "not." To do something with impunity is to do it without fear of punishment or consequences.

1 The thousand injuries of Fortunato I had borne as I best could, but when he ventured upon insult, I vowed revenge. You, who so well know the nature of my soul, will not suppose, however, that I gave utterance to a *threat*. At *length* I would be **avenged**; this was a point definitively settled—but the very definitiveness with which it was resolved precluded the idea of risk. I must not only punish, but punish with impunity. A wrong is **unredressed** when **retribution** overtakes its redresser. It is equally unredressed when the avenger fails to make himself felt as such to him who has done the wrong.

2 It must be understood that neither by word nor deed had I given Fortunato cause to doubt my good will. I continued as was my wont, to smile in his face, and he did not perceive that my smile *now* was at the thought of his **immolation**.

3 He had a weak point—this Fortunato—although in other regards he was a man to be respected and even feared. He prided himself on his **connoisseurship** in wine. Few Italians have the true virtuoso spirit. For the most part their enthusiasm is adopted to suit the time and opportunity to practice **imposture** upon the British and Austrian millionaires. In painting and gemmary, Fortunato, like his countrymen, was a quack, but in the matter of old wines he was sincere. In this respect I did not differ from him materially; I was skillful in the Italian vintages myself, and bought largely whenever I could.

avenged: punished

unredressed: not corrected or set right
retribution: revenge

immolation: killing, as a sacrifice

connoisseurship: expertise

imposture: deceit, dishonesty

My Notes

_____

_____

_____

_____

_____

_____

_____

_____

_____

_____

_____

_____

_____

Chunk 1

4 It was about dusk, one evening during the supreme madness of the carnival season, that I encountered my friend. He accosted me with excessive warmth, for he had been drinking much. The man wore motley[1]. He had on a tight-fitting parti-striped dress and his head was surmounted by the conical cap and bells. I was so pleased to see him that I thought I should never have done wringing his hand.

5 I said to him, "My dear Fortunato, you are luckily met. How remarkably well you are looking today! But I have received a pipe of what passes for Amontillado, and I have my doubts."

6 "How?" said he, "Amontillado? A pipe? Impossible! And in the middle of the carnival?"

7 "I have my doubts," I replied; "and I was silly enough to pay the full Amontillado price without consulting you in the matter. You were not to be found, and I was fearful of losing a bargain."

---

[1] motley is the traditional costume of the court jester

Irony in the Vaults

My Notes

8 "Amontillado!"

9 "I have my doubts."

10 "Amontillado!"

11 "And I must satisfy them."

12 "Amontillado!"

13 "As you are engaged, I am on my way to Luchesi. If anyone has a critical turn, it is he. He will tell me— "

14 "Luchesi cannot tell Amontillado from sherry."

15 "And yet some fools will have it that his taste is a match for your own."

16 "Come, let us go."

17 "Whither?"

18 "To your vaults."

19 "My friend, no; I will not impose upon your good nature. I perceive you have an engagement. Luchesi— "

20 "I have no engagement; come."

21 "My friend, no. It is not the engagement, but the severe cold with which I perceive you are afflicted. The vaults are insufferably damp. They are encrusted with nitre."

22 "Let us go, nevertheless. The cold is merely nothing. Amontillado! You have been imposed upon; and as for Luchesi, he cannot distinguish sherry from Amontillado."

23 Thus speaking, Fortunato possessed himself of my arm. Putting on a mask of black silk and drawing a *roquelaire*[2] closely about my person, I suffered him to hurry me to my palazzo.

Chunk 2

24 There were no attendants at home; they had **absconded** to make merry in honour of the time. I had told them that I should not return until the morning and had given them explicit orders not to stir from the house. These orders were sufficient, I well knew, to insure their immediate disappearance, one and all, as soon as my back was turned.

25 I took from their sconces two flambeaux, and giving one to Fortunato, bowed him through several suites of rooms to the archway that led into the vaults. I passed down a long and winding staircase, requesting him to be cautious as he followed. We came at length to the foot of the descent, and stood together on the damp ground of the catacombs of the Montresors.

26 The gait of my friend was unsteady, and the bells upon his cap jingled as he strode.

27 "The pipe," said he.

28 "It is farther on," said I; "but observe the white webwork which gleams from these cavern walls."

29 He turned towards me and looked into my eyes with two filmy orbs that distilled the rheum of intoxication.

absconded: run away, fled

---

[2] *roquelaire* is a knee-length cloak, often trimmed with fur

30 "Nitre?" he asked, at length.

31 "Nitre," I replied. "How long have you had that cough?"

32 "Ugh! ugh! ugh!—ugh! ugh! ugh!—ugh! ugh! ugh!—ugh! ugh! ugh!"

33 My poor friend found it impossible to reply for many minutes.

34 "It is nothing," he said, at last.

35 "Come," I said, with decision, "we will go back; your health is precious. You are rich, respected, admired, beloved; you are happy as once I was. You are a man to be missed. For me it is no matter. We will go back; you will be ill, and I cannot be responsible. Besides, there is Luchesi—"

36 "Enough," he said; "the cough is a mere nothing; it will not kill me. I shall not die of a cough."

37 "True—true," I replied; "and, indeed, I had no intention of alarming you unnecessarily—but you should use all proper caution. A **draught** of this Medoc will defend us from the damps." Here I knocked off the neck of a bottle which I drew from a long row of its fellows that lay upon the mould.

38 "Drink," I said, presenting him the wine.

39 He raised it to his lips with a leer. He paused and nodded to me familiarly, while his bells jingled.

40 "I drink," he said, "to the buried that **repose** around us."

41 "And I to your long life."

Chunk 3

42 He again took my arm and we proceeded.

43 "These vaults," he said, "are extensive."

44 "The Montresors," I replied, "were a great and numerous family."

45 "I forget your **arms**."

46 "A huge human foot d'or, in a field azure; the foot crushes a serpent rampant whose fangs are imbedded in the heel."

47 "And the motto?"

48 "*Nemo me impune lacessit.*"[3]

49 "Good!" he said.

50 The wine sparkled in his eyes and the bells jingled. My own fancy grew warm with the Medoc. We had passed through walls of piled bones, with casks and puncheons intermingling, into the inmost recesses of the catacombs. I paused again, and this time I made bold to seize Fortunato by an arm above the elbow.

51 "The nitre!" I said: "see, it increases. It hangs like moss upon the vaults. We are below the river's bed. The drops of moisture trickle among the bones. Come, we will go back ere it is too late. Your cough—"

52 "It is nothing," he said; "let us go on. But first, another draught of the Medoc."

My Notes

draught: drink

repose: lie resting

arms: coat of arms

---

[3] *Nemo me impune lacessit* is Latin for "No one insults me with impunity."

Irony in the Vaults

gesticulation: gesture, motion

GRAMMAR & USAGE
Syntax

Syntax refers to the way words, phrases, and clauses are organized in a sentence. Writers vary their syntax to achieve different rhythms and emphases in their prose. For example, notice that Poe uses an inverted word order in this sentence: "Its termination the feeble light did not enable us to see." A more typical word order is subject, verb, object, yet this sentence begins with the object (termination) followed by the subject (light) and verb (enable). Consider how the inverted word order places emphasis on the word *termination*.

WORD CONNECTIONS

Etymology

A *Mason* (capital "M") is a member of a secret organization known as the Freemasons. The fraternity was started in the 14th century and is highly selective about who it allows into its ranks. A *mason* (lowercase "m") is a person whose job it is to build with bricks and mortar. The two different definitions of this word create a delightful opportunity for irony in the story.

trowel: a tool with a flat blade used for laying bricks
interval: gap, space
fettered: restrained, chained

53 I broke and reached him a flagon of De Grave. He emptied it at a breath. His eyes flashed with a fierce light. He laughed and threw the bottle upwards with a **gesticulation** I did not understand.

54 I looked at him in surprise. He repeated the movement—a grotesque one.

55 "You do not comprehend?" he said.

56 "Not I," I replied.

57 "Then you are not of the brotherhood."

58 "How?"

59 "You are not of the Masons."

60 "Yes, yes;· I said, "yes! Yes."

61 "You? Impossible! A Mason?"

62 "A mason." I replied.

63 "A sign," he said.

64 "It is this," I answered, producing from beneath the folds of my *roquelaire* a **trowel**.

65 "You jest," he exclaimed, recoiling a few paces. "But let us proceed to the Amontillado."

66 "Be it so," I said, replacing the tool beneath the cloak, and again offering him my arm. He leaned upon it heavily. We continued our route in search of the Amontillado. We passed through a range of low arches, descended, passed on, and descending again, arrived at a deep crypt, in which the foulness of the air caused our flambeaux rather to glow than flame.

Chunk 4

67 At the most remote end of the crypt there appeared another less spacious. Its walls had been lined with human remains piled to the vault overhead, in the fashion of the great catacombs of Paris. Three sides of this interior crypt were still ornamented in this manner. From the fourth the bones had been thrown down, and lay promiscuously upon the earth, forming at one point a mound of some size. Within the wall thus exposed by the displacing of the bones, we perceived a still interior recess, in depth about four feet, in width three, in height six or seven. It seemed to have been constructed for no special use in itself, but formed merely the **interval** between two of the colossal supports of the roof of the catacombs, and was backed by one of their circumscribing walls of solid granite.

68 It was in vain that Fortunato, uplifting his dull torch, endeavoured to pry into the depths of the recess. Its termination the feeble light did not enable us to see.

69 "Proceed," I said; "herein is the Amontillado. As for Luchesi—"

70 "He is an ignoramus," interrupted my friend, as he stepped unsteadily forward, while I followed immediately at his heels. In an instant he had reached the extremity of the niche, and finding his progress arrested by the rock, stood stupidly bewildered. A moment more and I had **fettered** him to the granite. In its surface were two iron staples, distant from each other about two feet, horizontally. From one of these depended a short chain, from the other a padlock. Throwing the links about his waist, it was but the work of a few seconds to secure it. He was too much astounded to resist. Withdrawing the key I stepped back from the recess.

71 "Pass your hand," I said, "over the wall; you cannot help feeling the nitre. Indeed it is *very* damp. Once more let me ***implore*** you to return. No? Then I must positively leave you. But I must first **render** you all the little attentions in my power."

72 "The Amontillado!" ejaculated my friend, not yet recovered from his astonishment.

73 "True," I replied; "the Amontillado."

Chunk 5

74 As I said these words I busied myself among the pile of bones of which I have before spoken. Throwing them aside, I soon uncovered a quantity of building stone and mortar. With these materials and with the aid of my trowel, I began vigorously to wall up the entrance of the niche.

75 I had scarcely laid the first tier of my masonry when I discovered that the intoxication of Fortunato had in a great measure worn off. The earliest indication I had of this was a low moaning cry from the depth of the recess. It was *not* the cry of a drunken man. There was then a long and obstinate silence. I laid the second tier, and the third, and the fourth; and then I heard the furious vibrations of the chain. The noise lasted for several minutes, during which, that I might hearken to it with the more satisfaction, I ceased my labours and sat down upon the bones. When at last the clanking subsided, I resumed the trowel, and finished without interruption the fifth, the sixth, and the seventh tier. The wall was now nearly upon a level with my breast. I again paused, and holding the flambeaux over the mason work, threw a few feeble rays upon the figure within.

76 A succession of loud and shrill screams, bursting suddenly from the throat of the chained form, seemed to thrust me violently back. For a brief moment I hesitated—I trembled. Unsheathing my rapier, I began to grope with it about the recess; but the thought of an instant reassured me. I placed my hand upon the solid fabric of the catacombs, and felt satisfaction. I reapproached the wall; I replied to the yells of him who clamored. I reechoed—I aided—I surpassed them in volume and in strength. I did this, and the clamorer grew still.

Chunk 6

77 It was now midnight, and my task was drawing to a close. I had completed the eighth, the ninth, and the tenth tier. I had finished a portion of the last and the eleventh; there remained but a single stone to be fitted and plastered in. I struggled with its weight; I placed it partially in its destined position. But now there came from out the niche a low laugh that erected the hairs upon my head. It was succeeded by a sad voice, which I had difficulty in recognizing as that of the noble Fortunato. The voice said—

78 "Ha! ha! ha!—he! he!—a very good joke indeed—an excellent jest. We will have many a rich laugh about it at the palazzo—he! he! he!—over our wine—he! he! he!"

79 "The Amontillado!" I said.

80 "He! he! he!—he! he! he!—yes, the Amontillado. But is it not getting late? Will not they be awaiting us at the palazzo, the Lady of Fortunato and the rest? Let us be gone."

81 "Yes," I said, "let us be gone!"

implore: beg
render: provide

GRAMMAR &USAGE
Parallel Structure

Writers create **parallel structure** by presenting ideas, descriptions, or actions of equal importance in the same grammatical forms. This emphasizes important ideas and creates rhythm. For example, Poe uses parallel structure in these sentences: "I had completed **the eighth, the ninth,** and **the tenth** tier. I had finished a portion of **the last** and **the eleventh** . . . ." Think about what this repetition emphasizes about the narrator's actions.

My Notes

_____
_____
_____
_____
_____
_____
_____
_____
_____
_____
_____
_____
_____

WORD CONNECTIONS

Etymology

In pace requiescat! is Latin for "Rest in peace." Fortunato is buried alive, which in no way conjures up thoughts of him resting in peace. Poe's choice to end the story with this final thought leaves the reader with an unsettled feeling.

aperture: narrow opening
rampart: barrier

GRAMMAR & USAGE
Verbals

A **verbal** is a form of a verb that is used as some other part of speech—a noun, an adjective, or an adverb. Verbals add variety and complexity to a text.

A **gerund** is a verbal that ends in *-ing* and functions as a noun. For example: "When at last the **clanking** subsided, I resumed ... ."

A **participle** is a verbal that ends in *-ing* or *-ed* and functions as an adjective. For example: "I thrust a torch through the **remaining** aperture and let it fall within."

An **infinitive** is a verbal that can be used as a noun, an adjective, or an adverb. An infinitive is usually formed by adding *to* to the simple form of the verb: *to eat, to sleep*. For example: "Unsheathing my rapier, I began **to grope** with it about the recess."

82 *"For the love of God, Montresor!"*

83 "Yes," I said, "for the love of God!"

84 But to these words I hearkened in vain for a reply. I grew impatient. I called aloud—

85 "Fortunato!"

86 No answer. I called again—

87 "Fortunato!"

88 No answer still. I thrust a torch through the remaining **aperture** and let it fall within. There came forth in return only a jingling of the bells. My heart grew sick—on account of the dampness of the catacombs. I hastened to make an end of my labor. I forced the last stone into its position; I plastered it up. Against the new masonry I reerected the old **rampart** of bones. For the half of a century no mortal has disturbed them.

89 *In pace requiescat!*

Second Read

- Reread the story to answer these text-dependent questions.
- Write any additional questions you have about the text in your Reader/Writer Notebook.

2. **Key Ideas and Details:** Reread the last two sentences in paragraph 1. Based on this text, what is the narrator's opinion of revenge? What does this reveal about his character?

3. **Key Ideas and Details:** To whom is the narrator telling his story? Support your answer with evidence from the text.

4. **Craft and Structure:** How does Poe create suspense leading up to Fortunato's inevitable death? Cite three examples from the story.

5. **Craft and Structure:** How does the setting of Carnival aid in Fortunato's fate?

6. **Craft and Structure:** Reread the first paragraph of Chunk 2. How does Poe use irony in this scene?

7. **Craft and Structure:** What message is the author sending the audience through the imagery of Montresor's coat of arms? What does it symbolize?

8. **Craft and Structure:** How does the author use verbal irony to enhance the story's suspense? Locate two examples of verbal irony in the story.

9. **Craft and Structure:** What effect does the chosen point of view have on this story?

10. **Key Ideas and Details:** What is the central theme of the story? How is this theme created?

Working from the Text

11. Scan "The Cask of Amontillado" and find the examples of irony you highlighted. Make sure you have at least three examples of each type of irony. Scan the text if you need additional examples. Record your examples in the graphic organizer.

My Notes

Irony in the Vaults

My Notes

Verbal Irony in "The Cask of Amontillado"

Verbal irony occurs when a speaker or narrator says one thing while meaning the opposite. For example, when Fortunato proposes a toast to the dead buried in the crypts around them, Montresor adds: "And I to your long life." Montresor is using verbal irony here, as he intends to end Fortunato's life very soon.

What is stated ...	What it means ...

Situational Irony in "The Cask of Amontillado"

Situational irony occurs when an event contradicts the expectations of the characters or the reader. For example, Fortunato expects to enjoy the rare Amontillado; however, he is killed.

What is expected ...	What happens ...

Dramatic Irony in "The Cask of Amontillado"

Dramatic irony occurs when the reader or audience knows more about circumstances or future events in the story than the characters within it do. For example, from the beginning of "The Cask of Amontillado," the reader knows that Montresor will kill Fortunato; Fortunato does not know this.

What the reader knows ...	What the character knows ...

Check Your Understanding

Briefly explain why a writer would include irony in his or her story. How might you incorporate situational, dramatic, and/or verbal irony into your story?

Explanatory Writing Prompt

In a well-supported paragraph, explain how Poe uses verbal irony in "The Cask of Amontillado" to emphasize the evil intentions of Montresor. Be sure to:

- Create a sentence that introduces your topic.
- Cite textual examples of verbal irony.
- Include commentary sentences that explain the importance or the effect of the irony.
- Use appropriate parallel structure of multiple ideas within a sentence.

My Notes

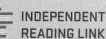

INDEPENDENT READING LINK

Read and Discuss

With a partner, share a plot summary of one of the stories you have read independently. Explain to your partner how the author uses imagery, symbolism, or irony in the story. Discuss how the author's use of the literary element(s) adds to the effectiveness of the story. Which specific literary element(s) that you have learned about make this a "good story"?

Connecting Symbolism to Meaning

Learning Targets
- Analyze how a poet explores the idea of revenge.
- Compare thematic elements and ideas across different texts and genres.

Preview
In this activity, you will read a poem with similar themes to "A Cask of Amontillado" and identify examples of imagery and symbolism.

Setting a Purpose for Reading
- Underline any examples of imagery, and draw a star next to types of irony.
- Circle unknown words and phrases. Try to determine the meaning of the words by using context clues, word parts, or a dictionary.

ABOUT THE AUTHOR
William Blake (1757–1827) was an artist as well as a poet. Born in London, he was apprenticed to an engraver when he was young. Blake claimed to have mystical visions, which he expressed in his poems and engravings. He engraved both the texts and illustrations for his poems. "A Poison Tree" is from his collection called *Songs of Experience*, which reflect his complex view of a world that includes good and evil, innocence and experience.

Poetry

A Poison Tree

by William Blake

> I was angry with my friend:
> I told my **wrath**, my wrath did end.
> I was angry with my foe:
> I told it not, my wrath did grow.
>
> 5 And I watered it in fears,
> Night and morning with my tears;
> And I sunned it with smiles,
> And with soft deceitful **wiles**.
>
> And it grew both day and night,
> 10 Till it bore an apple bright.
> And my foe beheld it shine.
> And he knew that it was mine,

My Notes

wrath: fierce anger; vengeance caused by anger

wiles: sneaky or clever behavior

And into my garden stole

When the night had veiled the pole;

15 In the morning glad I see

My foe outstretched beneath the tree.

Second Read

- Reread the poem to answer these text-dependent questions.
- Write any additional questions you have about the text in your Reader/Writer Notebook.

1. **Craft and Structure:** What does the tree symbolize? How can you tell?

2. **Key Ideas and Details:** Why does the speaker frequently reference day and night?

3. **Craft and Structure:** How does the structure of the poem enhance its message?

Working from the Text

4. You have learned and practiced important strategies to improve your reading and writing skills:

- Diffusing
- SIFT
- Levels of Questions

Using either SIFT or Levels of Questions, reread and analyze "A Poison Tree." Create a graphic organizer that includes an area for you to respond to or interpret the poem, based on your questions or your evidence.

My Notes

Connecting Symbolism to Meaning

Check Your Understanding

Write a thematic statement about the poem "The Poison Tree."

Writing to Sources: Explanatory Text

Explain how the authors of "The Cask of Amontillado" and "A Poison Tree" use literary elements, such as imagery and irony, to effectively convey the theme. How effective is each author's use of figurative language and symbolism? Provide examples that show each author's use of specific literary elements in developing the theme. Be sure to:

- Begin with a clear thesis that states your position.
- Include multiple direct quotations from the text to support your claims.
- Introduce and punctuate all quotations correctly.
- Include transitions between points and a statement that provides a conclusion.

Independent Reading Checkpoint

Review your independent reading. What have you learned and observed about authors' use of literary elements to develop theme and craft in a "good story"? Review any idea notes in your Reader/Writer Notebook. How can you use what you have learned to craft your own short story? Which narrative techniques will be most effective for you to use in developing your story and its theme?

Writing a Short Story

ASSIGNMENT

Your assignment is to write an original narrative from real or imagined experiences or events. Your story must include a variety of narrative techniques—such as foreshadowing, point of view, figurative language, imagery, symbolism, and/or irony—as well as effective details and a well-structured sequence of events.

Planning and Prewriting: Plan for your narrative.	■ Review the unit activities and your Reader/Writer Notebook for ideas. What activities have you completed that will help you as you create a short story with the required narrative techniques?
	■ What events or experiences do you want to write about? What prewriting strategies can you use to help you create ideas?
Drafting: Determine the structure and how to incorporate the elements of a short story.	■ What setting will you use? Point of view? Characters?
	■ Which additional narrative techniques will you use? Have you thought about including irony to create a sense of mystery, surprise, and tension?
	■ How does the story structure you created develop the events, characters, and plot of your story so that it engages your readers?
Evaluating and Revising: Create opportunities to review and revise to produce the best work.	■ When and how will you share and respond with others to get feedback on all elements of your narrative?
	■ What words and phrases, details, and sensory language have you used to create for the reader a vivid picture of the setting, events/experiences, and characters?
	■ Is your story developing as you want it to? Are you willing to change your story if you must? Once you get suggestions, are you creating a plan to include revision ideas in your draft?
	■ Does your conclusion reflect on experiences in the narrative and provide an effective resolution?
	■ Have you used the Scoring Guide to help you evaluate how well your draft includes the required elements of the assignment?
Checking and Editing for Publication: Confirm that the final draft is ready for publication.	■ How will you check for grammatical and technical accuracy? Cohesion?

Reflection

After completing this Embedded Assessment, think about how you set out and accomplished the tasks for this assignment. Write a reflection explaining how identifying and collecting information helped you create a short story. What did you do to review and revise your narrative, and how was the information you collected useful?

📶 Technology Tip

Storyboards are commonly used to sequence a story and to visualize events. If you want to use a storyboard, search for online storyboarding tools you might use to help you plan and write your story.

Writing a Short Story

Scoring Guide

Scoring Criteria	Exemplary	Proficient	Emerging	Incomplete
Ideas	The narrative • sustains focus on setting, character, events, and/or ideas to strengthen the unity of the story • presents thought-provoking details, conflict, and resolution to heighten reader interest • develops engaging and authentic characters that grow in complexity throughout the story.	The narrative • generally focuses on setting, character, events, and/or ideas to maintain the unity of the story • includes well-developed conflict and resolution with appropriate details to sustain reader interest • develops believable characters that grow in depth throughout the story.	The narrative • does not sustain a focus on setting, character, events, and/or ideas, limiting the unity of the story • contains unfocused conflict and resolution • contains characters that are not developed or are not believable.	The narrative • does not contain essential details to establish setting, character(s), events, and/or ideas • does not contain believable characters • does not provide a conflict or resolution.
Structure	The narrative • follows the structure of the genre • engages the reader and uses a variety of techniques to sequence events and create a coherent whole • provides an insightful conclusion with a clear and reasonable resolution.	The narrative • follows the structure of the genre • orients the reader and includes a sequence of events that create a coherent whole • provides a conclusion and clear resolution.	The narrative • may follow only parts of the structure of the genre • presents disconnected events with limited coherence • contains an underdeveloped conclusion with little or no resolution.	The narrative • does not follow the structure of the genre • includes few if any events and no coherence • does not contain a conclusion or does not provide a resolution.
Use of Language	The narrative • purposefully uses precise language, telling details, and sensory language to enhance mood or tone • effectively uses a range of narrative techniques and literary devices to enhance the plot • demonstrates technical command of spelling and standard English conventions.	The narrative • uses precise language and sensory details to define the mood or tone • uses a range of narrative techniques and literary devices to establish the plot • demonstrates general command of conventions and spelling; minor errors do not interfere with meaning.	The narrative • uses limited sensory details resulting in an unfocused or vague mood or tone • contains few or no narrative techniques and devices • demonstrates limited command of conventions and spelling; errors interfere with meaning.	The narrative • uses no sensory details to create mood or tone • contains few or no narrative techniques and devices • contains numerous errors in grammar and conventions that interfere with meaning.

Previewing Embedded Assessment 2: Thinking About Style

LEARNING STRATEGIES:
QHT, Graphic Organizer, Summarize, Marking the Text, Note-taking, Drafting

Learning Targets

- Identify the knowledge and skills needed to successfully complete Embedded Assessment 2 and reflect on prior learning that supports the knowledge and skills needed.
- Expand understanding of the elements that contribute to a writer's style.

Making Connections

In the first part of this unit, you read short stories and studied elements that help create a writer's style. By writing story starters and a short story, you also started developing your own writing style. In this last part of the unit, you will continue looking at style, but this time through the lens of film. By viewing a specific director's films, you will make connections between the choices that writers make with words and the choices that directors make with film techniques.

Essential Questions

Now that you have analyzed several short stories, how would you change your answer to the first Essential Question: What makes a good story?

The second Essential Question is: How does an artist define his or her style? Write a brief response in the following space.

My Notes

_____

_____

_____

_____

_____

_____

_____

_____

_____

_____

_____

_____

_____

_____

_____

Developing Vocabulary

Look at your Reader/Writer Notebook and review the Academic Vocabulary, Literary Terms, and language and writer's craft terms you have studied so far in this unit. Which terms can you now move to a new category on a QHT chart? Which could you now teach to others that you were unfamiliar with at the beginnig of the unit?

Unpacking Embedded Assessment 2

Read the assignment for Embedded Assessment 2: Writing a Style Analysis Essay:

> Think about the Tim Burton films that you have viewed and analyzed. Choose three or four stylistic devices (cinematic techniques) that are common to these films. Write an essay analyzing the cinematic style of director Tim Burton. Your essay should focus on the ways in which the director uses stylistic techniques across films to achieve a desired effect.

In your own words, summarize what you will need to know to complete this assessment successfully. With your class, create a graphic organizer to represent the skills and knowledge you will need to complete the tasks identified in the embedded assessment.

INDEPENDENT READING LINK

Read and Recommend

Think about stories that appear in print as well as in film. Make a plan for reading some of these stories and then viewing their film versions. Afterward, select one or more to recommend to a classmate, either orally or in writing. Be sure to include reasons for your recommendation. Reading articles about Tim Burton or viewing some of his films will be helpful to you when you do the style analysis in this unit.

Previewing Embedded Assessment 2: Thinking About Style

Style Analysis

In the first half of the unit, you learned about writing style. You learned that the choices a writer makes in subject matter, diction, syntax, imagery, point of view, and tone all help to characterize a writer's style. With a partner, review the definition of style and think about aspects of your style that you discovered as you wrote your own original short story.

1. Using these elements, how would you describe your writing style?

2. The following text analyzes elements of Edgar Allan Poe's writing style. Use the My Notes space to list each element of style listed previously, leaving space below each to add details from the essay. As you read the essay, mark key details that describe Poe's style. Be prepared to summarize and discuss the major points of the analysis of Poe's style.

Sample Style Analysis Essay

Although Poe wrote in many different genres, he is best remembered now as a writer of horror stories. Poe's style is characterized by an ability to create a mood of terror and ghastliness in his writing. His stories allow his reader to get lost in the mystery, the horror of the moment, and perhaps the fall into madness. Poe was more concerned about the effect he wanted to create in the reader than any kind of "moral lesson." "The Cask of Amontillado" exhibits Poe's concept that a story should be devoid of social, political, or moral teaching. In place of a moral, Poe creates a mood—terror, in this case—through his language. In this and many other of Poe's fictional and poetic pieces, the first-person narration compels the reader to identify with the narrator, in this case, Montresor, a revengeful murderer who, in his last act of revenge, insanely echoes his victim's screams for help.

The imagery of the story is mysterious and creates a perfect setting for a macabre act of revenge. The vaults or catacombs, populated with the bones of the dead, and whose damp walls are covered with the webbed whiteness of the nitre, create an ominous and forbidding setting characteristic of Poe's works. Poe's ornate prose also sets the tone by allowing the narrator to wield his ironic voice without much chance of the object of his revenge understanding. So when Montresor elegantly refers to the status of his victim, Fortunato, by saying, "You are rich, respected, admired, beloved; you are happy as once I was. You are a man to be missed. For me it is no matter," the irony of this carefully worded praise is lost on Fortunato and reminds the reader of the depth of Montresor's jealousy and hatred. Poe's ability to capture the imagination of his reader by creating a specific effect is his lasting legacy to the art of storytelling.

3. Based on the sample essay and your summary of the content, what are the stylistic characteristics of the work of Edgar Allan Poe?

4. Explain how the structure of Poe's language (syntax) contributes to his style.

Check Your Understanding

Write a brief summary of the literary and syntactical elements that contribute to a writer's style.

Working with Cinematic Techniques

Literary Terms

Cinematic techniques are the methods a director uses to communicate meaning and to evoke particular emotional responses from viewers.

WORD CONNECTIONS

Word Relationships

An analogy shows how pairs of words are related. The first pair of words is related to the second pair of words in the same ways. Some common analogy types include:

- part to whole— leaf : tree :: feather : bird
- item to purpose— ruler : measure :: pen : write
- synonyms— fragile : delicate :: gigantic : huge
- antonyms— fast : slow :: easy : difficult

Complete the following analogy.

film : visual images :: _____ : words on a page

My Notes

_____

_____

_____

_____

_____

_____

_____

Learning Targets

- Identify cinematic techniques and explain the effects of these techniques in visual text.
- Compare key stylistic elements in written and filmed texts and make connections between style in a writer's and a film director's texts.

Analyzing Film

Film can be analyzed by understanding both literary elements and **cinematic techniques** that create effects for the audience. To learn to "read" a film, you must understand how film and written texts are similar and different. Style in film has to do with how the visual images of the story are presented to create a certain effect. There are explicit connections between an author's choice of literary techniques and a director's choice of cinematic techniques.

1. In your Reader/Writer Notebook, draw a large Venn diagram with "Film" in one circle and "Text" in the other circle. At the top, label the middle overlapping section "Similarities." Above the "Text" circle write "Literary Techniques," and above the "Film" circle write "Cinematic Techniques."

2. With a partner, using the middle section, brainstorm elements shared by short stories, novels, and filmed stories.

3. Next, in the "Text" circle, write all the terms you know that relate to stylistic elements in written literary texts.

Cinematic Techniques

The following chart provides an overview of cinematic elements and specific techniques used in creating film texts. Use the chart to review these elements.

Shots and Framing	Camera Angles	Camera Movements	Lighting	Editing	Music/ Sound
Shot	Eye level	Pan	High key	Cut	Diegetic
Establishing shot	High angle	Tilt	Low key	Fade	Non-diegetic
Long shot	Low angle	Zoom	Bottom or side lighting	Dissolve/wipe	
Medium shot		Dolly/ tracking	Front or back lighting	Flashback	
Close-up		Boom/crane		Shot-reverse-shot	
Extreme close-up				Cross cutting	
Two shot				Eye-line match	

4. You will now view a television commercial or film clip. Choose one of the cinematic techniques listed on the previous page, and take notes on how the clip uses that technique to create an effect. After viewing the film clip, form an expert group with others who chose techniques from the same category (e.g., lighting), and together write a paragraph that explains the effects created in the clip by the techniques in your category. Each group member will write one sentence to develop the explanation. Continue around the table until your group has written a well-supported paragraph.

Your paragraph organization might follow this outline:

Topic sentence that introduces the category of techniques
 1. Detail
    a. Explanation of the importance of this detail
 2. Another Detail
    a. Explanation of the improtance of this detail
 3. Another detail
    a. Explanation of the importance of this detail
Concluding sentence

5. After writing, select a spokesperson for your group to read your paragraph to the class. As you listen to other groups present their explanation, take notes to help you understand how all cinematic techniques work together to create an effect.

Check Your Understanding

How are literary texts and film "texts" similar? How are they different? Write a brief response in the space below.

Writing to Sources: Explanatory Text

From your notes, choose what you consider the three most significant and/or effective cinematic techniques used in the commercial or film clip you watched. Write a paragraph to explain what makes these cinematic techniques effective in the film text. Be sure to:

- Include a well-stated topic sentence.
- Identify one or more cinematic techniques and explain the effects in the film.
- Cite the best details from the film text to prove your opinion.
- Provide a concluding statement that summarizes and supports your opinion.

My Notes

Film in Context: An Authorial Study

My Notes

_____

_____

_____

_____

_____

Literary Terms

A **biography** is a description or account of someone else's life or significant events from that person's life. In contrast, an **autobiography** is an account written by a person about his or her own life.

notoriously: famously
grisly: horrific
lore: tradition
classic: highest quality

_____

_____

_____

_____

revisioning: new version

_____

_____

_____

_____

Learning Targets

- Identify the subject and important details in a main-idea statement.
- Write main-idea statements.

Preview

In this activity, you will read a biographical essay on filmmaker Tim Burton and summarize the main idea of the essay.

Setting a Purpose for Reading

- As you read the essay, underline key facts and details that might contribute to the main idea.
- Circle unknown words and phrases. Try to determine the meaning of the words by using context clues, word parts, or a dictionary.
- Draw a star next to Burton's influences.

Biographical Essay

Tim Burton: Wickedly Funny, Grotesquely Humorous

"There's a naughtiness in Tim that's similar to Roald Dahl. A little bit of wickedness, a little bit of teasing, a subversiveness. Both of them never lost the gift of knowing what it's like to be a child—a very rare gift ..."—Felicity 'Liccy' Dahl[1]

1   Stories written for children haven't always been as tame as the stories created by Walt Disney. Grimm's fairy tales are **notoriously** violent and **grisly**, especially considering the sheer number of abandoned and mistreated children that populate the **lore** of fairy tales. Roald Dahl, who wrote the **classic** children's book, *James and the Giant Peach*, is as famous for his cruelly ironic adult short stories as he is for his popular and dark stories like *Charlie and the Chocolate Factory*, written for and about children. These are just two of the direct sources and inspirations for Tim Burton's films that have influenced his imagination and cinematic style.

2   Tim Burton's style is clearly influenced by his fascination with fairy tales and children's stories. Whether bringing to life his own literary creations such as *Frankenweenie* (2012) or *The Nightmare Before Christmas* (1993), or adapting popular works such as *Charlie and the Chocolate Factory* (2005) or *Alice in Wonderland* (2010), Burton offers a dark and delightful **revisioning** of childhood stories. Like fairy tales, Burton's stories encourage escapism into worlds of fantasy and the supernatural while often reminding his audience of traditional morals and lessons. Some of Burton's most important and recurring inspirations have come from children's books.

3   Burton grew up loving Dr. Seuss. He thought Dr. Seuss's books were a perfect blend of subversive storytelling with a playful, innocent use of rhythm and rhyme. It is easy to see the influence of Seuss's imagination in Burton's *The Nightmare Before Christmas*. Based upon Burton's original three-page poem and drawings as well as inspired by the well-known poem *The Night Before Christmas* (1823), the film is a gentle horror story.

[1] **Liccy Dahl** was the executive producer of *Charlie and the Chocolate Factory* (2005) and is the widow of author Roald Dahl. This quote is from Leah Gallo, *The Art of Tim Burton*, Los Angeles: Steeles Publishing, 2009.

4 Burton worked for many years at Walt Disney Studios, whose approach to adapting fairy tales tends to understate the more sinister elements. Burton, however, embraces the dark elements. His first project as an **apprentice** was a six-minute film called, *Vincent* (1982), a tribute to actor Vincent Price and author Edgar Allan Poe, two significant childhood influences. Burton says he related deeply to these two icons of horror fiction and film. The film features a seven-year-old boy, Vincent Malloy, who fantasizes about acting out Poe's gothic horror stories and dreams of being an **anguished** character like Price. In many ways this first short film anticipates many of the common themes and influences that Burton has continued to explore throughout his cinematic career.

5 In his 2005 adaptation of *Charlie and the Chocolate Factory*, Burton brings to life Roald Dahl's subversive vision of childhood innocence. All of the children in the story, save Charlie, are undeserving **wretches**. Burton delights in including Dahl's graphic rhyming songs celebrating the fates of the repulsive and ungrateful children of the story.

> *We very much regret that we*
> *Shall simply have to wait and see*
> *If we can get him back his height.*
> *But if we can't—it serves him right.*

6 Just as classic children's literature can be enjoyed by adults with new appreciation, so too can Tim Burton's films be enjoyed and appreciated after multiple revisits. By examining and understanding the influence of writers such as E.A. Poe and Roald Dahl, as well as Dr. Seuss and classic fairy tales, the sources of Burton's cinematic style become clear. Characterized by a childlike innocence and playfulness coupled with a dark and somewhat grotesque sensibility, Burton's films have already become classics.

Second Read

- Reread the biographical essay to answer these text-dependent questions.
- Write any additional questions you have about the text in your Reader/Writer Notebook.

1. **Key Ideas and Details:** How does the essay describe Burton's cinematic style? Explain how it first developed.

2. **Key Ideas and Details:** How does Burton's cinematic style compare and contrast with Walt Disney's style?

3. **Key Ideas and Details:** Where can you see Edgar Allan Poe's influence on Burton's work?

apprentice: a person learning a trade

anguished: showing excruciating distress

wretches: annoying people

My Notes

___

INDEPENDENT READING LINK

Read and Discuss

Discuss with classmates a story you have read that has a film version. Consider the cinematic techniques used in the film version and how they contribute to the filmmaker's style. Refer to what you learned about Tim Burton's style in the biographical essay to guide your discussion.

Film in Context: An Authorial Study

Literary Terms
A **main idea** is a statement (often one sentence) that summarizes the key details of a text.
A **theme** is the central message of a literary work.

My Notes

Working from the Text

Now that you have read a biographical essay on film director Tim Burton, you will spend the rest of this unit exploring his unique style. An understanding of his life and background will help you understand his directorial choices that define his style.

A statement of a **main idea** is not the same as a text's subject or the **theme** of a literary work. For instance, the biographical essay has a specific subject: Tim Burton's style as a filmmaker. The main-idea statement summarizes the important points of a text, usually informational in nature. Identifying the main idea of a text should begin with identifying the key points, or subjects, within the text. Now that you have read the essay, identify the main idea of the text by summarizing its key points in the following space.

Summarize the key points of this text into one main-idea sentence. You might use this sentence frame to guide your writing:

Because Tim Burton was influenced by _____,
_____ *(subject/key point)*
_____, and _____, his films are
(subject/key point) _____ *(subject/key point)*

characterized by _____ and _____.
(adjective phrase) _____ *(adjective phrase)*

Check Your Understanding

Choose one of the subjects that influenced director Tim Burton. Explain how this subject influenced him and how it impacted his style.

Writing to Sources: Explanatory Text

Once you have written and shared your main-idea statement, use your notes to write a paragraph that supports your topic sentence. Explain how specific details contribute to Tim Burton's cinematic style and what makes it effective. Be sure to:

- Revise your main-idea statement if needed.
- Choose details about Tim Burton and his style that support your topic sentence.
- Organize the sentences in your paragraph, and use correct grammar.
- Provide a conclusion to your paragraph that follows logically from the points presented.

Setting the Mood and Understanding Tone: Wonka Two Ways

Learning Targets
- Compare written and film texts and identify how mood and tone are created in each.
- Cite textual evidence from written and film texts to support an interpretation.

Preview
In this activity, you will read two novel excerpts and watch film clips. This is an opportunity to see style in action through a comparative study of written and film texts. Both authors and directors thoughtfully consider the **mood** and tone they create.

Setting a Purpose for Reading
- As you read the novel excerpt, highlight diction, imagery, and any adjectives that help you identify the predominant mood.
- Circle unknown words and phrases. Try to determine the meaning of the words by using context clues, word parts, or a dictionary.

ABOUT THE AUTHOR
Roald Dahl (1916–1990) was born in Wales to Norwegian parents. The stories he heard as a child greatly influenced his love of stories and books. Dahl wrote stories for adults and children. Many of his children's stories came about from the bedtime stories he made up for his daughters. *James and the Giant Peach* was his first book, followed by *Charlie and the Chocolate Factory*, both of which enjoyed huge success in the United Kingdom and the United States.

Novel Excerpt

from
Charlie and the
Chocolate Factory

by Roald Dahl

PASSAGE 1

1 The whole of this family—the six grownups (count them) and little Charlie Bucket—live together in a small wooden house on the edge of a great town.

2 The house wasn't nearly large enough for so many people, and life was extremely uncomfortable for them all. There were only two rooms in the place altogether, and there was only one bed. The bed was given to the four old grandparents because they were so old and tired. They were so tired, they never got out of it.

LEARNING STRATEGIES:
Rereading, Close Reading, Graphic Organizer, Note-taking, Word Map

Literary Terms
Mood is the atmosphere or predominant emotion in a literary work, the effect of the words on the audience.

My Notes

Setting the Mood and Understanding Tone: Wonka Two Ways

3   Grandpa Joe and Grandma Josephine on this side, Grandpa George and Grandma Georgina on this side.

4   Mr. and Mrs. Bucket and little Charlie Bucket slept in the other room, upon mattresses on the floor.

drafts: gusts of wind

5   In the summertime, this wasn't too bad, but in the winter, freezing cold **drafts** blew across the floor all night long, and it was awful.

6   There wasn't any question of them being able to buy a better house—or even one more bed to sleep in. They were far too poor for that.

My Notes

7   Mr. Bucket was the only person in the family with a job. He worked in a toothpaste factory, where he sat all day long at a bench and screwed the little caps onto the tops of the tubes of toothpaste after the tubes had been filled. But a toothpaste cap-screwer is never paid very much money, and poor Mr. Bucket, however hard he worked, and however fast he screwed on the caps, was never able to make enough to buy one-half of the things that so large a family needed. There wasn't even enough money to buy proper food for them all. The only meals they could afford were bread and margarine for breakfast, boiled potatoes and cabbage for lunch, and cabbage soup for supper. Sundays were a bit better. They all looked forward to Sundays because then, although they had exactly the same, everyone was allowed a second helping.

8   The Buckets, of course, didn't starve, but every one of them—the two old grandfathers, the two old grandmothers, Charlie's father, Charlie's mother, and especially little Charlie himself—went about from morning till night with a horrible empty feeling in their tummies.

9   Charlie felt it worst of all. And although his father and mother often went without their own share of lunch or supper so that they could give it to him, it still wasn't nearly enough for a growing boy. He desperately wanted something more filling and satisfying than cabbage and cabbage soup. The one thing he longed for more than anything else was ... CHOCOLATE.

Second Read

- Reread the story to answer these text-dependent questions.
- Write any additional questions you have about the text in your Reader/Writer Notebook.

1. **Craft and Structure:** What is the mood of this passage? Identify at least three details the author uses to set the mood.

2. **Key Ideas and Details:** How would you characterize the Bucket family? Why might the author have chosen to describe the family this way?

3. **Key Ideas and Details:** What is the author's attitude toward Charlie and his family? How can you tell?

Working from the Text

4. Complete the table with the examples of diction and imagery that you highlighted. List specific adjectives you noted that describe mood.

Diction, Imagery, Details/ Textual Evidence	Adjectives Describing Mood

Setting a Purpose for Reading

- As you read the second excerpt, highlight words that help you identify the author's tone and attitude toward the children he describes.

- Circle unknown words and phrases. Try to determine the meaning of the words by using context clues, word parts, or a dictionary.

My Notes

Novel Excerpt

Novel Excerpt

from

Charlie and the Chocolate Factory

by Roald Dahl

PASSAGE 2

1   The very next day, the first Golden Ticket was found. The finder was a boy called Augustus Gloop, and Mr. Bucket's evening newspaper carried a large picture of him on the front page. The picture showed a nine-year-old boy who was so enormously fat he looked as though he had been blown up with a powerful pump. Great flabby folds of fat bulged out from every part of his body, and his face was like a monstrous ball of dough with two small greedy **curranty** eyes peering out upon the world. The town in which Augustus Gloop lived, the newspaper said, had gone wild with excitement over their hero. Flags were flying from all the windows, children had been given a holiday from school, and a parade was being organized in honor of the famous youth.

2   "I just *knew* Augustus would find a Golden Ticket," his mother had told the newspapermen. "He eats so *many* candy bars a day that it was almost *impossible* for him *not* to find one. Eating is his hobby, you know. That's *all* he's interested in. But still, that's better than being a **hooligan** and shooting off **zip guns** and things like that in his spare time, isn't it? And what I always say is, he wouldn't go on eating like he does unless he *needed* **nourishment**, would he? It's all *vitamins*, anyway. What a *thrill* it will be for him to visit Mr. Wonka's marvelous factory! We're just as *proud* as can be!"

3   "What a **revolting** woman," said Grandma Josephine.

4   "And what a **repulsive** boy," said Grandma Georgina.

5   ... Suddenly, on the day before Charlie Bucket's birthday, the newspapers announced that the second Golden Ticket had been found. The lucky person was a small girl called Veruca Salt who lived with her rich parents in a great city far away. Once again, Mr. Bucket's evening newspaper carried a big picture of the finder. She was sitting between her beaming father and mother in the living room of their house, waving the Golden Ticket above her head, and grinning from ear to ear.

6   Veruca's father, Mr. Salt, had eagerly explained to the newspapermen exactly how the ticket was found. "You see, fellers," he had said, "as soon as my little girl told me that she simply *had* to have one of those Golden Tickets, I went out into the town and started buying up all the Wonka candy bars I could lay my hands on. *Thousands* of them, I must have bought. *Hundreds* of thousands! Then I had them loaded onto trucks and sent directly to my *own* factory. I'm in the peanut business, you see, and I've got about a hundred women working for me over at my **joint**, shelling peanuts for roasting and salting. That's what they do all day long, those women, they sit there **shelling** peanuts. So I says to them, 'Okay, girls,' I says, 'from now on, you can stop shelling peanuts and

curranty: having the appearance of currants, which are small dried fruits

hooligan: child who breaks the law
zip guns: homemade guns
nourishment: food

revolting: horrible

repulsive: gross

joint: place
shelling: removing shells

start shelling the wrappers off these crazy candy bars instead!' And they did. I had every worker in the place yanking the paper off those bars of chocolate full speed ahead from morning till night.

7 "But three days went by, and we had no luck. Oh, it was terrible! My little Veruca got more and more upset each day, and every time I went home she would scream at me, *"Where's my Golden Ticket! I want my Golden Ticket!"* And she would lie for hours on the floor, kicking and yelling in the most disturbing way. Well, sir, I just hated to see my little girl feeling unhappy like that, so I **vowed** I would keep up the search until I'd got her what she wanted. Then suddenly ... on the evening of the fourth day, one of my women workers yelled, 'I've got it! A Golden Ticket!' And I said, 'Give it to me, quick!' and she did, and I rushed it home and gave it to my darling Veruca, and now she's all smiles, and we have a happy home once again."

8 "That's even worse than the fat boy," said Grandma Josephine.

9 "She needs a real good spanking," said Grandma Georgina.

Second Read

- Reread the story to answer these text-dependent questions.
- Write any additional questions you have about the text in your Reader/Writer Notebook.

5. **Key Ideas and Details:** How does the author characterize Augustus and Veruca?

6. **Key Ideas and Details:** What inference can you make about the message the author is sending the audience about parenting?

7. **Key Ideas and Details:** Why does the author include Charlie's grandparents' reactions to the golden ticket finders' interviews?

GRAMMAR & USAGE
Nuance in Word Meanings

Writers pay attention to the small differences, or **nuances**, between words that have similar meanings. Careful word choice helps them add interest and clarity to their writing. Notice that in Passage 2 from *Charlie and the Chocolate Factory*, Grandma Josephine calls Augustus's mother "revolting" while Grandma Georgina calls Augustus "repulsive." Dahl uses these two words, which have nearly the same meaning, to show how strongly both women feel about Augustus's mother and to create humor. Using the words *awful* and *horrible* would not have had the same impact. Think about how word choice affects the way readers respond to the characters.

vowed: promised

My Notes

_____
_____
_____
_____
_____
_____
_____
_____
_____
_____
_____
_____
_____
_____

Setting the Mood and Understanding Tone: Wonka Two Ways

Working from the Text

8. Complete the table with the examples of words or phrases that you highlighted. List specific adjectives you noted that describe the tone of the passage.

Words/Phrases/Textual Evidence	Adjectives for Tone

The Language of Style Analysis

There are common literary elements to consider when examining an author's style in a text: tone and mood, diction, imagery, organization, syntax, and point of view. These elements can also be expressed through cinematic techniques. For the literary elements listed on the left side of the graphic organizer, fill in the right side of the chart with cinematic techniques a director can use for the same purpose.

The Language of Style Analysis

Literary Element	Cinematic Technique
Tone: The writer's or speaker's attitude toward a subject, character, or audience; it is conveyed through the author's choice of words and detail. **Mood:** The atmosphere or predominant emotion in a literary work	

Diction: Word choice intended to convey a certain effect	
Imagery: Words or phrases appealing to the senses, which a writer uses to represent persons, objects, actions, feelings, and ideas	
Organization: The narrative structure of a piece—how a text begins, ends, and is sequenced, paced, or arranged	
Syntax: The arrangement of words and the order of grammatical elements in a sentence	
Point of View: The perspective from which a narrative is told	

My Notes

Comparing Texts

Just as you did a close reading of passages from *Charlie and the Chocolate Factory*, now you will do a close "reading" of the beginning of Tim Burton's film version of that text. While viewing, pay special attention to the ways in which a director creates mood and tone through cinematic techniques such as lighting, sound, angles, framing and shots, editing, and camera movement.

As you watch this first segment, you might jigsaw this task with members of your viewing group so that each of you focuses on one technique and watches closely to understand Burton's manipulation of this technique.

Setting the Mood and Understanding Tone: Wonka Two Ways

Consider these questions as you watch the film:

- How does Burton create mood and tone? What does a director have at his disposal that an author does not?
- In terms of mood and tone, how is the film version similar to and different from the written version? What specific elements contribute to the mood/tone?

Film Notes on Burton's Style

Cinematic Technique	Textual Evidence	Mood/Tone
Framing or Camera Angles		
Setting		
Sound		
Other		

If you have jigsawed this activity with your group, take time to share around your group what each of you noticed. As you listen to the discoveries of group members, add details to your graphic organizer.

Language and Writer's Craft : Combining Sentences

Sentence combining is the process of joining two shorter sentences into one longer one. Writers combine sentences to vary sentence length, to create a slower pace through longer sentences, and to show relationships between events and ideas.

For example, look at the first sentence in paragraph 7 from Passage 2 of *Charlie and the Chocolate Factory*. Dahl's sentence is a compound sentence with two independent clauses. Had Roald Dahl written the following two simple sentences, the effect would have been choppy, hesitant writing: "Three days went by. We had no luck."

However, Dahl uses a comma and the coordinating conjunction *and* to join the two. He also starts the sentence with the coordinating conjunction *But*: "But three days went by, and we had no luck." The conjunction *But* shows contrast between what is expected (success in a short period of time) and what actually happens. The conjunction *and* allows the second clause to give additional information about the first.

You could also use a semicolon to imply a relationship between the two clauses without stating it directly: "Three days went by; we had no luck."

You could join two short sentences to make a complex sentence by making one part an independent clause and one a dependent clause: "Although three days went by, we had no luck." This would emphasize the fact that even though they continue working for several days, they do not have success.

PRACTICE Read the following sentences:

"Well, sir, I just hated to see my little girl feeling unhappy like that. I vowed I would keep up the search until I'd got her what she wanted."

Combine these sentences in two different ways. Then, reread Passage 2 from *Charlie and the Chocolate Factory*, and notice how Roald Dahl combines them. Identify the method he uses.

Check Your Understanding

Choose a literary technique Dahl uses to create mood and tone. How does this technique contribute to his style and create a specific effect?

Explanatory Writing Prompt

As you watched the film, you considered two questions. Select either Question 1 or Question 2. Think about your observation and analysis of mood and tone in the novel excerpt and the film. Explain your answer to the question you have chosen. Be sure to:

- Answer the question in the topic sentence.
- Cite textual evidence from both the written text and the film that relates to mood or tone.
- Include a clear explanation of how the textual details support your topic sentence.
- Provide a conclusion that supports your explanation.

My Notes

Revisiting Wonka: Thinking About Effect

LEARNING STRATEGIES:
Close Reading, Drafting,
Graphic Organizer,
Quickwrite, Role Playing

My Notes

Learning Targets

- Apply cinematic techniques to design a scene that creates an intended effect.
- Interpret the effect of a director's cinematic choices.

You have seen examples of how Burton translated Roald Dahl's writing style into his own unique cinematic style by making cinematic choices in what and how he filmed the story. In this activity, you will study two more scenes from *Charlie and the Chocolate Factory* and take notes.

Viewing the Film Clips

As you watch these scenes, identify as many film techniques as you can. Using the information from the cinematic technique chart, your group may want to divide up the cinematic techniques in order to take better notes.

1. **Quickwrite:** After viewing the film clips, draft brief responses:

   a. What effect does Burton want to create in the scene at home and in the scene in front of the factory?

   b. What choices does Burton make to create these effects?

2. Now you will consolidate your understanding of cinematic techniques by taking on the role of director. With your group, you will create a scene and then apply five cinematic techniques to that scene. Describe the scene you and your group plan to demonstrate using the cinematic techniques either assigned to you or chosen by you. You may want to create a graphic organizer in your Reader/Writer Notebook. In one column, identify the cinematic technique. In the second column, describe the intended effect of each technique.

   Present this scene to your class and explain your directorial choices by answering the following questions.

   a. In your scene, what effect did you want to have on your audience?

   b. What choices did you make in your direction to achieve your desired effect?

Check Your Understanding

Of the cinematic techniques you and your group chose, which was the most successful at producing your intended effect? Why?

Narrative Writing Prompt

Rewrite the scene your group created as a narrative. Refer to the comparison chart in Activity 2.13 and use narrative techniques that correspond to the cinematic techniques you incorporated in your group's scene. Think about the intended effect of your scene as you write your narrative. Be sure to:

- Introduce the characters and setting of the scene.
- Use descriptive words and details to set a tone and mood.
- Include imagery that allows the reader to visualize the scene.
- Include a logical sequence of actions that allows readers to move through the events of the scene.

INDEPENDENT READING LINK

Read and Research

Locate and read one or more articles about Tim Burton's filmmaking and how he uses cinematic techniques to create specific effects in his films. Apply what you have learned to revise and expand your answers to the Quickwrite Questions you answered in the activity.

More About Stylistic Effect

Learning Targets

- Create meaningful interpretive questions about stylistic elements.
- Make interpretive inferences about the effect of cinematic techniques

Analyzing Style in Film

You will first view a segment of *Charlie and the Chocolate Factory* for its visual effects without hearing the sound track. In this first viewing, pay close attention to the following shots and lighting:

- **long shots** to establish the setting
- **medium shots** to display the body language of the characters
- **close-up shots** to display facial expressions of the characters
- **shot-reverse-shot** to show a conversation between characters and to build tension
- **lighting** to establish mood

1. As you view the film clip without sound, take notes in the second column ("Observations") of the graphic organizer on the next page. Then, share your observations with your class. If another class member identifies a detail that you missed, add it to your notes.

2. Next, you will view the film for its visual effects combined with the sound track. As you view the film this time, pay close attention to any shots or lighting that you might have missed. Also, listen closely to the sound track and distinguish between the following:

- **diegetic sound**, which could logically be heard by the characters (including dialogue and background noises)
- **non-diegetic sound**, which only the audience can hear (includes the film's musical track)

Note also the use of this visual plot device:

- **flashbacks**—a shift in a narrative to an earlier event that interrupts the normal chronological development of the story

LEARNING STRATEGIES:
Close Reading, Graphic Organizer, Levels of Questions, Think-Pair-Share

My Notes

More About Stylistic Effect

Charlie and the Chocolate Factory	Observations: Note what you observe in this scene—camera movement, angles, shots, sound, lighting, setting, characters, etc.	Interpretation: What can you infer about the intended effect from your observations?
First viewing, without sound Scenes 14–16 40:24–49:40		
Second viewing, with sound		
Final viewing (optional)		

Levels of Questions

Questioning the text is an active reading strategy that keeps you alert and connected with the text as you read. Following is a review of the three Levels of Questions and examples of each level that you could ask about *Charlie and the Chocolate Factory*:

- **literal**—recall questions for which you can find answers in the text

  Example: *Who are the people living with Charlie Bucket?*

- **interpretive**—questions that require you to use text information to make inferences, draw conclusions, compare or contrast details, or consider the author's purpose

  Example: *Why does Burton use a close-up shot of the Golden Ticket?*

- **universal**—questions that are text-related but go beyond the text by making text-to-world or text-to-self connections

  Example: *Have you ever wished hard for something, and your wish came true?*

3. Using your observations from the graphic organizer, pose questions that relate to Burton's film style. (Write your questions in the My Notes space.)

   - First, generate three Level 2 questions that would help you understand why certain film techniques were used.

   - With a partner, share your questions during a pair-share, and answer the questions by making inferences based on your observations.

   - Take turns asking and answering your questions with your partner until you have each shared all three of your questions.

Remember: A well-supported response includes proving your answer with textual details.

4. After you have discussed your questions and answers, complete the third column of the graphic organizer, "Interpretation." Work in your discussion groups to share details and understandings of what you saw. If someone mentions a detail that you have not noted, add this information to your chart.

Check Your Understanding

How does Burton manipulate camera angles and lighting to create his intended effects?

Writing to Sources: Explanatory Text

Write an explanatory paragraph to explore in more detail why Tim Burton uses a flashback scene. What does the director accomplish by including such a scene at this point in the film? Be sure to:

- Include a well-stated topic sentence.
- Include a description of the sequence of events the flashback interrupts.
- Cite important details and evidence from the film to support your claims.
- Provide a conclusion that supports your claims.

My Notes

Interpreting Style: Tim Burton's *Edward Scissorhands*

My Notes

Learning Targets

- Identify the tone, mood, and imagery created by cinematic techniques in a film.
- Make inferences or predictions based on observations and context.

Segment One: Opening Credits

As you learned when watching *Charlie and the Chocolate Factory*, Burton creates a "fantastical world" by manipulating cinematic features. You will now begin a study of another film directed by Tim Burton, *Edward Scissorhands*. As the first segment begins, look at the opening credits. Viewers often overlook the opening credits and title sequence of a film. However, Burton presents a great deal of information in this part of the segment.

1. Study the opening sequence closely and, in the "Observations" column of the following graphic organizer, note what you see.

2. Apply your critical thinking skills to (a) make predictions, (b) identify the mood (effect on audience), and (c) identify the tone (attitude of director). Write your responses in the "Interpretations" column.

Segment of Film	Observations: What is happening in this scene?	Interpretations: What can you infer or predict based on your observations?
The Opening Credits	Images and Shapes	Predictions
		Mood
		Tone
	Music	

Segment Two: Frame Story—Grandmother and Granddaughter

3. The story of Edward Scissorhands is introduced in the "frame story" of the movie; an old woman prepares to narrate the story of Edward to her granddaughter. View this section closely, being especially observant of the camera movements—such as tilting, panning, dollying—and the kinds of shots, such as long shots, close-ups, and boom/crane shots. Watch the frame story closely, and note in the following "Observations" column what you see.

INDEPENDENT READING LINK

Read and Connect

Create a chart similar to the one shown in the activity to observe and analyze the opening credits from a film you watched independently, preferably a Tim Burton film. As you complete the chart, compare and contrast the opening credits with those in *Edward Scissorhands*. What are the similarities? What are the differences? How do the similarities and differences affect the mood and tone of the film?

4. After watching this frame story segment, apply your critical thinking skills to interpret (a) musical changes, (b) camera movements, and (c) frame story and to make predictions. Write your responses in the "Interpretations" column.

Segment of Film	Observations: What is happening in this scene?	Interpretations: What can you infer or predict based on your observations?
The Frame Story: **Grandmother with Granddaughter**		

Check Your Understanding

How do the opening credits exemplify Burton's style and establish the tone and mood of the film?

Writing to Sources: Explanatory Text

Write a brief explanatory essay about the possible mood of the film as suggested by the frame story sequence in *Edward Scissorhands*. Think about the mood of a bedtime story and compare it to your initial prediction of the mood of the film. Be sure to:

- Begin with a clear thesis that states your revised prediction of the mood of the film.
- Include specific examples and detailed evidence from the film to support your claims.
- Use a logical organizational structure that accurately reflects any scene events referred to in your explanation.
- Provide a concluding statement that supports your claim.

My Notes

Analyzing Burton's Style: Supporting with Textual Evidence

My Notes

Learning Targets

- Determine a director's purpose for his choice of cinematic techniques.
- Write an analytical statement that includes textual evidence for a claim.

First Viewing—Cinematic and Story Elements

You will now view the first chunk of *Edward Scissorhands*, Scenes 3–5. Give this segment a close viewing and focus on the camera angles, dialogue, and lighting to understand character development and plot. To study this segment, you will work in discussion groups. The first group will be your "home base" and the second group the "expert" group.

1. Study this segment closely for character, setting, and plot development, as well as cinematic techniques. Then, respond to the questions that follow.

Discussion Questions for the Home Base Group

2. In your home base group, conduct a discussion of the following five questions. Be sure to cite textual details to support your responses. As group members share responses, decide what is relevant and accurate support and record information in your Reader/Writer Notebook.

   a. How does Burton use color and costuming to create character?

   b. What do you know about Peg from this segment?

   c. How is Edward developed as a character? What conflict is being set up?

   d. How has the director established a connection between Edward and Kim?

   e. How is the neighborhood portrayed? How is the audience supposed to feel about it?

Second Viewing

You will now form expert groups to analyze cinematic techniques. You will become an expert on one of the five techniques listed as column heads in the following graphic organizer.

As you watch the key sequence in this segment, closely view the film and record your observations on the graphic organizer so you can be prepared for discussion. Pay attention to the music and the shots in the castle.

3. In the graphic organizer, note particularly interesting or effective examples of your assigned cinematic technique. You may need to put additional notes on a separate sheet of paper.

Framing/Angles	Lighting	Camera Movement	Music/Sound	Editing

Analyzing Burton's Style: Supporting with Textual Evidence

4. After you have completed your individual notes for this segment, share your thoughts with your group. As part of a collaborative discussion, all members should participate by presenting examples of their observations about cinematic techniques and the inferences they made. As a group, consider the accuracy and insights as everyone shares, and record notes when the group has agreed on what to record. Add any new details or ideas to your own list.

Writing an Analytical Statement with Textual Support

The first step in writing a style analysis paper is writing an analytical statement. Writing an analytical statement requires you to understand and identify style and effect, so review these terms with your group members. As you develop your analytical statement, keep the following in mind:

> **author's purpose:** the use of a device (literary, rhetorical, or cinematic) to create an intended effect or suggest an intended meaning
>
> **effect:** the result or influence of using a specific device

5. In the following space, describe the specific cinematic technique you studied, its effect, and an example from the film.

Cinematic technique:

Example(s) of this cinematic technique:

Effect(s) of this cinematic choice:

6. The following model is a helpful tool for creating analytical statements. Complete these sentences using your cinematic technique and example.

Tim Burton, in *Edward Scissorhands*, uses _____
                                                        (cinematic element)

to _____. For example,
    (achieve what purpose)

_____

(evidence from the text to support the topic sentence)

_____.

7. Using the sentence frame, each member of your group will write an analytical statement using different examples of the assigned cinematic technique. Remember to focus on the effect. After completing your statements, take turns reading each sentence. Respond to your peers by answering the following questions for each sentence. Groups should decide how they will incorporate peer responses into any revisions of the analytical statements.

- Does the statement identify the cinematic technique assigned to your group?
- Does the statement clearly present an accurate effect?
- Does the evidence accurately support the statement of effect?

8. Now, return to your home base group to share your expertise and analytical statements, with textual support, from your expert group. As each group member presents, respond thoughtfully to the multiple perspectives presented. Make notes to help you get a full picture of all the cinematic techniques presented in this segment.

Check Your Understanding

Write a new analytical statement featuring a different cinematic technique. Use textual evidence to support your statement.

Writing to Sources: Argument

Write an argumentative paragraph about a cinematic technique that you think Burton uses best to create a dramatic effect in these opening scenes. What is his purpose in using this technique? Explain the effectiveness of the technique in achieving the filmmaker's purpose. Be sure to:

- Identify the filmmaker and title of the film in an opening statement.
- Support your claim by including a specific cinematic technique, its effect, and other related evidence from the film.
- Incorporate appropriate terminology to discuss cinematic techniques.
- Provide a concluding statement that supports your argument.

My Notes

Analyzing Burton's Style: Explaining with Commentary

LEARNING STRATEGIES:
Close Reading, Discussion Groups, Graphic Organizer, Predicting

My Notes

Learning Targets

- Demonstrate understanding of the effect of specific cinematic techniques in film.
- Write an analytical statement, including reflective commentary explaining the supporting textual evidence

First Viewing

Watch the second chunk of *Edward Scissorhands*, Scenes 5–13. Focus on the camera angles, dialogue, and lighting to understand character development and plot. For a study of this segment, you will continue to work in groups.

1. Study this segment closely for character and plot development and cinematic techniques. Make notes as needed.

Discussion Questions for the Home Base Group

2. In your home base group, conduct a discussion of the following five questions. Be sure to come to the discussion prepared to cite textual details to support your response. As group members share their responses, record answers in your Reader/Writer Notebook.

   a. Why does the neighborhood welcome Edward into their lives so quickly?

   b. How does the neighborhood seem to change after Edward's arrival?

   c. Kim's reaction to Edward is played for humor, but in what way is hers the most natural or realistic response?

   d. What hints in this segment indicate that all will not work out well?

   e. What did you notice in the plot sequence that was a purposeful editing decision by Burton?

Second Viewing

After forming expert groups, choose a new cinematic technique to watch for.

3. Using a graphic organizer like the one in Activity 2.17, note particularly interesting or effective examples of your chosen or assigned cinematic element.

4. After you have completed your notes for this segment, share your discoveries with your group. Each person in the group should read one example that he or she has found. As you discuss, work with your peers to clarify examples and connect the techniques to their effects. Continue around your group until everyone has shared lists. Add any new details or ideas to your list.

Writing an Analytical Statement with Textual Support and Reflective Commentary

5. In this writing exercise, you will add reflective commentary to your analytical statement. The reflective commentary comes after the example. The job of the commentary is to show your understanding of the relationship between your example and your original claim. You can make a comment, explain the connection, illustrate the point you made, or perhaps prompt a realization in the mind of the reader. In other words, if your example is the "what," then the reflective commentary is the "so what."

Complete this statement for your assigned cinematic technique. Each member of your group will write an individual statement. Remember to use details from the film to describe the purpose and effect of the technique.

Tim Burton, in *Edward Scissorhands*, uses _____
  (cinematic element)

to _____. For example,
  (achieve what purpose)

_____

_____
  (evidence from the text to support the topic sentence)

_____

_____.
  (reflective commentary)

Analyzing Burton's Style: Explaining with Commentary

6. Share your sentences with the group. Respond to your peers by answering these questions for each statement:

   a. Does the statement identify the cinematic technique assigned to your group?

   b. Does the statement clearly present an accurate effect?

   c. Does the evidence accurately support the statement of effect?

   d. Does the statement include a reflective commentary that logically extends the explanation of the effect?

7. Now, return to your home base group to share your expertise and analytical statements, with textual support, from your expert group. As each group member presents, make notes so that you get a full picture of all of the cinematic techniques present in this segment.

Check Your Understanding

Think about the scenes from *Edward Scissorhands* you have watched. Which cinematic technique appears most frequently? Does it exemplify Tim Burton's style? Briefly explain.

Writing to Sources: Explanatory Text

Write an explanatory paragraph about how Burton uses a specific cinematic technique. In your reflective commentary, show the relationship between your claim and the evidence that supports it. Your reflection should logically extend your explanation of the technique and its effect. Be sure to:

- Begin with a clear thesis that identifies a cinematic technique Burton uses effectively and his purpose in doing so.
- Cite specific examples to describe the purpose and effect of the cinematic technique.
- Use a logical organizational structure that shows the relationship between your claim, the provided supporting evidence, and your conclusion.
- Use appropriate terminology knowledgeably to discuss Burton's cinematic style.

Analyzing Burton's Style: Bringing to Closure

Learning Targets

- Analyze cinematic techniques for character and plot development.
- Create a complete analytical statement with textual evidence, commentary, and closure that demonstrates an understanding of cinematic techniques in film.

LEARNING STRATEGIES:
Close Reading, Discussion Groups, Graphic Organizer, Drafting, Sharing and Responding, Oral Reading

First Viewing

Study the third chunk of *Edward Scissorhands*, Scenes 13–19. Give this segment a close reading and focus on the camera angles, dialogue, and lighting to understand character development and plot. You will continue to work in groups. In your home base group, review what you have learned about cinematic techniques from the first two viewings of *Edward Scissorhands*.

1. Study this segment closely for character and plot development and cinematic techniques. Make notes to help you remember specific techniques, examples, and effects.

Discussion Questions for the Home Base Group

2. After viewing this segment, with your home base group, conduct a discussion of the following five questions. Be sure to cite textual details to support your responses. As group members share responses, record answers in your Reader/Writer Notebook.

- How would you describe Edward's personality and attitude toward others?
- What is different about the neighborhood's treatment of Edward?
- What is the effect of the scene with Kim dancing in the ice crystals? How have her feelings about Edward changed? Why?
- How has Edward tried to fit in? Why has he failed?
- What does the "ethics lesson" reveal about Edward?

Second Viewing

3. In your expert groups, choose a different cinematic technique to watch for. Record your observations using a note-taking graphic organizer like the one in Activity 2.17. Listen closely to the music and watch the framing of each scene. Note particularly interesting or effective uses of your assigned cinematic technique.

4. After you have completed your notes for this segment, share your discoveries with your group. Continue around your group until everyone has shared lists. Add any new details or ideas to your list.

Analytical Statement with Textual Support, Reflective Commentary, and Closure

5. Now you will add a sentence of closure to your analytical statement. The job of the closure is to make clear the relationship between your example and your original claim. You can summarize, highlight key examples in your statement, or remind readers of your claim, but do not just repeat the claim. Use the following sentence frame to write an analytical statement that includes all of these parts:

- claim statement that includes cinematic element and explanation of purpose
- evidence from the text
- reflective commentary
- statement of closure that summarizes the key idea

Analyzing Burton's Style: Bringing to Closure

GRAMMAR &USAGE
Parallel Structure

Using **parallel structure**—expressing similar ideas in the same grammatical form—can help bring clarity and coherence to your writing.

In this sentence, the three verbs are listed in a sequence that shows the mounting frustration of the speaker: "The speaker *cajoled*, *remonstrated*, and *threatened*, but the audience remained unmoved."

Listen for parallel structure when you are watching films, and consider how you can add it to your writing for effect.

Tim Burton, in *Edward Scissorhands*, uses _____

(cinematic element)

to _____. For example,

(achieve what purpose)

_____

(provide evidence from the text to support the topic sentence)

_____.

_____

(reflective commentary)

_____

_____

(sentence of closure)

_____.

My Notes

_____

_____

_____

_____

_____

_____

_____

_____

_____

_____

_____

_____

_____

_____

_____

_____

_____

_____

_____

_____

Language and Writer's Craft: Transitions

Transitions help writers connect the ideas in a text. Transitional words, phrases, and clauses show the connections among ideas or events and help readers follow the writer's train of thought.

Transitional words such as *however* and *therefore* introduce ideas that contrast with (*however*) or follow from (*therefore*) previous ideas. The transitional phrase *for example* is used to introduce supporting ideas or evidence. The phrase *in contrast* introduces contrasting information:

> The Cowardly Lion lacks courage. *In contrast*, the Tin Man is extremely intelligent, lacking only a heart.

A transitional clause is often a dependent clause added to the beginning of a sentence:

> *While Dorothy's home in Kansas is dull and tedious*, her experiences in Oz are vibrant and full of adventure.

Look back at the sentence frame about *Edward Scissorhands*, and notice the phrase *For example*. This phrase introduces the evidence from the film. Other transitions that can be used to introduce evidence are *For instance*, *In particular*, and *In addition* (for an additional piece of evidence).

PRACTICE As you review your analytical writing, notice ideas that, in your own thoughts, link back to other ideas or pieces of evidence. Then, use transitions to show readers those links. Make sure to use a variety of transitional words, phrases, or clauses that show the logical progression of your ideas.

6. Using the sentence frame, each member of your group will write an analytical statement. Remember to focus on your chosen or assigned cinematic technique. Rotate around your group, reading each sentence. Respond to your peers by answering these questions for each analytical statement:

- Does the claim statement identify the assigned cinematic technique?
- Does the statement accurately present a specific effect?
- Does the evidence accurately support the statement of effect?
- Does the statement include a reflective commentary that logically extends the explanation of the effect?
- Does the last sentence provide appropriate closure without repeating the first sentence?

7. Now, return to your home base group to share your expertise and analytical statements, with textual support, from your expert group. As each group member presents, make notes so that you get a full picture of all of the cinematic techniques present in this segment.

Check Your Understanding

What cinematic technique is most apparent in Burton's *Edward Scissorhands*, and what effects does he create with his manipulation of this technique? Write an analytical statement to answer the question.

Argument Writing Prompt

Write a paragraph to support the analytical statement you wrote to check your understanding. Use the textual evidence and support from your notes. Be sure to:

- Show the relationship between the claim and the provided textual evidence.
- Explain the effect of each cinematic technique discussed.
- Use transitional devices to link the claim and the evidence.
- Provide a conclusion that supports your argument.

INDEPENDENT READING LINK

Read and Respond

Observe one or more cinematic techniques used in a film you have watched independently. Consider the purpose of the technique and its effectiveness in achieving that purpose. For example, a specific technique might be used to create a mood or convey the filmmaker's tone. Write a response using what you have learned about writing analytic statements.

Analyzing Burton's Style: Writing the Analytical Paragraph

LEARNING STRATEGIES:
Close Reading, Discussion Groups, Graphic Organizer, Note-taking, Sharing and Responding

My Notes

Learning Targets

- Understand the director's purpose for cinematic choices in order to interpret visual text.
- Write an extended paragraph of analysis.

First Viewing

You will now view the last chunk of *Edward Scissorhands*, Scenes 19–24. Focus on the camera angles, dialogue, and lighting to understand character development and plot. For a study of this segment, you will continue to work in groups.

1. In your home base group, review what you have learned about cinematic techniques from the first three viewings of *Edward Scissorhands*.

2. Read this segment closely for character and plot development and cinematic techniques. Make notes as needed to support your group discussions.

Discussion Questions for the Home Base Group

3. After viewing this segment, with your home base group conduct a discussion of the five questions that follow. Be sure to cite textual details to support your response. As group members share their responses, record answers in your Reader/Writer Notebook.

- Does Edward's action seem justified?
- How does Edward appear to feel about Jim's death?
- How does Kim appear to feel?
- Why do you think Edward cuts his clothes off?
- Most fairy tales have a lesson or a moral to teach. What does Kim want her granddaughter to learn from her story?

Second Viewing

4. In your expert groups, choose a different cinematic technique to watch for. By this time you should have taken expert notes on three other cinematic techniques used in the film. Listen closely to the music and watch the framing of each scene. Record your observations using a graphic organizer. Note the scenes in which you see particularly interesting or effective uses of your chosen cinematic element.

5. After you have completed your notes for this segment, share your discoveries with your group. Continue around your group until each member has shared one example. Add any new details or ideas to your list. Your detailed list wil help as you write an extended analytical statement about the purpose and effect of Burton's use of specific cinematic techniques.

The analytical statements that you have completed in previous activities are a mini-outline for a well-supported, well-organized paragraph. Notice how each piece of an analytical statement reflects the organizational parts of a paragraph. The paragraph should repeat the support and elaboration sections to explore more than one example or more than one piece of textual evidence. Link these examples, details, and commentaries with transitional devices.

Analytical Statement	Paragraph
Sentence that makes a claim about a cinematic technique	Topic sentence that introduces the main idea of the paragraph
Textual evidence	Support by example or textual evidence
Reflective commentary	Elaboration, discussion, or explanation of the significance of the support
Closure statement	Closure, clincher, or summarizing sentence that draws the paragraph to an end

6. Before you return to your home base group, as a group, participate in the writing of an extended paragraph that analyzes your groups's assigned cinematic technique. Because this is a group effort, it is especially important that all members share information, determine what evidence is best, and agree on appropriate commentary about the significant effects. This is an opportunity to exchange ideas and actively challenge each other's thinking.

7. Now, return to your home base group to share your expertise and analytical statements, with textual support and closure, from your expert group. As each group member presents, make notes so you get a full picture of all of the cinematic techniques present in this segment.

Check Your Understanding

Choose a cinematic technique. Compare and contrast two scenes where Burton uses this technique. Is one instance more successful than the other? Explain why or why not in the following space.

Drafting the Embedded Assessment

Write a well-developed paragraph analyzing Burton's use of one specific cinematic element in *Edward Scissorhands*. Consider the purpose he has in using that technique and the effect in has on the audience. Include all the features that you have practiced. Be sure to:

- Include at least two examples of the use and effect of the cinematic technique.
- Use reflective commentary to explain the significance of the support you use
- Use transitional devices to show the relationship between examples and commentaries.
- End with a conclusion that summarizes the thesis.

Independent Viewing

My Notes

Learning Targets

- Discover connections between cinematic techniques and their effects in multiple texts by the same director.
- Explain the effects of cinematic techniques on the audience.

You have viewed two Tim Burton movies and analyzed them for their overall effect on the audience. You will now view another Tim Burton film and work individually to identify film techniques and their effects, in order to:

- Ensure that you can recognize film techniques and their effects.
- Ensure that you understand how these techniques influence the audience.
- Prepare you for success by ensuring that you have knowledge of three films by Burton to complete Embedded Assessment 2.

Use the following double-entry journal or create your own for your individual notes, identifying film techniques and their effects in the next Tim Burton film. You will use these examples in your final writing assessment, so identify as many examples as you can. Use notebook paper if you need additional space.

Film Technique and Example (Framing/Angles, Lighting, Camera Movement, Music/Sound, and Editing)	Effect
1. In *Big Fish*, a dolly/tracking shot allows viewers to see the movement of the fish through its own eyes rather than those of an omniscient (all-seeing) observer.	1. Establishes a first-person point of view and helps the viewer to understand the perspective of the animal as a character rather than an object
2. In *Edward Scissorhands*, a tracking shot follows movement out the window with a boom/crane shot over the neighborhood to the mansion on the hill.	

Film Technique and Example (Framing/Angles, Lighting, Camera Movement, Music/Sound, and Editing)	Effect	My Notes

Check Your Understanding

Now that you've watched three films by Tim Burton, think about how his background and interests shape his style and his choice of cinematic techniques. Choose one thing that influenced Burton and provide an example from each film that clearly illustrates this influence.

Writing to Sources: Explanatory Text

Write a brief explanatory essay comparing and contrasting the style and themes of the Tim Burton films you have watched. Use your notes to help you. What similarities in style and/or theme do you notice? What differences in style and/or theme are there between the films? Be sure to:

- Include specific details and evidence from the films to support your claims.
- Use a coherent organizational structure and employ transitions effectively to highlight similarities and differences.
- Use an appropriate voice and a variety of phrases to add interest to your writing.
- Provide a concluding statement that supports your claim.

Planning a Draft

LEARNING STRATEGIES:
Graphic Organizer,
Prewriting

My Notes

Learning Targets
- Draft a thesis statement.
- Plan a well-organized style analysis essay by completing a content frame for comparison of text.

1. Consider all of the films you have viewed in class. Fill in the following content frame with details that help you understand how each element is used in each film. You will use this content frame organizer to synthesize similarities and differences among the films that you have studied. Refer to your previous notes to help you cite details.

Cinematic Technique	Charlie and the Chocolate Factory	Edward Scissorhands	Independent Film Title
Framing			
Lighting			
Camera movements			
Music/sound			
Editing			

2. How does Tim Burton use cinematic techniques to achieve a particular effect? Cite examples from at least two films.

3. Return to the comparison of the analytical statement and the paragraph. Just as the analytical statement is a "mini" paragraph in organization, so is the paragraph a "mini" essay in organizational pattern. Study the following chart to identify the differences and the similar components among the three types of organization.

My Notes

Analytical Statement	Analytical Paragraph	Analytical Essay
Sentence that makes a claim about a cinematic technique	Topic sentence that introduces the main idea of the paragraph	Thesis sentence that summarizes the main idea of the essay; the thesis sentence is usually in the essay's first paragraph.
Textual evidence	Support by example or textual evidence (often introduced by transitional devices)	Body paragraphs in which each idea is organized in the manner described in the "Paragraph" column. These paragraphs are linked with effective transitional devices.
Reflective commentary	Elaboration, discussion, or explanation of the significance of the support (often connected by transitional devices)	
Closure statement	Closure, clincher, or summarizing sentence that draws the paragraph to an end	Conclusion that summarizes the main idea and often answers these three questions: What did you say? (Literal) What does It mean? (Interpretive) Why does it matter? (Universal)

Check Your Understanding

Draft an analytical thesis statement that makes a claim about Tim Burton's style as represented by the effective use of specific cinematic techniques. From your completed content frame graphic organizer, select three or four of the cinematic techniques for which you have clear, relevant, and effective examples.

Thesis Statement:

Planning a Draft

My Notes

Use the following topic outline to guide you as you craft your plan for a multiple-paragraph analytical essay. Use the space in the outline for your notes.

Body Paragraph: Topic Outline

Focus on one cinematic technique for each paragraph, and outline its effect in multiple films. For the topic sentence, think about the transition you could use to focus the reader's attention. You do not need to write complete sentences for your planning; include idea statements only.

Topic sentence:

Evidence:

Commentary:

Evidence:

Commentary:

Evidence:

Commentary:

Statement of closure:

For each body paragraph, develop your ideas following this organizational pattern. You should plan to write as many paragraphs as you need to prove the claim in your thesis statement.

Independent Reading Checkpoint

You have viewed film versions of various stories and observed the effect of different cinematic techniques. What have you learned from your observations that will help you as you complete the Embedded Assessment? How can you use this information to strengthen your essay?

Writing a Style Analysis Essay

ASSIGNMENT

Think about the Tim Burton films that you have viewed and analyzed. Choose three or four stylistic devices (cinematic techniques) that are common to these films. Write an essay analyzing the cinematic style of director Tim Burton. Your essay should focus on the ways in which the director uses stylistic techniques across films to achieve a desired effect.

Planning and Prewriting: Take time to gather and organize your ideas.	▪ What films, graphic organizers, and notes will you need in order to write an analysis of Tim Burton's cinematic style? ▪ How can you use your Writing Group to help you craft an effective thesis statement and refine your thinking about the examples you will include for each stylistic element?
Drafting: Determine the structure of your essay.	▪ How will you be sure all the components of an expository essay—the thesis, introduction, body paragraphs, and conclusion—are coherently and clearly connected? ▪ What is the most effective textual evidence you can use to develop your topic and create a powerful commentary? ▪ How can you use your practice writing from *Edward Scissorhands* as a model for developing your body paragraphs?
Evaluating and Revising the Draft: Create opportunities to review and revise in order to make your work the best it can be.	▪ What questions and discussion starters can you use to guide sharing your draft with your Writing Group? ▪ How can you use the Scoring Guide criteria to guide responses and suggestions for revision?
Checking and Editing for Publication: Confirm that your final draft is ready for publication.	▪ How will you use available resources (e.g., spell-checker, digital dictionaries, Writer's Checklist) to edit for correctness of grammar and conventions and prepare your essay for publication? ▪ Your focus for editing should be on the skills that you have studied in this unit, including sentence variety, syntax, sentence combining, parallel structure, punctuation of quotations, colon, semicolon, and conjunctive adverb with comma.

Reflection

Consider how your understanding of organizing and structuring your writing has guided your use of detail and commentary in writing an essay of analysis.

- How has the close analysis of film techniques in this unit changed the way you view non-print texts outside of class?

- How could your understanding of how directors use cinematic techniques for effect help you analyze author's purpose in a literary text?

Writing a Style Analysis Essay

Scoring Guide

Scoring Criteria	Exemplary	Proficient	Emerging	Incomplete
Ideas	The essay • clearly identifies and analyzes Burton's style, uses evidence from multiple films, and provides insightful commentary • displays in-depth understanding of cinematic techniques and how they create specific effects.	The essay • clearly identifies and describes the director's style, using support from more than one film • displays a clear understanding of the effect of the director's cinematic choices.	The essay • shows limited understanding of the director's style; support is insufficient or inaccurate • confuses how the director achieves an intended effect and/or may include a plot summary rather than an analysis.	The essay • summarizes the plot with little attention to elements of style • does not show an understanding of the director's cinematic choices and their intended effect.
Structure	The essay • is logically organized • introduces the topic clearly and develops a strong thesis; body paragraphs develop the topic with examples and details leading to a perceptive conclusion • uses transitions effectively to clarify ideas and create cohesion.	The essay • is well-organized • introduces a clear thesis, uses detailed body paragraphs, and provides a conclusion that supports the explanation • uses transitions to create clarity and cohesion.	The essay • is not well-organzied • may have an unfocused thesis, undeveloped body paragraphs, and/or inadequate conclusion • uses few, if any, transitions to create clarity or cohesion.	The essay • is confusing and/or is missing key parts • omits the thesis or does not develop it • uses no transitions to create clarity or cohesion.
Use of Language	The essay • uses a formal style and demonstrates a precise and sophisticated use of terminology to knowledgeably discuss cinematic style • has few or no errors in standard English usage.	The essay • maintains a formal style and demonstrates correct use of film and literary vocabulary to discuss style • is generally error free.	The essay • uses informal or inappropriate diction and demonstrates limited use of film vocabulary to discuss style • contains errors that distract from meaning.	The essay • shows little use of the vocabulary of literary and style analysis • contains multiple errors in language and conventions that interfere with meaning.

Coming of Age in Changing Times

Visual Prompt: What do you think is the context for this photograph? What clues help you make inferences about the setting?

Unit Overview

Of Harper Lee's *To Kill a Mockingbird*, Oprah Winfrey said, "I think it is our national novel." The book's narrator, Scout Finch, reflects on her coming-of-age experiences as a young girl confronting prejudice in her own community and learning how to live in a less-than-perfect world. In this unit, you will examine how social, cultural, geographical, and historical context can affect both the writer's construction of a text and readers' responses to it. You will conduct and present research to understand both the setting of the novel *To Kill a Mockingbird* and the civil rights struggles that surrounded its controversial publication. While reading the novel, you will analyze literary elements in selected passages in order to discover how an author develops the overall themes of the work. Every part of *To Kill a Mockingbird* contributes to the whole—from a little girl rolling down the street inside a tire to a black man standing trial for his life.

Coming of Age in Changing Times

GOALS:
- To gather and integrate relevant information from multiple sources to answer research questions
- To present findings clearly, concisely, and logically, making strategic use of digital media
- To analyze how literary elements contribute to the development of a novel's themes
- To write a literary analysis, citing textual evidence to support ideas and inferences

ACADEMIC VOCABULARY
context
primary source
secondary source
plagiarism
parenthetical citations
valid
rhetoric
bibliography
annotated bibliography
evaluate
censor
censorship

Literary Terms
symbol
motif
plot
subplot
flat/static character
round/dynamic character

Contents

Activities

Texts not included in these materials

Language and Writer's Craft

- Citing Sources (3.4)
- Footnotes and Endnotes (3.7)
- Incorporating Quotations (3.16)
- Topic Sentences and Transitions (3.20)

MY INDEPENDENT READING LIST

_____
_____
_____
_____
_____
_____
_____
_____
_____
_____
_____
_____
_____
_____
_____
_____
_____
_____
_____
_____
_____
_____

Previewing the Unit

pich

LEARNING STRATEGIES:
Marking the Text, Skimming/
Scanning, Summarizing,
Graphic Organizer

My Notes

Learning Targets

- Explore preliminary thinking by writing responses to the Essential Questions.
- Identify the skills and knowledge required to complete Embedded Assessment 1 successfully.

Making Connections

In this unit, you will study the novel *To Kill a Mockingbird* in depth. As part of this study, you will examine the historical and cultural context of the novel and analyze literary elements that develop the themes of the novel. You will also apply your knowledge of film techniques as you examine clips from the film *To Kill a Mockingbird*, analyze the director's choices, and make comparisons between the film and literary elements in the novel.

Essential Questions

Based on your current knowledge, write your answers to these questions:

1. How can context contribute to the understanding of a novel?

2. How does a key scene from a novel contribute to the work as a whole?

Developing Vocabulary

Review the terms listed on the Contents page for Academic Vocabulary and Literary Terms. Use a QHT or other strategy to analyze and evaluate your knowledge of those words. Use your Reader/Writer Notebook to make notes about meanings you know already. Add to your notes as you study this unit and gain greater understanding of each of these words.

Unpacking Embedded Assessment 1

Read the assignment for Embedded Assessment 1: Historical Investigation and Presentation.

> Your assignment is to research the historical, cultural, social, and/or geographical context of the novel *To Kill a Mockingbird* and investigate how individuals, organizations, and events contributed to change in the United States during the Civil Rights Movement. You will work collaboratively to create an oral presentation of your findings with multimedia support and guiding questions for your audience.

In your own words, summarize what you will need to know to complete this assessment successfully. With your class, create a graphic organizer to represent the skills and knowledge you will need to complete the tasks identified in the Embedded Assessment.

**INDEPENDENT
READING LINK**

Read and Discuss
The focus of this unit is the novel *To Kill a Mockingbird*. For independent reading, choose informational texts about the United States between the 1930s and the 1960s. Once you have selected texts, discuss one or more of your selections with peers, explaining a few facts you learned about the time period. Record notes from your discussion in your Reader/Writer Notebook.

Picturing the Past

Learning Targets
- Identify the historical, cultural, social, and geographical contexts of the setting, writing, and publication of the novel *To Kill a Mockingbird*.
- Summarize observations about context from visual images.

Developing Context

In this unit, you will read the novel *To Kill a Mockingbird*. In order to understand and grasp the significance of the story, it is important to analyze the **context** of the novel. Understanding the context of a novel can deepen your understanding of the story and its themes. Read and answer the following questions in your Reader/Writer Notebook:

1. Think about the context of your classroom. Where is it located? Who is in your class?

2. What is the context of your town? Where is it? What are some unique or identifiable things about your town?

3. Your country?

With a partner, compare your answers and complete the context web graphic organizer. Add branches for historical, cultural, social, and geographical. Discuss what each term describes in relation to context. Then discuss how context can shape your understanding of a story.

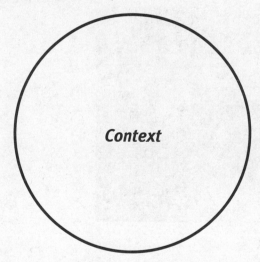

4. To further develop an understanding of the context for the novel *To Kill a Mockingbird*, view the following photographs. Keep in mind that the novel is set in the 1930s, but it was written years later and first published in 1960.

Note your observations and questions about the images in the table.

> **LEARNING STRATEGIES:**
> Graphic Organizer,
> Word Maps, Drafting,
> Discussion Groups

> **ACADEMIC VOCABULARY**
> When reading a text, you may find words that you do not know. You can use the **context**—the words around the text—to infer meaning. In the same way, the context of a novel or a situation refers to the circumstances or conditions in which the thing exists or takes place. Knowing context helps you understand the novel or situation better.

> **My Notes**

Picturing the Past

5. Examine the photographs and make observations about the context. Write any observations, reflections, and questions you have about each photograph in the table.

Topic: Segregation and Desegregation in America: 1930s through 1960s

Photo #	Observation (Note the details of the image in the photograph.)	Reflection (What is your response to the images in the photograph?)	Questions (What questions come to mind that might lead to further exploration or research?)
Unit Opener photo			

Picturing the Past

6. **Discussion Groups:** After viewing the photographs, meet with your group to discuss the questions you have created. You may want to use these questions to prompt your research for the Embedded Assessment. Share and respond to others' questions, and add new questions to your own list.

Check Your Understanding

How does analyzing the context of a novel help you gain a greater understanding of the story?

Explanatory Writing Prompt

As you review the photographs, choose one image that stood out to you. Summarize what you learned from this photograph about the context of the setting, writing, and publication of *To Kill a Mockingbird*. Be sure to:

- Begin with a topic sentence summarizing what you learned from the photograph.
- Include specific, relevant details about the image that stood out or informed your understanding.
- Provide commentary on what you saw and learned.

Learning Targets

- Analyze a secondary and a primary source to understand the cultural, social, and legal contexts of the novel *To Kill a Mockingbird*.
- Examine the historical impact of Jim Crow in the United States.

Preview

In this activity, you will read two informational passages that will provide additional context about the social, cultural, and legal setting of *To Kill a Mockingbird*.

Setting a Purpose for Reading

- Underline words or phrases that define the term *Jim Crow*.
- Circle unknown words and phrases. Try to determine the meaning of the words by using context clues, word parts, or a dictionary.

Informational Text

Jim Crow:
Shorthand for **Separation**

by Rick Edmonds

1 "Jim Crow" the term, like Jim Crow the practice, settled in over a long period of time. By the 1950s, Jim Crow was the **colloquialism** whites and blacks routinely used for the complex system of laws and customs separating the races in the South. Hardly anyone felt a particular need to define it or explore its origins.

2 The term appears to date back at least to the eighteenth century, though there is no evidence that it refers to an individual. Rather it was mildly **derogatory** slang for a black everyman (Crow, as in black like a crow). A popular American **minstrel** song of the 1820s made sport of a **stereotypic** Jim Crows. "Jump Jim Crow" was a sort of jig. By the mid-1800s, a segregated rail car might be called the "Jim Crow." As segregation laws were put into place—first in Tennessee, then throughout the South—after Reconstruction, such diverse things as separate public facilities and laws restricting voting rights became known collectively as Jim Crow.

3 A bit like "political correctness" in recent years, the term was particularly popular with opponents of the practice. It was a staple of NAACP conversations of the '30s and '40s. Ralph Bunche once said he would turn down an appointment as ambassador to Liberia because he "wouldn't take a Jim Crow job." A skit at Morehouse College during Martin Luther King's student days portrayed a dramatic "burial" of Jim Crow. And ... at the eventful Republican National Convention in 1964 in San Francisco, picketers outside the hall chanted, "Jim Crow (clap, clap) must go." ...

From material in *American Heritage Dictionary, Safire's Political Dictionary,* and *From Slavery to Freedom*.

LEARNING STRATEGIES:
Marking the Text, Metacognitive Markers, Previewing, Drafting, Discussion Groups

GRAMMAR&USAGE
Prepositional Phrases

A **preposition** shows the relationship or connection between its object and another word. A **prepositional phrase** consists of a preposition, its object, and any modifiers of the object. Common prepositions include *about, across, in, by, after, on, for, until, at,* and *up.* They are used to add detail to a sentence.

The second sentence in this essay begins with a prepositional phrase, "By the 1950s." In this sentence, *by* shows the relationship between "1950s" and the term "Jim Crow," giving an important detail about the passage of time. Look at the prepositions *for, of,* and *in* that appear in this same sentence. Consider how the reader's understanding would change if these prepositional phrases were not used.

colloquialism: informal speech
derogatory: disrespectful
minstrel: group of comedians that traditionally dress in black-face
stereotypic: based on an oversimplified idea about a group of people

My Notes

_____

_____

Setting the Context

WORD CONNECTIONS

Content Connections

The *NAACP* (The National Association for the Advancement of Colored People) is a civil rights organization. Its main focus is to ensure the political, educational, social, and economic equality of all persons, regardless of race.

Second Read

- Reread the text to answer these text-dependent questions.
- Write any additional questions you have about the text in your Reader/Writer Notebook.

1. **Key Ideas and Details:** Why were Jim Crow laws put in place, and why did opponents want to overturn the laws?

2. **Craft and Structure:** How did Jim Crow laws get their name?

Setting a Purpose for Reading

- As you read, use metacognitive markers to respond to the text as follows:

  Put a ? next to lines that are confusing or bring up questions.

  Put a * next to lines that are interesting or reinforce what you already know.

  Put a ! next to lines that are surprising or help you make predictions.

- Circle unknown words and phrases. Try to determine the meaning of the words by using context clues, word parts, or a dictionary.

My Notes

wards: large hospital rooms housing several patients

Informational Text

Jim Crow Laws

Martin Luther King, Jr. National Historic Site

Compiled by the National Park Service, US Department of the Interior

1 **Nurses** No person or corporation shall require any white female nurse to nurse in **wards** or rooms in hospitals, either public or private, in which negro men are placed. *Alabama*

2 **Buses** All passenger stations in this state operated by any motor transportation company shall have separate waiting rooms or space and separate ticket windows for the white and colored races. *Alabama*

3 Restaurants It shall be unlawful to conduct a restaurant or other place for the serving of food in the city, at which white and colored people are served in the same room, unless such white and colored persons are **effectually** separated by a solid **partition** extending from the floor upward to a distance of seven feet or higher, and unless a separate entrance from the street is provided for each compartment. *Alabama*

4 Pool and Billiard Rooms It shall be unlawful for a negro and white person to play together or in company with each other at any game of pool or billiards. *Alabama*

5 Intermarriage The marriage of a person of **Caucasian** blood with a **Negro**, Mongolian, Malay, or Hindu shall be **null** and void. *Arizona*

6 Intermarriage All marriages between a white person and a negro, or between a white person and a person of negro descent to the fourth generation inclusive, are hereby forever prohibited. *Florida*

7 Education The schools for white children and the schools for negro children shall be conducted separately. *Florida*

8 Mental Hospitals The Board of Control shall see that proper and distinct apartments are arranged for said patients, so that in no case shall Negroes and white persons be together. *Georgia*

9 Barbers No colored barber shall serve as a barber [to] white women or girls. *Georgia*

10 Burial The officer in charge shall not bury, or allow to be buried, any colored persons upon ground set apart or used for the burial of white persons. *Georgia*

11 Restaurants All persons licensed to conduct a restaurant shall serve either white people **exclusively** or colored people exclusively and shall not sell to the two races within the same room or serve the two races anywhere under the same license. *Georgia*

12 Amateur Baseball It shall be unlawful for any **amateur** white baseball team to play baseball on any **vacant** lot or baseball diamond within two blocks of a playground devoted to the Negro race, and it shall be unlawful for any amateur colored baseball team to play baseball in any vacant lot or baseball diamond within two blocks of any playground devoted to the white race. *Georgia*

13 Parks It shall be unlawful for colored people to frequent any park owned or maintained by the city for the benefit, use and enjoyment of white persons ... and unlawful for any white person to frequent any park owned or maintained by the city for the use and benefit of colored persons. *Georgia*

14 Reform Schools The children of white and colored races committed to the houses of reform shall be kept entirely separate from each other. *Kentucky*

15 Circus Tickets All circuses, shows, and tent exhibitions, to which the attendance of ... more than one race is invited or expected to attend shall provide for the convenience of its **patrons** not less than two ticket offices with individual ticket sellers, and not less than two entrances to the said performance, with individual ticket takers and receivers, and in the case of outside or tent performances, the said ticket offices shall not be less than twenty-five (25) feet apart. *Louisiana*

effectally: adequately
partition: barrier; wall person

Caucasian: a white
Negro: a black person
null: without value

My Notes

_____
_____
_____
_____
_____
_____
_____
_____

exclusively: available to only one person or group

amateur: not professional
vacant: not in use

_____
_____
_____
_____
_____
_____

patrons: customers

_____
_____
_____
_____
_____

Setting the Context

My Notes

_____

_____

_____

_____

urging: pushing forward

mulatto: derogatory term for a person with both black and white ancestors

_____

_____

_____

_____

_____

_____

prohibited: not allowed
pupils: students
periodicals: magazines or newspapers

WORD CONNECTIONS

Roots and Affixes

The word *transportation* means "a method of moving passengers or goods from one place to another." The Latin prefix trans- means "across" or "beyond." The Latin root *port* means "to carry" or "to bear."

The root *port* is found in many other English words, such as *portable, portfolio, import, export, report,* and *support.*

Some of the words in which the prefix trans- appears are *transfer, transform, translate,* and *transparent.*

16 The Blind The board of trustees shall ... maintain a separate building ... on separate ground for the admission, care, instruction, and support of all blind persons of the colored or black race. *Louisiana*

17 Railroads All railroad companies and corporations, and all persons running or operating cars or coaches by steam on any railroad line or track in the State of Maryland, for the transportation of passengers, are hereby required to provide separate cars or coaches for the travel and transportation of the white and colored passengers. *Maryland*

18 Promotion of Equality Any person ... who shall be guilty of printing, publishing or circulating printed, typewritten or written matter **urging** or presenting for public acceptance or general information, arguments or suggestions in favor of social equality or of intermarriage between whites and negroes, shall be guilty of a misdemeanor and subject to fine not exceeding five hundred (500.00) dollars or imprisonment not exceeding six (6) months or both. *Mississippi*

19 Intermarriage The marriage of a white person with a negro or **mulatto** or person who shall have one-eighth or more of negro blood, shall be unlawful and void. *Mississippi*

20 Hospital Entrances There shall be maintained by the governing authorities of every hospital maintained by the state for treatment of white and colored patients separate entrances for white and colored patients and visitors, and such entrances shall be used by the race only for which they are prepared. *Mississippi*

21 Prisons The warden shall see that the white convicts shall have separate apartments for both eating and sleeping from the negro convicts. *Mississippi*

22 Education Separate free schools shall be established for the education of children of African descent; and it shall be unlawful for any colored child to attend any white school, or any white child to attend a colored school. *Missouri*

23 Intermarriage All marriages between ... white persons and negroes or white persons and Mongolians ... are **prohibited** and declared absolutely void. ... No person having one-eighth part or more of negro blood shall be permitted to marry any white person, nor shall any white person be permitted to marry any negro or person having one-eighth part or more of negro blood. *Missouri*

24 Education Separate rooms [shall] be provided for the teaching of **pupils** of African descent, and [when] said rooms are so provided, such pupils may not be admitted to the school rooms occupied and used by pupils of Caucasian or other descent. *New Mexico*

25 Textbooks Books shall not be interchangeable between the white and colored schools, but shall continue to be used by the race first using them. *North Carolina*

26 Libraries The state librarian is directed to fit up and maintain a separate place for the use of the colored people who may come to the library for the purpose of reading books or **periodicals**. *North Carolina*

27 Transportation The ... Utilities Commission ... is empowered and directed to require the establishment of separate waiting rooms at all stations for the white and colored races. *North Carolina*

28 Teaching Any instructor who shall teach in any school, college or institution where members of the white and colored race are received and enrolled as pupils for instruction shall be deemed guilty of a misdemeanor, and upon conviction thereof, shall be fined in any sum not less than ten dollars ($10.00) nor more than fifty dollars ($50.00) for each offense. *Oklahoma*

29 Fishing, Boating, and Bathing The [Conservation] Commission shall have the right to make **segregation** of the white and colored races as to the exercise of rights of fishing, boating and bathing. *Oklahoma*

30 Telephone Booths The Corporation Commission is hereby vested with power and authority to require telephone companies ... to maintain separate booths for white and colored patrons when there is a demand for such separate booths. That the Corporation Commission shall determine the necessity for said separate booths only upon complaint of the people in the town and **vicinity** to be served after due hearing as now provided by law in other complaints filed with the Corporation Commission. *Oklahoma*

31 Lunch Counters No persons, firms, or corporations, who or which **furnish** meals to passengers at station restaurants or station eating houses, in times limited by common carriers of said passengers, shall furnish said meals to white and colored passengers in the same room, or at the same table, or at the same counter. *South Carolina*

32 Libraries Any white person of such county may use the county free library under the rules and regulations prescribed by the commissioners court and may be entitled to all the privileges thereof. Said court shall make proper provision for the negroes of said county to be served through a separate branch or branches of the county free library, which shall be administered by [a] custodian of the negro race under the supervision of the county librarian. *Texas*

33 Education [The County Board of Education] shall provide schools of two kinds; those for white children and those for colored children. *Texas*

34 Railroads The conductors or managers on all such railroads shall have power, and are hereby required, to assign to each white or colored passenger his or her **respective** car, coach or compartment. If the passenger fails to disclose his race, the conductor and managers, acting in good faith, shall be the sole judges of his race. *Virginia*

35 Theaters Every person ... operating ... any public hall, theatre, opera house, motion picture show or any place of public entertainment or public **assemblage** which is attended by both white and colored persons, shall separate the white race and the colored race and shall set apart and **designate** ... certain seats therein to be occupied by white persons and a portion thereof, or certain seats therein, to be occupied by colored persons. *Virginia*

36 Intermarriage All marriages of white persons with Negroes, Mulattos, Mongolians, or Malayans hereafter contracted in the State of Wyoming are and shall be illegal and void. *Wyoming*

My Notes

segregation: separation based on race

vicinity: area

furnish: provide

respective: particular
assemblage: meeting
designate: specify

WORD CONNECTIONS

Multiple Meaning Words

The word *provision* has multiple meanings. As a verb, it can mean "to supply," as in to provision a campsite. As a noun, it can mean "a stipulation or a qualification," such as a clause in a document or agreement. In this article, however, *provision* means "something provided or supplied." In Texas, the court will supply what is needed for black people to access their own library, administered by only black workers.

Setting the Context

My Notes

Second Read

- Reread the text to answer these text-dependent questions.
- Write any additional questions you have about the text in your Reader/Writer Notebook.

3. **Integration of Knowledge and Ideas:** Why is it significant that many Jim Crow laws reference gender as well as race?

4. **Integration of Knowledge and Ideas:** Why did Mississippi likely make it illegal to promote racial equality?

5. **Craft and Structure:** What does the word *promotion* mean within the context of this article?

6. **Integration of Knowledge and Ideas:** Each Jim Crow law in this article also lists the name of the state where the law was put into effect. What do the state names tell you about the scope of Jim Crow?

7. **Key Ideas and Details:** How did Jim Crow laws affect black citizens' basic human rights?

8. **Integration of Knowledge and Ideas:** How does it change your understanding of the laws to read them as a primary source rather than just a summary of the laws?

My Notes

_____

_____

_____

_____

_____

_____

Working from the Text

9. With your group, sort the Jim Crow laws into three or four categories. Work with your group to create a poster that represents the categories and includes brief summaries of several laws that fall into each category.

10. Which of the sources in this activity is a **primary source**?

ACADEMIC VOCABULARY
A **primary source** is an original document containing firsthand information about a subject. A **secondary source** is a discussion about or commentary on a primary source; the key feature of a secondary source is that it offers an interpretation of information gathered from primary sources.

11. What are the benefits of a primary source?

12. Which is a **secondary source**?

13. What are the benefits of a secondary source?

14. Which source was more helpful to you in answering the research questions about Jim Crow laws, and why?

Setting the Context

Check Your Understanding

Define *Jim Crow* and briefly explain its importance in American history.

Writing to Sources: Explanatory Text

Cite three examples of Jim Crow laws that would have presented financial hardships to a local government or institution. What can you infer from the fact that these laws went unchallenged for many years? Be sure to:

- Cite direct quotations and specific examples from the text.
- Use prepositional phrases correctly.
- Use an appropriate voice and a variety of sentence structures to add interest to your writing.

INDEPENDENT READING LINK

Read and Connect

As you read the informational texts you have chosen, look for descriptions of the Jim Crow laws. What recurring themes and issues do you notice? What are the similarities and differences? How will reading about these laws help you better understand the events in *To Kill a Mockingbird*?

Researching and Presenting Information

Learning Targets

- Conduct research by exploring a website and gathering information for a presentation on the rise and fall of Jim Crow laws.
- Organize information into a coherent piece and make an oral presentation.

> **LEARNING STRATEGIES:**
> KWHL, Note-taking, Graphic Organizer, Think-Pair-Share

Organizing Information

1. Based on the photographs and sources you examined in the previous activities, fill out the first two columns of the following KWHL chart. A KWHL chart is an effective tool to help focus and refine research activity by determining which topics need further research and where to find the needed information.

K: What do I know about Jim Crow?	W: What more do I want to know about Jim Crow?	H: How will I find information?	L: What have I learned about Jim Crow?

Researching and Presenting Information

2. Choose at least three questions that you will use to guide your investigation of the PBS website "The Rise and Fall of Jim Crow": www.pbs.org/wnet/jimcrow. As you explore the website, complete the graphic organizer as follows:

- In the "H" column, record the URLs of the page or pages where you find information to answer your questions so that you can easily find them again.
- In the "L" column, take notes to summarize the answers to your questions.
- Add new questions generated by your research to the "W" column.

3. Select one question that you were able to answer in your investigation of the website. Copy the following onto an index card:

- the research question and webpage URL
- a brief summary of the information you learned
- at least one new question generated by the answers

4. Present your findings to at least two of your peers. Display the appropriate webpage as a visual for your audience, but use your index cards so that you can maintain eye contact instead of reading information from the computer screen. Be prepared to answer any questions your audience may have about the information you are presenting.

5. As you listen to your peers' presentations, evaluate how well each presenter summarizes the information on the webpage in a clear and concise manner, faces the audience, and uses eye contact. Take notes in the graphic organizer on the next page. After each presentation, be sure to ask questions to clarify your understanding of the information presented.

Presenter Name and Research Question	Information Learned from the Investigation	My Thoughts and Questions	Evaluation of Presenting Skills

Language and Writer's Craft: Citing Sources

When you quote a source word for word or include information that is not common knowledge, you must cite the source to avoid **plagiarism**. Several different style guides provide information on how to cite sources, such as the *Chicago Manual of Style*, the *Publication Manual of the APA* (American Psychological Association), and the *MLA Handbook for Writers of Research Papers*. This book uses MLA style; you should be consistent and use only one style in a document.

A **parenthetical citation** gives basic information about the source of a quote immediately after the quote, in the same sentence. The information in the parenthetical citation will correspond to an entry on your works cited page, which will include more complete information about the source, such as publisher and date.

To use a parenthetical citation, write the author's last name (and a page number if available) in parentheses at the end of the sentence. If no author is given, use the title or (for a very long title) the first words of the title. If the author's name is used to introduce the quote, give only the page number in parentheses. Place your citation outside the quotation marks, but inside the closing punctuation of the sentence.

Examples:

"... became known collectively as Jim Crow" (Edmonds 7).

As Rick Edmonds notes, "such diverse things as separate public facilities and laws restricting voting rights became known collectively as Jim Crow" (7).

"... was actually supported by *Plessy v. Ferguson*" ("The Rise and Fall of Jim Crow").

PRACTICE Choose a nonfiction book or article on a topic of your choice, and quote a sentence from it using the correct MLA-style parenthetical citation.

ACADEMIC VOCABULARY
Plagiarism is using another person's ideas without giving credit. Researchers must always give credit by citing sources. **Parenthetical citations** are used for citing sources directly in an essay. In contrast, some writers place citations in footnotes or endnotes.

My Notes

_____

Check Your Understanding

Choose one question you asked in your KWHL Chart at the beginning of this activity. Describe how how you were able to answer this question through research.

Expository Writing Prompt

Explain how Jim Crow laws and practices deprived American citizens of their civil rights. Use information from the website you researched as well as from the two informational texts in Activity 3.3. Avoid plagiarism by using precise citations. Be sure to:

- Define the term *Jim Crow* in your topic sentence.
- Include well-chosen textual evidence with parenthetical citations from at least two sources.
- Provide commentary on the specific civil rights violations: educational rights, social freedoms, and voting rights.

A Time for Change

LEARNING STRATEGIES:
SOAPSTone, Marking the Text,
Drafting, Discussion Groups

Learning Targets
- Analyze a historical document for its purpose, audience, claims, and evidence.
- Identify how a historical document provides context.

Preview
In this activity, you will read a letter from Martin Luther King, Jr. and analyze the rhetorical devices and appeals he uses to convey his message.

Setting a Purpose for Reading
- Underline strong examples of diction and imagery.
- Circle unknown words and phrases. Try to determine the meaning of the words by using context clues, word parts, or a dictionary.
- Draw a star next to any instances of ethos, logos, or pathos.

ABOUT THE AUTHOR
Martin Luther King, Jr. (January 15, 1929–April 4, 1968) was an American clergyman, activist, and leader in the Civil Rights Movement. In 1964, King became the youngest person to receive the Nobel Peace Prize for his work to end racial segregation and racial discrimination through civil disobedience and other nonviolent means.

King's letter is a response to a statement made by eight white Alabama clergymen on April 12, 1963, titled "A Call for Unity." The clergymen agreed that social injustices existed but argued that the battle against racial segregation should be fought solely in the courts, not in the streets.

My Notes

Letter

from
"Letter from Birmingham Jail"
by **Martin Luther King, Jr.**

16 April 1963

My Dear Fellow **Clergymen**:

1   While confined here in the Birmingham city jail, I came across your recent statement calling my present activities "unwise and untimely." Seldom do I pause to answer criticism of my work and ideas. If I sought to answer all the criticisms that cross my desk, my secretaries would have little time for anything other than such correspondence in the course of the day, and I would have no time for constructive work. But since I feel that you are men of genuine good will and that your criticisms are sincerely set forth, I want to try to answer your statement in what I hope will be patient and reasonable terms.

clergymen: ministers

2 I think I should indicate why I am here in Birmingham, since you have been influenced by the view which argues against "outsiders coming in." I have the honor of serving as president of the Southern Christian Leadership Conference, an organization operating in every southern state, with headquarters in Atlanta, Georgia. We have some eighty five affiliated organizations across the South, and one of them is the Alabama Christian Movement for Human Rights. Frequently we share staff, educational and financial resources with our **affiliates**. Several months ago the affiliate here in Birmingham asked us to be on call to engage in a nonviolent direct action program if such were deemed necessary. We readily consented, and when the hour came we lived up to our promise. So I, along with several members of my staff, am here because I was invited here. I am here because I have organizational ties here.

3 But more basically, I am in Birmingham because injustice is here. Just as the prophets of the eighth century B.C. left their villages and carried their "thus saith the Lord" far beyond the boundaries of their home towns, and just as the Apostle Paul left his village of Tarsus and carried the gospel of Jesus Christ to the far corners of the Greco Roman world, so am I compelled to carry the gospel of freedom beyond my own home town. Like Paul, I must constantly respond to the Macedonian call for aid.

4 Moreover, I am **cognizant** of the **interrelatedness** of all communities and states. I cannot sit idly by in Atlanta and not be concerned about what happens in Birmingham. Injustice anywhere is a threat to justice everywhere. We are caught in an inescapable network of **mutuality**, tied in a single **garment** of destiny. Whatever affects one directly, affects all indirectly. Never again can we afford to live with the narrow, **provincial** "outside **agitator**" idea. Anyone who lives inside the United States can never be considered an outsider anywhere within its bounds.

5 You **deplore** the demonstrations taking place in Birmingham. But your statement, I am sorry to say, fails to express a similar concern for the conditions that brought about the demonstrations. I am sure that none of you would want to rest content with the **superficial** kind of social analysis that deals merely with effects and does not grapple with underlying causes. It is unfortunate that demonstrations are taking place in Birmingham, but it is even more unfortunate that the city's white power structure left the Negro community with no alternative . . .

6 We know through painful experience that freedom is never voluntarily given by the **oppressor**; it must be demanded by the oppressed. Frankly, I have yet to engage in a direct action campaign that was "well timed" in the view of those who have not suffered unduly from the disease of segregation. For years now I have heard the word "Wait!" It rings in the ear of every Negro with piercing familiarity. This "Wait" has almost always meant "Never." We must come to see, with one of our distinguished jurists, that "justice too long delayed is justice denied."

7 We have waited for more than 340 years for our constitutional and God given rights. The nations of Asia and Africa are moving with jetlike speed toward gaining political independence, but we still creep at horse and buggy pace toward gaining a cup of coffee at a lunch counter. Perhaps it is easy for those who have never felt the stinging darts of segregation to say, "Wait." But when you have seen vicious mobs lynch your mothers and fathers at will and drown your sisters and brothers at whim; when you have seen hate filled policemen curse, kick and even kill your black brothers and sisters; when you see the vast majority of your twenty million Negro brothers smothering in an airtight cage of poverty in the midst of an **affluent** society; when you suddenly find your tongue twisted and your speech stammering as you seek to explain to your six year old daughter why she can't go to the public amusement park that has just been advertised on television, and see tears welling up in her eyes when she is told that Funtown is closed to colored children, and see **ominous** clouds of **inferiority** beginning to form in her little mental

affiliates: people linked to an organization

My Notes

cognizant: aware
interrelatedness: connectedness

mutuality: dependency
garment: cloth
provincial: local
agitator: person who stirs up trouble
deplore: hate

superficial: on the surface

WORD CONNECTIONS

Roots and Affixes

The word *lynch* means "to put to death (usually by hanging) a suspected criminal without a trial." The word originates from Charles Lynch, a planter in the 1700s. He and his neighbors took the law into their own hands and punished British sympathizers by plundering their property, often without proof or trial.

oppressor: person or organization that holds others down
affluent: rich
ominous: threatening
inferiority: state of being lower status than others

A Time for Change

My Notes

harried: harassed

legitimate: lawful
diligently: carefully

sublime: outstanding
provocation: attempts to irritate or anger
noble: distinguished

profundity: depth

prejudice: unfavorable opinion about someone

scintillating: brilliant

sky, and see her beginning to distort her personality by developing an unconscious bitterness toward white people; when you have to concoct an answer for a five year old son who is asking: "Daddy, why do white people treat colored people so mean?"; when you take a cross country drive and find it necessary to sleep night after night in the uncomfortable corners of your automobile because no motel will accept you; when you are humiliated day in and day out by nagging signs reading "white" and "colored"; when your first name becomes "nigger," your middle name becomes "boy" (however old you are) and your last name becomes "John," and your wife and mother are never given the respected title "Mrs."; when you are **harried** by day and haunted by night by the fact that you are a Negro, living constantly at tiptoe stance, never quite knowing what to expect next, and are plagued with inner fears and outer resentments; when you are forever fighting a degenerating sense of "nobodiness"—then you will understand why we find it difficult to wait. There comes a time when the cup of endurance runs over, and men are no longer willing to be plunged into the abyss of despair. I hope, sirs, you can understand our **legitimate** and unavoidable impatience. You express a great deal of anxiety over our willingness to break laws. This is certainly a legitimate concern. Since we so **diligently** urge people to obey the Supreme Court's decision of 1954 outlawing segregation in the public schools, at first glance it may seem rather paradoxical for us consciously to break laws. One may well ask: "How can you advocate breaking some laws and obeying others?" The answer lies in the fact that there are two types of laws: just and unjust. I would be the first to advocate obeying just laws. One has not only a legal but a moral responsibility to obey just laws. Conversely, one has a moral responsibility to disobey unjust laws. I would agree with St. Augustine that "an unjust law is no law at all."

8 ... I wish you had commended the Negro sit inners and demonstrators of Birmingham for their **sublime** courage, their willingness to suffer and their amazing discipline in the midst of great **provocation**. One day the South will recognize its real heroes. They will be the James Merediths, with the **noble** sense of purpose that enables them to face jeering and hostile mobs, and with the agonizing loneliness that characterizes the life of the pioneer. They will be old, oppressed, battered Negro women, symbolized in a seventy two year old woman in Montgomery, Alabama, who rose up with a sense of dignity and with her people decided not to ride segregated buses, and who responded with ungrammatical **profundity** to one who inquired about her weariness: "My feets is tired, but my soul is at rest." They will be the young high school and college students, the young ministers of the gospel and a host of their elders, courageously and nonviolently sitting in at lunch counters and willingly going to jail for conscience' sake. One day the South will know that when these disinherited children of God sat down at lunch counters, they were in reality standing up for what is best in the American dream and for the most sacred values in our Judaeo Christian heritage, thereby bringing our nation back to those great wells of democracy which were dug deep by the founding fathers in their formulation of the Constitution and the Declaration of Independence.

9 Never before have I written so long a letter. I'm afraid it is much too long to take your precious time. I can assure you that it would have been much shorter if I had been writing from a comfortable desk, but what else can one do when he is alone in a narrow jail cell, other than write long letters, think long thoughts and pray long prayers?

10 ... Let us all hope that the dark clouds of racial **prejudice** will soon pass away and the deep fog of misunderstanding will be lifted from our fear drenched communities, and in some not too distant tomorrow the radiant stars of love and brotherhood will shine over our great nation with all their **scintillating** beauty.

Yours for the cause of Peace and Brotherhood,

Martin Luther King, Jr.

Second Read

- Reread the letter to answer these text-dependent questions.
- Write any additional questions you have about the text in your Reader/Writer Notebook.

1. **Key Ideas and Details:** What is the central purpose of Martin Luther King, Jr.'s letter?

2. **Craft and Structure:** How do the allusions that King uses in his letter help the audience relate to him and what he is saying?

3. **Integration of Knowledge and Ideas:** What evidence does King give as to why he deserves to be in Birmingham?

4. **Key Ideas and Details:** To King, what is the difference between just and unjust laws?

5. **Integration of Knowledge and Ideas:** How does this letter help summarize the atmosphere in Birmingham in the early 1960s?

6. **Craft and Structure:** What metaphor does King use to close the letter, and why is it appropriate?

A Time for Change

Working from the Text

7. Complete a SOAPSTone analysis using the graphic organizer.

SOAPSTone	Analysis	Textual Evidence
Speaker:		
Occasion:		
Audience:		
Purpose:		
Subject:		
Tone:		

8. Then, go back to the text and highlight words, phrases, clauses, or sentences that stand out as being **valid**, important, profound, and/or moving. Look for the following:

- examples of **rhetoric** and powerful diction, particularly words with strong connotations
- imagery, sensory detail, and figurative language
- rhetorical appeals to emotion, ethics, or logic

9. Revisit the photographs from Activity 3.2. Use your analysis of the photos to decide how quotations from Martin Luther King, Jr.'s letter could serve as captions for those photographs.

   What other words would you need to add to the caption in order to link the quotation to the image?

ACADEMIC VOCABULARY
"Letter from Birmingham Jail" is a blend of exposition, narrative, and argument. An analysis of King's writing must determine whether he makes valid points. In this sense, **valid** refers to reasoning, examples, and facts that support a main point.
Using rhetorical appeals is part of the art of **rhetoric**, or using words to persuade in writing or speaking.

10. **Group Discussion:** With the members of your group, discuss responses to the following questions:

- How does King use rhetoric to achieve his purpose? Give specific examples of his rhetorical appeals to logic, emotion, and ethos.
- How does he appeal to a specific audience with his language and details?
- How can you use rhetoric and an awareness of your audience to enhance your oral presentation?

Check Your Understanding

Explain King's purpose in writing this letter. What does he hope to achieve?

Writing to Sources: Argument

Martin Luther King, Jr. uses several rhetorical devices in "Letter from Birmingham Jail." Choose the rhetorical device that you think is most effective. State King's purpose for using this device and explain the effectiveness of the rhetorical device In achieving this purpose. Be sure to:

- Write a precise claim and support it with valid reasoning and relevant evidence from the text.
- Acknowledge counterclaims and refute evidence for those claims.
- Maintain a formal tone, vary sentence types, and use effective transitions.

My Notes

Voices of Change

LEARNING STRATEGIES:
Skimming/Scanning, Marking
the Text, Drafting

My Notes

Learning Targets

- Analyze a timeline to understand how social change occurred during the Civil Rights Movement.
- Make inferences and connections using multiple sources of information.

Preview

In this activity, you will read a timeline of significant events that eventually led to the Civil Rights Act of 1968.

Setting a Purpose for Reading

- Highlight the names of significant individuals, organizations, groups, events, places, and laws.
- Circle unknown words and phrases. Try to determine the meaning of the words by using context clues, word parts, or a dictionary.

Timeline

Civil Rights Timeline

1863 President Lincoln issues the Emancipation Proclamation.

1868 The 14th Amendment, which requires equal protection under the law to all persons, is ratified.

1870 The 15th Amendment, which bans racial discrimination in voting, is ratified.

1948 President Truman issues Executive Order 9981 outlawing segregation in the U.S. military.

1954 The Supreme Court declares school segregation unconstitutional in *Brown v. Board of Education of Topeka, Kansas*.

1955 Rosa Parks refuses to give up her seat on a Montgomery bus. Bus boycott begins and lasts for more than a year. Buses desegregated in 1956.

1957 The National Guard is called in to block "The Little Rock Nine" from integrating Little Rock High School. President Eisenhower sends in federal troops to allow the black students to enter the school.

1960 Four black college students begin sit-ins at the lunch counter of a Greensboro, North Carolina, restaurant where black patrons are not served.

To Kill a Mockingbird **is published on July 11**.

1961 CORE (Congress of Racial Equality) and SNCC (Student Nonviolent Coordinating Committee) sponsor "Freedom Rides," which bus student volunteers into Southern states to test new laws prohibiting segregation.

To Kill a Mockingbird **wins the Pulitzer Prize for literature**.

1962 James Meredith becomes the first black student to enroll at the University of Mississippi. The Supreme Court rules that segregation is unconstitutional in all transportation facilities.

1963 Gregory Peck wins an Academy Award for best actor in the film *To Kill a Mockingbird*.

1964 Congress passes the Civil Rights Act, declaring discrimination based on race illegal.

1965 A march from Selma to Montgomery, Alabama, leads to the signing of a new Voting Rights Act.

1967 Thurgood Marshall becomes the first black Supreme Court justice. In *Loving v. Virginia*, the Supreme Court rules that prohibiting interracial marriage is unconstitutional.

1968 President Lyndon B. Johnson signs the Civil Rights Act of 1968, which prohibits discrimination in the sale, rental, and financing of housing.

Second Read

- Reread the timeline to answer these text-dependent questions.
- Write any additional questions you have about the text in your Reader/Writer Notebook.

1. **Key Ideas and Details:** What can you infer from this timeline about the context for the publication of *To Kill a Mockingbird*?

2. **Key Ideas and Details:** Based on this timeline, what is suggested about how *To Kill a Mockingbird* was received by the public?

My Notes

Voices of Change

Working from the Text

Consider the following quotations by American presidents.

> "Every segment of our population, and every individual, has a right to expect from his government a fair deal." —*Harry S. Truman*, 1945

> "The final battle against intolerance is to be fought—not in the chambers of any legislature—but in the hearts of men." —*Dwight D. Eisenhower*, 1956

> "There are no 'white' or 'colored' signs on the foxholes or graveyards of battle." —*John Fitzgerald Kennedy*, 1963

> "The vote is the most powerful instrument ever devised by man for breaking down injustice and destroying the terrible walls which imprison men because they are different from other men." —*Lyndon B. Johnson*, 1965

What do they tell you about the progress toward equal rights for all races during this period of time in the United States?

Check Your Understanding

How do the quotes reflect what is happening on the timeline? What can you infer about the American Civil Rights Movement from this timeline?

Writing to Sources: Explanatory Text

Explain how Martin Luther King, Jr.'s letter relates to the Civil Rights Timeline. Which past events from the timeline does King reference? How did his letter influence the events that occurred after it was written? Be sure to:

- Begin with a clear thesis statement that states your position.
- Include multiple direct quotations from the text to support your claims.
- Include transitions between points and a statement that provides a conclusion.

INDEPENDENT READING LINK

Read and Connect

As you read the informational texts you have chosen, identify a cause-and-effect relationship between two significant events or situations. Write a sentence or two of commentary explaining the cause and effect.

Historical Research and Citation

Learning Targets

- Write research questions, conduct research to choose a focus for a historical investigation, and begin to gather evidence.
- Create an annotated bibliography that conforms to the guidelines of a style manual.

LEARNING STRATEGIES:
Graphic Organizer, Brainstorming, Drafting, Summarizing

Writing Research Questions

1. Review the first sentence of the assignment for Embedded Assessment 1: Historical Investigation and Presentation.

   > Your assignment is to research the historical, cultural, social, or geographical context of the novel *To Kill a Mockingbird* and investigate how individuals, organizations, and events contributed to change in the United States during the Civil Rights Movement.

   Rewrite the sentence as a question (or questions) that could guide your research.

ACADEMIC VOCABULARY
A **bibliography** is a list of the sources used for research. This list may also be called a works cited list.
An **annotated bibliography** includes comments about or summaries of each of the sources and the information found there.

Citing Sources

2. An **annotated bibliography** is a tool for tracking and giving credit to sources used for your research. Entries typically consist of two parts: a *citation* that follows the guidelines of a style manual—such as MLA—for the source, and an *annotation* (a brief summary of and commentary about the source). Examine the following model entry. Then, mark the text to identify the key elements of an annotated bibliography entry: information and details, evaluation of usefulness, and source description.

Edmonds, Rick. "Jim Crow: Shorthand for Separation." FORUM Magazine. Summer 1999: 7.

Edmonds reviews the origins of the term Jim Crow *and the significance of Jim Crow laws and customs as a social factor in the South. He also traces how awareness of the term's meaning has changed over time as our society has become more politically correct. This source is useful for understanding how racial attitudes led to the creation of the "separate but equal" laws that existed in the South before the Civil Rights Movement. This magazine article is a secondary source that draws from other reliable sources, such as the* American Heritage Dictionary.

My Notes

Historical Research and Citation

3. Complete the **bibliography** that follows by annotating each of the sources listed. Explain how each of the texts you have analyzed in this unit so far could help you address the research question(s) that you just wrote. Under the citation, write a summary that includes the following:

- specific information learned from the source, including key details
- an evaluation of the source's usefulness in answering the research question(s)
- a description of the type of source, including its relevance and authority

"Jim Crow Laws," Martin Luther King Jr. National Historic Site. National Park Service. 21 July 2012. Web. 06 Aug. 2012. <http://www.nps.gov/malu/forteachers/jim_crow_laws.htm/index.htm>

Annotation:

King, Martin Luther, Jr. "Letter from Birmingham Jail." The Norton Anthology of African-American Literature. Eds. Henry Louis Gates, Jr. and Nellie Y. McKay. New York: Norton, 1997.

Annotation:

4. Work with your class to brainstorm some of the people, organizations, and events that contributed to positive social change in the United States during the Civil Rights Movement. Write your notes in the following graphic organizer.

People	Organizations	Events

My Notes

5. Explore a website about the Civil Rights Movement to identify more subjects and add them to your research list.

6. With a partner or group of three, choose a subject as the focus of your historical investigation and presentation. Generate at least three research questions to guide your investigation. (You can revise these later if needed.) Include at least one of each of the following:

- a question that explores a **cause** by setting the context; for example, *What factors influenced what life was like for African Americans in Birmingham, Alabama, before the Civil Rights Movement?*

- a question that explores your **subject**; for example, *What were sit-ins, and where did they take place?*

- a question that explores an **effect** by evaluating the change; for example, *How did the "Freedom Riders" help enforce antisegregation laws?*

Historical Research and Citation

7. Write a research proposal that includes the following:
   - your group members' names
   - the subject of your investigation
   - at least three research questions

8. After your proposal is approved, assign a different research question to each group member. As you conduct research, think about the following questions:
   - Is the research question too broad or too narrow? Revise if needed.
   - Do the sources provide useful information to answer your question?
   - Are you using both print and digital sources for research? Are they reliable?
   - Does the initial information lead you to advanced research beyond your preliminary information?

9. **Evaluate** how well each source answers your questions. Then, complete a note card for each different source you use in your research, noting each site's usefulness in answering the research questions. You will use these note cards to create your annotated bibliography.

ACADEMIC VOCABULARY

When you **evaluate** something, you are making a judgment—one that most likely results from some degree of analysis about the value or worth of the information, idea, or object.

Language and Writers Craft: Footnotes and Endnotes

As you learned in Activity 3.4, writers often use MLA (Modern Language Association) style for art- and literature-focused academic papers. MLA uses parenthetical citations rather than footnotes and endnotes to cite sources within a research paper. If you are writing to the MLA style, use footnotes and endnotes only when you want to refer your reader to other publications that may be informative or helpful. A less common use for footnotes is when you want to provide additional information that may digress from the main information in your paper.

If you are writing a research paper using the Chicago style (based on the Chicago Manual of Style), use footnotes and endnotes instead of parenthetical citations. To cite a source within your paper, add a superscript footnote[1] to the end of quotation or piece of information you are citing. The footnote should correspond to a bibliography entry at the bottom of that page of your paper or, as in MLA, refer to a separate document known as the Notes page. The Notes page is a list of all of the sources you used in the paper and comes before your Works Cited page. Your sources should be listed in the order in which they appear in the paper. Word processing programs such as Microsoft Word offer tools to manage footnotes and endnotes within your paper.

As with MLA style, there are specific formatting guidelines to the Chicago style. Be sure to read these guidelines closely if you are asked to write a research paper using this style. Ask your teacher if he or she has any specific style or citation requirements before starting your research paper.

Creating Research Note Cards

On one side of an index card, include the citation for each source, according to the MLA guidelines provided by your teacher or an appropriate guide such as the Purdue OWL (Online Writing Lab) website or the *MLA Handbook for Writers of Research Papers*.

On the other side of the index card, include the following:

- quotes, paraphrases, and summaries of the information from the source
- a description of the type of source and an evaluation of its usefulness
- ideas for how to use the source in a presentation, including specific notes about integrating images and multimedia

10. Before creating your own note cards, work with your class to create a sample note card for the website "The Rise and Fall of Jim Crow" based on the notes you took during Activity 3.4.

Example

Front:

Back:

Reaching an Audience

LEARNING STRATEGIES:
Graphic Organizer, Levels of
Questions, Note-taking, Sharing
and Responding

Learning Target

- Analyze photo essays, videos, and multimedia presentations in order to plan effective ways to reach an audience of my peers in a presentation.

Elements of Effective Presentations

1. As you view at least three different types of presentations, take notes in the following graphic organizer to evaluate the effectiveness of each.

Subject and Type of Presentation (photo essay, video, multimedia, etc.)	Facts and Information (What claim was being made by the presenter? Was the reasoning convincing and the evidence relevant to the claim?)	Audio and Visual Components (How did the kind of media used determine which details were emphasized?)	Effectiveness of the Presentation (How engaging was the presentation? Did it grab and hold my attention? Did it feel relevant and important?)

2. **Discuss:** Which of the presentations were effective and why?

My Notes

3. Based on your class discussion on the effectiveness of the presentations, work with your group to analyze an audience of your peers. Include answers to the following questions:

- What does my audience already know about my subject, and how is my presentation going to expand that knowledge?

- What audio and visual components appeal to my audience, and how will I use these in my presentation?

- What connections can I make between my subject and my target audience to make my presentation relevant to their lives?

4. Meet with another group to share and respond to each other's analysis of the audience. Consider suggestions for improvement.

5. Create guiding questions for your audience's note-taking during your presentation. You will incorporate these questions into the media you choose (for example, as titles of slides), write them clearly on a poster to display during your presentation, or make copies for the class.

Levels of Questions

6. Work with your group to write questions that will guide both the organization and the audience's note-taking on your presentation.

Start with your research questions and generate at least two more questions for each, using a variety of levels.

Level 1 Questions: Literal (Questions of Fact)

Example: *In what ways did Jim Crow laws affect schools?*

For my subject:

Level 2 Questions: Interpretive (Questions of Meaning)

Example: *Why was* Brown v. Board of Education *such a landmark case?*

For my subject:

Level 3 Questions: Universal (Questions of Relevance)

Example: *Does everyone in the United States today receive the same quality education? In the world? What still needs to change to make that happen?*

For my subject:

My Notes

Reaching an Audience

Drafting the Embedded Assessment

Draft an explanatory text that explains how an individual, an organization, or an event facilitated the changes that occurred during the Civil Rights Movement. Remember to take the historical, cultural, social, and geographical context of *To Kill a Mockingbird* into account as you write. Be sure to:

- Identify the individual, organization, or event in your first sentence.
- Describe events in the correct chronological order.
- Include multiple direct quotations from the multimedia you used to support your claims.
- Provide a conclusion that summarizes your explanation.

Independent Reading Checkpoint

Review your independent reading. What have you learned and observed about the United States during the 1930s or 1960s? How did the events you read about connect to the texts you read? Were any of the events you read about also listed on the Civil Rights Timeline? Review any notes you took. How can you use what you have learned as you complete the writing prompt and the Embedded Assessment?

Historical Investigation and Presentation

ASSIGNMENT

Your assignment is to research the historical, cultural, social, or geographical context of the novel *To Kill a Mockingbird* and investigate how individuals, organizations, and events contributed to change in the United States during the Civil Rights Movement. You will work collaboratively to create an oral presentation of your findings with multimedia support and guiding questions for your audience.

Planning: Take time to plan, conduct, and record your research.	▪ What individual, organization, or event will your group investigate? ▪ What research questions will help you explore the subject and investigate your subject's contribution to change (cause and effect)? ▪ How will you record citations, information, and source evaluations as you gather answers and evidence? ▪ How will you record sources to create an alphabetized annotated bibliography?
Creating and Rehearsing: Collaborate with your group to create and prepare a multimedia oral presentation.	▪ How will you select the most relevant facts and sufficient details to develop your presentation for your audience? ▪ How will you organize your presentation to emphasize the cause-and-effect relationship between the 1930s context of the novel *To Kill a Mockingbird* and the Civil Rights Movement? ▪ How will you divide the speaking responsibilities and make smooth transitions between speakers? ▪ How will you collaborate to create an audience analysis and plan how to present your findings to your peers? ▪ How will you select and incorporate audio and visual components into your presentation? What is your plan for rehearsing your presentation delivery and getting feedback from your peers to revise and improve your presentation?
Presenting and Listening: Use effective speaking and listening as a presenter and audience member.	▪ How will you use notes for your talking points so that you can maintan eye contact with your audience? ▪ During your peers' presentations, how will you use the guiding questions to organize your notes on the subject of each presentation?

Reflection

As you read and study *To Kill a Mockingbird*, take notes on how your topic (or another that interests you more) surfaces in the novel. Record both textual evidence and personal commentary. After you have finished the novel, reflect on the following questions: How did the class presentations enhance your understanding and appreciation of the novel?

Historical Investigation and Presentation

SCORING GUIDE

Scoring Criteria	Exemplary	Proficient	Emerging	Incomplete
Ideas	The presentation • is thoughtful and well-organized • demonstrates a comprehensive understanding of significant aspects of the topic and its relevance to the novel.	The presentation • is organized and displays a solid understanding of the topic • clearly connects the topic and the novel for the audience.	The presentation • is somewhat organized • contains information that shows a limited understanding of the topic or how it connects to the novel.	The presentation • is not well-organized and/or does not contain relevant content • provides few or no clear facts and details to help the audience connect the topic and the novel.
Structure	The presentation • skillfully uses a variety of audio/visual resources to keep the audience engaged • includes media resources that are used creatively to enhance understanding of the topic • includes a well-organized audience guide with thoughtful questions to focus information for the audience and adequate space for recording responses.	The presentation • uses audio/visual resources to engage the audience • uses media effectively to support information about the topic and ideas connecting it to the novel.	The presentation • uses some audio/visual resources that do not engage the audience • uses media choices that are distracting and do not serve the group's purpose.	The presentation • does not use audio/visual resources.
Use of Language	The presentation • demonstrates accomplished oral communication skills and rehearsal to create a well-planned delivery • includes participation by all group members.	The presentation • demonstrates adequate oral communication skills and rehearsal to plan the delivery • includes participation by all group members, although some may present more than others.	The presentation • demonstrates inadequate oral communication skills and shows little evidence of rehearsal • is delivered by only some of the group members.	The presentation • shows inadequate oral communication skills and no evidence of rehearsal • is not delivered by all group members.

Previewing Embedded Assessment 2: Writing a Literary Analysis Essay

Learning Targets

- Identify and analyze the knowledge and skills needed to complete Embedded Assessment 2 successfully.
- Revise, refine, and reflect on understanding of vocabulary words and the Essential Questions.

Making Connections

To Kill a Mockingbird is set in the 1930s before the major changes brought about by the Civil Rights Movement. At that time, Jim Crow laws governed the civil rights of minorities, and segregation was the law of the land. In this second part of the unit, you will begin reading the novel and exploring the historical, social, and cultural contexts of its setting.

Developing Vocabulary

Return to the Table of Contents and note the Academic Vocabulary and Literary Terms you have studied so far in this unit. Which words/terms can you now move to a new category on a QHT chart? Which could you now teach to others that you were unfamiliar with at the beginning of the unit?

Essential Questions

How would you answer each of these questions now?

1. How can context contribute to the understanding of a novel?

2. How does a key scene from a novel contribute to the work as a whole?

Unpacking Embedded Assessment 2

Read the assignment for Embedded Assessment 2: Writing a Literary Analysis Essay.

> Your assignment is to write a passage analysis of a key coming-of-age scene from *To Kill a Mockingbird*. After annotating the text to analyze Harper Lee's use of literary elements in your selected passage, write an essay explaining how the literary elements in this passage help develop a theme of the novel.

In your own words, summarize what you will need to know to complete this assessment successfully. With your class, create a graphic organizer to represent the skills and knowledge you will need to complete the tasks identified in the Embedded Assessment.

My Notes

INDEPENDENT READING LINK

Read and Discuss

The second section of the unit also focuses on *To Kill a Mockingbird*, which is a coming-of-age novel. For independent reading, choose novels or biographies or autobiographies with coming-of-age themes. Discuss one or more of your independent reading selections with peers, explaining a few facts you learned about the time period of the book.

A Story of the Times

My Notes

_____

_____

_____

_____

_____

_____

📖 **WORD
CONNECTIONS**

Multiple-Meaning Words

To *buck* a system, tradition,
or trend means "to fight
against it." The word *buck* is
also used in reference to the
way bulls try to kick a cowboy
or cowgirl off their back in a
rodeo. This is a helpful image
when considering the way
characters in the novel fought
against the tradition of racism
in their town.

_____

_____

_____

petition: formal request that
people sign

integrate: bring together

opposition: resistance

_____

_____

_____

_____

_____

_____

Learning Targets

- Analyze reflective texts for tone and to understand context.
- Write an objective summary of a passage.

Preview

In this activity, you will read reflective texts from a variety of readers responding to
the novel *To Kill a Mockingbird*.

Setting a Purpose for Reading

- Highlight words or phrases that identify the reader's tone or attitude toward
  the novel.
- Circle unknown words and phrases. Try to determine the meaning of the words
  by using context clues, word parts, or a dictionary.

ABOUT THE AUTHOR

Mary McDonagh Murphy is an Emmy award–winning American writer, producer,
and director whose work has appeared on CBS, NBC, and PBS. She primarily
focuses on independent documentaries, creating long and short features on a
variety of subjects. Her bestselling book *Scout, Atticus, and Boo: A Celebration
of Fifty Years of* To Kill A Mockingbird is based on interviews she completed for
the documentary *Harper Lee: From Mockingbird to Watchman*. In the
interviews, she asked each person to discuss a favorite scene from the novel.

Reflective Texts

from Scout, Atticus, and Boo:
A Celebration *of* To Kill a Mockingbird

by Mary McDonagh Murphy

Reverend Thomas Lane Butts, pastor, born in Alabama in 1930:

1 I was in Mobile as a pastor of the Michigan Avenue Methodist Church. I had gone
through an encounter with the Ku Klux Klan. They were after me because I'd signed
a **petition** to **integrate** the buses there. This was in 1960 when *To Kill a Mockingbird*
came out, and it was a great comfort to those of us who had taken some stand on this
particular issue.

2 The book was written in a way that it could not be refuted. It was a soft **opposition**
to people who were against civil rights. It was just a great comfort to those of us who
had been involved in the civil rights movement that somebody from the Deep South
had given us a book that gave some comfort to us in what we had done.

3 I understood the context in which the book was written, because that's how I grew
up. It was a rural, poverty-stricken situation during the Depression, where people did
not have much. It was hardscrabble for most people to make a living. It was a time in
which black people were treated terribly and people took in racism with their mother's
milk. Here in this novel, you have a person bucking the tradition in order to advocate
the rights of a person without regard to color.

James Patterson, author of over 50 novels including the Maximum Ride series, born in New York in 1947:

1   I read *To Kill a Mockingbird* in high school, and it was one of the few books I really liked. Part of my problem with going to this particular high school is they just didn't give us many books that would turn us on. I was a good student, but I just didn't get turned on to reading. What I remember most about *To Kill a Mockingbird* was—and I think this probably is more of an American trait than in other places—I think we are particularly **attuned** to **injustice**. The stories that deal with injustice are really powerful here. I think we have more of a sense of that than they do in some places where injustice is more a fact of life. I loved the narration, how it went from a pleasant story to a quite horrifying one.

2   Sometimes people will criticize *To Kill a Mockingbird* because of certain language, but it expresses views of how certain people thought in the 1930s. Similarly people will write books about us now, and I am sure [in the future] people will be **scandalized** by the way we eat and the fact we're still having all these ridiculous wars and whatever. But I think it's useful to kids, and it was useful to me to look back on an earlier time and see how different things were.

3   My connection was more to Jem, because he was a boy. I found the drama just kept building and building and building. In the beginning, you are suspecting something about Boo, which should tell you something about yourself, that you suspect him for no reason.

Oprah Winfrey, talk show host, TV/film producer, actress, philanthropist, born in Mississippi in 1954:

1   At the time that I read *To Kill a Mockingbird*, I was living with my mother in Milwaukee. I would not have had any money to buy it, so I would undoubtedly have chosen it from the library ... I remember starting it and just **devouring** it, not being able to get enough of it, because I fell in love with Scout. I wanted to be Scout. I thought I was Scout. I always took on or wanted to take on the characteristics of whoever I was reading about, so I wanted to be Scout and I wanted a father like Atticus.

2   I remember watching the movie with my father many years after I read the book. The impact of the movie on my father caused me to see the book differently and experience the book differently. I am right after the cusp of the civil rights movement. I wasn't a child of the civil rights movement. I am one of those people who has been one of the greatest **beneficiaries** of the civil rights movement. I don't know what it is like to be told to go to the back door.

3   I did not live a Jim Crow segregated life, because I was one of the fortunate ones who were able to escape Mississippi. And I do mean escape—1960, when this book was published, was about the time I was leaving Mississippi.

4   I left for Milwaukee and left my grandmother when I was six years old, so I never experienced the segregation of the South. I moved to an integrated school and was the smartest kid in the class, and when you are the smartest kid in the class, you always get a lot of attention. I never felt any of the oppressiveness of racism. I always recognize that life would have been so different for me had I been raised in a segregated environment, if I had to experience even secondhand what was happening in that environment.

My Notes

attuned: able to recognize
injustice: wrong

scandalized: shocked or horrified

devouring: swallowing hungrily

beneficiaries: people who gain something

A Story of the Times

My Notes

Second Read

* Reread the texts to answer these text-dependent questions.
* Write any additional questions you have about the text in your Reader/Writer Notebook.

1. **Key Ideas and Details:** What is the main reason Reverend Thomas Lane Butts finds comfort in *To Kill A Mockingbird*?

2. **Key Ideas and Details:** What aspect does James Patterson find most moving about *To Kill a Mockingbird*?

3. **Key Ideas and Details:** How did the civil rights movement affect Oprah Winfrey's life?

Working from the Text

4. Write a brief, objective summary of one of the passages. Meet with a group of students who read different passages. Introduce each passage by reading your summary and sharing textual evidence related to the questions below:

- How did each reader's personal experiences impact his or her reaction to the novel?

- How were the responses similar? How were they different?

- What predictions can you make about the novel based on these passages?

Check Your Understanding

How might your response to the novel differ from that of someone who read the book in the 1960s?

A Scouting Party

LEARNING STRATEGIES:
Graphic Organizer,
Marking the Text,
Visualizing, Sketching,
Discussion Groups

Learning Target

- Analyze the first chapter of a novel to identify details that establish point of view, character, and setting.

Opening Credits

1. View the opening clip of *To Kill a Mockingbird,* noting your observations on the graphic organizer.

My Notes

Viewing the Opening Credits of *To Kill a Mockingbird*

What do you observe? What images did you see on screen?	What do you notice about the lighting?	What do you notice about the sound?	What predictions can you make?

2. **Collaborative Discussion:** Refer to and add to your notes as you discuss the following with your classmates:

- Usually the opening credits of a film set a mood and provide clues about conflicts or themes. What predictions can you make based on the opening credits of this film?

- From the sounds and images, what can you infer about the perspective or point of view from which this story will be told?

- When this film was made, color film technology was available. Why do you think the director chose to shoot this film in black and white?

Preview

In this activity, you will read two excerpts from *To Kill a Mockingbird* and look for details about character, point of view, and setting.

Setting a Purpose for Reading

- Highlight words and phrases that give you clues about the narrator's personality and establish her voice.

- Circle unknown words and phrases. Try to determine the meaning of the words by using context clues, word parts, or a dictionary.

- Underline the names of characters who are related to the narrator as well as the words that tell you how they are related.

ABOUT THE AUTHOR

American writer Nelle Harper Lee (1926–2016) was born and grew up in Alabama. As an adult, she moved to New York City, where she wrote and published several short stories. She then took a year off from work to write *To Kill a Mockingbird*, using her father as a model for Atticus Finch. *To Kill a Mockingbird* won much acclaim when it was published and a Pulitzer Prize in 1961.

Novel

from

To Kill a Mockingbird

(Chapter 1)

by Harper Lee

1   When he was nearly thirteen, my brother Jem got his arm badly broken at the elbow. When it healed, and Jem's fears of never being able to play football were **assuaged**, he was seldom self-conscious about his injury. His left arm was somewhat shorter than his right; when he stood or walked, the back of his hand was at right angles to his body, his thumb **parallel** to his thigh. He couldn't have cared less, so long as he could pass and punt.

2   When enough years had gone by to **enable** us to look back on them, we sometimes discussed the events leading to his accident. I maintain that the Ewells started it all, but Jem, who was four years my senior, said it started long before that. He said it began the summer Dill came to us, when Dill first gave us the idea of making Boo Radley come out.

3   I said if he wanted to take a broad view of the thing, it really began with Andrew Jackson. If General Jackson hadn't run the Creeks up the creek, Simon Finch would never have paddled up the Alabama, and where would we be if he hadn't? We were far too old to settle an argument with a fist-fight, so we **consulted** Atticus. Our father said we were both right.

Second Read

- Reread the novel excerpt to answer these text-dependent questions.
- Write any additional questions you have about the text in your Reader/Writer Notebook.

3. **Craft and Structure:** What is the point of view of the novel, and what do we know about the novel's narrator?

My Notes

assuaged: soothed; calmed

parallel: extending in the same direction

enable: make possible

consulted: sought advice from

A Scouting Party

4. **Craft and Structure:** What can you infer about the novel's setting based on the first few paragraphs of the novel?

Setting a Purpose for Reading

- Highlight details that reveal characterization, such as a character's appearance, thoughts, actions, or words.
- Circle unknown words and phrases. Try to determine the meaning of the words by using context clues, word parts, or a dictionary.

Novel

from

To Kill a Mockingbird

(Chapter 1)

by Harper Lee

1 Early one morning as we were beginning our day's play in the back yard, Jem and I heard something next door in Miss Rachel Haverford's **collard** patch. We went to the wire fence to see if there was a puppy—Miss Rachel's rat terrier was expecting—instead we found someone sitting looking at us. Sitting down, he wasn't much higher than the collards. We stared at him until he spoke:

2 "Hey."

3 "Hey yourself," said Jem pleasantly.

4 "I'm Charles Baker Harris," he said. "I can read."

5 "So what?" I said.

6 "I just thought you'd like to know I can read. You got anything needs readin' I can do it. ..."

7 "How old are you," asked Jem, "four-and-a-half?"

8 "Goin' on seven."

9 "Shoot no wonder, then," said Jem, jerking his thumb at me. "Scout **yonder**'s been readin' ever since she was born, and she ain't even started to school yet. You look right **puny** for goin' on seven."

10 "I'm little but I'm old," he said.

11 Jem brushed his hair back to get a better look. "Why don't you come over, Charles Baker Harris?" he said. "Lord, what a name."

collard: leafy vegetable

yonder: over there

puny: small

12 "'s not any funnier'n yours. Aunt Rachel says your name's Jeremy Atticus Finch."

13 Jem scowled. "I'm big enough to fit mine," he said. "Your name's longer'n you are. Bet it's a foot longer."

14 "Folks call me Dill," said Dill, struggling under the fence.

15 "Do better if you go over it instead of under it," I said. "Where'd you come from?"

16 Dill was from Meridian, Mississippi, was spending the summer with his aunt, Miss Rachel, and would be spending every summer in Maycomb from now on. His family was from Maycomb County originally, his mother worked for a photographer in Meridian, had entered his picture in a Beautiful Child contest and won five dollars. She gave the money to Dill, who went to the picture show twenty times on it.

17 "Don't have any picture shows here, except Jesus ones in the courthouse sometimes," said Jem. "Ever see anything good?"

18 Dill had seen *Dracula*, a **revelation** that moved Jem to eye him with the beginning of respect. "Tell it to us," he said.

19 Dill was a curiosity. He wore blue linen shorts that buttoned to his shirt, his hair was snow white and stuck to his head like duck-fluff; he was a year my senior but I towered over him. As he told us the old tale his blue eyes would lighten and darken; his laugh was sudden and happy; he **habitually** pulled at a **cowlick** in the center of his forehead.

20 When Dill reduced Dracula to dust, and Jem said the show sounded better than the book, I asked Dill where his father was: "You ain't said anything about him."

21 "I haven't got one."

22 "Is he dead?"

23 "No..."

24 "Then if he's not dead you've got one, haven't you?"

25 Dill blushed and Jem told me to hush, a sure sign that Dill had been studied and found acceptable. Thereafter the summer passed in routine **contentment**.

Second Read

- Reread the novel excerpt to answer these text-dependent questions.
- Write any additional questions you have about the text in your Reader/Writer Notebook.

5. **Key Ideas and Details:** Compare and contrast the characters of Jem and Dill. How are their characters the same? How are they different?

My Notes

revelation: something revealed

habitually: regularly
cowlick: tuft of hair that grows in a different direction to the rest of the hair

contentment: state of being satisfied

A Scouting Party

GRAMMAR&USAGE
Clauses

A **relative clause** is a type of dependent clause that begins with a relative pronoun: *who, whom, that, which,* or *whose.* A relative clause modifies a noun much like an adjective does.

These clauses can be **restrictive** (essential) or **nonrestrictive** (nonessential). Commas are usually used to set off nonrestrictive clauses. Consider these examples:

Nonrestrictive: "She gave the money to Dill, *who went to the picture show twenty times on it.*" The relative clause tells more about what Dill did with the money, but it is not essential to understanding the sentence.

Restrictive: "He wore blue linen shorts *that buttoned to his shirt* ..." Consider why the author stating that Dill's shorts buttoned to his shirt is an essential part of this sentence.

My Notes

_____

_____

_____

_____

_____

_____

_____

_____

_____

_____

_____

_____

6. **Key Ideas and Details:** How can you tell that Dill is an outsider in the Maycomb community?

7. **Key Ideas and Details:** Why does Jem tell Scout to hush, and what does this action reveal about their characters?

Working from the Text

8. From what point of view is the novel told?

9. How is it both similar to and different from the point of view established in the opening credits of the film?

10. Why is each point of view appropriate for its medium—film or literature?

11. As a group, sketch the characters and the scene you just read, indicating the relationships among the children in your drawing. Annotate the sketch with textual evidence to support your analysis of the scene. Include details about how your character looks, acts, speaks, and thinks as well as other characters' reactions.

Check Your Understanding

Summarize the sketches you made of the characters. What can you infer about the characters based on the text evidence you chose?

Visual Prompt: As you read the rest of Chapter 1, choose a passage that describes a setting, such as the town of Maycomb or the Radley house. Visualize and sketch the setting, and then annotate your sketch with textual evidence.

In addition to details about the setting's appearance, include examples of the diction and imagery that help to create the author's attitude or tone.

Narrative Writing Prompt

Think about the scene you just read. Write an "unseen scene" that either comes before or goes after the scene. Or, continue one of the excerpted scenes. Use both dialogue and description in your scene. Be sure to:

• Include a new conflict for the unseen scene, or a continuation of the conflict from the excerpted scene.

• Write dialogue that creates a vivid picture of the characters and conflict.

• Create a consistent point of view.

Conflict with Miss Caroline

Learning Targets
- Analyze fictional text and make connections to characters and plot events.
- Demonstrate understanding of conflict in writing.

LEARNING STRATEGIES:
Graphic Organizer, Drafting

Exploring Conflict

1. Think about the different kinds of **conflicts** you have studied. **Internal conflict** occurs when a character struggles between opposing needs, desires, or emotions within his or her own mind. **External conflict** occurs when a character struggles against an outside force, such as another character, society, or nature. Using the graphic organizer below, brainstorm examples of conflicts from your life, the world, books, television, or films.

Internal Conflict: Person vs. Self (Struggles against one's own opposing needs, desires, emotions)	External Conflict: Person vs. Person (Struggles against another person)	External Conflict: Person vs. Society (Struggles against laws or expectations)	External Conflict: Person vs. Nature (Struggles against the physical world)

My Notes

Working from the Text: Chapters 2–3

2. After you read Chapter 2, work with a partner or small group to locate textual evidence of the conflict between Scout and Miss Caroline. Write quotes below with commentary to explain why these two are "starting off on the wrong foot in every way."

Scout's Side	Caroline's Side

Conflict with Miss Caroline

3. Fill in the circles below, making connections to Scout's first-day-of-school experiences. As you read Chapter 3, fill in the circles with more connections:

- Text-to-self: when the text makes you think of your own life
- Text-to-text: when the text makes you think of another text
- Text-to-world: when the text makes you think of world events

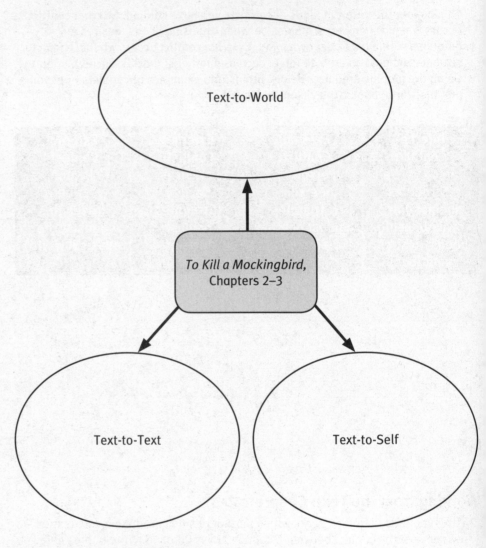

Check Your Understanding

What type of conflict is happening between Scout and Miss Caroline? Support your answer with text evidence.

Explanatory Writing Prompt

Write an introduction to an essay analyzing the conflict between Scout and Miss Caroline in Chapter 2 of *To Kill a Mockingbird*. Be sure to:

- Begin with a QQAS (question, quote, anecdote, or statement of intrigue) that introduces a connection to Scout's experiences.
- Provide a brief summary of the chapter.
- End with a statement about the conflict and what Scout learns from it.

INDEPENDENT READING LINK

Read and Connect

Create a graphic organizer similar to the one in this activity to make connections with the events in your independent coming-of-age reading. Under the graphic organizer, write a few sentences to compare the different conflicts.

Analyzing Boo

Learning Targets

- Analyze subplot and motif in a text to determine how characters develop through coming-of-age experiences.
- Make predictions, form inferences, draw conclusions, and find evidence to support an analysis of a literary text.

The Story of Boo Radley

1. Return to the pages in Chapter 1 that introduce the story of Boo Radley. Complete the graphic organizer below to separate fact from rumor, and provide textual evidence of each. Add your own questions about Boo's story and your personal commentary.

My Notes

_____

_____

_____

_____

Boo Radley's Story	Textual Evidence	Questions/Commentary
Facts		
Rumors		

Analyzing Boo

hastily: quickly

Preview

In this excerpt, notice how the children begin to question their assumptions about Boo and the Radley place.

Setting a Purpose for Reading

- Underline any details about Boo or the Radley place.
- Circle unknown words and phrases. Try to determine the meaning of the words by using context clues, word parts, or a dictionary.
- Write any inferences or conclusions you draw from "reading between the lines" in the My Notes section.

Novel

from

To Kill a Mockingbird

(Chapter 4)

by Harper Lee

1   As the year passed, released from school thirty minutes before Jem, who had to stay until three o'clock, I ran by the Radley Place as fast as I could, not stopping until I reached the safety of our front porch. One afternoon as I raced by, something caught my eye and caught it in such a way that I took a deep breath, a long look around, and went back.

2   Two live oaks stood at the edge of the Radley lot; their roots reached out into the side-road and made it bumpy. Something about one of the trees attracted my attention.

3   Some tinfoil was sticking in a knot-hole just above my eye level, winking at me in the afternoon sun. I stood on tiptoe, **hastily** looked around once more, reached into the hole, and withdrew two pieces of chewing gum minus their outer wrappers.

4   My first impulse was to get it into my mouth as quickly as possible, but I remembered where I was. I ran home, and on our front porch I examined my loot. The gum looked fresh. I sniffed it and it smelled all right. I licked it and waited for a while. When I did not die I crammed it into my mouth: Wrigley's Double-Mint.

5   When Jem came home he asked me where I got such a wad. I told him I found it.

6   "Don't eat things you find, Scout."

7   "This wasn't on the ground, it was in a tree."

8   Jem growled.

9   "Well it was," I said. "It was sticking in that tree yonder, the one comin' from school."

10   "Spit it out right now!"

11   I spat it out. The tang was fading, anyway. "I've been chewin' it all afternoon and I ain't dead yet, not even sick."

12   Jem stamped his foot. "Don't you know you're not supposed to even touch the trees over there? You'll get killed if you do!"

13 "You touched the house once!"

14 "That was different! You go gargle—right now, you hear me?"

15 "Ain't neither, it'll take the taste outa my mouth."

16 "You don't 'n' I'll tell Calpurnia on you!" Rather than risk a tangle with Calpurnia, I did as Jem told me. For some reason, my first year of school had **wrought** a great change in our relationship: Calpurnia's **tyranny**, unfairness, and meddling in my business had faded to gentle grumblings of general disapproval. On my part, I went to much trouble, sometimes, not to **provoke** her.

wrought: worked

tyranny: absolute rule by a leader

provoke: anger

17 Summer was on the way; Jem and I awaited it with impatience. Summer was our best season: it was sleeping on the back screened porch in cots, or trying to sleep in the treehouse; summer was everything good to eat; it was a thousand colors in a **parched** landscape; but most of all, summer was Dill.

parched: dry

18 The authorities released us early the last day of school, and Jem and I walked home together. "Reckon old Dill'll be coming home tomorrow," I said.

My Notes

_____

_____

_____

_____

19 "Probably day after," said Jem. "Mis'sippi turns 'em loose a day later."

20 As we came to the live oaks at the Radley Place I raised my finger to point for the hundredth time to the knot-hole where I had found the chewing gum, trying to make Jem believe I had found it there, and found myself pointing at another piece of tinfoil.

21 "I see it, Scout! I see it—"

22 Jem looked around, reached up, and **gingerly** pocketed a tiny shiny package. We ran home, and on the front porch we looked at a small box patchworked with bits of tinfoil collected from chewing-gum wrappers. It was the kind of box wedding rings came in, purple velvet with a minute catch. Jem flicked open the tiny catch. Inside were two scrubbed and polished pennies, one on top of the other. Jem examined them.

gingerly: carefully

23 "Indian-heads," he said. "Nineteen-six and Scout, one of 'em's nineteen-hundred. These are real old."

24 "Nineteen-hundred," I echoed. "Say—"

25 "Hush a minute, I'm thinkin'."

26 "Jem, you reckon that's somebody's hidin' place?"

27 "Naw, don't anybody much but us pass by there, unless it's some grown person's—"

28 "Grown folks don't have hidin' places. You reckon we ought to keep 'em, Jem?"

29 "I don't know what we could do, Scout. Who'd we give 'em back to? I know for a fact don't anybody go by there—Cecil goes by the back street an' all the way around by town to get home."

30 Cecil Jacobs, who lived at the far end of our street next door to the post office, walked a total of one mile per school day to avoid the Radley Place and old Mrs. Henry Lafayette Dubose. Mrs. Dubose lived two doors up the street from us; neighborhood opinion was **unanimous** that Mrs. Dubose was the meanest old woman who ever lived. Jem wouldn't go by her place without Atticus beside him.

unanimous: agreed on by everyone

31 "What you **reckon** we oughta do, Jem?"

reckon: think

32 Finders were keepers unless title was proven. Plucking an occasional camellia, getting a squirt of hot milk from Miss Maudie Atkinson's cow on a summer day, helping ourselves to someone's scuppernongs was part of our **ethical** culture, but money was different.

ethical: moral

Analyzing Boo

slicked: polished

33 "Tell you what," said Jem. "We'll keep 'em till school starts, then go around and ask everybody if they're theirs. They're some bus child's, maybe—he was too taken up with gettin' outa school today an' forgot 'em. These are somebody's, I know that. See how they've been **slicked** up? They've been saved."

34 "Yeah, but why should somebody wanta put away chewing gum like that? You know it doesn't last."

35 "I don't know, Scout. But these are important to somebody. ..."

36 "How's that, Jem. ...?"

37 "Well, Indian-heads—well, they come from the Indians. They're real strong magic, they make you have good luck. Not like fried chicken when you're not lookin' for it, but things like long life 'n' good health, 'n' passin' six-weeks tests ... these are real valuable to somebody. I'm gonna put 'em in my trunk."

38 Before Jem went to his room, he looked for a long time at the Radley Place. He seemed to be thinking again.

Second Read

- Reread the novel excerpt to answer these text-dependent questions.
- Write any additional questions you have about the text in your Reader/Writer Notebook.

2. **Key Ideas and Details:** What does Scout's changing relationship with Calpurnia suggest about Scout's coming of age?

3. **Key Ideas and Details:** Why do the children struggle with what to do with the pennies they find? What does this suggest about their characters?

4. **Key Ideas and Details:** At the end of this excerpt, Jem is **"thinking again."** What might Jem be considering that the younger Scout hasn't thought of?

5. **Craft and Structure:** How does language help characterize the children?

Working from the Text

6. The character of Boo Radley is a **motif** in *To Kill a Mockingbird*, and the incidents involving the children's fascination with him form one of the major **subplots** of the novel. In your discussion group, divide the following passages that explore this motif and subplot in further depth.

   Passage 1: Chapter 4 (from "Let's roll in the tire …" to the end of Chapter 4)

   Passage 2: Chapter 5 (from "Next morning when I …" to the end of Chapter 5)

   Passage 3: Chapter 6 (from "What are you gonna do?" to "Settle it yourselves.")

   Form an expert group with other students who have selected the same passage. Conduct a close reading of your passage, using sticky notes to mark textual evidence and record your questions, commentary, predictions, inferences, and conclusions.

   Work together to complete the appropriate row of the graphic organizer on the following page.

7. Return to your discussion group and share your expert group's observations, interpretations, and evidence. Take notes in the appropriate row as you listen to the other group members analyze their passage.

8. **Independent Practice:** As you read the rest of Chapters 4–6, revisit this graphic organizer to add additional details, commentary, and evidence, and to evaluate whether or not you agree with the "expert" analysis.

Check Your Understanding

Construct an interpretive statement about how the experience of finding gifts in the knothole of the Radley live oak tree has helped Jem and Scout come of age.

Writing to Sources: Explanatory Text

Write a paragraph to explain how the experience of finding gifts in the knothole of the Radley live oak tree has helped Jem and Scout come of age. Be sure to:

- Include a well-stated topic sentence.
- Include direct quotations and specific examples from the text.
- Use a coherent organization structure and make connections between specific words, images, and ideas conveyed.

Literary Terms

A **symbol** is anything (object, animal, event, person, or place) that represents itself but also stands for something else on a figurative level.

A **motif** is a recurring image, symbol, theme, character type, subject, or narrative detail that becomes a unifying element in an artistic work.

The **plot**, or sequence of events that make up a story, is often accompanied by a **subplot**, or secondary or side story, that develops from and supports the main plot and usually involves minor characters.

My Notes

Analyzing Boo

Objective Summary of the Passage	Statement About How This Is a Coming-of-Age Experience	Key Textual Evidence to Support Your Interpretation
Passage 1:		
Passage 2:		
Passage 3:		

Questions and Conclusions

Learning Targets
- Use Levels of Questions to identify themes in Chapters 7–9.
- Write thematic statements and a conclusion paragraph.

Levels of Questions

1. Themes in literature usually revolve around ideas that apply to multiple situations. Using Levels of Questions can help you identify those universal themes in a text.

   Sample: *What does Harper Lee have to say about prejudice through Boo Radley's character?*

First Read: Chapter 7

2. Read and analyze the first chunk of Chapter 7 with your class, generating questions at all three levels. Share your responses to the questions in a class discussion.

Chunk 1: From the start of Chapter 7 to "I'd have the facts."

Level 1 Question: Literal Questions ("What does the text say?")

Level 2 Question: Interpretive Questions ("What does the text mean?")

Level 3 Question: Universal Questions ("Why does it matter?")

---

3. Read and analyze the second and third chunks with a small group, and generate three Levels of Questions for each chunk. Share your responses to the questions in a group discussion.

LEARNING STRATEGIES:
Chunking the Text, Levels of Questions, Discussion Groups

My Notes

Questions and Conclusions

Chunk 2: From "There are no clearly defined seasons ..." to "Huh?"

Level 1 Question: Literal Questions ("What does the text say?")

Level 2 Question: Interpretive Questions ("What does the text mean?")

Level 3 Question: Universal Questions ("Why does it matter?")

Chunk 3: From "You reckon we oughta write a letter ..." to the end of the chapter.

Level 1 Question: Literal Questions ("What does the text say?")

Level 2 Question: Interpretive Questions ("What does the text mean?")

Level 3 Question: Universal Questions ("Why does it matter?")

Working from the Text: Chapter 7

4. Work with your discussion group to identify several topics and thematic statements that can be made by examining the character of Boo Radley and how the children interact with him. What coming-of-age lessons have the children learned from these experiences?

5. Good conclusions support the information and explanations presented in an essay. One way to write a conclusion is to connect the thesis statement to literal, interpretive, and universal statements. Read the following model conclusion from a passage analysis. Mark the text as follows:

- Highlight the thesis statement.
- Put an "L" in the margin next to literal statements.
- Put an "I" in the margin next to interpretive statements.
- Put a "U" in the margin next to universal statements.

Model Conclusion

In this passage, Harper Lee uses the motif of Boo Radley to convey the theme that sometimes sterotypes limit our expectations. When Jem goes back to the Radley Place to retrieve his lost pants, his pants are folded across the fence, waiting for him. The way that they are sewn—all crooked—shows that someone inexperienced with sewing is trying to help him stay out of trouble: the same someone who has been watching the children, leaving them gifts, and laughing when a tire rolls into his yard carrying a dizzy and frightened little girl. Jem and Scout had come to expect only evil from Boo Radley, so Boo's friendliness and helpfulness are unexpected. The message we might all take away from this passage is that peoples' actions are more important than what others say about them.

6. **Independent Practice:** As you read Chapters 8 and 9, chunk each chapter into at least three sections and use sticky notes to generate Levels of Questions for each chunk.

Check Your Understanding

After you read Chapters 8 and 9, return to your discussion group to share and respond to one another's questions. Work together with your class to identify topics introduced in these chapters, and write thematic statements that show Harper Lee's opinion.

Explanatory Writing Prompt

Choose one of the topics that is introduced in a passage from Chapters 7–9 and write a conclusion to an essay analyzing how motif (Boo), subplot (the fire), conflict (Scout vs. Francis), setting (Finch's Landing), or character (Uncle Jack) contributes to that theme. Be sure to:

- Begin with a statement that reflects the thesis of the essay as in the model above.
- Include factual, interpretive, and universal statements.
- Use the present tense, literary vocabulary, and formal style consistently.

GRAMMAR & USAGE
Present Tense

One use of **present tense** is called the "literary present," and it is a characteristic of the formal style used for a literary analysis. Using the literary present means referring to events in a written work using the present tense—as if they are currently happening. For example, in a summary or analysis of *To Kill a Mockingbird*, a writer might note: "When Jem goes back to the Radley place, his pants are folded …" The literary present reminds us that each time we open a book, the story takes place anew for the reader.

My Notes

_____

_____

_____

INDEPENDENT READING LINK

Read and Discuss

Choose three chunks of text from one of your independent reading selections. Make them about the same length as the chunks from *To Kill a Mockingbird*. As you answer the following questions for each chunk, notice how each level adds a layer of complexity to your understanding of the material. (Level 1) What does the text say? (Level 2) What does the text mean? (Level 3) Why does it matter?

Two Views of "One Shot"

LEARNING STRATEGIES:
Close Reading, Discussion
Groups, Graphic Organizer

Learning Targets

- Analyze how an author uses multiple literary elements in one passage to develop a theme.
- Compare a key scene in text and film to identify how literary elements are portrayed in each medium.

Preview

In this passage from *To Kill a Mockingbird*, you will read a short but important scene and compare this scene to the film version.

Setting a Purpose for Reading

- Highlight references to the title of the novel.
- Circle unknown words and phrases. Try to determine the meaning of the words by using context clues, word parts, or a dictionary.

My Notes

rudiments: basics

Novel

from

To Kill a Mockingbird

(Chapter 10)

1   When he gave us our air rifles Atticus wouldn't teach us to shoot. Uncle Jack instructed us in the **rudiments** thereof; he said Atticus wasn't interested in guns. Atticus said to Jem one day, "I'd rather you shot at tin cans in the back yard, but I know you'll go after birds. Shoot all the bluejays you want, if you can hit 'em, but remember it's a sin to kill a mockingbird."

2   That was the only time I ever heard Atticus say it was a sin to do something, and I asked Miss Maudie about it.

3   "Your father's right," she said. "Mockingbirds don't do one thing but make music for us to enjoy. They don't eat up people's gardens, don't nest in corncribs, they don't do one thing but sing their hearts out for us. That's why it's a sin to kill a mockingbird."

Collaborative Discussion: Chapter 10

- Based on your understanding of Atticus's character, why do you think he isn't interested in guns?
- How does Miss Maudie's information about mockingbirds add to Atticus's comment that "it's a sin to kill a mockingbird"?
- Based on this passage, what might a mockingbird symbolize?

1. Work with a small group to conduct a close reading of Chapter 10. Choose one of the following literary elements to focus on: character, conflict, or setting. Use sticky notes to mark the text for evidence of the importance of your chosen literary element.

Working from the Text

2. After you discuss each of the literary elements and textual evidence with your group, you will view a film clip of the scene. Take notes below on how each of the elements is portrayed similarly or differently in the film.

Setting	Conflict	Character

3. Compare the two versions of the scene. Why is each appropriate for the medium of film or literature?

4. If the mad dog symbolizes the madness of racism, what is a possible theme introduced in this chapter?

My Notes

_____

_____

_____

_____

_____

_____

_____

_____

_____

_____

_____

Two Views of "One Shot"

Check Your Understanding

Consider the following thesis statement:

In Chapter 10, Harper Lee uses the killing of the mad dog as a symbolic act to develop the theme that racism is a dangerous threat to any peaceful community.

Write your own thesis statement about how the literary element that you analyzed from Chapter 10 contributes to a theme.

Writing to Sources: Explanatory Text

Compare and contrast the scene in the book vs. the depiction in the film. Explain how they are alike and where they differ. Be sure to:

- Include a well-developed topic sentence.
- Include elements that are both similar and different.
- Cite details from the text and the film to support your explanation.

Pin the Quote on Atticus

Learning Targets
- Write an interpretive statement about the significance of literary elements.
- Gather textual evidence to generate theme statements.

Preview
In this activity, you will read an excerpt from Chapter 11 in order to analyze conflict and character.

Setting a Purpose for Reading
- Underline descriptions of settings and character.
- Circle unknown words and phrases. Try to determine the meaning of the words by using context clues, word parts, or a dictionary.
- Draw a star next to any indications of conflict.

Novel

from

To Kill a Mockingbird

(Chapter 11)

1 When we were small, Jem and I **confined** our activities to the southern neighborhood, but when I was well into the second grade at school and tormenting Boo Radley became **passé**, the business section of Maycomb drew us frequently up the street past the real property of Mrs. Henry Lafayette Dubose. It was impossible to go to town without passing her house unless we wished to walk a mile out of the way. Previous minor encounters with her left me with no desire for more, but Jem said I had to grow up some time.

2 Mrs. Dubose lived alone except for a Negro girl in constant attendance, two doors up the street from us in a house with steep front steps and a dog-trot hall. She was very old; she spent most of each day in bed and the rest of it in a wheelchair. It was rumored that she kept a CSA pistol concealed among her numerous shawls and wraps.

3 Jem and I hated her. If she was on the porch when we passed, we would be raked by her **wrathful** gaze, subjected to ruthless interrogations regarding our behavior, and given a **melancholy** prediction on what we would amount to when we grew up, which was always nothing. We had long ago given up the idea of walking past her house on the opposite side of the street; that only made her raise her voice and let the whole neighborhood in on it.

4 We could do nothing to please her. If I said as sunnily as I could, "Hey, Mrs. Dubose," I would receive for an answer, "Don't you say hey to me, you ugly girl! You say good afternoon, Mrs. Dubose!"

GRAMMAR & USAGE
Independent Clauses

An **independent clause** is a group of words that contains a subject and a verb and can stand alone as a sentence. A sentence having more than one independent clause is a compound sentence. One way to combine two such clauses is to use a coordinating conjunction: *and, or, but.* Most sentences with multiple independent clauses need a comma before the coordinating conjunction.

Example: *I did not remember our mother, but Jem did … .*

---

confined: restricted
passé: out of fashion

wrathful: angry
melancholy: gloomy

My Notes

LEARNING STRATEGIES:
Skimming/Scanning, Diffusing, Marking the Text, Drafting, Discussion Groups

Pin the Quote on Atticus

apoplectic: extremely angry

livid: enraged

My Notes

5   She was vicious. Once she heard Jem refer to our father as "Atticus" and her reaction was **apoplectic**. Besides being the sassiest, most disrespectful mutts who ever passed her way, we were told that it was quite a pity our father had not remarried after our mother's death. A lovelier lady than our mother never lived, she said, and it was heartbreaking the way Atticus Finch let her children run wild. I did not remember our mother, but Jem did—he would tell me about her sometimes—and he went **livid** when Mrs. Dubose shot us this message.

Working from the Text

1. Consider the significance of character, conflict, and setting in the passage you just read. Ask yourself: Why are these literary elements important? How do they connect to the larger issues in the novel?

   Use the following sentence stems to generate an interpretive statement about each of these elements.

   - The character of Mrs. Dubose represents ...

   - The conflict between the children and Mrs. Dubose is similar to ...

   - The setting of Mrs. Dubose's house, halfway between the Finch home and the town, is significant because ...

2. In the following quotation, Atticus gives Jem advice on how to deal with Mrs. Dubose. Consider what this advice might be foreshadowing.

   "You just hold your head high and be a gentleman. Whatever she says to you, it's your job not to let her make you mad."

   Rewrite Atticus's advice as a statement or "life lesson."

3. **Independent Practice:** As you read the rest of Chapter 11, use sticky notes to record textual evidence of Atticus's advice to Jem and Scout concerning Mrs. Dubose.

Identifying Themes

4. Work with your class to gather evidence of Atticus's "life lessons" from other chapters. Create and illustrate a poster with the quotes and life lessons.

5. Use the quotes to identify themes based on the lessons Atticus wants his children to learn as they come of age. Create a web of these and other themes Harper Lee explores in Part One of *To Kill a Mockingbird*.

When identifying themes, keep in mind the following:

• A theme is a message, not just a topic, and it cannot be just a word, such as *prejudice*. A theme from *To Kill a Mockingbird* would be "Prejudice is based on fear."

• Avoid clichés such as "Blood is thicker than water."

• Don't state a theme as an order: "People must not be racist."

• Themes should be universal, not limited to the characters in a novel. "Scout is a tomboy" is not a theme.

Part One:
Themes
Connected to
Coming of Age

Pin the Quote on Atticus

pick

My Notes

Language and Writer's Craft: Incorporating Quotations

Quotations are powerful pieces of text evidence that can be used to support your literary analysis. However, quotations must be integrated into the body of your analysis smoothly and carefully, so that it is clear how the quoted text relates to the logical flow of ideas in your writing.

Use the **TLQC** (Transition, Lead-in, Quote, Commentary) method to integrate your quotes, with commentary, in a literary analysis essay:

- **Transition:** A transitional word, phrase, or clause can be used to begin introducing your quote. The type of transition will depend on how the quotation follows from the previous idea. Some commonly used transitions are *for example, in addition, as a result, regardless,* and *after all.*

- **Lead-in:** Give background for the quote by identifying the situation in which it occurs, who is speaking, or any other information necessary to set the quote in context.

- **Quote:** Place quoted text in quotation marks, and remember to include a parenthetical citation.

- **Commentary:** Follow up the quote with an explanation of what the quote shows or how it is relevant to the point you are making.

PRACTICE Identify the transition, lead-in, quote, and commentary in the following example:

> For example, Jem never loses his calm as he reads to Mrs. Dubose. Scout observes that "Through the weeks he had cultivated an expression of polite and detached interest, which he would present to her in answer to her most blood-curdling inventions" (146). Jem is taking his father's advice and growing into the kind of man who will not get dragged down by other people's anger.

Check Your Understanding

Choose a literary element (character, conflict, or setting) from Chapter 11 and explain how it connects to the larger issues in the novel.

INDEPENDENT READING LINK

Read and Research

Choose one of your independent reading selections. Identify the themes in the selection. Make a web like the one you made for the themes in *To Kill a Mockingbird*. Record your observations about your independent reading selection.

Explanatory Writing Prompt

Analyze how character, conflict, or setting contribute to a coming-of-age theme in Chapter 11. Be sure to:

- Begin with a topic sentence that connects your chosen literary element to a theme.

- Include textual evidence in the form of direct quotations from Chapter 11.

- Provide commentary explaining how your quotes support your analysis.

Shifting Perspectives

Learning Targets
- Create an outline for an analytical essay about how literary elements contribute to a theme.
- Analyze the purpose of literary elements and the effects they have on readers.

LEARNING STRATEGIES:
Brainstorming, Close Reading, Marking the Text

Research Reflections
1. **Discuss:** Before you begin Part 2 of the novel, review your notes from the first half of this unit in which you researched and presented the context of the novel's setting and publication.
   - How did the experience of researching and presenting context enhance your understanding of the novel?
   - How has it informed your understanding of how readers would have responded to the text in 1960?
   - What specific topics from the presentations are relevant to the issues raised so far in the novel?

2. Part of coming of age is understanding that your perspective of the world is not the only one—that other perspectives based on different cultures, nationalities, religions, political beliefs, customs, languages, and values are just as real and valid as your own. Brainstorm experiences that you have had that have exposed you to different perspectives.

My Notes

Close Reading: Chapter 12
3. You will conduct a close reading of a passage from Chapter 12, marking the text for evidence of how setting, character, and conflict contribute to following theme:
Coming of age involves recognizing different perspectives.

Working from the Text
4. Work with your class to complete the outline that follows for an essay about how literary elements in this passage contribute to the theme "Coming of age involves recognizing different perspectives."

Shifting Perspectives

Outline for a Passage-Analysis Essay

I. **Introduction:**

   Hook: Anecdote, Quote, Question, or Statement of Intrigue

   Thesis:

II. **Body (Support Paragraph)**

   Topic Sentence:

   Textual Evidence:

III. **Body (Support Paragraph):**

   Topic Sentence:

   Textual Evidence:

V. **Body (Support Paragraph):**

   Topic Sentence:

   Textual Evidence:

VI. **Conclusion:**

   Restate Thesis:

   Literal/Interpretive/Universal Statements:

5. Look for more textual evidence in Chapter 12 to support the topic sentences in your outline.

Check Your Understanding

How can perspective and context enhance your understanding of the novel?

Drafting the Embedded Assessment

Draft an explanatory paragraph that analyzes two different literary elements from the text. Consider the purpose the author had in using those literary elements and the effect they have on readers. Remember to include all the features that you have practiced. Be sure to:

- Begin with an analytical claim about the use of two different literary elements.
- Include at least one example of each of the literary elements.
- Use transitional devices to show the relationship between examples and commentaries.
- Provide a conclusion that summarizes the thesis.

6. **Independent Practice:** After you read Chapters 13–14, choose a passage to reread and mark for at least two different literary elements. Use the outline above as a model of an outline for your passage analysis.

A Solitary Light

My Notes

Learning Targets

- Compare and contrast how a theme is developed in a key scene in film and text.
- Conduct a close read and analyze significant literary elements.

Making Inferences

1. **Quickwrite:** Your teacher will show you a photo (or photos) of Atticus and Scout as a visual prompt for exploring how character, setting, and conflict are conveyed in a film text. What can you infer from the image about each of these literary elements?

Close Reading: Chapter 15

2. Conduct a close reading of the passage in Chapter 15 that begins with a description of the Maycomb jail and continues until the end of the chapter. Work with a small group to record textual evidence of significant literary elements in the graphic organizer below.

Setting

Conflict

Character

Other (plot, symbol, motif)

Working from the Text

3. Work together to identify a theme. Ask yourself what Scout, Dill, or Jem could learn from this experience, even if they may not recognize it yet.

4. Write at least two interpretive statements about how different literary elements contributed to the theme.

5. As you view a film version of this scene, use the graphic organizer below to take notes on the cinematic techniques. Review cinematic techniques in Unit 2 if necessary.

Angles/Framing	Lighting	Sound	Other
(High/low angles, eye level, close-up, two shot, long shot)	(Bottom/side/front/back, high/low key)	(Diegetic [including dialogue], non-diegetic)	(Camera movements, editing techniques)

6. **Discuss:** What are some of the differences between the film and text versions? What changes in dialogue were made?

My Notes

A Solitary Light

Check Your Understanding

Why might changes have been made in the transformation from text to film?

Explanatory Writing Prompt

Compare and contrast the text and film versions of this scene. How do different literary and cinematic elements contribute to a theme? Which do you think is more effective? Be sure to:

- Begin with a topic sentence or thesis that clearly states a theme.
- Include textual evidence from the text and the film.
- Provide commentary comparing and contrasting the use of literary elements and cinematic techniques.

7. **Independent Practice:** Read Chapter 16 and choose a key scene to visualize and sketch. Annotate your scene with textual evidence and commentary to explain the choices you made in details, angles, framing, and background.

Analyzing Atticus's Closing Argument

Learning Targets
- Recognize the rhetorical appeals used in a speech.
- In a written paragraph, compare and contrast the use of rhetorical appeals in a key scene in two mediums.

LEARNING STRATEGIES:
Rereading, Marking the Text, SMELL, Graphic Organizer, Drafting

Working from the Text: Chapters 17–19

1. Review the testimony presented in Chapters 17–19. Which rhetorical appeals do the lawyers and witnesses use? Find textual evidence of each of the following:

    Logos: an appeal to logic or reason

    Ethos: an appeal to ethics or the character of the speaker

    Pathos: an appeal to senses or emotions

Discuss:
- Which speakers rely primarily on pathos?
- Which speakers would have had difficulty appealing to ethos?
- What evidence comes to light through appeals to logos?

Preview
In this activity, you will read, take note of rhetorical appeals, and analyze Atticus's closing argument from Chapter 20.

Setting a Purpose for Reading
- Highlight rhetorical appeals (ethos, logos, and pathos).
- Circle unknown words and phrases. Try to determine the meaning of the words by using context clues, word parts, or a dictionary.
- Draw a star next to any elements of an argument (hook, claim, evidence, counterclaims, and call to action).

My Notes

Analyzing Atticus's Closing Argument

minute: tiny
sifting: sorting

iota: small quantity

persisted: continued with
determination
contraband: something
forbidden by the law

GRAMMAR & USAGE
Parallel Structure

Parallel structure is often used in persuasive speech because it emphasizes an important aspect of the related ideas, creates a pleasing rhythm, and helps the speaker build to a point.

Consider this part of Atticus's argument: "... the assumption ... that *all* Negroes lie, that *all* Negroes are basically immoral beings, that *all* Negro men are not to be trusted...." This sentence uses parallel relative clauses beginning with *that*. Consider how Atticus's use of parallel structure adds to the force of his argument.

Novel

from

To Kill a Mockingbird

(Chapter 20)

by Harper Lee

1 "Gentlemen," he was saying, "I shall be brief, but I would like to use my remaining time with you to remind you that this case is not a difficult one, it requires no **minute sifting** of complicated facts, but it does require you to be sure beyond all reasonable doubt as to the guilt of the defendant. To begin with, this case should never have come to trial. This case is as simple as black and white.

2 "The state has not produced one **iota** of medical evidence to the effect that the crime Tom Robinson is charged with ever took place. It has relied instead upon the testimony of two witnesses whose evidence has not only been called into serious question on cross-examination, but has been flatly contradicted by the defendant. The defendant is not guilty, but somebody in this courtroom is.

3 "I have nothing but pity in my heart for the chief witness for the state, but my pity does not extend so far as to her putting a man's life at stake, which she has done in an effort to get rid of her own guilt.

4 "I say guilt, gentlemen, because it was guilt that motivated her. She has committed no crime, she has merely broken a rigid and time-honored code of our society, a code so severe that whoever breaks it is hounded from our midst as unfit to live with. She is the victim of cruel poverty and ignorance, but I cannot pity her: she is white. She knew full well the enormity of her offense, but because her desires were stronger than the code she was breaking, she **persisted** in breaking it. She persisted, and her subsequent reaction is something that all of us have known at one time or another. She did something every child has done—she tried to put the evidence of her offense away from her. But in this case she was no child hiding stolen **contraband**: she struck out at her victim—of necessity she must put him away from her—he must be removed from her presence, from this world. She must destroy the evidence of her offense.

5 "What was the evidence of her offense? Tom Robinson, a human being. She must put Tom Robinson away from her. Tom Robinson was her daily reminder of what she did. What did she do? She tempted a Negro.

6 "She was white, and she tempted a Negro. She did something that in our society is unspeakable: she kissed a black man. Not an old Uncle, but a strong young Negro man. No code mattered to her before she broke it, but it came crashing down on her afterwards.

7 "Her father saw it, and the defendant has testified as to his remarks. What did her father do? We don't know, but there is circumstantial evidence to indicate that Mayella Ewell was beaten savagely by someone who led almost exclusively with his left. We do know in part what Mr. Ewell did: he did what any God-fearing, persevering, respectable white man would do under the circumstances—he swore out a warrant, no doubt signing it with his left hand, and Tom Robinson now sits before you, having taken the oath with the only good hand he possesses—his right hand.

8 "And so a quiet, respectable, humble Negro who had the unmitigated **temerity** to 'feel sorry' for a white woman has had to put his word against two white people's. I need not remind you of their appearance and conduct on the stand—you saw them for yourselves. The witnesses for the state, with the exception of the sheriff of Maycomb County, have presented themselves to you gentlemen, to this court, in the **cynical** confidence that their testimony would not be doubted, confident that you gentlemen would go along with them on the assumption—the evil assumption—that *all* Negroes lie, that *all* Negroes are basically immoral beings, that *all* Negro men are not to be trusted around our women, an assumption one associates with minds of their **caliber**.

9 "Which, gentlemen, we know is in itself a lie as black as Tom Robinson's skin, a lie I do not have to point out to you. You know the truth, and the truth is this: some Negroes lie, some Negroes are immoral, some Negro men are not to be trusted around women— black or white. But this is a truth that applies to the human race and to no particular race of men. There is not a person in this courtroom who has never told a lie, who has never done an immoral thing, and there is no man living who has never looked upon a woman without desire."

10 Atticus paused and took out his handkerchief. Then he took off his glasses and wiped them, and we saw another "first": we had never seen him sweat—he was one of those men whose faces never **perspired**, but now it was shining tan.

11 "One more thing, gentlemen, before I quit. Thomas Jefferson once said that all men are created equal, a phrase that the Yankees and the distaff side of the Executive branch in Washington are fond of hurling at us. There is a **tendency** in this year of grace, 1935, for certain people to use this phrase out of context, to satisfy all conditions. The most ridiculous example I can think of is that the people who run public education promote the stupid and **idle** along with the industrious—because all men are created equal, educators will gravely tell you, the children left behind suffer terrible feelings of inferiority. We know all men are not created equal in the sense some people would have us believe—some people are smarter than others, some people have more opportunity because they're born with it, some men make more money than others, some ladies make better cakes than others—some people are born gifted beyond the normal scope of most men.

12 "But there is one way in this country in which all men are created equal—there is one human institution that makes a **pauper** the equal of a Rockefeller, the stupid man the equal of an Einstein, and the ignorant man the equal of any college president. That institution, gentlemen, is a court. It can be the Supreme Court of the United States or the humblest J.P. court in the land, or this honorable court which you serve. Our courts have their faults, as does any human institution, but in this country our courts are the great levelers, and in our courts all men are created equal.

13 "I'm no **idealist** to believe firmly in the integrity of our courts and in the jury system—that is no ideal to me, it is a living, working reality. Gentlemen, a court is no better than each man of you sitting before me on this jury. A court is only as sound as its jury, and a jury is only as sound as the men who make it up. I am confident that you gentlemen will review without passion the evidence you have heard, come to a decision, and restore this defendant to his family. In the name of God, do your duty."

14 Atticus's voice had dropped, and as he turned away from the jury he said something I did not catch. He said it more to himself than to the court. I punched Jem. "What'd he say?"

15 "'In the name of God, believe him,' I think that's what he said."

temerity: recklessness

WORD CONNECTIONS

Roots and Affixes

Circumstantial is an adjective meaning "having to do with certain facts or conditions." The prefix circum- derives from the Latin word *circum*, meaning "around." English has many words beginning with circum-. They include *circumference*, *circumnavigate*, and *circumvent*.

cynical: distrusting the motives of others
caliber: quality
perspired: sweat

tendency: inclination to do something

idle: not working

My Notes

_____
_____

pauper: very poor person

_____
_____

idealist: person who pursues noble principles

_____
_____
_____
_____
_____
_____

Analyzing Atticus's Closing Argument

Second Read

- Reread the novel excerpt to answer these text-dependent questions.
- Write any additional questions you have about the text in your Reader/Writer Notebook.

2. **Key Ideas and Details:** What does Atticus mean when he says, "This case is as simple as black and white"?

3. **Key Ideas and Details:** What tone does Atticus use when describing Mayella to the court?

4. **Key Ideas and Details:** Why is it significant that Atticus is sweating while delivering his closing statement?

5. **Key Ideas and Details:** According to Atticus, what is the one way that all men are created equal?

6. **Key Ideas and Details:** How does Atticus feel about Tom Robinson? How can you tell?

Working from the Text

7. Perform a close reading of Atticus's closing statement. Use the SMELL strategy to complete your analysis.

S = Sender-receiver relationship. Atticus is the sender. The jury and the audience are the receivers. What is the relationship among Atticus, the jury, and the audience? Whom does Atticus mean to influence with his statement? What attitudes and assumptions does his target audience hold toward his subject? Toward Atticus himself?

M = Message. What is Atticus's message? Summarize the statements made in his closing argument.

E = Emotional strategies. Does Atticus use any statements that are meant to get an emotional reaction from his audience? Explain. If so, what is the desired effect?

L = Logical strategies. Does Atticus use any statements or appeals that are logical? Explain. How does the logic (or its absence) affect the message?

L = Language. Look for specific words and phrases used by Atticus, and consider how the language affects his message.

My Notes

_____

_____

_____

_____

_____

_____

_____

_____

_____

_____

_____

_____

_____

_____

_____

_____

_____

_____

_____

_____

INDEPENDENT READING LINK

Read and Respond

Examine the texts you have read independently to analyze the voice of the main character and one or two of the most important supporting characters. Since they are all coming-of-age texts, what similarities, if any, did you notice in the voices? How does the voice contribute to your understanding of the character? Is the voice of a main character in one text stronger than those in the other texts? Why?

Analyzing Atticus's Closing Argument

8. As you watch the film version of the courtroom scene, fill out the chart below with specific details from the scene.

What images does the director present to the audience?	What images does the director consciously choose NOT to present to the audience?	What do you notice about the relationship between the speech and the images?	What changes or deletions do you notice in the text of Atticus's speech?

My Notes

Check Your Understanding

Which rhetorical appeal does Atticus rely on most heavily for his closing argument? Why?

Writing to Sources: Argument

Which version of Atticus's appeal is more effective—the one in the text or the one in the film? Write an argument that addresses the question and supports your position with evidence from the text and the film. Be sure to:

- Write a precise claim and support it with valid reasoning and evidence from the film and the text.
- Integrate quotes from the text using the TLQC method (transition, lead-in, quote, and commentary).
- Provide a concluding statement that follows from the argument you have presented.

9. **Independent Practice:** As you read Chapters 21–23, take notes on the different characters' reactions to the verdict.

Aftermath and Reflection

Learning Targets

- Analyze the significance of literary elements in a passage in relation to a theme of the novel.
- Write a thesis statement and topic sentences for an essay that explains how literary elements contribute to a theme of the novel.

Socratic Seminar

1. Your teacher will lead you in a Socratic Seminar in which you discuss the verdict of the trial. Read the questions and write your responses below. Then, write at least one question at each Level to use in the discussion.

   - Why is Jem so optimistic before he hears the verdict?

   - How and why is Scout's reaction to the verdict different from Jem's?

2. After your discussion, work with your group to co-construct a statement synthesizing your response to the question(s):

3. Work with your class to co-construct a statement about how the trial was a coming-of-age experience for Jem.

4. Revisit the theme web that you created in Activity 3.16, and consider the lessons Scout and Jem learn in Part 2 as they interact with the world outside their neighborhood. Add more thematic statements related to coming of age to your web.

LEARNING STRATEGIES:
Socratic Seminar, Levels of Questions, Graphic Organizer, Revising

My Notes

Aftermath and Reflection

Working from the Text: Chapter 24

5. As you read Chapter 24, consider the significance of the chapter to the meaning of the novel as a whole. Complete the graphic organizer below by analyzing how different literary elements contribute to a recurring theme of the novel.

Analysis of a Literary Element in Chapter 24	Textual Evidence (Quote from text)	Theme of the Novel as a Whole	Evidence of This Theme in Another Chapter
Character: Grace Merriweather's character represents the irony of someone who claims to be religious but is actually a hypocrite.		Racism is a disease that infects a person's mind and soul.	
Setting: The setting of the missionary tea in the Finches' living room			
Conflict:			
Plot event:			

6. **Discuss:** How does Scout's perspective on what it means to be a lady evolve during this scene? How are the events in this chapter a coming-of-age experience for her?

Language and Writer's Craft: Topic Sentences and Transitions

Topic sentences and transitions are important ways of bringing structure and flow to your writing. Your thesis—your assertion about the topic—will be stated in the introduction of your essay. Body paragraphs then explain the main ideas that work together to support your thesis. A **topic sentence** of a body paragraph is a statement of the main idea of that paragraph.

Transitions guide readers through your essay by showing how ideas are connected. Some transitions, such as *for example* and *therefore*, often work to provide coherence among sentences—to link one sentence to the next. Common transitions are shown in the table below.

Similarity	Contrast	Cause/Effect	Introduction
Likewise	In contrast	As a result	For example
Similarly	However	Therefore	For instance
In the same way	Conversely	Consequently	In particular
		Accordingly	To illustrate

Other transitions help you link paragraphs and main ideas to your thesis. A **three-fold transition** is an example of this type of transition.

Three-fold transitions help you make logical connections between your points in an essay. They are typically used to introduce the second, third, and remaining body paragraphs, as a way to call the reader's mind back to the thesis. A three-fold transition sentence does the following:

- refers subtly to the idea discussed in the previous paragraph
- refers briefly to the overall thesis idea
- refers more specifically to the new idea to be discussed in this paragraph

PRACTICE Add at least two transitions to the following paragraph.

To Kill a Mockingbird highlights the difference between two methods of education. Miss Caroline favors a structured, inflexible method in which students must all meet the same set of expectations. "We don't write in the first grade, we print. You won't learn to write until you're in the third grade" (27). Atticus favors a flexible approach to education that reflects the unique gifts of each child.

Aftermath and Reflection

7. Work with your discussion group to write a thesis statement and topic sentences for an essay about how the literary elements in Chapter 24 contribute to a theme of the work as a whole.

Thesis:

Topic Sentence:

Topic Sentence:

Topic Sentence:

8. Work with your group to revise at least one of your topic sentences using three-fold transitions. Sample: *After recognizing the irony in her society, Scout matures even further as she recognizes the strength of Miss Maudie's quiet, calm responses to her conflict with Grace Merriweather.*

Check Your Understanding

Explain the significance of Chapter 24 and how it relates to the novel as a whole.

Drafting the Embedded Assessment

Draft an introductory paragraph for your essay about how the literary elements in Chapter 24 contribute to a theme of the work as a whole. Be sure to:

- State your thesis clearly in the first sentence.
- Present your main supporting details.
- Provide a transition to the body paragraphs.

9. **Independent Practice:** As you read Chapters 25–27, consider passages that you could analyze to show how literary elements contribute to a theme of the novel as a whole.

Standing in Borrowed Shoes

Learning Targets
- Identify character traits and create a character profile poster collaboratively.
- Evaluate how primary and secondary characters and their interactions contribute to the development of a novel's themes.

LEARNING STRATEGIES:
Quickwrite, Graphic Organizer, Marking the Text

Analyzing Characters

1. **Quickwrite:** Consider the following quote from the novel:

   "Atticus was right. One time he said you never really know a man until you stand in his shoes and walk around in them."—*Scout*

   When have Scout, Jem, or Dill had to look at the world from other people's perspectives? What have they learned from other residents of Maycomb?

2. Work in a small group to list the *primary* (major) and *secondary* (minor) characters you can identify from the novel. Indicate whether these characters are **static** or **dynamic**. When you have finished, make notes on the thematic subjects that secondary characters might represent in the novel.

Literary Terms
A **flat** or **static character** is uncomplicated, staying the same without changing or growing during the story. A **round** or **dynamic character** evolves and grows in the story and has a complex personality.

Primary Characters	Static or Dynamic	Secondary Characters and Thematic Topics They Represent

WORD CONNECTIONS

Roots and Affixes

The word *dynamic* comes from the Greek word meaning "powerful." The root *dyna* appears in *dynamo*, *dynamite*, and *dynasty*. *Static* also comes from a Greek word, *statikos*, referring to something firm or fixed. Other English words with the root *stat* include *status*, *station*, *statistics*, and *statue*.

My Notes

_____

_____

_____

_____

_____

_____

_____

_____

Standing in Borrowed Shoes

3. Working with a partner, create a character profile poster. Your poster should include the following elements:

- a picture or graphic representation of the character
- a physical description from the novel
- a list of several adjectives describing the character's personality, values, and/ or motives
- a description of the plot events in which this character is involved
- a quotation about him or her from another character
- a quotation by the character that reveals his or her values

4. As you view the posters your class creates, take notes in the graphic organizer below on at least two characters other than your own.

Character and Description	Events Involving the Character	Textual Evidence	Theme Related to This Character

Check Your Understanding

Work with a partner to review the Events column of your graphic organizer. Choose an event that you think is important and locate the most significant passage describing that event. Explain why this passage is important using text evidence to support your answer.

Writing to Sources: Explanatory Text

Explain how the author uses the voices of her characters to develop and distinguish their personalities. Be sure to:

- Describe the voice of each character you write about.
- Include multiple direct quotations from the text to support your claims.
- Include transitions between points and a statement that provides a conclusion.

5. **Independent Practice:** As you read Chapter 28, annotate each page with sticky notes. Pay close attention to the literary elements, and note how the tone shifts with different plot events.

Controversy in Context

Learning Targets
- Analyze a nonfiction text about various controversies surrounding the novel *To Kill a Mockingbird*.
- Evaluate the techniques and effectiveness of an argument.
- Use the RAFT strategy to compose an argument in writing.

Literal and Figurative
1. **Quickwrite:** Chapter 27 ended with the line "Thus began our longest journey together." What are the literal and figurative meanings of the word "journey"? How is reading a novel similar to and different from taking a journey?

Preview
In this activity, you will read an essay about the controversies in *To Kill a Mockingbird* and analyze the historical context in which it's set.

Setting a Purpose for Reading
- Underline the evidence in the arguments for and against the novel.
- Circle unknown words and phrases. Try to determine the meaning of the words by using context clues, word parts, or a dictionary.

ABOUT THE AUTHOR
Nicholas J. Karolides is an associate lecturer and professor emeritus of English at the University of Wisconsin-River Falls. The author and editor of books for young adults, he has also written about the topics of the politics of suppression and **censorship** of literary works.

> **LEARNING STRATEGIES:**
> Quickwrite, Marking the Text, RAFT

> **My Notes**

Essay

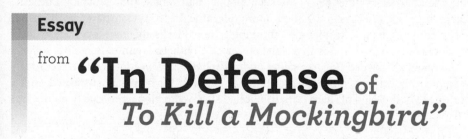

from **"In Defense** of *To Kill a Mockingbird"**

by Nicholas J. Karolides, et al.

1   The critical career of *To Kill a Mockingbird* is a late twentieth-century case study of censorship. When Harper Lee's novel about a small southern town and its prejudices was published in 1960, the book received favorable reviews in professional journals and the popular press. Typical of that opinion, Booklist's reviewer called the book "**melodramatic**" and noted "traces of sermonizing," but the book was recommended for

> **ACADEMIC VOCABULARY**
> The word **censor** means "to examine materials for objectionable content." *Censor* is a noun when used to describe a person and a verb when used to describe the action of censoring. The word **censorship** (*n.*) derives from *censor* and describes the act of suppressing public speech or publication of materials deemed to be offensive by the censor.

melodramatic: emotionally exaggerated

Controversy in Context

wit: intelligent humor

My Notes

restrained: held back

sporadic: occasional

espoused: supported
assassinated: murdered

orator: speaker

tolerable: bearable
sustained: kept alive
laden: filled
profanity: swearing

WORD CONNECTIONS

Roots and Affixes

The word *psychological* (*adj.*) means "mental" or "of the mind." The prefix psycho- comes from the Greek word *psychē*, meaning "soul" or "spirit." Other words with the prefix psycho- include *psychoanalysis*, *psychobabble*, and *psychodrama*.

library purchase, commending its "rare blend of **wit** and compassion." Reviewers did not suggest that the book was young-adult literature, or that it belonged in adolescent collections; perhaps that is why no one mentioned the book's language or violence. In any event, reviewers seemed inclined to agree that *To Kill a Mockingbird* was a worthwhile interpretation of the South's existing social structures during the 1930s. In 1961 the book won the Pulitzer Prize Award, the Alabama Library Association Book Award, and the Brotherhood Award of the National Conference of Christians and Jews. It seemed that Harper Lee's blend of family history, local custom, and **restrained** sermonizing was important reading, and with a young girl between the ages of six and nine as the main character, *To Kill a Mockingbird* moved rapidly into junior and senior high school libraries and curriculum. The book was not destined to be studied by college students. Southern literature's critics rarely mentioned it; few university professors found it noteworthy enough to "teach" as an exemplary southern novel.

2 By the mid-sixties *To Kill a Mockingbird* had a solid place in junior and senior high American literature studies. Once discovered by southern parents, the book's solid place became shaky indeed. **Sporadic** lawsuits arose. In most cases the complaint against the book was by conservatives who disliked the portrayal of whites. Typically, the Hanover County School Board in Virginia first ruled the book "immoral," then withdrew their criticism and declared the ruckus "was all a mistake" (*Newsletter on Intellectual Freedom* 1966). By 1968 the National Education Association listed the book among those which drew the most criticism from private groups. Ironically it was rated directly behind *Little Black Sambo* (*Newsletter* 1968). And the seventies arrived.

3 Things had changed in the South during the sixties. Two national leaders who had supported integration and had **espoused** the ideals of racial equality were **assassinated** in southern regions. When John F. Kennedy was killed in Texas on November 27, 1963, many southerners were shocked. Populist attitudes of racism were declining, and in the aftermath of the tragedy southern politics began to change. Lyndon Johnson gained the presidency: blacks began to seek and win political offices. Black leader Martin Luther King had stressed the importance of racial equality, always using Mahatma Gandhi's strategy of nonviolent action and civil disobedience. A brilliant **orator**, King grew up in the South; the leader of the [Southern Christian Leadership Conference], he lived in Atlanta, Georgia. In 1968, while working on a garbage strike in Memphis, King was killed. The death of the 1965 Nobel Peace Prize winner was further embarrassment for white southerners. Whites began to look at public values anew, and gradually southern blacks found experiences in the South more **tolerable**. In 1971 one Atlanta businessman observed [in *Ebony*], "The liberation thinking is here. Blacks are more together. With the doors opening wider, this area is the mecca. ..." Southern arguments against *To Kill a Mockingbird* subsided. *The Newsletter on Intellectual Freedom* contained no record of southern court cases during the seventies or eighties. The book had **sustained** itself during the first period of sharp criticism; it had survived regional protests from the area it depicted.

4 The second onslaught of attack came from new groups of censors, and it came during the late seventies and early eighties. Private sectors in the Midwest and suburban East began to demand the book's removal from school libraries. Groups, such as the Eden Valley School Committee in Minnesota, claimed that the book was too **laden** with **profanity** (*Newsletter* 1978). In Vernon, New York, Reverend Carl Hadley threatened to establish a private Christian school because public school libraries contained such "filthy, trashy sex novels" as *A Separate Peace* and *To Kill a Mockingbird* (*Newsletter* 1980). And finally, blacks began to censor the book. In Warren, Indiana, three blacks resigned from the township Human Relations Advisory Council when the Warren County school administration refused to remove the book from Warren junior high

school classes. They contended that the book "does psychological damage to the positive integration process and represents institutionalized racism" (*Newsletter* 1982). Thus, censorship of *To Kill a Mockingbird* swung from the conservative right to the liberal left. Factions representing racists, religious **sects**, concerned parents, and minority groups vocally demanded the book's removal from public schools. ...

sects: small groups

5   The censors' reactions to *To Kill a Mockingbird* were reactions to issues of race and justice. Their moves to ban the book derive from their own **perspectives** of the book's theme. Their "reader response" criticism, usually based on one reading of the book, was personal and political. They needed to ban the book because it told them something about American society that they did not want to hear. That is precisely the problem facing any author of realistic fiction. Once the story becomes real, it can become grim. An author will use first-person flashback in a story in order to let the reader lie in another time, another place. Usually the storyteller is returning for a second view of the scene. The teller has experienced the events before and the story is being retold because the scene has left the storyteller uneasy. As the storyteller recalls the past, both the listener and the teller see events in a new light. Both are working through troubled times in search of meaning. In the case of *To Kill a Mockingbird* the first-person retelling is not pleasant, but the underlying significance is with the narrative. The youthful personalities who are recalled are hopeful. Scout tells us of a time past when white people would lynch or convict a man because of the color of his skin. She also shows us three children who refuse to believe that the system is right, and she leaves us with the thought that most people will be nice if seen for what they are: humans with **frailties**. When discussing literary criticism, Theo D'Haen suggested [in *Text to Reader*] that the good literary work should have a life within the world and be "part of the ongoing activities of that world." *To Kill a Mockingbird* continues to have life within the world; its ongoing activities in the **realm** of censorship show that it is a book which deals with regional moralism. The children in the story seem very human; they worry about their own identification, they **defy** parental rules, and they cry over injustices. They mature in Harper Lee's novel, and they lose their innocence. So does the reader. If the readers are young, they may believe Scout when she says, "nothin's real scary except in books." If the readers are older they will have learned that life is scary, and they will be prepared to meet some of its realities.

perspectives: views

My Notes

_____

_____

_____

_____

_____

_____

frailties: weaknesses

realm: world
defy: disobey

Second Read

- Reread the essay to answer these text-dependent questions.
- Write any additional questions you have about the text in your Reader/Writer Notebook.

2. **Key Ideas and Details:** What is the central claim of the essay?

3. **Key Ideas and Details:** What were the main reasons white critics felt *To Kill a Mockingbird* should be banned in schools?

GRAMMAR & USAGE
Active and Passive Voice
Verbs have active and passive voice in all six tenses. When the subject of the verb does the acting, the verb is in the **active voice**: "Lyndon Johnson gained the presidency: blacks began to seek and win political offices." Using active voice emphasizes the person or group that does the action.

When the subject of the verb receives the action, the verb is in the **passive voice**. A passive-voice verb always contains a form of *be* along with the past participle of the verb: "When John F. Kennedy was killed in Texas on November 27, 1963, many southerners were shocked." Using passive voice emphasizes the receiver of the action.

4. **Key Ideas and Details:** Why is it significant to note that there was a large population of black audiences who felt the novel should be banned?

5. **Key Ideas and Details:** How does *To Kill a Mockingbird* remain "part of the ongoing activities" of our world?

Working from the Text

6. Use the RAFT strategy to compose an argument defending or challenging the use of the novel *To Kill a Mockingbird* in the ninth-grade curriculum of your high school.

Role: Student

Audience: Parent, teacher, censor, administrator, school board member

Format: Letter, speech, or e-mail

Topic: Whether or not the novel *To Kill a Mockingbird* should be part of the ninth-grade curriculum

As you write your argument, be sure to do the following:

- Start with a claim defending or challenging the use of *To Kill a Mockingbird* in the ninth-grade curriculum.

- Use textual evidence from your research, your reading of the novel, and/or the Karolides article.

- Raise at least one counterargument and rebut it.

Check Your Understanding

Using evidence from the article, explain how the experience of reading *To Kill a Mockingbird* in the 1960s would be different from the experience of reading it now.

"Hey, Boo"

Learning Targets
- Analyze and annotate a literary passage.
- Support inferences with text evidence.
- Write an essay about how literary elements contribute to a theme.

LEARNING STRATEGIES:
Graphic Organizer,
Discussion Groups

Impressions of Boo

1. Before reading Chapters 29 and 30, complete the first row of the graphic organizer below, which asks about Scout's mental picture of Boo Radley from the early chapters of the book.

Close Reading: Chapters 29–31

2. As you read Chapters 29–31, complete the rest of the graphic organizer. In the Textual Evidence column, first write the inference you are making from the topic of the commentary, and then provide the textual evidence to support that inference.

Commentary	Textual Evidence
Scout's mental picture of Boo before Chapter 29	
The reality of Boo	
Scout's understanding of Boo after she meets him	

My Notes

"Hey, Boo"

Working from the Text

3. With a small group, brainstorm a list of the literary elements you have studied in this unit and take turns explaining their meaning so that you can use them in your writing and also for Embedded Assessment 2.

4. Conduct a close reading of the passage in Chapter 31 that begins "I led him to the front porch" and ends with "Just standing on the Radley porch was enough." Use sticky notes to annotate the text with your interpretation and analysis.

Drafting the Embedded Assessment

Work together with your group to write an essay about how the literary elements in the passage you have just annotated help develop a theme of the novel. If you have computers, try using something like Google docs or a wiki to compose the analysis and your essay together. Be sure to:

- Include an introduction with a hook that connects to a thesis.
- Provide multiple support paragraphs with topic sentences, textual evidence, and commentary.
- End with a conclusion that makes connections between the literal, interpretive, and universal.

Independent Reading Checkpoint

Review your independent reading. What have you learned and observed about the main characters in coming of age novels, biographies, and autobiographies? Review any idea notes you made. How can you use what you have learned as you read additional coming-of-age literature? Which techniques will be most effective if you choose to write a coming-of-age piece?

Writing a Literary Analysis Essay

ASSIGNMENT

Your assignment is to write a passage analysis of a key coming-of-age scene from *To Kill a Mockingbird*. After annotating the text to analyze Harper Lee's use of literary elements in your selected passage, write an essay explaining how the literary elements in this passage help develop a theme of the novel.

Planning and Prewriting: Take time to select and annotate a passage.	▦ Which passage from the novel will you choose to illustrate a significant coming-of-age moment? ▦ How will you be sure you understand all the literary elements that you have studied in this unit? (See the list you created in Activity 3.22.) ▦ How can you be sure readers know what passage you have chosen to mark and annotate to analyze literary elements? ▦ How will you use your annotations to generate a working thesis that shows the significance of the passage to a theme of the book?
Drafting: Determine the structure of your essay and how to incorporate necessary elements.	▦ How will you organize your essay? What tools will you use to help you organize? ▦ What is your thesis? Do your topic sentences support your thesis? ▦ What textual evidence do you need to support your thesis and topic sentences? ▦ What elements do you need to include in your introduction and conclusion?
Evaluating and Revising: Create opportunities to review and gain feedback for revisions.	▦ How will you ask for feedback on your draft? Whom will you ask? ▦ How will you revise your draft for seamless integration of quotations using the TLQC method (transition, lead in, quote, and commentary)?
Editing for Publication: Confirm that the final draft is ready for publication.	▦ How will you proofread and edit your draft to demonstrate command of the conventions of standard English (capitalization, punctuation, spelling, grammar, and usage)? ▦ How will you use the Scoring Guide to be sure you have met all of the criteria for this assignment?

Reflection

After completing this Embedded Assessment, think about how you went about accomplishing this task, and respond to the following question: What have you learned about the significance of individual passages to a novel as a whole?

Writing a Literary Analysis Essay

SCORING GUIDE

Scoring Criteria	Exemplary	Proficient	Emerging	Incomplete
Ideas	The essay • includes a well-chosen passage that reveals the complex relationship between the literary elements and the major ideas and concepts of the entire work • provides supporting details to enhance understanding of the writer's position • relates commentary directly to the thesis.	The essay • reflects a careful choice of passage to show the relationship between a scene and the major ideas and concepts of the novel • provides relevant details to explain the writer's position • uses appropriate commentary.	The essay • attempts to link a passage to a major theme of the novel • presents supporting details that may be fully developed or provide an understanding of the writer's position • has commentary that may not relate directly to the thesis or may be a plot summary.	The essay • a passage that does not represent a major theme of the novel • is missing supporting details or presents undeveloped ideas • is missing commentary or includes commentary that does not relate directly to the thesis.
Structure	The essay • has multiple paragraphs and a clear and precise thesis that directs the organization of the body • uses transitions to clarify and connect ideas • provides relevant and insightful commentary; the conclusion follows from the ideas presented.	The essay • has multiple paragraphs and is organized with an introduction, detailed body paragraphs, and a conclusion • uses transitions to establish connections between ideas.	The essay • attempts to organize ideas but key pieces are lacking • may be missing an introduction, detailed body paragraphs, and/or a conclusion • uses few or no transitions to connect ideas.	The essay • does not have a focus with a clear organization of introduction, body paragraphs, and conclusion • does not use transitions to connect paragraphs and/or ideas.
Use of Language	The essay • uses a formal style • seamlessly incorporates literary analysis vocabulary • is mostly error-free, with proper punctuation and capitalization to embed quotations into the text.	The essay • uses diction that is appropriate for an academic topic • incorporates some literary analysis vocabulary • has few errors.	The essay • uses simple language that is not appropriate for an academic topic • includes little literary analysis vocabulary • has errors that interfere with meaning.	The essay • uses slang or informal words that are not appropriate for an academic topic • includes little or no literary analysis vocabulary • has numerous errors that interfere with meaning.

Exploring Poetic Voices

Visual Prompt: Authors write poetry about almost any subject. What do you see in this image that might inspire a poem?

Unit Overview

Poetry evokes the power of words, feelings, and images. We are surrounded by poetry in its various forms on a daily basis—popular music, billboards, and advertising jingles. Poetry allows us to stop and appreciate the mystery of daily life, as Walt Whitman noted in *Leaves of Grass:*

Stop this day and night with me, and you
    shall possess the origin of all poems;
You shall possess the good of the earth and
    sun ... (there are millions of suns left,)
You shall no longer take things at second or
    third hand, nor look through eyes of the
    dead, nor feed on the spectres in books;
You shall not look through my eyes
either, nor take things from me,
You shall listen to all sides, and filter them
    from yourself.
    —Walt Whitman, *Leaves of Grass*

Exploring Poetic Voices

GOALS:

- To develop the skills and knowledge to analyze and craft poetry
- To analyze the function and effects of figurative language
- To write original poems that reflect personal voice, style, and an understanding of poetic elements
- To write a style-analysis essay
- To present an oral interpretation of a poem

ACADEMIC VOCABULARY

complementary
emulate
interpretation
oral interpretation
elaborate (v.)

Literary Terms

free verse
repetition
anaphora
form
stanza
rhyme scheme
musical devices
sound devices
cacophonous
euphonious
catalog poem
rhythm
extended metaphor
ode
quatrain
couplet
iambic pentameter

Contents

Activities

Texts not included in these materials.

Language and Writer's Craft
- Verbals (4.6)

MY INDEPENDENT READING LIST

Previewing the Unit

My Notes

_____

_____

_____

_____

_____

_____

_____

ACADEMIC VOCABULARY
Complementary elements are elements that are combined in a way that enhances all the elements.

INDEPENDENT READING LINK

Read and Discuss
The focus of this unit is poetry. As you begin your study of the unit, discuss with peers two or three poets whose works you would like to explore. They may be poets in this unit or other poets you and your peers know. Use an online resource or a print poetry anthology to get more information about poets if you need it. Make a plan for reading in which you decide which poets to read. Then choose three or four of each poet's poems and decide on a regular time you will set aside for reading.

Learning Targets
- Preview the literary terms and poetic devices introduced in this unit.
- Analyze the skills and knowledge needed to complete Embedded Assessment 1 successfully.

Making Connections

Careful attention to the works of published poets will help you to explore your own poetic voice. In this unit, you will explore the function and effect of poetic structure and poetic devices; that is, figurative language, diction, imagery. Once you understand the specific effects of poetic devices, you will be able to use those same devices to create poems that express your experiences about coming of age.

Essential Questions

Based on your current knowledge, write your answers to these questions:
1. What is poetry?
2. What can a writer learn from studying an author's craft and style?

Developing Vocabulary

Go back to the Contents page and use a QHT or other strategy to analyze and evaluate your knowledge of the Academic Vocabulary and Literary Terms for the unit.

Unpacking the Embedded Assessment

Read the following assignment for Embedded Assessment 1. Mark the text to show the skills and knowledge you will need to successfully accomplish this task.

> Your assignment is to create a thematic poetry anthology that will include an introduction to the collection, seven or eight original poems with **complementary** visuals, and a reflection that explains the style and content of the work presented.

With your class, create a graphic organizer to identify the skills and knowledge you will need to accomplish this task, and plan how you will acquire them to complete the assignment. To help you complete your graphic organizer, be sure to review the criteria in the Scoring Guide on page 326.

What Is Poetry?

Learning Targets

- Read and analyze a free verse poem closely to interpret meaning.
- Analyze one author's creative approaches to writing poetry to find ideas for poems.
- Write an original free verse poem.

Perspectives on Poetry

1. Read the quotations below and select one that is meaningful to you. Copy the quote onto one side of an index card, and write a brief interpretation on the other side.

Poets' Perspectives on Poetry

1.	"We don't read and write poetry because it's cute. We read and write poetry because we are members of the human race. And the human race is filled with passion. And medicine, law, business, engineering, these are noble pursuits and necessary to sustain life. But poetry, beauty, romance, love, these are what we stay alive for."—*Dead Poet's Society*
2.	"Poetry is what gets lost in translation." —Robert Frost
3.	"Out of the quarrel with others we make rhetoric; out of the quarrel with ourselves we make poetry." —W. B. Yeats
4.	"Poetry is man's rebellion against being what he is." —James Branch Cabell
5.	"Poetry is the revelation of a feeling that the poet believes to be interior and personal which the reader recognizes as his own." —Salvatore Quasimodo
6.	"Mathematics and poetry are ... the utterance of the same power of imagination, only that in the one case it is addressed to the head, in the other, to the heart." —Thomas Hill
7.	"Poetry is an orphan of silence. The words never quite equal the experiences behind them." —Charles Simic

2. Listen as your teacher explains how you will participate in a "poetry mixer." Be prepared to share your quotation and interpretation with other students and listen as others share with you. Your classmates may have different interpretations of their quotations. Listen to their reasoning and be prepared to respond with further clarification or explanation of your interpretation. You may also want to adjust your interpretation based on your classmates' ideas.

LEARNING STRATEGIES:
Brainstorming, Close Reading, Marking the Text, Oral Reading, Summarizing

My Notes

What Is Poetry?

Literary Terms

Free verse describes poetry without a fixed pattern of meter and rhyme.

Form refers to the particular structure or organization of a work. Free verse is a form of poetry.

My Notes

Preview

In this activity, you will read a **free verse** poem that explore the question, "What is poetry?"

Setting a Purpose for Reading

- Mark the text by highlighting or underlining images that Neruda uses to describe how "poetry arrived in search of me."
- Circle unknown words and phrases. Try to determine the meaning of the words by using context clues, word parts, or a dictionary.
- Underline ideas you think might be helpful to a new writer of poetry.

ABOUT THE AUTHOR

Chilean author Pablo Neruda (1904–1973) contributed his first poem to a literary journal when he was 13 years old and published his first collection of poems in 1923. Throughout his life, his poems reflected his world and his work. He wrote political poems, an epic poem about the South American continent, and a series of odes that reflect everyday life—things, events, relationships. In 1971, he was awarded the Nobel Prize in Literature.

Poetry

Poetry

by Pablo Neruda
Translated by Alastair Reid

And it was at that age ... poetry arrived
in search of me. I don't know, I don't know where
it came from, from winter or a river.
I don't know how or when,
5 no they were not voices, they were not
words, nor silence,
but from a street I was **summoned**,
from the branches of night,
abruptly from the others,
10 among violent fires
or returning alone,
there I was without a face
and it touched me.

summoned: called

abruptly: suddenly; without warning

I did not know what to say, my mouth

15 had no way

with names,

my eyes were blind,

and something started in my soul,

fever or forgotten wings,

20 and I made my own way,

deciphering

that fire,

and I wrote the first faint line,

faint, without substance, pure

25 nonsense,

pure wisdom

of someone who knows nothing,

and suddenly I saw

the heavens

30 unfastened and open,

planets

palpitating plantations,

shadow **perforated**,

riddled

35 with arrows, fire, and flowers,

the winding night, the universe.

And I, **infinitesimal** being,

drunk with the great starry

void,

40 likeness, image of mystery,

felt myself a pure part

of the abyss,

I wheeled with the stars,

my heart broke loose on the wind.

My Notes

deciphering: figuring out; decoding

palpitating: pulsating or throbbing rapidly
perforated: pierced with holes

infinitesimal: so small as to be almost nothing

Second Read

- Reread the poem to answer these text-dependent questions.
- Write any additional questions you have about the text in your Reader/Writer Notebook.

3. **Craft and Structure:** How does the author use personification in this poem?

WORD CONNECTIONS

Word Relationships

An *abyss* is a bottomless depth, or an immeasurable, infinite space. Neruda conjures up an image of the abyss alongside the words *infinitesimal* (extremely small) and *void* (an empty space). These three words, used in such close proximity to each other, suggest the way poetry opened the universe to Neruda, making him feel tiny in comparison.

What Is Poetry?

My Notes

4. **Craft and Structure:** What is the effect of **anaphora** in this poem?

5. **Key Ideas and Details:** What does the author mean when he says, "I did not know what to say, my mouth / had no way / with names, / my eyes were blind"?

Literary Terms

A **stanza** is a group of lines, usually similar in length and pattern, that form a unit within a poem.

Anaphora is a particular kind of repetition in which the same word or group of words is repeated at the beginnings of two or more successive clauses or lines.

Repetition is the use of any element of language—a sound, a word, a phrase, a line, or a stanza—more than once.

Working from the Text

Use your ideas about poetry to complete the frame poem below. Try to incorporate imagery and **repetition** into your poem.

A Poem About Poetry

Poetry is _____

Poetry is like _____

Poetry is about _____

Poetry is as important as _____

Poetry is as pointless as _____

Poetry means _____

Poetry is _____

Preview

Now you will read a creative essay about writing poetry.

Setting a Purpose for Reading

- Underline any advice or methods you might find helpful when writing a poem.
- Circle unknown words and phrases. Try to determine the meaning of the words by using context clues, word parts, or a dictionary.

ABOUT THE AUTHOR

Susan Wooldridge is a teacher of creative writing. Her work has been published in numerous journals, though she is best known for her collection of essays, *poemcrazy*. As an observer of nature and the world around her, she is inspired in her writing by everyday events and shares her stories in a distinctive writing style.

Essay

from Poemcrazy

by Susan Goldsmith Wooldridge

3

collecting words and creating a wordpool

1   I have a strong gathering instinct. I collect boxes, hats, rusty flattened bottle caps for collages and creek-worn sticks to color with my **hoard** of Berol prisma color pencils. When I was a kid I'd lie in bed imagining I was a squirrel who lived in a hollow tree, **foraging** for acorns, twigs and whatever it takes to make squirrel furniture.

2   Most of us have collections. I ask people all the time in workshops, Do you collect anything? Stamps? Shells? '57 Chevys? Raccoons? Money? Leopards? Meteorites? Wisecracks? What a **coincidence**, I collect them, too. Hats, coins, cougars, old Studebakers. That is, I collect the words. Pith helmet, fragment, Frigidaire, quarrel, love seat, lily. I gather them into my journal.

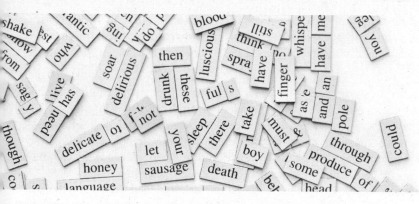

3   The great thing about collecting words is they're free; you can borrow them, trade them in or toss them out. I'm trading in (and literally composting) some of my other collections—driftwood, acorns and bits of colored Easter egg shell—for words. Words are lightweight, unbreakable, portable, and they're everywhere. You can even make them up. *Frebrent, bezoncular, zurber.* Someone made up the word *padiddle.*

4   A word can trigger or inspire a poem, and words in a stack or thin list can make up poems.

5   Because I always carry my journal with me, I'm likely to jot down words on trains, in the car, at boring meetings (where I appear to be taking notes), on hikes and in bed.

6   I take words from everywhere. I might *steal* steel, spelled both ways. *Unscrupulous.* I'll toss in *iron, metal* and *magnolias.* Whatever flies into my mind. *Haystack, surge, sidewinder.* A sound, *splash.* A color, *magenta.* Here's a chair. *Velvet. Plush.*

My Notes

hoard: a hidden collection of something
foraging: searching for food

coincidence: two events happening at the same time, by chance

 WORD CONNECTIONS

Word Relationships

Homonyms are words that sound alike but have different meanings: *steal* (to take something that is not yours) and *steel* (iron metal) is an example of the use of homonyms in this essay.

What Is Poetry?

ballad: a sentimental love song

My Notes

laborious: requiring a lot of work

idolized: worshiped
irreverent: not respectful
antiestablishment: opposed to working with the government

profound: having deep insight

7 Dylan Thomas loved the words he heard and saw around him in Wales. "When I experience anything," he once said, "I experience it as a thing and a word at the same time, both equally amazing." Writing one **ballad**, he said, was like carrying around an armload of words to a table upstairs and wondering if he'd get there in time.

8 Words stand for feelings, ideas, mountains, bees. Listen to the sound of words. I line up words I like to hear, *Nasturtiums buzz blue grass catnip catalpa catalog.*

9 I borrow words from poems, books and conversations. *Politely.* Take *polite.* If I'm in a classroom, I just start chalking them onto the board. I don't worry about spelling or meaning. *Curdle. Cantankerous. Linoleum. Limousine.* Listen. *Malevolent. Sukulilli,* the Maidu Indian word for silly. *Magnet cat oven taste tilt titter.*

10 I call gathering words this way creating a *wordpool.* ...

11 When I'm playing with words, I don't worry about sounding dumb or crazy. And I don't worry about whether or not I'm writing "a poem." *Word pool. World pool, wild pool, whipoorwill, swing.* Words taken out of the **laborious** structures (like this sentence) where we normally place them take on a spinning life of their own.

5

most mad and moonly

12 Things I love have a way of turning up in my life in unexpected ways. In high school I **idolized** e. e. cummings because he was **irreverent** and made me feel free. He played with language and broke all the rules, nourishing my *Catcher in the Rye,* **antiestablishment** side.

13 I memorized most of "What if a much of a which of a wind" and several other Cummings poems. My favorite for years was "Somewhere I have never traveled," with the unexpected line that moved me most, "and no one, not even the rain, has such small hands."

14 During my freshman year of college in New York City I met a Columbia student named Simon Roosevelt, who played Lysander in a production of *A Midsummer Night's Dream.* I painted viney leaves for the set as part of a stage crew that played loud rock music all hours of the night. I helped mend and fit costumes, happiest hanging out behind the scenes. Simon and I went to movies and studied together in the Columbia library. One evening I noticed a worn photo of e. e. cummings in Simon's wallet. "He was my grandfather," Simon told me. e. e. cummings—who died while I was in high school—was turning up again in my world. Life can be like a poem that way, with the unexpected appearing in the room, not just on the page.

15 cummings plays with words, spacing and capital letters, often putting all the punctuation somewhere unexpected. He experiments with opposites. His poems are both goofy and **profound**, soft and sharp at the same time, tender and fierce. "What if a much of a which of a wind" opens gently, but soon we're shocked as the wind "bloodies with dizzying leaves the sun / and yanks immortal stars awry."

16 cummings's words, often like the trail of an acrobat tumbling down the page, invite us to put our own words down. Filled with open, white space, his poems leave room for us to enter. We feel we can do this too. cummings's writing inspired a passion in me to create my own world, poke around and explore my boundaries, see how many shades of unnamed color and sound I might find there.

. . . .

17 cummings reminds me to allow poems to swagger, soar or tiptoe in unexpectedly. I need to be open and ready for them. Poems aren't written from ideas, like essays, and they're not overly controlled. In a poem's "most mad and moonly" spell, out of time, I can break rules and expectations about who I am as well as about writing.

18 My journal has a memorial page both for e. e. cummings and for his grandson Simon, killed on his red motorcycle the year after we met. At Simon's memorial service someone read a cummings poem that helped us with our shock and sadness,

> love is more thicker than forget
>
> more thinner than recall
>
> more seldom than a wave is wet
>
> more frequent than to fail
>
> it is most mad and moonly
>
> and less it shall unbe
>
> than all the sea which only
>
> is deeper than the sea
>
> love is less always than to win
>
> less never than alive
>
> less bigger than the least begin
>
> less littler than forgive
>
> it is most sane and sunly
>
> and more it cannot die
>
> than all the sky which only
>
> is higher than the sky.

19 The unexpected brings us light and darkness, joy and sorrow, life and death. And it brings discovery. Some of our most important discoveries are made when we're not looking.

Literary Terms
Rhyme scheme refers to the consistent pattern of rhyme throughout a poem. Although the rhyme is slightly off, the rhyme scheme of cummings's poem is abab/cdcd/efef/ghgh.

My Notes

What Is Poetry?

My Notes

6

gas, food, longing

20 ... Image is the root word of imagination. It's from Latin *imago*, "picture," how you see things. Images carry feelings. Saying, "I'm angry," or "I'm sad," has little impact. Creating images, I can make you feel how I feel.

21 When I read the words of a young student named Cari—"I'm a rose in the shape of a heart / with nineteen days of nothing / but the pouncing of shoes on my dead petals"—I experience desperation through her image. Cari doesn't even have to name the feeling—nineteen days, a pale green sky, a pouch of seed held against a sower's heart.

22 Writing poems using images can create an experience allowing others to feel what we feel. Perhaps more important, poems can put us in touch with our own often buried or unexpected feelings.

23 Shoua discovered her frustration by using the image of a man shooting pool,

> I hear bang, click, shoosh
>
> feeling like the white ball
>
> that does all the work.

24 Tori used images from a landscape to indicate hopelessness,

> the clouds collapsed,
>
> they're touching the ground
>
> trying to come alive,
>
> but they can't.

25 Sometimes word tickets magically fit with the images in the paintings. One of Tori's words was *jingle*. It helped her convey her developing feeling of hope,

> the glowing water shows shadow
>
> till we all hear
>
> the *jingle* of dawn.

26 Images we create in our poem can not only help us discover our feelings, but can help us begin to transform them.

PRACTICE

27 Make a wordpool of feeling words, going for opposites: *psychotic stable, laughable sober drab vibrant bored blissful frantic calm fragile invincible*.

28 Find a postcard of a painting, a reproduction in a magazine or book, or a poster on a wall. Any painting will do.

29 Choose a feeling. Look closely at your painting and find a detail that seems to express your feeling, perhaps one color or the **gesture** of someone's arm. Perhaps a jug in the corner. Let your words paint the feeling. *I feel as still as a white water jug*.

30 Say your painting is a landscape. You feel *powerless*. What does that gray cloud look like that expresses your feeling? You might write that the cloud is dissolving, losing its shape. Or you feel *powerful*. Now the cloud is gathering electricity to snap out as lightning

gesture: movement of the body

31 You might feel *unimportant*, like that tiny leaf on top of the tree, lost in all the others. You might feel like you're *fading* like the last bit of pink light on top of the mountain.

32 Choose a variety of paintings so you can begin to express the full range of your feelings in one or several poems.

8

it looks like

33 ... I think we naturally see things metaphorically. We're always comparing the way one thing looks to another. Comparison is built into our language. I've noticed that on a highway a hairpin turn, from above, *looks like* a hairpin. Cattails in a swampy area along Lonestar Road *look like* cat's tails. In my garden foxglove looks like a wee "folk's glove," with a pouch for a tiny hand. Georgia O'Keeffe said she painted individual flowers and made them huge so we'd be forced to look closely and notice what flowers really look like. Whether she intended this or not, O'Keeffe's paintings lend themselves to metaphor. Inside her white flower I see

> a gown with long white sleeves,
>
> a curled satin slipper with grey on the toe,
>
> a Chinese lantern on low,
>
> a bowl of silver bells, ringing.

34 Wilfred Funk writes in *Word Origins and Their Romantic Stories* that originally all words were poems, since our language is based, like poems, in metaphor. The names of flowers makes this easier to see. This flower looks like a shooting star. Maybe the next time I see one I'll make the shift from simile to full metaphor and think, This flower is a shooting star, or a bird's-eye, a paintbrush, butter and eggs.

35 In some words we can still see the poem/metaphor, especially flowers and trees like ladyslipper, redbud, spinster blue-eyed Mary. My married name, Wooldridge, must have come from the image of lambs on a ridge.

36 Metaphor is a bridge bringing things together. The world is a stage. Life is a dream. The navel is a belly button. When she lived in Athens years ago, a friend Sally tells me, some of the delivery bikes had the word METAPHOR printed on their sides—probably a company name. In Greek *metaphor* literally means to bear or carry over.

37 Sometimes part of writing a poem is as simple as looking carefully and bringing things together through simile and metaphor. This bit of moon looks like a canoe. The moon is a cradle, a wolf's tooth, a fingernail, snow on a curved leaf or milk in the bottom of a tipped glass.

PRACTICE

38 Take an object and think about what it *looks like*. Describe exactly what you see.

39 Look around you. Does your lampshade look like a ballerina's illuminated pink pleated skirt? Not exactly, but it's a start. Let yourself go for the farfetched and the ridiculous when you make comparisons.

40 If you can find a flower, look inside. What does it look like?

41 Find a painting, abstract or realistic. Choose a detail and stare at it. Focusing on that detail, write,

My Notes

I see

It looks like

it looks like

I see

It looks like (repeat)

42 For more practice, list what you see around you and write down what it looks like.

The pine tree looks like a torpedo

That folded piece of paper looks like a flattened sail

The curled telephone cord looks like an earthworm

That man's curly hair looks like ...

The moth's wing ...

43 Keep going.

Second Read

- Reread the essay to answer these text-dependent questions.
- Write any additional questions you have about the text in your Reader/Writer Notebook.

6. **Key Ideas and Details:** What is the central purpose of this essay?

7. **Craft and Structure:** What is a "wordpool," and why is it important?

8. **Key Ideas and Details:** What does the author mean when she says, "Life can be like a poem that way" (paragraph 14)?

9. **Key Ideas and Details:** To Wooldridge, what is the importance of imagery?

Working from the Text

10. Summarize what Wooldridge is saying about the importance of words. In your Reader/Writer notebook, start your own "wordpool." Here are some ideas:

   • Notice that Wooldridge mentions homonyms in Part 3: "I might steal steel ..." Write 10 more sets of homonyms in your notebook.

   • Create a personal thesaurus of synonyms for the verb "to walk or move." Try to find one synonym for each letter of the alphabet. Use this list to vary your verbs in your writing.

11. Read the suggestions for ideas in the "Practice" from Part 6 to help you increase your wordpool of images that might help you write a poem. Choose one or more suggestions you would like to experiment with, and write your response in your Reader/Writer Notebook.

12. In Part 8, the "Practice" asks you to think about what an object looks like. In your notebook, list what you see around you and describe some of the items using creative descriptions and details.

Check Your Understanding

How does writing free verse poetry allow for creativity?

Drafting the Embedded Assessment

Write an original free verse poem you might use for your anthology. Be sure to:

• Use imagery.

• Experiment with free verse.

• Use repetition.

My Notes

Literary Devices in Poetry

pic

My Notes

_____

_____

_____

_____

_____

_____

_____

_____

_____

Literary Terms

Musical or **sound devices** convey and reinforce the meaning or experience of poetry through the use of sound. Just as in music, some words have a **cacophonous** or unpleasant effect, while other combinations of words are **euphonious** with a harmonious or pleasing effect.

**INDEPENDENT
READING LINK**

Read and Connect

As you read the poems you have chosen, use the terms in your Personal Poetry Glossary to identify the literary devices the poets use. Make a chart showing the literary devices and compare/contrast them with examples from your poems.

Learning Targets

- Work with a group to learn literary terminology.
- Apply literary terminology while analyzing and creating poetry.

The Sounds of Poetry

1. In your Reader/Writer Notebook, create a QHT chart and categorize the poetry terms in the following graphic organizer according to how well you know the definitions:

   Q = Don't know the word

   H = Heard of the word

   T = Can teach the word to someone else

2. After categorizing the terms, proceed as follows:
   - Share your "T" words with a partner, discussing and perhaps revising definitions. Write your revised definition for each word you know in the graphic organizer.
   - Share your "H" words, consulting appropriate resources for definitions. Add definitions for these words to the graphic organizer.
   - Create groups of four and share definitions and examples. Discuss and research the "Q" words to find agreed-upon definitions, and then add those to the graphic organizer.

3. **Visualizing Vocabulary:** There are 16 words on this list. Your group will be assigned three or four words. For each word assigned, create a graphic representation in your Reader/Writer Notebook that captures the essence of the term.

4. The second page of the Personal Poetry Glossary contains words that are referred to as **musical devices**. The following are also words that refer to sound:
   - **euphony:** pleasing combination of sounds
   - **cacophony:** harsh, discordant effect of sound

These sounds produce opposite effects. Copy these terms to your Reader/Writer Notebook and write an explanation of why poets would use musical devices to create euphony or cacophony in a poem.

Personal Poetry Glossary

Literary Device	Definition	Example from Text and Explanation of Function and Use	Original Example for My Reader/Writer Notebook
Connotation			
Tone			
Imagery			
Diction			
Hyperbole			
Allusion			
Symbol			
Extended metaphor			
Anaphora			
Theme			

Literary Devices in Poetry

Literary Device	Definition	Example from Text and Explanation of Function and Use	Original Example for My Reader/Writer Notebook
Refrain			
Onomatopoeia			
Alliteration			
Rhyme			
Assonance			
Consonance			

Examining Experiences and Poetic Structure

Learning Targets
- Analyze and write an autobiographical catalog poem.
- Conduct a close reading of a poem by generating and answering levels of questions.
- Identify how sound and structural elements create an effect in a poem.

Memorable Experiences
1. **Quickwrite:** In your Reader/Writer Notebook, make a list of memorable childhood experiences.

Preview
In this activity, you will read a **catalog poem** and a free verse poem. Both poems use specific poetic devices and structures to express themes and meaning.

Setting a Purpose for Reading
- Notice the way Giovanni punctuates and capitalizes in order to control the way the poem is read.
- Circle unknown words and phrases. Try to determine the meaning of the words by using context clues, word parts, or a dictionary.
- When reading, pause where there seems to be a natural break and draw a backslash (/) where you paused.

LEARNING STRATEGIES:
Quickwrite, Marking the Text, Note-taking, Levels of Questions, Think-Pair-Share

Literary Terms
A **catalog poem** uses repetition and variation in the creation of a list, or catalog, of objects, desires, plans, or memories.

My Notes

ABOUT THE AUTHOR
Yolanda Cornelia "Nikki" Giovanni (b. 1943) is a popular American poet and Emmy Award nominee known for her writing on the black experience. She has received a variety of awards for her work, including the Reverend Martin Luther King Jr. Award, three NAACP Image Awards, the Langston Hughes award, and more than twenty honorary degrees from colleges and universities. As one of the foremost authors of the Black Arts Movement, her work first came to light in the 1960s, and she is now one of the world's best known African American authors. Giovanni's advice to young writers is, "The authority of the writer always overcomes the skepticism of the reader. If you know what you're talking about, or if you feel that you do, the reader will believe you."

The poet Nikki Giovanni

Examining Experiences and Poetic Structure

My Notes

Poetry

Nikki-Rosa

by Nikki Giovanni

childhood remembrances are always a drag
if you're Black
you always remember things like living in Woodlawn
with no inside toilet
5   and if you become famous or something
they never talk about how happy you were to have
your mother
all to yourself and
how good the water felt when you got your bath
10 from one of those
big tubs that folk in Chicago barbecue in
and somehow when you talk about home
it never gets across how much you
understood their feelings
15 as the whole family attended meetings about Hollydale
and even though you remember
your **biographers** never understand
your father's pain as he sells his stock
and another dream goes
20 and though you're poor it isn't poverty that
concerns you
and though they fight a lot
it isn't your father's drinking that makes any difference
but only that everybody is together and you
25 and your sister have happy birthdays and very good
Christmases
and I really hope no white person ever has cause
to write about me
because they never understand
30 Black love is Black wealth and they'll
probably talk about my hard childhood
and never understand that
all the while I was quite happy.

biographers: writers of someone's life story

Second Read

- Reread the poem to answer these text-dependent questions.
- Write any additional questions you have about the text in your Reader/Writer Notebook.

2. **Craft and Structure:** Who is the speaker of this poem, and to whom is the speaker speaking?

3. **Key Ideas and Details:** What is the biggest misunderstanding the speaker assumes white biographers would make about her life?

4. **Key Ideas and Details:** According to themes of this poem, what is the most important thing children need in order to be happy?

Working from the Text

5. Review the definitions of the three Levels of Questions:

- literal: questions that can be answered by going to a resource or back to the text
- interpretive: questions that are significant to the meaning and usually begin with "how" or "why"
- universal: questions that go beyond the text

Read the poem again and write at least two interpretive questions in your Reader/Writer Notebook. Then, exchange questions with another student. Meet with another two students and discuss your responses to the questions.

Drafting the Embedded Assessment

Try your hand at creating a catalog poem of your own memorable experiences. Refer to the list of memorable childhood experiences you compiled at the beginning of this activity. Be sure to:

- Use imagery to create vivid sensory pictures.
- Experiment with forms of repetition and variation.
- Order your catalog of memories in a meaningful way.

My Notes

Examining Experiences and Poetic Structure

Literary Terms
Rhythm in poetry is the pattern of stressed and unstressed syllables.

WORD CONNECTIONS

Content Connections

Jazz is a genre of music that evolved from slave songs and spirituals (religious African American folk songs) in New Orleans, Louisiana. Jazz is considered to be a rebellious genre—experimental and improvisational—because it doesn't follow traditional musical rules. **June** is the sixth month of the year and traditionally when schools let out for the summer. As such, the month is associated with freedom. By putting the two words together, the author suggests that these characters have embraced their freedom in an unconventional way.

lurk: to hang around a place, hidden from view

My Notes

_____
_____
_____
_____
_____
_____
_____
_____
_____
_____
_____

Setting a Purpose for Reading

- As you read, pay attention to the poem's **rhythm**, sound devices, and poetic structure.
- Circle unknown words and phrases. Try to determine the meaning of the words by using context clues, word parts, or a dictionary.
- Underline examples of repetition and alliteration.

ABOUT THE AUTHOR
Gwendolyn Brooks (1917–2000) grew up and lived in Chicago. While still in her teens, she published poems in an African American newspaper in Chicago. It wasn't long before her poetry became recognized nationally, and she won the Pulitzer Prize for Poetry in 1950, the first African American to win a Pulitzer. Poetry was the focus of Brooks's life, and she continued to be a prolific writer as well as a teacher and advocate of poetry. She taught creative writing at a number of colleges and universities. Her publications and awards were numerous, including an appointment as Consultant in Poetry to the Library of Congress.

Poetry

We Real Cool

by Gwendolyn Brooks

> *The Pool Players.*
> *Seven at the Golden Shovel.*
>
> We real cool. We
> Left school. We
>
> 5   **Lurk** late. We
> Strike straight. We
> Sing sin. We
> Thin gin. We
> Jazz June. We
> 10   Die soon.

Second Read

- Reread the poem to answer these text-dependent questions.
- Write any additional questions you have about the text in your Reader/Writer Notebook.

6. **Key Ideas and Details:** Why is it significant that the boys have dropped out of school?

7. **Craft and Structure:** What is the effect of the broken sentences, with each line ending in the word "We"?

Working from the Text

8. In your Reader/Writer Notebook, write a summary of the poem "We Real Cool."

9. Examine the painting below called *The Pool Game* by Jacob Lawrence. Notice how the artist creates a feeling about his subject. Compare the representation of the pool players in "We Real Cool" versus *The Pool Game*. What is emphasized in each version? How are the portrayals different?

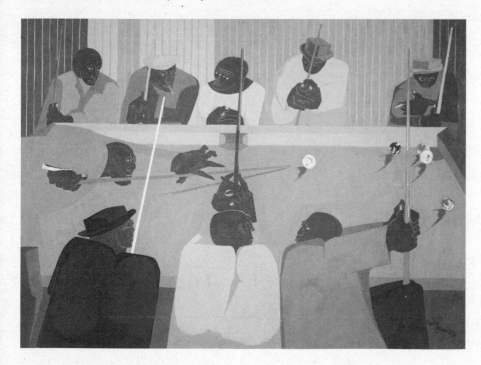

My Notes

Examining Experiences and Poetic Structure

Check Your Understanding

Use the TAG sentence stem to write an analytical statement connecting Brooks's use of form or imagery to theme and tone. (Example: *In "Poetry," a poem by Neruda, the imagery and verse form convey a sense of surprise and pleasure at the discovery of poetry in his life.*)

In " _____ ," a poem by _____ , the imagery and verse form convey _____.

Writing to Sources: Explanatory Text

You have already written a summary of the poem "We Real Cool." Now, expand on that summary by writing an analytical statement that explains how the poetic elements in the poem create an effect. Be sure to:

- Start with a thesis statement that introduces your ideas.
- Use relevant quotations from the text to support your ideas.
- Finish with a conclusion that follows from your explanation.

Exploring Diction and Imagery

Learning Targets
- Read a poem to understand how diction and imagery create effect and tone.
- Write a poem in the style of "Fast Break" that conveys appreciation of a favorite pastime.

LEARNING STRATEGIES:
Freewriting, Marking the Text, TWIST

Preview
In this activity, you will analyze how the poet uses precise diction and imagery to create tone and effect.

Setting a Purpose for Reading
- Underline the verbs in the poem.
- Circle unknown words and phrases. Try to determine the meaning of the words by using context clues, word parts, or a dictionary.
- You might highlight any basketball jargon that shows the poet is familiar with the sport.

ABOUT THE AUTHOR
Edward Hirsch (b. 1950) is a professor of English and a published author of many poems, essays, and books. His collection of verse, *Wild Gratitude*, was awarded the National Book Critics Circle Award in 1986; Hirsch has also earned a Guggenheim Fellowship and a MacArthur Foundation Fellowship. One of Hirsch's most popular books has been his surprise best seller, *How to Read a Poem and Fall in Love with Poetry*.

My Notes

Poetry

Fast Break

In Memory of Dennis Turner, 1946–1984
by Edward Hirsch

> A hook shot kisses the rim and
> hangs there, helplessly, but doesn't drop,
>
> and for once our **gangly** starting **center**
> boxes out his man and times his jump
>
> 5 perfectly, gathering the orange leather
> from the air like a **cherished** possession
>
> and spinning around to throw a strike
> to the outlet who is already shoveling

gangly: tall, thin, and awkward

cherished: beloved

Exploring Diction and Imagery

My Notes

tandem: two things working in partnership

an underhand pass toward the other guard
10 scissoring past a flat-footed defender

who looks stunned and nailed to the floor
in the wrong direction, trying to catch sight

of a high, gliding dribble and a man
letting the play develop in front of him

15 in slow motion, almost exactly
like a coach's drawing on the blackboard,

both forwards racing down the court
the way that forwards should, fanning out

and filling the lanes in **tandem**, moving
20 together as brothers passing the ball

between them without a dribble, without
a single bounce hitting the hardwood

25 until the guard finally lunges out
and commits to the wrong man

while the power-forward explodes past them
in a fury, taking the ball into the air

by himself now and laying it gently
30 against the glass for a lay-up,

but losing his balance in the process,
inexplicably falling, hitting the floor

with a wild, headlong motion
for the game he loved like a country

and swiveling back to see an orange blur
floating perfectly through the net.

Second Read

- Reread the poem to answer these text-dependent questions.
- Write any additional questions you have about the text in your Reader/Writer Notebook.

1. **Craft and Structure:** What is the effect of writing this poem as one long sentence?

2. **Key Ideas and Details:** This poem was written to honor Dennis Turner, the author's friend who died. How does this information affect your understanding of the poem's closing image?

3. **Craft and Structure:** Why might the author have chosen to write this poem in couplets?

Working from the Text

4. Apply the TWIST strategy to "Fast Break," using the following graphic organizer to record your analysis of the poem.

Introducing the Strategy: TWIST

The TWIST strategy (tone, word choice, imagery, style, and theme) is used to create a thesis statement in response to a text. When using this strategy, think specifically about how the tone, word choice (diction), imagery, and style convey theme.

My Notes

Exploring Diction and Imagery

My Notes

Literary Element	Analysis
Tone: What is the writer's attitude toward the topic?	
Word choice: What specific words does the writer use to help convey the topic and the attitude?	
Imagery: What imagery is especially significant for conveying the attitude and topic?	
Style: How do syntax, imagery, and diction work together to communicate the main idea of the poem?	
Theme: What is the author's comment on the subject of the poem?	

INDEPENDENT READING LINK

Read and Connect

Choose one of the poems you have read for independent reading. Use the TWIST strategy to create a thesis statement in response to the poem. Complete a graphic organizer like the one on this page to record your analysis before you create your thesis statement.

Check Your Understanding

Explain the effect of the diction and imagery in the poem. Think about the tense of the verbs and the adjectives the poet chose to use.

Drafting the Embedded Assessment

Write a free verse poem about a pastime you are passionate about. To begin, jot down some ideas. Then write your poem. Be sure to:

- Consider carefully how you create line breaks in your free verse poem.
- Choose precise words (especially verbs) to convey the activities of this pastime.
- Use specific diction and imagery to create an effect.

Extended Metaphor and Hyperbolic Me

Learning Targets
- Explain the relationship between the title of a poem and its central images.
- Analyze a poem to understand how hyperbole and allusion enhance the meaning of a literary text.
- Write a poem using an extended metaphor.

Preview
In this activity, you will read and analyze two poems that explore the theme of identity.

Setting a Purpose for Reading
- Note how the **extended metaphor** develops throughout the poem.
- Circle unknown words and phrases. Try to determine the meaning of the words by using context clues, word parts, or a dictionary.
- Underline any images related to a *weed*.

> **LEARNING STRATEGIES:**
> Graphic Organizer, Marking the Text, Oral Reading, Discussion Groups, TWIST

> **Literary Terms**
> An **extended metaphor** is a metaphor that extends over several lines or the whole poem.

ABOUT THE AUTHOR
Julio Noboa Polanco was born in New York City. He began writing poetry at a young age, writing "Identity" when he was in the eighth grade. His work focuses on Latino identity, particularly the identity of Latinos blending in with white culture. This theme is reflected in Polanco's language, as he writes his poems in both English and Spanish.

My Notes

Poetry

Identity

by Julio Noboa Polanco

Let them be as flowers
always watered, fed, guarded, **admired**,
but harnessed to a pot of dirt.

I'd rather be a tall, ugly weed,
5   clinging on cliffs, like an eagle
wind-wavering above high, **jagged** rocks.

To have broken through the surface of stone,
to live, to feel exposed to the madness
of the **vast**, eternal sky.

admired: took pleasure in

jagged: having sharp edges

vast: immense; huge

bizarre: strange

shunned: avoided

fertile: capable of producing vegetation

My Notes

10   To be swayed by the breezes of an ancient sea,

carrying my soul, my seed,

beyond the mountains of time or into the abyss of the **bizarre**.

I'd rather be unseen, and if

then **shunned** by everyone,

15   than to be a pleasant-smelling flower,

growing in clusters in the **fertile** valley,

where they're praised, handled, and plucked

by greedy human hands.

I'd rather smell of musty, green stench

20   than of sweet, fragrant lilac.

If I could stand alone, strong and free,

I'd rather be a tall, ugly weed.

Second Read

- Reread the poem to answer these text-dependent questions.
- Write any additional questions you have about the text in your Reader/Writer Notebook.

1. **Key Ideas and Details:** What is the relationship between the central image and the title of Polanco's poem?

2. **Key Ideas and Details:** Polanco wrote this poem when he was in eighth grade. Knowing this, who might the "they" be in the poem? How can you tell?

3. **Craft and Structure:** What is the tone of this poem?

Working from the Text

4. Create a T-chart that identifies the two central images of the poem. Highlight lines about one image in one color and the other image in another color.

Language and Writer's Craft: Verbals

A verbal is a verb form that is used as another part of speech—an adjective, noun, or adverb. Verbals include participles, infinitives, and gerunds.

A participle, which functions as an adjective, is the present or past participle of a verb:

A *clinging* weed

A *watered* flower

An infinitive is a verb form beginning with *to*. A present perfect infinitive begins with *to have*, and a passive infinitive with *to be*. Infinitives can function as nouns, adjectives, or adverbs:

To cling to life is the nature of weeds. (infinitive as a noun, the subject of the sentence)

The desire *to stay* alive motivates all living things. (infinitive as an adjective, modifying *desire*)

The flower bends *to bask* in the light of the sun. (Infinitive as an adverb, modifying *bends*)

A gerund is the *-ing* form of a verb used as a noun.

Clinging to the soil keeps the weed alive.

PRACTICE Identify a present participle, an infinitive, and a gerund in the following paragraph:

In the poem "Fast Break," Edward Hirsch uses vivid imagery to describe a few fleeting moments of a basketball game. Forcing so many actions— *fanning, filling*—into just a few lines gives readers a sense that these momentary events occurred in slow motion. The final image of a floating basketball enhances this feeling of slow motion.

5. Go back to the poem "Identity" and mark the verbals. Add them in the appropriate columns to your T-chart, indicating where they are used in creating the contrasting images.

Setting a Purpose for Reading

- Underline allusions to famous people, places, or events.
- Circle unknown words and phrases. Try to determine the meaning of the words by using context clues, word parts, or a dictionary.
- Draw a star next to any images that seem like an exaggeration.

Poetry

Ego Tripping
(there may be a reason why)

by Nikki Giovanni

I was born in the Congo

I walked to the fertile crescent and built the sphinx

I designed a pyramid so tough that a star

that only glows every one hundred years falls

5   into the center giving **divine** perfect light.

I am bad.

I sat on the throne

drinking **nectar** with allah

I got hot and sent an ice age to Europe

10   to cool my thirst.

My oldest daughter is nefertiti

the tears from my birth pains

created the nile

I am a beautiful woman.

15   I gazed on the forest and burned

out the sahara desert

With a packet of goat's meat

and a change of clothes

I crossed it in two hours

20   I am a gazelle so **swift**

so swift you can't catch me.

For a birthday present when he was three

I gave my son hannibal an elephant

He gave me rome for mother's day

25   My strength flows ever on

WORD CONNECTIONS

Multiple Meaning Words

The word *bad* is most often used as the opposite of good. In street slang, however, especially in the 1970s when this poem was written, the word *bad* actually means *awesome*. When the speaker says that she is bad, she is saying that she is proud of her accomplishments.

divine: relating to God

nectar: the liquid in a flower that attracts bees

My Notes

_____

_____

_____

swift: quick

WORD CONNECTIONS

Content Connections

An *ego trip* is an act carried out simply for one's sense of self-importance. The word *trip* in the title could be referencing an ego so large that the speaker is tripping over it. *Trip* might also be referencing the act of losing one's mind.

My son noah built a new/ark and
I stood proudly at the **helm**
as we sailed on a soft summer day

I turned myself into myself and was
30   jesus
Men **intone** my loving name
All praises All praises
I am the one who would save

I sowed diamonds in my back yard
35   My bowels delivered uranium
The filings from my fingernails are
semi-precious jewels

On a trip north
I caught a cold and blew
40   My nose giving oil to the arab world
I am so hip even my errors are correct.
I sailed west to reach east and had to round off
the earth as I went
The hair from my head thinned and gold was laid
45   across three continents.

I am so perfect, so divine so **ethereal** so surreal
I cannot be **comprehended** except by my permission

I mean ... I ... can fly
like a bird in the sky...

helm: steering wheel

intone: chant

My Notes

ethereal: heavenly
comprehended: understood

Second Read

- Reread the poem to answer these text-dependent questions.
- Write any additional questions you have about the text in your Reader/Writer Notebook.

6. **Key Ideas and Details:** Who is the speaker of this poem, and what does she think of herself?

Extended Metaphor and Hyperbolic Me

7. **Craft and Structure:** What is the effect of hyperbole in this poem?

8. **Key Ideas and Details:** What does the speaker mean when she says, "I am so perfect, so divine so ethereal so surreal / I cannot be comprehended except by my permission"?

9. **Craft and Structure:** How do the religious references strengthen the poem's theme?

Working from the Text

10. Use the chart below to conduct a TWIST analysis of "Ego Tripping."

Literary Element	Analysis
Tone:	
Word Choice:	
Imagery:	
Style:	
Theme:	

Check Your Understanding

Write an interpretive sentence that explains how the title of the poem relates to the hyperbole and allusions in "Ego Tripping."

Drafting the Embedded Assessment

Write an **emulation** of either "Identity" or "Ego Tripping," creating your own two contrasting central images as an extended metaphor. Use different types of verbals in your poem. Be sure to:

- Create two central contrasting images.
- Extend the metaphor to include multiple comparisons.
- Use free verse.

ACADEMIC VOCABULARY
When you **emulate** someone or something, you are trying to equal or excel the quality of the original through imitation.

My Notes

Exploring Theme

LEARNING STRATEGIES:
Discussion Groups, Rereading,
Marking the Text, TWIST, SIFT,
Levels of Questions

Learning Targets
- Develop a thematic statement to use as a topic sentence in an analysis of a poem.
- Write a paragraph that connects the effect of literary devices to the theme of the poem.

Preview
In this activity, you will read and analyze a poem for theme and determine the effects of literary devices.

Setting a Purpose for Reading
- Notice the lack of punctuation. Make note of places where you would typically add punctuation, such as a question mark or period.
- Circle unknown words and phrases. Try to determine the meaning of the words by using context clues, word parts, or a dictionary.

My Notes

ABOUT THE AUTHOR
Born in Harlem in New York, Audre Lorde (1934–1992) was a poet and essayist. Her first poem was published in *Seventeen* magazine while she was in high school. Lorde's writing, especially her poetry, explores personal, political, and social issues, focusing on the emotions of relationships, especially in urban life. She was serving as the New York State poet laureate when she died.

Poetry

Hanging Fire

by Audre Lorde

> I am fourteen
> and my skin has betrayed me
> the boy I cannot live without
> still sucks his thumb
> 5 in secret
> how come my knees are
> always so ashy
> what if I die
> before the morning comes
> 10 and momma's in the bedroom
> with the door closed.

WORD CONNECTIONS

Content Connections

Hanging fire is a phrase used to describe a lack of progress, or stalled action. Originally, the phrase was used to describe the brief moment between when the trigger of a gun is pulled and when the gunpowder actually ignites.

I have to learn how to dance

in time for the next party

my room is too small for me

15 suppose I die before graduation

they will sing sad melodies

but finally

tell the truth about me

There is nothing I want to do

20 and too much

that has to be done

and momma's in the bedroom

with the door closed.

Nobody even stops to think

25 about my side of it

I should have been on Math Team

my marks were better than his

why do I have to be

the one

30 wearing braces

I have nothing to wear tomorrow

will I live long enough

to grow up

and momma's in the bedroom

35 with the door closed.

Second Read

- Reread the poem to answer these text-dependent questions.
- Write any additional questions you have about the text in your Reader/Writer Notebook.

1. **Key Ideas and Details:** What relationship does the speaker have with her mother?

GRAMMAR &USAGE
Clauses and Phrases

Independent clauses can stand alone as a complete sentence. Dependent clauses have a subject and a verb but are not a complete thought. **Prepositional phrases** add important details. This poem is a collection of clauses and phrases, and in such a situation line breaks become an important tool for the poet. Notice the line "I have to learn how to dance." This independent clause expresses a grand longing, one without boundaries. Consider how the next line—a prepositional phrase—changes the feeling or meaning of this idea.

My Notes

_____

_____

_____

_____

_____

_____

_____

_____

_____

_____

_____

_____

_____

_____

_____

_____

_____

_____

_____

Exploring Theme

My Notes

2. **Key Ideas and Details:** What is the central theme of this poem?

3. **Craft and Structure:** What is the tone of this poem?

Working from the Text

Read the poem again silently. Then engage in a group reading and discussion. With your group, reread the poem several times, marking and annotating the text for images and significant repetition. Use TWIST, SIFT, or Levels of Questions to help you understand and discuss the poem.

Check Your Understanding

As a group, develop a thematic statement that can be used as a topic sentence in an analysis of the poem "Hanging Fire."

Writing to Sources: Explanatory Text

Using your thematic statement, explain one of the themes of Audre Lorde's poem "Hanging Fire." Use the results from the TWIST, SIFT, or Levels of Questions strategy as a starting point. Be sure to:

- Begin by clearly stating the theme.
- Include multiple direct quotations from the poem to support your claims. Introduce and punctuate all quotations correctly.
- Use appropriate transitions and correct grammar, spelling, and punctuation.

INDEPENDENT READING LINK

Read and Discuss

Choose one of the poems you have read independently. Then review the strategies you have learned in this unit: TWIST, SIFT, and Levels of Questions. Analyze your poem using the most appropriate of the three strategies. Use your analysis to draft a thematic statement for the poem.

Odes to Special Things

Learning Targets
- Analyze odes for figurative language.
- Create an original ode.

Preview
In this activity, you will read two lyric poems, or **odes**, and analyze them for figurative language.

Setting a Purpose for Reading
- Underline the reasons the poet gives for writing an ode to his socks.
- Circle unknown words and phrases. Try to determine the meaning of the words by using context clues, word parts, or a dictionary.
- Highlight similes and metaphors.

LEARNING STRATEGIES:
Marking the Text, Sharing and Responding

Literary Terms
An **ode** is a lyric poem expressing the feelings or thoughts of a speaker, often celebrating a person, event, or thing.

WORD CONNECTIONS

Etymology
An *ode* is a poem written to formally praise a person, event, or object. Odes, first called *oldes*, were first written by the ancient Greeks, who would chant or sing praises. The word shares the same root with the musical words *melody* and *rhapsody*.

Poetry

Ode to My Socks

by Pablo Neruda
translated by Robert Bly

Mara Mori brought me
a pair of socks
which she knitted herself
with her sheepherder's hands,
5   two socks as soft as rabbits.
I slipped my feet into them
as if they were two cases
knitted with threads of twilight and goatskin,
Violent socks,
10 my feet were two fish made of wool,
two long sharks
sea blue, shot through
by one golden thread,
two **immense** blackbirds,
15 two cannons,

my feet were honored in this way
by these heavenly socks.
They were so handsome for the first time
my feet seemed to me unacceptable

My Notes
_____
_____
_____
_____
_____

immense: huge

_____
_____
_____
_____

Odes to Special Things

decrepit: worn out by long use

My Notes

20 like two **decrepit** firemen,
firemen unworthy of that woven fire,
of those glowing socks.

Nevertheless, I resisted the sharp temptation
to save them somewhere as schoolboys
25 keep fireflies,
as learned men collect
sacred texts,
I resisted the mad impulse to put them
in a golden cage and each day give them
30 birdseed and pieces of pink melon.
Like explorers in the jungle
who hand over the very rare green deer
to the spit and eat it with remorse,
I stretched out my feet and pulled on
35 the magnificent socks and then my shoes.

The moral of my ode is this:
beauty is twice beauty
and what is good is doubly good
when it is a matter of two socks
40 made of wool in winter.

Second Read

- Reread the poem to answer these text-dependent questions.
- Write any additional questions you have about the text in your Reader/Writer Notebook.

1. **Key Ideas and Details:** What is the moral message of this poem?

2. **Craft and Structure:** How does the poem's form support its moral?

3. **Craft and Structure:** How is the poem's tone conveyed through figurative language?

4. **Craft and Structure:** What is the effect of alliteration in the poem?

Setting a Purpose for Reading

- Underline the images that show the speaker's attitude toward "Abuelito."
- Circle unknown words and phrases. Try to determine the meaning of the words by using context clues, word parts, or a dictionary.

ABOUT THE AUTHOR

Sandra Cisneros (b. 1954) grew up in Chicago and now lives in San Antonio, Texas. Cisneros has written extensively about the experiences of growing up as a Latina. In talking about her writing, Cisneros says she creates stories from things that have touched her deeply: "... in real life a story doesn't have shape, and it's the writer that gives it a beginning, a middle, and an end."

Poetry

Abuelito Who

by Sandra Cisneros

Abuelito[1] who throws coins like rain
and asks who loves him
who is dough and feathers
who is a watch and glass of water
5 whose hair is made of fur
is too sad to come downstairs today
who tells me in Spanish you are my diamond
who tells me in English you are my sky
whose little eyes are string
10 can't come out to play

---

[1] **Abuelito:** Spanish term for "grandfather"

Odes to Special Things

sleeps in his little room all night and day

who used to laugh like the letter k

is sick

is a doorknob tied to a sour stick

15 is tired shut the door

doesn't live here anymore

is hiding underneath the bed

who talks to me inside my head

is blankets and spoons and big brown shoes

20 who snores up and down up and down up and down again

is the rain on the roof that falls like coins

asking who loves him

who loves him who?

Second Read

- Reread the poem to answer these text-dependent questions.
- Write any additional questions you have about the text in your Reader/Writer Notebook.

5. **Key Ideas and Details:** What is the significance of the poem's title?

6. **Key Ideas and Details:** What relationship does the speaker of the poem have with her *abuelito*?

7. **Craft and Structure:** How does the poem's tone reflect its central message?

Working from the Text

8. In the My Notes section, create a list of your favorite people, places, things, or experiences. Share these items with a group.

9. Why or why not would these items make a good ode?

Check Your Understanding

Odes have a long tradition and in ancient times were accompanied by music and dance. How are odes similar to songs in the way they express their "lyrics" and emotions?

Drafting the Embedded Assessment

Review the list of favorite things you made, and choose one of the items—something that you treasure. Write an ode, a poem of praise or respect, to honor the person, place, thing, or experience you have chosen. Be sure to:

- Use repetition or a refrain for effect.
- Use images, figurative language, such as similes and metaphors, and vivid verbs to create a feeling.
- Use free verse, carefully choosing effective line breaks.

LEARNING STRATEGIES:
Diffusing, Paraphrasing,
Marking the Text

Literary Terms

A **quatrain** is a four-line stanza in a poem.
A **couplet** is two consecutive lines of verse with end rhyme. A couplet usually expresses a complete unit of thought.
Iambic pentameter describes a rhythmic pattern: five feet (or units), each consisting of one unstressed syllable followed by a stressed syllable.

My Notes

_____
_____
_____
_____
_____
_____

thee: you

temperate: mild

_____
_____
_____

untrimmed: stripped of beauty

eternal: never ending

fair thou ow'st: beauty you possess

Learning Targets
- Examine the structure of a sonnet to infer the relationship between structure and meaning.
- Write an original sonnet.

Preview

In this activity, you will read a sonnet, which is a fixed form of poetry with 14 lines consisting of three **quatrains** and a **couplet**, and is written in **iambic pentameter**.

Setting a Purpose for Reading
- Draw lines to separate the quatrains and the couplet.
- Circle unknown words and phrases. Try to determine the meaning of the words by using context clues, word parts, or a dictionary.
- Mark the rest of the poem's rhyme scheme and note its regularity.

ABOUT THE AUTHOR

Little is known about the early life of William Shakespeare (1564–1616) except that he was born and grew up in Stratford-upon-Avon in England. He is considered one of the greatest playwrights who ever lived. In addition to 37 plays (comedies, tragedies, and histories), he also wrote a series of 154 sonnets in a style that has become known as the Shakespearean sonnet.

Poetry

Sonnet 18

by William Shakespeare

Shall I compare **thee** to a summer's day?	A
Thou art more lovely and more **temperate**.	B
Rough winds do shake the darling buds of May,	A
And summer's lease hath all too short a date.	B
5 Sometime too hot the eye of heaven shines,	C
And often is his gold complexion dimmed;	—
And every fair from fair sometime declines,	—
By chance, or nature's changing course **untrimmed**.	—
But thy **eternal** summer shall not fade	—
10 Nor lose possession of that **fair thou ow'st**;	—
Nor shall death brag thou wand'rest in his shade,	—
When in eternal lines to time thou grow'st,	—
So long as men can breathe or eyes can see,	—
So long lives this, and this gives life to thee.	—

Second Read

- Reread the sonnet to answer these text-dependent questions.
- Write any additional questions you have about the text in your Reader/Writer Notebook.

1. **Key Ideas and Details:** How does the speaker of this poem feel about summer?

2. **Key Ideas and Details:** What does the speaker appreciate most about his beloved, and how can you tell?

3. **Key Ideas and Details:** How does the tone of the speaker's praise shift in the final couplet?

Working from the Text

4. Work in your discussion groups to paraphrase each quatrain and the couplet. Use the My Notes section of the page for your paraphrases. To aid in your understanding, try to paraphrase each sentence in the poem. In your groups, respond to the following:

- What is the purpose of each quatrain?

- How does the couplet bring closure to ideas presented in the poem?

- Write a thematic statement that expresses the main idea of the poem.

My Notes

Coming of Age in Sonnets

Check Your Understanding

How do the couplets and quatrains in a sonnet help the poet express a theme or main idea?

Drafting the Embedded Assessment

Transform one of the free verse poems you have written into a sonnet, or write an original sonnet on a topic of your choice. Be sure to:

- Follow the rhyme scheme and structural elements of the type of poem you choose.
- Give your poem a title that relates to its central image or images.
- Use figurative language and specific words to convey your topic and the attitude in your poem.

Independent Reading Checkpoint

Review your independent readings. Write a short paragraph explaining what you have learned about the various forms of poetry and how each contributes to the overall theme of the poem, as well as to your enjoyment and understanding. Then choose one of the poems you read and briefly explain what you liked most about it.

Creating a Poetry Anthology

ASSIGNMENT

Your assignment is to create a poetry anthology that will include an introduction to the collection, seven or eight original poems with complementary visuals, and a reflection that explains the style and content of the work presented. Use technology to create your anthology and to present it in a polished format.

Planning: Create a plan for writing.	▦ How can you use your Reader/Writer Notebook as a source of ideas for your collection? ▦ Have you reviewed the different poetry structures (sonnet, free verse, catalog, ode) presented in the unit as possible models for your original poetry? ▦ How will you show your use and understanding of literary devices and their effects as part of your original collection? ▦ Have you included imagery and symbolism in your poetry that can be represented by pictures, photographs, or sketches?
Drafting: Revise poems and write additional ones to create a collection.	▦ How will you arrange your poetry in an anthology to best reflect your efforts? ▦ What will you write in your introduction or preface to help your reader understand your poetry? What does the reader need to know about your life to better understand your work? ▦ What must you include in a reflection to highlight your deliberate and purposeful use of poetic forms and elements? ▦ How will you include a discussion of your creative process and inspiration?
Revising: Finalize the anthology for publication.	▦ How will you ensure that you take your poetry through an active process of revision that includes soliciting feedback from others? ▦ How can you use the strategies of adding and deleting as you choose diction and figurative language and structure stanzas and lines? ▦ How can consulting the Scoring Guide help you revise?
Editing for Publication: Prepare your final draft as a polished work ready to be shared.	▦ How will you make your anthology visually appealing? ▦ How will you organize your collection to include all the components of an anthology (cover page, table of contents, introduction, annotated original poems with visuals, and reflection)? ▦ How might you use technology to illustrate, produce, and publish your anthology?

Reflection

Describe how you have grown as a writer in the process of creating this poetry anthology. Have you discovered anything new about yourself as a writer? If so, what? If not, why?

Creating a Poetry Anthology

SCORING GUIDE

Scoring Criteria	Exemplary	Proficient	Emerging	Incomplete
Ideas	The anthology • presents original poems with a clear tone • uses annotations to identify literary devices and to provide insightful analysis of purpose • insightfully introduces the collection of work • clearly explains and provides examples of purpose, creative process, challenges, and use of symbolic visuals.	The anthology • presents original poems with a clear tone • uses annotations to identify some literary devices and to analyze purpose • clearly introduces relevant information that helps the reader understand the collection of work • explains the poet's purpose, creative process, challenges, and use of symbolic visuals.	The anthology • presents some poems that are not original or do not present clear tone • does not use annotations to identify the literary devices used or provide appropriate analysis of purpose • includes a vague introduction that does not connect life events • does not adequately explain the process, product, or learning of poetic form, style, and content.	The anthology • presents few, if any, poems; poems presented may not be original • is missing annotations or annotations do not identify literary devices used (if any) • has no introduction or the introduction does not present related information • does not include a reflection or the reflection does not relate to the process or product.
Structure	The anthology • contains all required elements, including a creative cover page and title, a complete table of contents, and symbolic visuals • shows appropriate and consistent poetic form.	The anthology • contains a cover page and title, table of contents, and complementary visuals • generally uses appropriate and consistent poetic form.	The anthology • is not well-organized or may be missing a cover page and title, a table of contents, or visuals • does not carefully use poetic format or structure.	The anthology • is confusing or may be missing a cover page and title, a table of contents, or visuals • shows little attention to the use of poetic format or structure.
Use of Language	The anthology • uses connotative words, figurative language, and compelling verbs to reinforce theme and to achieve a specific effect.	The anthology • generally uses descriptive words, figurative language, and verbs to reinforce theme and to achieve a specific effect.	The anthology • does not use precise words or figurative language; verbs are weak or inconsistent.	The anthology • uses confusing words and lacks figurative language or relevant verbs.

Unpacking Embedded Assessment 2: Analyzing and Presenting a Poet

Learning Targets
- Identify the knowledge and skills needed to complete Embedded Assessment 2 successfully and reflect on prior learning that supports the knowledge and skills needed.
- Examine tone and write an analysis of the way tone is created.

LEARNING STRATEGIES:
Summarizing, Graphic Organizer, Close Reading

Making Connections

In the first part of this unit, you read and analyzed a variety of poems written in different styles and using varied poetic structures. You practiced using poetic style and structure by writing your own poems. In this part of the unit, you will expand your analysis of poetry by examining tone in depth and writing an analysis of one poet's style.

Essential Questions

Now that you have read and analyzed several poems, how would you change your answer to the Essential Question "What is poetry?"

Consider the second Essential Question: What can a writer learn from studying an author's craft and style?

My Notes

Developing Vocabulary

Look at your Reader/Writer Notebook and review the new vocabulary you learned in the first part of this unit. Which words do you now know thoroughly, and which do you need to learn more about? Make a plan to review vocabulary and add to your notes about new words as you study the rest of this unit.

Unpacking Embedded Assessment 2

Read the assignment for Embedded Assessment 2: Analyzing and Presenting a Poet.

> Your assignment is to analyze a collection of work from a poet and write a style-analysis essay. You will then select one of the poems you analyzed and present an oral interpretation of the poem to the class.

In your own words, summarize what you will need to know to complete this assignment successfully. With your class, create a graphic organizer to represent the skills and knowledge you will need to complete the tasks identified in the Embedded Assessment.

Unpacking Embedded Assessment 2: Analyzing and Presenting a Poet

Tone Review

1. "Smells Like Teen Spirit" is a song originally written and recorded by Nirvana. Later, Tori Amos recorded it with her own signature style. Listen to both artists' versions of the song, and use the following graphic organizer to note words or phrases that may describe the tone the artists convey in the song.

Nirvana's Version: "Smells Like Teen Spirit"	Tori Amos's Version: "Smells Like Teen Spirit"
Comments About Tone:	Comments About Tone:

2. Respond to the following questions:

   • What are the differences between these two versions of one song?

   • What tone (attitude) does each version create? Note phrases and images from the song that support your opinion.

   • Where in each version do you see or hear a shift? Explain.

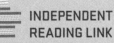

INDEPENDENT READING LINK

Read and Research

For independent reading during this half of the unit, you may want to look at the works of several poets. You will memorize, present, and analyze the works of one of these poets for your Embedded Assessment. From the poets you have researched, choose the one you want to use for your Embedded Assessment. Make a list of the poems you plan to read.

Writing to Sources: Explanatory Text

Write a style-analysis paragraph in which you identify the tone and explain how it differs between the two songs. Refer to the graphic organizer you completed as you develop your paragraph. Be sure to:

• Start with a topic sentence that identifies the two songs and their differing tones.

• Use textual evidence to support the opinion stated in the topic sentence.

• Incorporate quoted material smoothly in your analysis.

Analyzing a Persona Poem

LEARNING STRATEGIES:
Close Reading, Paraphrasing,
Predicting

Learning Targets

- Identify and interpret key ideas and tone in a poem.
- Write a paragraph analyzng how imagery and diction create tone.

Preview

In this activity, you will read a persona poem in which a poet writes from the perspective of his mother, who was taken to an internment camp during World War II.

Setting a Purpose for Reading

- Mark the shift in the poem's tone with an exclamation point (!).
- Circle unknown words and phrases. Try to determine the meaning of the words by using context clues, word parts, or a dictionary.

ABOUT THE AUTHOR

Dwight Okita (b. 1958) was born and continues to live in Chicago. His first book of poems, *Crossing with the Light*, was published in 1992. He continues to be an active writer, working on poetry, stage plays, a screenplay, and fiction—both short stories and novels.

My Notes

Poetry

In Response to Executive Order 9066:
All Americans of Japanese Descent
Must Report to Relocation Centers

by Dwight Okita

Dear Sirs:

Of course I'll come. I've packed my galoshes

and three packets of tomato seeds. Denise calls them

love apples. My father says where we're going

5 they won't grow.

I am a fourteen-year-old girl with bad spelling

and a messy room. If it helps any, I will tell you

I have always felt funny using chopsticks

and my favorite food is hot dogs.

10 My best friend is a white girl named Denise—

we look at boys together. She sat in front of me

all through grade school because of our names:

O'Connor, Ozawa. I know the back of Denise's head very well.

Analyzing a Persona Poem

I tell her she's going bald. She tells me I copy on tests.

15 We're best friends.

I saw Denise today in Geography class.

She was sitting on the other side of the room.

"You're trying to start a war," she said, "giving secrets

away to the Enemy.[1] Why can't you keep your big

20 mouth shut?"

I didn't know what to say.

I gave her a packet of tomato seeds

and asked her to plant them for me, told her

when the first tomato ripened

25 she'd miss me.

Second Read

- Reread the poem to answer these text-dependent questions.
- Write any additional questions you have about the text in your Reader/Writer Notebook.

1. **Craft and Structure:** What is the effect of having a 14-year-old narrate this poem?

2. **Key Ideas and Details:** What do the tomato seeds symbolize in the poem?

3. **Key Ideas and Details:** How does life change for the speaker after the executive order?

[1] **the Enemy:** Japan, which was at war with the United States during World War II

Working from the Text

4. How does the title of the poem affect its tone?

5. The poem is written as a letter in direct response to Executive Order 9066. Why would Okita structure his poem as a letter?

6. How does having an understanding of the actual Executive Order 9066 signed by President Franklin D. Roosevelt provide context and deepen your understanding of the poem?

Check Your Understanding

Write a thematic statement about how diction and imagery create tone in "In Response to Executive Order 9066."

Explanatory Writing Prompt

Using your thematic statement, write an analysis of the function of diction and imagery in creating tone in "In Response to Executive Order 9066." Be sure to:

- Identify the tone and include textual evidence that shows how tone is created by diction and imagery.
- Include multiple direct quotations from the poem to support your claim.
- Use correct grammar, spelling, and punctuation, and finish with a conclusion paragraph.

My Notes

Poetry Analysis of "Young"

LEARNING STRATEGIES:
Marking the Text, Skimming/
Scanning, TP-CASTT,
Discussion Groups

My Notes

Learning Targets
- Analyze a poem using the vocabulary of literary analysis.
- Use the TP-CASTT strategy to analyze a poem.

Preview
In this activity, you will read a free verse coming-of-age poem and conduct a close analysis of its style and theme.

Setting a Purpose for Reading
- Underline examples of imagery.
- Circle unknown words and phrases. Try to determine the meaning of the words by using context clues, word parts, or a dictionary.
- Make note of the punctuation and the poet's use of literary devices.

ABOUT THE AUTHOR
Anne Sexton (1928–1974) discovered her poetic voice as an adult when she joined writing groups and met other poets who encouraged her work. She published several successful collections of poetry and was awarded a Pulitzer Prize for Poetry in 1967. Much of her work explores personal issues or issues specific to women.

Poetry

Young

by Anne Sexton

A thousand doors ago
when I was a lonely kid
in a big house with four
garages and it was summer
5 as long as I could remember,
I lay on the lawn at night,
clover wrinkling under me,
the wise stars bedding over me,
my mother's window a funnel
10 of yellow heat running out,
my father's window, half shut,
an eye where sleepers pass,
and the boards of the house
were smooth and white as wax

15 and probably a million leaves
    sailed on their strange stalks
    as the crickets ticked together
    and I, in my brand new body,
    which was not a woman's yet,
20 told the stars my questions
    and thought God could really see
    the heat and the painted light,
    elbows, knees, dreams, goodnight.

Second Read

- Reread the poem to answer these text-dependent questions.
- Write any additional questions you have about the text in your Reader/Writer Notebook.

1. **Craft and Structure:** How does the author capture the isolation of a teenager's coming of age in this poem?

2. **Key Ideas and Details:** What is the speaker's relationship to nature?

3. **Craft and Structure:** How does the poem's form reflect its central message?

Working from the Text

4. Complete the TP-CASTT note-taking organizer on the following page with your small group.

My Notes

Poetry Analysis of "Young"

Introducing the Strategy: TP-CASTT

TP-CASTT is an acronym for a strategy used to analyze poetry by breaking the analysis down into parts and then synthesizing thinking into one cohesive interpretation. The letters stand for **T**itle, **P**araphrase, **C**onnotation, **A**ttitude, **S**hift, **T**itle, and **T**heme.

TP-CASTT Analysis
Title of Poem:
Author:

Title: Make a prediction before you read the poem. What do you think the title means?

Paraphrase: Restate the important sentences or lines of the poem in your own words.

Connotation: What words or phrases suggest something beyond their literal meanings? What do you think the poet is saying in this poem? Go beyond the literal meanings or the plot of the poem.

Attitude: Describe the speaker's attitude. Use specific adjectives to describe your ideas.

Shifts: Describe where the poem appears to shift, either in subject, speaker, or tone.

Title: Re-examine the title. What do you think it means now, in the context of the poem?

Theme: What do you think is the underlying message about life expressed in this poem?

Check Your Understanding

Write a thematic statement about the poem "Young." Consider Sexton's diction and the structure of the poem. How does the lack of punctuation contribute to the coming-of-age theme?

**INDEPENDENT
READING LINK**

Read and Discuss

Choose one of the poems from your independent reading. Apply a TP-CASTT analysis to the poem. Share your analysis with peers. Explain how using the TP-CASTT analysis helped you better understand the poem.

Poetry Café

ACTIVITY
4.13

Learning Targets
- Independently analyze a poem for its poetic elements.
- Present an oral interpretation that demonstrates an understanding of the structure and ideas of a poem.

Preview
In this activity, you will work with a group to develop **oral interpretations** of a poem.

Setting a Purpose for Reading
- Underline poetic elements such as diction, imagery, allusion, and hyperbole.
- Circle unknown words and phrases. Try to determine the meaning of the words by using context clues, word parts, or a dictionary.

ABOUT THE AUTHOR
Gladys Cardiff (b. 1942) is an American poet and writer of Irish, Welsh, and Cherokee descent. Her poetry tends to reflect her heritage. She has published two books of poems, *To Frighten a Storm* and *A Bare Unpainted Table*. She is an associate professor of poetry, American literature, and Native American literature at Oakland University, Michigan.

LEARNING STRATEGIES:
TP-CASTT, Close Reading, Oral Interpretation, Discussion Groups

ACADEMIC VOCABULARY
The word **interpretation** can be applied in many situations. Interpreting is the act of explaining or showing the meaning of something, and it can be applied to data, poetry, or historical events. An **oral interpretation** specifically refers to the interpretation of a text through an oral reading.

Poetry

Combing

by Gladys Cardiff

Bending, I bow my head
And lay my hand upon
Her hair, combing, and think
How women do this for
5 Each other. My daughter's hair
Curls against the comb.
Wet and **fragrant** — orange
Parings. Her face, downcast,
Is quiet for one so young.

10 I take her place. Beneath
My mother's hands I feel
The braids drawn up tight
As a piano wire and singing,
Vinegar-rinsed. Sitting
15 before the oven I hear

My Notes

fragrant: sweet smelling

Unit 4 • Exploring Poetic Voices **331**

coils: spirals

plaiting: braiding

The orange **coils** tick
The early hour before school.

She combed her grandmother
Mathilda's hair using
20 A comb made out of bone.
Mathilda rocked her oak-wood
Chair, her face downcast,
intent on tearing rags
In strips to braid a cotton
25 Rug from bits of orange
And brown. A simple act,

Preparing hair. Something
Women do for each other,
Plaiting the generations.

ABOUT THE AUTHOR
William Wordsworth (1770–1850) was a British poet who lived in the Lake District in Northern England. He was an innovator in that he wrote lyric poetry in the language of ordinary people rather than in the "poetic" diction that was common at the time. His wrote about his love of nature in a way that later came to be known as Romanticism.

Poetry

i Wandered Lonely as a Cloud

by William Wordsworth

I wandered lonely as a cloud
That floats on high o'er **vales** and hills,
When all at once I saw a crowd,
A host, of golden daffodils;
5 Beside the lake, beneath the trees,
Fluttering and dancing in the breeze.

Continuous as the stars that shine
And twinkle on the milky way,
They stretched in never-ending line
10 Along the **margin** of a bay:
Ten thousand saw I at a glance,
Tossing their heads in **sprightly** dance.

The waves beside them danced; but they
Outdid the sparkling waves in glee:
15 A poet could not but be gay,
In such a **jocund** company:
I gazed—and gazed—but little thought
What wealth the show to me had brought:

For oft, when on my couch I lie
20 In vacant or in **pensive** mood,
They flash upon that inward eye
Which is the bliss of solitude;
And then my heart with pleasure fills,
And dances with the daffodils.

vales: valleys

margin: border

sprightly: lively

jocund: cheerful

pensive: dreamy; thoughtful

Poetry Café

My Notes

Working from the Text

1. Create and present an oral interpretation of your assigned poem (either "Combing" or "I Wandered Lonely as a Cloud"). Then, present research that connects the writer's biography to your understanding of the poem.

2. Your teacher will next assign your group one of the following five poems. Your group will prepare and present an oral interpretion of the assigned poem. Rehearse, and follow this format for your presentation:

   • Introduce the author and title of the poem.

   • Present the group's oral interpretation.

   • Conclude with a statement connecting the group's analysis to the oral interpretation and sharing information about the writer that relates to the poem.

ABOUT THE AUTHOR

Langston Hughes (1902–1967) was born in the Midwest but went to New York to attend Columbia University. He became a prominent figure in the period of American literature known as the Harlem Renaissance. Much of his work—poetry, prose, and plays—evoked life in the Harlem section of New York. In fact, he was known as the "poet laureate of Harlem." In his work, he focused on the struggles and feelings of ordinary individuals.

Poetry

Harlem

by Langston Hughes

deferred: postponed

fester: rot

What happens to a dream **deferred**?

Does it dry up

like a raisin in the sun?

Or **fester** like a sore—

5 And then run?

Does it stink like rotten meat?

Or crust and sugar over—

like a syrupy sweet?

Maybe it just sags

10 like a heavy load.

Or does it explode?

ABOUT THE AUTHOR

Emily Dickinson (1830–1886) lived her entire life in her father's house in Amherst, Massachusetts. She was somewhat reclusive, yet her imagination was extremely active. Using her own peculiar style of punctuation and capitalization, she wrote more than 1,700 short poems, of which only a few were published (anonymously) in her lifetime. The others were found after her death. She is regarded as one of America's greatest poets.

My Notes

Poetry

"Hope" is the thing with feathers

by Emily Dickinson

"Hope" is the thing with feathers—
That perches in the soul—
And sings the tune without the words—
And never stops—at all—

5 And sweetest—in the **Gale**—is heard;
And sore must be the storm—
That could **abash** the little Bird
That kept so many warm—

I've heard it in the chillest land—
10 And on the strangest Sea—
Yet, never, in Extremity,
It asked a crumb—of me.

Gale: wind

abash: embarrass

Poetry Café

My Notes

_____
_____
_____
_____
_____
_____
_____
_____

evoke: to call up; summon

_____
_____
_____

endure: to continue to exist

ruthless: without pity or compassion

branding: a mark made on the skin by burning

_____
_____
_____
_____
_____
_____
_____
_____
_____
_____
_____

ABOUT THE AUTHOR
Daniel Halpern (b. 1945) is a literary editor, translator, and writer. He has published eight collections of his own poetry. He has also edited two collections of international short stories and several collections of writings on a variety of topics, such as nature and artists.

Poetry

Scars

_by_ Daniel Halpern

> They are the short stories of the flesh,
> can **evoke** the entire event
> in a moment—the action, the scent
> and sound—place you there a second time.
>
> 5   It's as if the flesh decides to hold
> onto what threatens its well-being,
> They become part of the map marking
> the pain we've had to **endure**.
>
> If only the heart were so **ruthless**,
> 10 willing to document what it lived
> by **branding** even those sensitive
> tissues so information might flow back.
>
> It's easy to recall what doesn't heal,
> more difficult to call back what leaves
> 15 no mark, what depends on memory
> to bring forward what's been gone so long,
>
> The heart's too gentle. It won't hold
> **before us what we may still need to see.**

ABOUT THE AUTHOR
Percy Bysshe Shelley (1792–1822) is one of the best-known English romantic poets of the 19th century. He is best known for works such as "Ode to the West Wind," "The Masque of Anarchy," "Queen Mab," and "Alastor." Shelley's wife Mary, also a writer, wrote the influential novel *Frankenstein*.

Poetry

Ozymandias

by Percy Bysshe Shelley

I met a traveler from an antique land
Who said: "Two vast and trunkless legs of stone
Stand in the desert ... Near them, on the sand,
Half sunk, a shattered **visage** lies, whose frown,

5 And wrinkled lip, and sneer of cold command,
Tell that its sculptor well those passions read
Which yet survive, stamped on these lifeless things,
The hand that mocked them and the heart that fed;
And on the **pedestal** these words appear:

10 "My name is Ozymandias, King of Kings,
Look on my works, ye Mighty, and despair!"
Nothing beside remains. Round the decay
Of that **colossal** wreck, boundless and bare
The lone and level sands stretch far away.

visage: face

pedestal: a supporting base

colossal: huge

ABOUT THE AUTHOR

Essex Hemphill (1957–1995) was a poet, essayist, and editor. He began writing when he was 14 years old, and, over time, he published three volumes of poetry. His poetry also appeared in a variety of magazines and in several films and documentaries. Some of his poems, like "American Hero," reflect on self-acceptance and social acceptance or denial.

Poetry

American Hero

by Essex Hemphill

I have nothing to lose tonight.
All my men surround me, panting,
as I spin the ball above our heads
on my middle finger.
5   It's a shimmering club light
and I'm dancing, slick in my sweat.
Squinting, I aim at the hole
fifty feet away. I let the tension go.
Shoot for the net. Choke it.
10 I never hear the ball
slap the backboard. I slam it
through the net. The crowd goes wild
for our win. I scored
thirty-two points this game
15 and they love me for it.
Everyone hollering
is a friend tonight.
But there are towns,
certain neighborhoods
20 where I'd be hard pressed
to hear them cheer
if I move on the block.

Writing to Sources: Explanatory Text

Write an analysis of a poem of your choice. Identify the key ideas and tone. Include an explanation of all of the poetic elements. Be sure to:

- Include the title and author of your poem.
- Include multiple direct quotations from the poem to exemplify your analysis. Introduce and punctuate all quotations correctly.
- Use an appropriate voice and a variety of sentence structures.

Exploring and Analyzing a Poet's Work

Learning Targets
- Identify elements of an author's style.
- Connect biographical information to an understanding of a poet's work.
- Compose a thesis connecting style and meaning.

Preview
In this activity, you will read and analyze two poems by the poet Leslie Marmon Silko. Notice the influence her heritage has had on her poetry by paying close attention to her use of imagery, diction, and theme.

Setting a Purpose for Reading
- Underline parts of the poem that evoke a specific image.
- Circle unknown words and phrases. Try to determine the meaning of the words by using context clues, word parts, or a dictionary.
- Look for poetic devices and similarities between the poems.

> **ABOUT THE AUTHOR**
> American author and poet Leslie Marmon Silko (b. 1948) is regarded as one of the most important contemporary Native American writers alive today. Her work is renowned for portraying the life, struggles, and culture of modern Native Americans. Silko herself has mixed ancestry, but she identifies largely with her Laguna heritage. Silko grew up on the edge of the Laguna reservation where she attended school through the fifth grade, learning about Laguna spirituality, traditions, and myths. After fifth grade, she transferred to a Catholic school that banned her from speaking her native language. This transition profoundly affected Silko, and the struggle between cultures resonates deeply in her work.

LEARNING STRATEGIES:
Graphic Organizer, Marking the Text, Discussion Groups

My Notes

Poetry

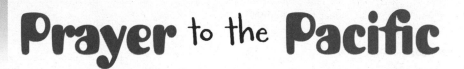

Prayer to the Pacific

by Leslie Marmon Silko

> I traveled to the ocean
>   distant
>   from my southwest land of sandrock
>   to the moving blue water
> 5   Big as the myth of origin.
>
> Pale
> pale water in the yellow-white light of
>   sun floating west
>   to China

My Notes

10   where ocean herself was born.
    Clouds that blow across the sand are wet.

    Squat in the wet sand and speak to the Ocean:
            I return to you turquoise the red coral you sent us,
                        sister spirit of Earth.
15 Four round stones in my pocket I carry back the ocean
                        to suck and to taste.

    Thirty thousand years ago
                Indians came riding across the ocean
                carried by giant sea turtles.
20 Waves were high that day
            great sea turtles waded slowly out
                        from the gray sundown sea.
    Grandfather Turtle rolled in the sand four times
            and disappeared
25   swimming into the sun.

    And so from that time
        immemorial,
                as the old people say,
    rain clouds drift from the west
30   gift from the ocean.

    Green leaves in the wind
    Wet earth on my feet
            swallowing raindrops
                clear from China.

immemorial: long ago

Second Read
- Reread the poem to answer these text-dependent questions.
- Write any additional questions you have about the text in your Reader/Writer Notebook.

1. **Key Ideas and Details:** How does this poem reflect the author's Native American culture?

2. **Key Ideas and Details:** Why is this poem called a prayer?

3. **Craft and Structure:** What is the effect of the poem's form on its central message?

Poetry

In Cold Storm Light

by Leslie Marmon Silko

In cold storm light
I watch the sandrock
   canyon rim.
The wind is wet
5   with the smell of **piñon**.
The wind is cold
    with the sound of juniper.
      And then
         out of the thick ice sky
10   running swiftly
           pounding
           swirling above the treetops
The snow elk come,
Moving, moving
15   white song
            storm wind in the branches.
And when the elk have passed
    behind them
      a crystal train of snowflakes
20   strands of mist
        tangled in rocks
        and leaves.

piñon: a small pine tree in Mexico

Exploring and Analyzing a Poet's Work

Second Read

- Reread the poem to answer these text-dependent questions.
- Write any additional questions you have about the text in your Reader/Writer Notebook.

4. **Key Ideas and Details:** What is this poem about?

5. **Craft and Structure:** How does the poem's form reflect the central theme?

6. **Key Ideas and Details:** What is the effect of synesthesia—or blended senses—in the poem?

Working from the Text

7. Brainstorm a list of elements that characterize Silko's poetic style.

ACADEMIC VOCABULARY
To **elaborate** on a point is to expand or to add information or detail and thus to develop the point more fully.

8. Complete the following chart, listing elements of and **elaborating** on the author's style.

Poet or Lyricist: _____ Leslie Marmon Silko _____

Author's Style	Example from the Poems	Analysis

Check Your Understanding

Using TWIST (tone, word choice/diction, imagery, style, theme), compose a thesis that conveys your understanding of the connection between Silko's style and the meaning of her poetry.

Writing to Sources: Explanatory Text

Write an analysis of the poet's style. Explain how poetic structure and elements contribute to this style. Use your completed style chart to help generate ideas. Be sure to:

- Identify the poetic structure and elements the author uses.
- Include direct quotations and specific examples and details from your source text to support your analysis. Introduce and punctuate all quotations correctly.
- Provide a concluding statement that summarizes your main points.

My Notes

INDEPENDENT READING LINK

Read and Respond

Choose two of your independent reading poems written by the same author. Compare the two poems for theme, style, tone, and use of poetic elements. Explain how the writer's craft and style differ and stay the same.

Choosing and Researching a Poet

My Notes

Learning Targets

- Choose a poet and a selection of his or her poetry to study and analyze in depth.
- Make stylistic and thematic connections among the poet's poems.

Choosing a Poet to Research

1. You are now ready to select poetry by one author to study in depth. Brainstorm a list of possible authors and poems. In this unit, you have studied multiple works by three poets: Pablo Neruda, Nikki Giovanni, and Leslie Marmon Silko. Use these poets and the poetry presented in this unit as a springboard.

2. Based on your own interests and the directions provided by your teacher, find a poet whose work you would like to study in more depth. Select three to five of their poems. List them here.

3. Using the strategies you have learned in this unit, analyze the poems you have chosen, and find thematic and stylistic connections among them. Use the following graphic organizer to take notes and make connections among the poems.

Poet or Lyricist: _____

Author's Style	Example from the Poems	Analysis

Independent Reading Checkpoint

After completing your independent readings, think about which poet's works you might choose to further analyze. With a group, discuss why this poet's works best lend themselves to analysis and an oral interpretation.

Generating a Rhetorical Plan

Learning Targets
- Create a strong thesis statement for an essay of analysis.
- Unpack the thesis statement to develop a plan for an essay of analysis.

Planning an Analysis Essay

1. Based on the analysis you have done of your poet's work, create a working thesis to use as you develop an organizational plan for an essay of analysis.

   Criteria for a thesis statement:
   - Include author and genre.
   - Identify stylistic techniques and their connection to meaning.

   Sample Thesis and Topic Outline:

   Thesis: *Giovanni's unconventional use of line breaks, punctuation, capitalization, and imagery emphasizes her persona as unconventional and unrestrained by rules.*
   - Topic Sentence 1: *Giovanni's unconventional use of punctuation and capitalization emphasizes her emotional and unconventional voice.*
     - Possible examples for support:

   - Topic Sentence 2: *Giovanni weaves unique and unconventional imagery together to assert a strong and passionate speaker.*
     - Possible examples for support:

2. Develop a rhetorical plan for your essay analyzing the poems of your chosen author. Draft a thesis statement, topic sentences for paragraphs that develop the thesis statement, and a conclusion. This outline will be the basis for your literary analysis of the collection of three to five poems by one author.

My Notes

Generating a Rhetorical Plan

Your Outline:

I. Thesis

II. Topic Sentence 1:

    Possible examples:

III. Topic Sentence 2:

    Possible examples:

IV. Conclusion

Analyzing and Presenting a Poet

ASSIGNMENT

Your assignment is to analyze a collection of work from a poet and write a style-analysis essay. You will then select one of the poems you analyzed and present an oral interpretation of the poem to the class.

Planning: Create a plan.	▪ How will you select poems that are of sufficient quality to benefit from a close analysis? ▪ What criteria will you use to choose a poem for oral interpretation that will provide your audience with an understanding of meaning and structure?
Drafting: Write the analysis.	▪ How will you make notes about your analysis of the poem? Do you see recurring patterns? What diction and stylistic techniques contribute to the poet's style? ▪ How will you organize and structure ideas for the essay?
Revising: Finalize your essay for publication.	▪ How will you share your draft with peers and revise to reflect feedback on your analysis of style, clarity of ideas, and support for your analysis (such as through quotations)? ▪ How will you evaluate your draft for final organization, use of transitions, and coherence? ▪ How can you use the Scoring Guide to help you revise your draft and add any missing elements?
Editing for Publication: Prepare a final draft as a polished work ready to share.	▪ What edits do you need to make to your draft for seamless integration of quotations and for correct grammar, punctuation, and spelling? ▪ Have you chosen an appropriate title and prepared your draft for publication?
Planning for Presentation: Rehearse and time your presentation.	▪ Which poem will you select for your oral interpretation? Mark and annotate this poem for use of gestures, inflection, props, sound effects, and so on. ▪ What format will you use to organize your performance (for example, brief introduction of the poet and his or her style, presentation of your interpretation, brief rationale for your interpretation)? ▪ What is your rehearsal plan? How much time will you need to rehearse? Rehearse your oral interpretation in front of a mirror, and then practice with a group of your peers. Ask for suggestions to refine your oral interpretation.

Reflection

Describe how you used your knowledge of poetic structure and the elements that contribute to an author's style to create your style-analysis essay. What more do you need to learn about writers' styles?

Analyzing and Presenting a Poet

SCORING GUIDE

Scoring Criteria	Exemplary	Proficient	Emerging	Incomplete
Ideas	The essay • demonstrates an insightful analysis of the poet's style • portrays a deep understanding of the poem • is accompanied by an oral interpretation that is convincingly performed with skillful use of movement, gestures, inflection, props, and/or sound effects.	The essay • shows a generally accurate analysis of the poet's style • shows a clear understanding of the poem • is accompanied by an oral interpretation that is performed with purposeful use of movement, gestures, inflection, props, and/or sound effects.	The essay • consistently misinterprets the text and/or relies primarily on summary • shows an unclear understanding of the poem • is accompanied by an oral interpretation that lacks performance elements.	The essay • is missing significant elements (e.g., thesis), and the analysis is missing or too limited to be useful • shows little understanding of the poem • may not be accompanied by an oral interpretation and/or appropriate performance elements.
Structure	The essay • has a well-written introduction with an engaging lead and sophisticated thesis • includes coherent and concise body paragraphs with complex topic sentences, strong textual support, and insightful commentary • uses transitions to show clear relationships between ideas • concludes by extending key ideas.	The essay • contains a clear introduction and thesis • includes body paragraphs that are coherent and contain topic sentences, adequate textual support, and relevant commentary • uses transitions to show relationships between ideas • concludes by extending most key ideas.	The essay • has an unclear thesis and/or introduction • includes body paragraphs without topic sentences and lacks support for the thesis, textual evidence, or relevant commentary • uses few or no transitions • concludes with repetitive ideas and/or no extension of ideas.	The essay • provides an unclear thesis and/or introduction • includes some body paragraphs that do not have topic sentences and lacks support for the thesis, textual evidence, or relevant commentary • uses no transitions • concludes by repeating the thesis or lacks a conclusion.
Use of Language	The essay • uses a clear, consistent academic voice and seamless integration of quotations woven into commentary.	The essay • uses an academic voice and integrates quotations with commentary.	The essay • uses an inconsistent voice, ineffective sentence structure, or quotations not connected with commentary.	The essay • uses an inconsistent voice and incomplete sentences and/or is missing quotations or commentary.

Coming of Age on Stage

Visual Prompt: The balcony scene is one of the most famous in *Romeo and Juliet*. How do you visualize this scene?

Unit Overview

Romeo and Juliet, a coming-of-age drama about two young star-crossed lovers, was one of William Shakespeare's most popular plays in his lifetime. To this day, it is one of his most widely performed plays, and it has inspired countless artists, musicians, and filmmakers to bring to life their own visions of this timeless tragedy. In this unit, you will join their ranks by planning and performing your own collaborative interpretation of a scene. After reflecting on this experience, you will conduct research to support an argument about the relevance of Shakespeare in today's world.

Coming of Age on Stage

Contents

Activities

*Texts not included in these materials

Language and Writer's Craft
- Rhetorical Questions (5.16)
- Using and Citing Sources (5.17)

MY INDEPENDENT READING LIST

_____
_____
_____
_____
_____
_____
_____
_____
_____
_____
_____
_____
_____
_____
_____
_____
_____
_____
_____
_____
_____

Previewing the Unit

LEARNING STRATEGIES:
QHT, Marking the Text,
Skimming/Scanning

My Notes

Learning Targets

- Preview the big ideas and vocabulary for the unit.
- Identify the skills and knowledge required to complete Embedded Assessment 1 successfully.

Making Connections

In this unit, you will focus on drama. You will learn the elements of drama and of staging a play, and you will engage in a debate about the relevance of William Shakespeare. As you work through the activities, you will apply your skills of analysis, interpretation, research, writing, and collaboration.

Essential Questions

To get started thinking about drama and theater, answer the Essential Questions. Based on your current knowledge, write your answers to these questions.

1. How do actors and directors use theatrical elements to create a dramatic interpretation?

2. Why do we study Shakespeare?

Developing Vocabulary

Look at the vocabulary terms on the Contents page. Use a QHT strategy to analyze your knowledge of each term and your ability to explain and use each term correctly.

Unpacking Embedded Assessment 1

Read the assignment for Embedded Assessment 1: Presenting a Dramatic Interpretation.

> Your assignment is to work collaboratively with your acting company to interpret, rehearse, and perform a scene from William Shakespeare's *Romeo and Juliet*. In preparation, each member of the acting company will create a staging notebook providing textual evidence and commentary on the planned interpretation. Finally, you will write a reflection evaluating your final performance.

In your own words, summarize what you will need to know to complete this assessment successfully. With your class, create a graphic organizer to represent the skills and knowledge you will need to complete the tasks identified in the Embedded Assessment.

INDEPENDENT READING LINK

Read and Recommend

In this unit, you will be reading a play by William Shakespeare. For your independent reading, choose another play. You might want to read another of Shakespeare's plays, or a play by another author. Discuss your selection with a small group. Explain why you would recommend this particular play.

Shakespeare's Age

Learning Targets
- Analyze a monologue and make connections to the themes in the unit.
- Research Shakespeare to develop a context for the play.

Preview

In this activity, you will read a famous **monologue** known as the "Seven Ages of Man" speech from Shakespeare's play *As You Like It* and analyze its coming-of-age themes.

Literary Terms
A **monologue** is a dramatic speech delivered by a single character in a play.

Setting a Purpose for Reading
- Put an asterisk (*) next to each line that introduces a new "age of man."
- Next to each asterisk, put an age range that you think Shakespeare is describing (for example, 0–2 years).
- Circle unknown words and phrases. Try to determine the meaning of the words by using context clues, word parts, or a dictionary.

WORD CONNECTIONS

Roots and Affixes

The root *logue* comes from the Latin *logus* and means "to speak." Words that use this root and communicate different forms of speaking include *monologue*, *prologue*, *dialogue*, and *epilogue*.

ABOUT THE AUTHOR
British poet and playwright William Shakespeare (1564–1616) is perhaps the most famous writer of all time. Shakespeare began his theatrical life as an actor and writer. He eventually started an acting troupe and opened his own theater, The Globe, in London. Shakespeare was a favorite playwright of many royals and noblemen, yet his work was also beloved by the common man. After his death, speculation grew as to whether or not one man could have written such eloquent and varied works. Nevertheless, Shakespeare has remained one of the most widely read, published, and studied authors of all time.

My Notes

Drama

Monologue from *As You Like It*

by William Shakespeare

All the world's a stage,
And all the men and women merely players:
They have their exits and their entrances;
And one man in his time plays many parts,
5 His acts being seven ages. At first, the infant,
Mewling and puking in the nurse's arms.
And then the whining school-boy, with his **satchel**
And shining morning face, creeping like snail
Unwillingly to school. And then the lover,
10 Sighing like furnace, with a **woeful ballad**
Made to his mistress' eyebrow. Then a soldier,

mewling: crying

satchel: a bag with a shoulder strap

woeful: full of unhappiness
ballad: an emotional song

Shakespeare's Age

oaths: promises
pard: leopard

My Notes

pantaloon: pants

oblivion: being completely
forgotten or unknown
sans: without

Full of strange **oaths** and bearded like the **pard**,

Jealous in honour, sudden and quick in quarrel,

Seeking the bubble reputation

15 Even in the cannon's mouth. And then the justice,

In fair round belly with good capon lined,

With eyes severe and beard of formal cut,

Full of wise saws and modern instances;

And so he plays his part. The sixth age shifts

20 Into the lean and slipper'd **pantaloon**,

With spectacles on nose and pouch on side,

His youthful hose, well saved, a world too wide

For his shrunk shank; and his big manly voice,

Turning again toward childish treble, pipes

25 And whistles in his sound. Last scene of all,

That ends this strange eventful history,

Is second childishness and mere **oblivion**,

Sans teeth, sans eyes, sans taste, sans everything.

Second Read

- Reread the monologue to answer these text-dependent questions.
- Write any additional questions you have about the text in your Reader/Writer Notebook.

1. **Key Ideas and Details:** What is the central theme of this monologue?

2. **Craft and Structure:** What is the tone of this monologue?

3. **Craft and Structure:** What is the significance of the opening two lines of this monologue?

Working from the Text

4. In your group, assign a different research topic from the following list to each member. Visit the Folger Shakespeare Library website (www.folger.edu) to conduct research on your assigned topic by exploring the "Discover Shakespeare" link. On an index card, summarize the key points you learned. Copy the website address onto the back side of your note card.

- **Shakespeare's Life:** Stratford Beginnings, Success in London, Final Years, An Expansive Age, Shakespeare's Story, Questioning Shakespeare's Authorship
- **Shakespeare's Work:** The Plays, The Poems, Publication, First Folio
- **Shakespeare's Theater:** London Playhouses, Inside the Theaters, Staging and Performance, Business Arrangements

5. Present your findings to your group. Access and include visual or audio media in your presentation. Work together to generate a list of questions you still have about Shakespeare and his times.

Check Your Understanding

Based on this monologue, briefly explain what Shakespeare is trying to convey about coming of age.

Writing to Sources: Explanatory Text

Read the first four lines of the monologue. Identify the metaphor Shakespeare uses to describe human life. Explain how and why this is an appropriate comparison. Be sure to:

- Begin with a topic sentence summarizing your understanding of the metaphor.
- Cite direct quotations and specific examples from the metaphor. Introduce and punctuate all quotations correctly.
- Provide a conclusion that summarizes your explanation.

My Notes

A Sonnet Sets the Stage

LEARNING STRATEGIES:
Marking the Text, Diffusing,
Metacognitive Markers,
Visualizing, Previewing

Literary Terms

A **drama** is a play written for stage, radio, film, or television, usually about a serious topic or situation.

A **tragedy** is a dramatic play that tells the story of a character, usually of a noble class, who meets an untimely and unhappy death or downfall, often because of a specific character flaw or twist of fate.

WORD CONNECTIONS

The word *prologue* comes from the Greek word *prologos*, containing the prefix *pro-* (before) and root *logos* (saying). This literally translates to "before the speech" or "before the play."

dignity: rank

mutiny: rebellion against authority

fatal loins: unfortunate offspring

star-crossed lovers: lovers destined for an unhappy end
piteous: pathetic

continuance: remaining in the same place

toil: hard work

Learning Targets

- Analyze the prologue to *Romeo and Juliet* to preview and make inferences about the play.
- Define *drama* and *tragedy* in context of the play.
- Create a collaborative tableau to preview the characters and their relationships.

Preview

In this activity, you will read the prologue from Shakespeare's most famous **tragedies**, *Romeo and Juliet*.

Setting a Purpose for Reading

Use metacognitive markers to mark the text as follows:

- Put a question mark (?) next to lines that are confusing or bring up questions.
- Put an asterisk (*) next to lines that are interesting or reinforce what you already know.
- Put an exclamation mark (!) next to lines that are surprising or help you make predictions.

Drama

from Romeo and Juliet

by William Shakespeare

PROLOGUE

Enter Chorus

      Two households, both alike in **dignity**,

      In fair Verona, where we lay our scene,

      From ancient grudge break to new **mutiny**,

      Where civil blood makes civil hands unclean.

5   From forth the **fatal loins** of these two foes

      A pair of **star-crossed lovers** take their life,

      Whose misadventured **piteous** overthrows

      Doth with their death bury their parents' strife.

      The fearful passage of their death-marked love,

10 And the **continuance** of their parents' rage,

      Which, but their children's end, naught could remove,

      Is now the two hours' traffic of our stage;

      The which if you with patient ears attend,

      What here shall miss, our **toil** shall strive to mend.

Second Read

- Reread the prologue to answer these text-dependent questions.
- Write any additional questions you have about the text in your Reader/Writer Notebook.

1. **Key Ideas and Details:** What is the main purpose of the prologue?

2. **Craft and Structure:** How does the structure of the prologue reflect the play's central theme?

Working from the Text

The prologue serves as an introductory speech in which an actor, in this case probably just one man called the "Chorus," provides the audience with a brief outline of the plot.

In this play, the prologue is a 14-line poem with a defined structure that is called an English or Shakespearean **sonnet**. Note that this sonnet, like all of Shakespeare's sonnets, uses iambic pentameter to create a distinct rhythm. The most noticeable feature of this rhythmic pattern is the use of pentameter, which means that each line includes 10 syllables or 5 feet (pairs of syllables). Try counting the number of syllables for each line. Work with your class to label the lines of the prologue on the following page to show its rhythm and rhyme scheme.

3. Examine the masks, which are a common graphic representation of drama. What do the two masks represent?

4. List words that you associate with the term *tragedy*. Add a few key words from the prologue.

Literary Terms
A **sonnet** is a 14-line lyric poem, usually written in iambic pentameter and following a strict pattern of rhyme.

A Sonnet Sets the Stage

5. A *tableau* is a purposeful arrangement of characters frozen as if in a painting or a photograph. After you are assigned a character name, work with your class to create a tableau based on the information provided in the prologue and in the cast of characters in your copy of *Romeo and Juliet*. Think about the following as you prepare to assume your role in the class tableau:

- Body positions (who you stand next to, distance)
- Postures and poses
- Facial expressions and gestures

To help you keep track of the characters, create a bookmark to use while you are reading *Romeo and Juliet*. Fold a sheet of paper in half lengthwise, and list the Capulets on one side, the Montagues on the other side, and unaffiliated characters inside. Identify the characters using both images and text to describe what you know about them.

Check Your Understanding

Based on your reading of the prologue and the definition of a tragedy, make an inference about something that might happen in the play. Use evidence from the prologue to support your answer.

Conflict Up Close

Learning Targets
- Analyze the opening scene of *Romeo and Juliet* to understand Shakespeare's language.
- Annotate the text for vocal and visual delivery to communicate meaning in a performance.

LEARNING STRATEGIES:
Skimming/Scanning,
Close Reading, Visualizing,
Diffusing

Diffusing Shakespeare's Language

1. Working with a partner, skim and scan the text of the excerpt from Scene I and diffuse some of Shakespeare's unfamiliar language using the following translation table. What resources could you use to help diffuse Shakespeare's language?

Shakespeare	Translation	Shakespeare	Translation
Thee/Thou	You	Ay	Yes
Thy/Thine	Your	Would	Wish
Hath	Has	Alas	Unfortunately
Art	Are	'Tis	It is
Wilt/Wouldst	Will/Would	Marry	Really
An	If	Canst/Didst/Hadst/Dost	Can/Did/Had/Does

Preview

In this activity, you will read Scene I from *Romeo and Juliet* and annotate the text in order to present a vocal and visual performance.

Setting a Purpose for Reading
- Draw a star next to any questions the characters ask.
- Circle unknown words and phrases. Try to determine the meaning of the words by using context clues, word parts, or a dictionary.
- Underline words that imply a character is mad or angry.

Drama

from *Romeo and Juliet*

SAMPSON: My naked weapon is out: **quarrel**, I will back thee.

GREGORY: How! turn thy back and run?

SAMPSON: Fear me not.

quarrel: fight

My Notes

My Notes

35   GREGORY: No, marry; I fear thee!

SAMPSON: Let us take the law of our sides; let them begin.

GREGORY: I will frown as I pass by, and let them take it as they list.

SAMPSON: Nay, as they dare. I will bite my thumb at them, which is a disgrace to them, if they bear it.

40   *Enter ABRAHAM and BALTHASAR*

ABRAHAM: Do you bite your thumb at us, sir?

SAMPSON: I do bite my thumb, sir.

ABRAHAM: Do you bite your thumb at us, sir?

SAMPSON: [*Aside to GREGORY*] Is the law of our side, if I say ay?

45   GREGORY: No.

SAMPSON: No, sir, I do not bite my thumb at you, sir, but I bite my thumb, sir.

GREGORY: Do you quarrel, sir?

ABRAHAM: Quarrel sir! No, sir.

SAMPSON: If you do, sir, I am for you: I serve as good a man as you.

50   ABRAHAM: No better.

SAMPSON: Well, sir.

kinsmen: relatives

GREGORY: Say 'better:' here comes one of my master's **kinsmen**.

SAMPSON: Yes, better, sir.

ABRAHAM: You lie.

swashing: moving in a violent motion

55   SAMPSON: Draw, if you be men. Gregory, remember thy **swashing** blow.

   They fight. Enter BENVOLIO

BENVOLIO: Part, fools!

Put up your swords; you know not what you do. [*Beats down their swords.*]

   Enter TYBALT

60   TYBALT: What, art thou drawn among these heartless hinds?

Turn thee, Benvolio, look upon thy death.

BENVOLIO: I do but keep the peace: put up thy sword,

Or manage it to part these men with me.

TYBALT: What, drawn, and talk of peace! I hate the word,

65   As I hate hell, all Montagues, and thee:

Have at thee, coward!

   They fight.

Second Read

- Reread the scene to answer these text-dependent questions.
- Write any additional questions you have about the text in your Reader/Writer Notebook.

2. **Key Ideas and Details:** Why does Benvolio fight Tybalt at the end of this scene?

3. **Key Ideas and Details:** What does this scene suggest about masculinity?

4. **Craft and Structure:** How does this opening scene help set the stage for the play?

Working from the Text

5. In your groups, assume the roles of the characters. As you work with your class to make meaning of the first chunk of text, take notes in the margins to paraphrase what your character is saying in each line.

6. Once you have made meaning of the chunk, prepare to read it through aloud by annotating the text with tone cues to indicate the appropriate **vocal delivery** (angry, confused, bragging, laughing).

   Use punctuation as cues for vocal delivery. Pause briefly after commas, semicolons, colons, and periods. Adjust your pitch to indicate a question, and emphasize lines that end in an exclamation mark.

7. As you read the chunk, visualize how this scene would look onstage. When, where, and how would the actors use movement and gestures to communicate meaning to the audience? Add annotations to the text to indicate appropriate **visual delivery** for each character.

8. Form groups of six to read the following section of Scene I at least twice as you paraphrase and annotate the text for vocal and visual delivery. Assign the roles of Samson, Gregory, Abraham, Benvolio, Tybalt, and Balthasar (who has no lines but should still have gestures and movement).

9. Work with your group to rehearse a performance in which you use vocal and visual delivery to communicate meaning. Present to another group.

10. **Reflect:** Rate your comfort level with reading and performing Shakespeare on a scale of 1 (lowest) to 10 (highest). Explain your rating. What are your strengths and challenges?

    Reading Shakespeare: _____ Performing Shakespeare: _____

My Notes

ACADEMIC VOCABULARY
Vocal delivery refers to the way a performer on stage expresses the meaning of a text through volume, pitch, rate or speed of speech, pauses, pronunciation, and articulation.
Visual delivery refers to the way a performer on stage interprets plot, character, and conflict through movement, gestures, and facial expressions.

Conflict Up Close

11. Continue reading Act I in a small group as follows:
    - Chunk the text into manageable sections and assign roles.
    - Preview your lines before reading each chunk, using sticky notes to paraphrase and annotate for vocal delivery.
    - After each chunk, discuss and rehearse visual delivery.

Check Your Understanding

What parts of the text are important to consider when deciding how to vocally and visually deliver a scene?

Explanatory Writing Prompt

Work with a small group to write a paragraph explaining how you would stage this scene. Include details about both the vocal delivery and the visual delivery. Explain why you think your staging ideas would be effective. Be sure to:

- Include an explanation about how you developed your ideas for vocal and visual delivery.
- Support analysis with evidence from the scene.
- Explain your ideas using reflective commentary.

INDEPENDENT READING LINK

Read and Discuss

Choose a scene from your independent reading text. Annotate the text for vocal and visual delivery.

Talking by Myself

Learning Targets
- Make inferences about characters from textual evidence.
- Explore symbols, imagery, and figurative language within monologues.

LEARNING STRATEGIES:
Skimming/Scanning,
SIFT, Graphic Organizer,
Discussion Groups

Monologues: Act I

1. Review the literary term *monologue*. Then, skim and scan Act I of *Romeo and Juliet* looking for examples of monologues.

My Notes

2. Choose one of the monologues and describe a modern-day situation in which someone might give a similarly long speech.

Making Inferences

3. In Act I, Scene III, Lady Capulet has a monologue in which she uses figurative language to describe Paris in a way that she thinks will appeal to Juliet. Reread the monologue and make inferences about why Lady Capulet favors the match.

Textual Evidence	Inferences

Talking by Myself

4. Choose another monologue from Act I. Work in small groups to define each element of the SIFT strategy (using your glossary if needed) and complete the graphic organizer by citing textual evidence and making inferences.

Literary Element	Textual Evidence	Inference
Symbol:		
Imagery:		
Figurative Language:		
Tone and Theme:		

My Notes

Rehearse and Present

5. Rehearse and present your interpretation of a monologue from Act I to students in another group, each of whom has analyzed a different monologue from Act I.

Check Your Understanding

What purpose do monologues serve?

Explanatory Writing Prompt

Explain how you would use visual and vocal delivery in your monologue to communicate character, tone, and/or theme to the audience. Be sure to:

- Use a topic sentence that addresses the prompt.
- Provide a brief summary of the monologue.
- Cite textual evidence with commentary to support your analysis.

Party Blocking

Learning Targets

- Compare and contrast two interpretations of a scene.
- Visualize a stage performance of a text and make a plan for blocking a scene.

Comparing Film and Theater

1. How is a live performance different from a film? Thinking like an actor, use the following graphic organizer to compare/contrast and explore the benefits and challenges of each medium.

Film   **Live Performance**

2. **Discuss:** For the play to work, the audience has to believe in Romeo and Juliet's love. What are some of the challenges an actor or director faces in convincing the audience that the love between Romeo and Juliet is real? How could actors and directors overcome these challenges?

LEARNING STRATEGIES:
Graphic Organizer, Note-taking, Discussion Groups, Sketching

My Notes

Party Blocking

Literary Terms

Theatrical elements are elements used by dramatists and directors to tell a story and create an interpretation on stage (or in a filmed version of a staged play).

3. As you view the same scene from different film versions of *Romeo and Juliet*, take notes in the following graphic organizer to explore how the directors use **theatrical elements** to interpret the scene. These elements include costumes, makeup, props, set (the place where the action takes place, as suggested by objects, such as furniture, placed on a stage), and acting choices (gestures, movements, staging, and actors' vocal techniques to convey their characters and tell a story).

Act I, Scene V: The Capulet Party—first meeting between Romeo and Juliet

Director	Actors' Appearance: Costumes and Makeup	Actors' Choices: Vocal and Visual Delivery	Objects: Set Design and Props

4. Choose three different theatrical elements observed in the film clips, and explain why you think the director choose each one. What effect is the director trying to convey?

Director	Theatrical Element	Intended Effect

My Notes

_____

_____

_____

_____

_____

_____

_____

_____

_____

_____

_____

_____

_____

_____

_____

_____

5. Because there are no cameras for close-ups, one of the challenges faced in a live performance is **blocking** the scene so that the audience will focus on the speakers even when there are a number of people onstage (as in a party scene).

Literary Terms
Blocking is the way actors position themselves on stage in relation to one another, the audience, and the objects on the stage.

On a separate page, work with a partner to make a "playbook" sketch showing an aerial view of how you would block the Capulets' party on stage. Use an X for Juliet, an O for Romeo, and initials for the other key characters in the scene (Lord Capulet, Tybalt, the Nurse). Leave a one-inch margin at the bottom of the page and write the word "audience" inside the margin to remind you where the actors should be facing.

Party Blocking

Check Your Understanding

How can blocking a scene before a performance help with visual delivery?

Argument Writing Prompt

Now that you have viewed the same scene from different film versions of *Romeo and Juliet*, choose the version that you think succeeds in capturing the essence of Romeo and Juliet's first meeting and convincing the audience that their love is real. Write an argument explaining your reasoning for choosing this version. Be sure to:

- Introduce a clear thesis statement giving the name of the director of the film version you prefer.
- Use textual evidence of specific theatrical elements and their effect to support your position.
- Use effective organization and a logical progression of ideas to show how your ideas are related.

Acting Companies

Learning Targets
- Discuss and evaluate possible scenes for performance.
- Preview the requirements for the Staging Notebooks.

Choosing a Scene to Perform

1. With your acting company, preview and discuss the scenes in the chart that follows, and put an asterisk next to scenes that you agree to consider for your interpretation. **Note:** Some scenes have characters with very small roles; these can be assigned to a group member who wants to work primarily as the Director or Dramaturge, combined with another role, or be cut from the scene. Other scenes have long monologues that can be shortened with your teacher's direction or approval.

My Notes

_____

_____

_____

Performance Scenes

Act and Scene	Description	Characters	Research Suggestions
Act I, Scene I, lines 153–232: **80 lines** From "Good morrow, cousin" to "die in debt."	Benvolio tries to cheer up Romeo, who pines for Rosaline.	Benvolio Romeo	Family relationships, courtship, convents
Act I, Scene II, entire scene: **103 lines**	Paris asks Lord Capulet for Juliet's hand in marriage. Benvolio and Romeo find out about the Capulets' party from Peter, a servant.	Lord Capulet Paris Peter Benvolio Romeo	Servants, marriage customs, patriarchy
Act I, Scene III, entire scene: **107 lines**	Lady Capulet and the Nurse are discussing Paris with Juliet before the party.	Juliet Lady Capulet Nurse Peter	Marriage customs, nobility, nursemaids
Act I, Scene IV, lines 1–116: **116 lines** From "What, shall this speech" to "Strike, drum."	Romeo is worried about going to the party because he had a bad dream and Mercutio is teasing him.	Romeo Mercutio Benvolio	Superstitions, festivities
Act I, Scene V, lines 41–141: **101 lines** From "Oh, she doth teach" to "all are gone."	Romeo and Juliet meet and fall in love; meanwhile Tybalt complains to Lord Capulet about Romeo crashing the party.	Romeo Juliet Tybalt Capulet Nurse	Festivities, courtship, dancing
Act II, Scene II, lines 33–137: **105 lines**	Romeo visits Juliet after the party and overhears her declaring her love on the balcony.	Romeo Juliet	Courtship, architecture

Acting Companies

Act and Scene	Description	Characters	Research Suggestions
Act II, Scene III, entire scene: **94 lines**	Romeo visits the Friar to tell him about his love for Juliet and ask him to perform the wedding.	Romeo Friar Lawrence	Friars, herbal medicine
Act II, Scene IV, lines 1–85: **85 lines**	Mercutio and Benvolio discuss Tybalt's challenge and give Romeo a hard time.	Mercutio Benvolio Romeo	Dueling
Act II, Scene V, entire scene: **77 lines**	Juliet is trying to get the Nurse to tell her Romeo's message about their wedding plans.	Juliet Nurse	Nursemaids, marriage customs
Act III, Scene I, lines 34–132: **99 lines** From "Follow me close" to "I am fortune's fool!"	Mercutio, Tybalt, and Romeo engage in a street fight that has tragic consequences.	Mercutio Tybalt Romeo Benvolio	Fencing, banishment laws
Act III, Scene II, lines 37–143: **107 lines** From "Ay me" to "last farewell."	The Nurse delivers news of Romeo's banishment to Juliet.	Nurse Juliet	Nursemaids, banishment laws
Act III, Scene III, lines 1–108: **108 lines** From "Romeo, come," to "desperate hand."	Romeo receives word of his banishment, and the Friar is trying to calm him when the Nurse arrives.	Romeo Friar Nurse	Friars, banishment laws
Act III, Scene V, lines 112–205: **94 lines** From "Marry, my child" to "how shall this be prevented?"	Juliet, her parents, and the Nurse argue about her proposed marriage to Paris.	Lady Capulet Juliet Capulet Nurse	Courtship customs, female rights
Act IV, Scene I, lines 1–122: **122 lines** From "On Thursday, sir?" to "tell me not of fear!"	Juliet meets Paris on the way to church. The Friar gives her a potion to fake her death and avoid marriage.	Paris Friar Lawrence Juliet	Burial vaults, herbal potions

Act and Scene	Description	Characters	Research Suggestions
Act IV, Scene V, lines 1–95: **95 lines** From "Mistress" to "crossing their high will."	The Nurse thinks Juliet is dead, and she informs the household.	Nurse Capulet Lady Capulet Friar Paris	Funeral customs, astrology
Act V, Scene I, entire scene: **88 lines**	Balthasar tells Romeo of Juliet's "death." Romeo buys poison to kill himself.	Romeo Balthasar Apothecary	Apothecary, poisons
Act V, Scene III, lines 84–170: **87 lines** From "For here lies Juliet" to "let me die."	Romeo and Juliet commit suicide. Note: The exchange between Friar Lawrence and Balthasar may be deleted from this scene.	Romeo Juliet Friar Lawrence Balthasar	Burial customs

2. After you have selected your scene, brainstorm possible interpretations. Film adaptations of *Romeo and Juliet* have explored a variety of interpretations by casting rival gangs in *West Side Story*, garden gnomes in *Gnomeo and Juliet*, and kung fu cops and mobsters in *Romeo Must Die*. Consider the time, place, and characters that would enhance your scene.

3. In Shakespeare's day, acting companies named themselves just as bands do today. Shakespeare belonged first to the Lord Chamberlain's Men and later to the King's Men. Your acting company should think of a name that reflects the characteristics of your group.

Create a contract like the one below, and sketch a rough draft of a poster design advertising your performance. Include a performance date, cast (character and student name), director, and dramaturge, as well as words and images that reflect your interpretation.

We, the _____ (name of acting company), pledge to plan,

rehearse, and perform _____ (act and scene) from

William Shakespeare's *Romeo and Juliet*.

My Notes

_____

_____

_____

_____

_____

_____

_____

_____

_____

_____

_____

_____

_____

_____

_____

_____

_____

_____

Acting Companies

4. Every member of the Acting Company will complete a Staging Notebook to prepare for the performance. Based on your primary role in the performance, prepare an Actor's Notebook, Director's Notebook, or a Dramaturge Notebook. Read the description of your notebook, highlighting key elements. Create a "To Do" list that you can refer to as you work with your acting company.

Director's Notebook:

Interpretation: Write a paragraph describing the interpretation you have chosen for your scene. Provide textual evidence to explain the reasoning and plan for the theatrical elements that will create your interpretation.

Visuals: Decide whether you will use visuals for your scene (posters, large photographs, etc.), and create them.

Text: Print a copy of your scene and annotate it with suggestions for your actors' vocal and visual delivery. Be sure to describe interactions and reactions.

Set Diagram: Sketch the scene from the audience's perspective as well as an aerial view. Use the "playbook" approach to block your scene for character placement and movement.

Lighting, Sound, and Props: Create a plan for lighting and sound (effects or music) that will enhance your acting company's performance. Include an explanation of your intended effect. Make a list of the props for your scene and where you will get them.

Introduction: Write an introduction that provides context (what happened prior to your scene) and previews the content of your scene. Memorize and present the introduction before your performance. Like the Prologue, it could be in sonnet form.

Meeting Log: After every meeting, you will be responsible for writing a dated log that records how the meeting went. Some questions you might answer in your log include the following:

- What did the group accomplish?
- What obstacles were identified?
- Which problems have been resolved? How?
- What needs to be done before and at the next meeting?

Director's "To Do" List: This will be the first entry in your Director's Staging Notebook.

Actor's Notebook:

Interpretation: Write a paragraph describing the interpretation you have chosen for your character. Provide textual evidence to explain the reasoning and plan for the theatrical elements that will create your interpretation.

Text: Print out or make a copy of your scene and highlight your lines. Paraphrase each of your lines and annotate them with your plan for vocal and visual delivery. Annotate the other characters' lines with notes on your nonverbal reactions.

Costume: Decide on an appropriate costume for your character. Sketch, photograph, cut out of a magazine, or print out an online image of both your ideal costume and your real costume.

Character Analysis: Create a visual representation of your character's thoughts, desires, actions, and obstacles. Focus on your scene, but you can include evidence from other parts of the play.)

Actor's "To Do" List: This will be your first entry in your Actor's Staging Notebook.

Dramaturge's Notebook:

Research Questions: Generate research questions related to the scene. In addition to the suggestions in this activity, consider the following:

- the history and context of the play
- unfamiliar references or vocabulary in your scene
- theater and performance in Shakespeare's time

Note cards: Conduct research to answer questions and take careful notes.

Annotated Bibliography: Create a bibliography of the works you consulted in your research. Include annotations that summarize what you learned, and provide commentary on how this information enhances your understanding of Shakespeare, *Romeo and Juliet*, and/or your scene.

Suggestions: Based on your research findings, prepare a list of suggestions for the director and the actors. Present them to the group and be prepared to explain your reasons for the suggestions.

Interpretation: Write an explanation of how your research helped the acting company interpret its scene. Cite specific sources and quotes from your research. Memorize this explanation and present it after the performance.

Dramaturge's "To Do" List: This will be the first entry in the Dramaturge's Staging Notebook.

My Notes

Literary Terms

A **dramaturge** is a member of an acting company who helps the director and actors make informed decisions about the performance by researching information relevant to the play and its context.

What's in a Setting?

LEARNING STRATEGIES:
Graphic Organizer, Drafting

Learning Targets
- Analyze set designs, blocking, and other theatrical elements to compare and contrast two interpretations of a scene.
- Evaluate the effectiveness of a director's choices.

My Notes

_____

_____

_____

_____

_____

_____

_____

Preview
In this activity, you will explore the famous balcony scene from two different film versions of *Romeo and Juliet* and explore how the directors use set design, blocking, and other theatrical elements to convey the emotional impact Shakespeare intended.

Setting a Purpose for Viewing
- Think about how Romeo and Juliet interact with one another and with the balcony.
- Pay close attention to the set design, blocking, and other theatrical elements (sound effects, costumes, music, lighting).

Act II, Scene II: The Balcony Scene—Romeo and Juliet declare their love

Director	Set Design (everything you see in the scene including structures, nature, props)	Blocking (how the actors move and interact with the set and each other)	Other Theatrical Elements (sound effects, lighting, music, costumes)

Working from the Film

1. Describe one choice that each director made in set design or blocking, and reflect on its effect on you as an audience member. Does the director's choice effectively convey an emotional impact?

Director	Director's Choice	Effective? Why or why not?

My Notes

Shakespeare's Influence on Modern Works

One of the best-known modern works that draws on Shakespeare's *Romeo and Juliet* is the musical *West Side Story*. The story of feuding families in *Romeo and Juliet* becomes the story of warring street gangs in 1950s New York City. The Montagues and Capulets of Shakespeare's play become the Jets and Sharks of the West Side neighborhood. The Jets are white teenagers of European descent, while the Sharks are teens of Puerto Rican ancestry. Each group is determined to protect its side of the neighborhood.

Preview

Now you will read an excerpt from the script of *West Side Story*. This scene is an adaptation of the balcony scene *Romeo and Juliet*.

Setting a Purpose for Reading

- Highlight any similarities and differences in this scene from *Romeo and Juliet*.
- Circle unknown words and phrases. Try to determine the meaning of the words by using context clues, word parts, or a dictionary.
- Observe stage directions and think about how you would block this scene.

What's in a Setting?

My Notes

ABOUT THE AUTHOR

Arthur Laurents (1918–2011) was considered one of American theater's greatest writers for musical theater. Among the well-known plays he wrote are *West Side Story* (1957), *Gypsy* (1959), *The Way We Were* (1973), and *The Turning Point* (1977). Laurents grew up in Brooklyn, New York, and began his career by writing scripts for radio programs. After a stint in the Army during World War II, where he wrote training films, he wrote musicals for Broadway.

Script

from
West Side Story

SCENE FIVE. *Maria and Tony have just met at a dance. They danced and kissed and now Tony is looking for Maria.*

11:00 P.M. A back alley. A suggestion of buildings; a fire escape climbing to the rear window of an unseen flat. As Tony sings, he looks for where Maria lives, wishing for her. And she does appear, at the window above him, which opens onto the fire escape. Music stays beneath most of the scene.

TONY [*sings*]: Maria, Maria . . .

MARIA: Ssh!

TONY: Maria!

MARIA: Quiet!

5 TONY: Come down.

MARIA: No.

TONY: Maria . . .

MARIA: Please. If Bernardo—

TONY: He's at the dance. Come down.

10 MARIA: He will soon bring Anita home.

TONY: Just for a minute.

MARIA [*smiles*]: A minute is not enough.

TONY [*smiles*]: For an hour then.

MARIA: I cannot.

15 TONY: Forever!

MARIA: Ssh!

TONY: Then I'm coming up.

WOMAN'S VOICE [*from the offstage apartment*]: Maria!

MARIA: Momentito, Mama . . .

20 TONY [*climbing up*]: Maria, Maria—

MARIA: Cállate! [*reaching her hand out to stop him*] Ssh!

TONY [*grabbing her hand*]: Ssh!

MARIA: It is dangerous.

TONY: I'm not "one of them."

25 MARIA: You are; but to me, you are not. Just as I am one of them—[*She gestures toward the apartment.*]

TONY: To me, you are all the—[*She covers his mouth with her hand.*]

MAN'S VOICE [*from the unseen apartment*]: Maruca!

MARIA: Sí, ya vengo, Papa.

30 TONY: Maruca?

MARIA: His pet name for me.

TONY: I like him. He will like me.

MARIA: No. He is like Bernardo: afraid. [*suddenly laughing*] Imagine being afraid of you!

TONY: You see?

35 MARIA [*touching his face*]: I see you.

TONY: See only me.

MARIA [*sings*]:

Only you, you're the only thing I'll see forever.

In my eyes, in my words and in everything I do,

40 Nothing else but you

Ever!

TONY:

And there's nothing for me but Maria,

Every sight that I see is Maria

45 MARIA: Tony, Tony . . .

TONY:

Always you , every thought I'll ever know,

Everywhere I go, you'll be.

MARIA [*And now the buildings, the world fade away, leaving them suspended in space.*]:

50 All the world is only you and me!

Tonight, tonight,

It all began tonight,

I saw you and the world went away.

Tonight, tonight,

55 There's only you tonight,

What you are, what you do, what you say.

TONY:

Today, all day I had the feeling

My Notes

What's in a Setting?

A miracle would happen—

60 I know now I was right.

For here you are

And what was just a world is a star

Tonight!

BOTH:

65 Tonight, tonight,

The world is full of light,

With suns and moons all over the place.

Tonight, tonight,

The world is wild and bright,

70 Going mad, shooting stars into space.

Today the world was just an address,

A place for me to live in,

No better than all right,

But here you are

75 And what was just a world is a star

Tonight!

MAN'S VOICE [*offstage*]: Maruca!

MARIA: Wait for me! [*She goes inside as the buildings begin to come back into place.*]

TONY [*sings*]:

80 Tonight, tonight,

It all began tonight,

I saw you and the world went away.

MARIA [*returning*]: I cannot stay. Go quickly!

TONY: I'm not afraid.

85 MARIA: They are strict with me. Please.

TONY [*kissing her*]: Good night.

MARIA: Buenos noches.

TONY: I love you.

MARIA: Yes, yes. Hurry. [*He climbs down.*] Wait! When will I see you? [*He

90 starts back up.*] No!

TONY: Tomorrow.

MARIA: I work at the bridal shop. Come there.

TONY: At sundown.

MARIA: Yes. Good night.

95 TONY: Good night. [*He starts off.*]

MARIA: Tony!

TONY: Ssh!

MARIA: Come to the back door.

TONY: Sí. [*Again he starts out.*]

100 MARIA: Tony! [*He stops. A pause.*] What does Tony stand for?

TONY: Anton.

MARIA: Te adoro, Anton.

TONY: Te adoro, Maria.

[*Both sing as music starts again:*]

105 Good night, good night,

Sleep well and when you dream,

Dream of me

Tonight.

[*She goes inside; he ducks out into the shadows just as Bernardo and Anita enter.*]

Second Read

- Reread the scene to answer these text-dependent questions.
- Write any additional questions you have about the text in your Reader/Writer Notebook.

2. **Key Ideas and Details:** What is the significance of the setting where Maria and Tony agree to meet next? Why might the director have chosen this setting?

3. **Key Ideas and Details:** What comparisons can be made between the relationships of Romeo and Juliet and Tony and Maria?

4. **Craft and Structure:** Why is it significant that Tony and Maria repeat the phrase "tonight, tonight" over and over in their song?

My Notes

What's in a Setting?

Working from the Text

5. Using a Venn diagram or similar graphic organizer, compare this scene with the balcony scene in *Romeo and Juliet*. How are the scenes similar? How are they different?

Check Your Understanding

How did the writer of *West Side Story* use Shakespeare's play as inspiration for this scene?

Writing to Sources: Explanatory Text

Write a review stating a preference for one of the three balcony scenes you have watched or read. Compare and contrast how the set design, blocking, and/or other theatrical elements contribute to an emotional impact. Provide commentary on the three scenes. Be sure to:

- Clearly state your preference in a topic sentence or thesis.
- Include evidence in the form of details comparing and contrasting all three balcony scenes.
- Include appropriate transition words.

INDEPENDENT READING LINK

Read and Connect

Suppose that you are the director for a theatrical version of your independent reading play. Make a chart to block one scene. Explain how your choices convey the emotional impact you think the author intended for the scene.

Friends and Foils

Learning Targets
- Analyze the relationships between the protagonists and their foils, and emphasize interactions in vocal and visual delivery.
- Create a visual representation of a character's motivation: thoughts, desires, actions, and obstacles.

Practice Role-Play

1. Work with your acting company to take turns role-playing at least two of the following scenarios:

   a. A student shows up in his teacher's room one morning asking for help. He is madly in love and wants to get married in secret. The teacher is doubtful because this same student was in love with a different girl the day before.

   b. Two friends are talking about a third friend who ditched them mysteriously the previous night. The third friend shows up and they start teasing him about what he was doing the night before.

   c. A girl sent her best friend on a mission to find out if the boy she likes will go out with her. The best friend returns but will not answer the girl's questions. Instead, she just wants to talk about herself.

2. **Discuss:** How did you use vocal and visual delivery to express the relationships between the characters?

Preview

Now you and your acting group will conduct an oral reading of one of the scenes listed below from *Romeo and Juliet*.

Act II of *Romeo and Juliet*

3. Each of the scenarios at the beginning of this activity describe a situation similar to a scene from Act II in which one of the protagonists interacts with a **foil**. With your Acting Company, choose a scene from the following that you are not performing for your Embedded Assessment and conduct an oral reading.

   a. Act II, Scene III: Romeo and Friar Lawrence

   b. Act II, Scene IV: Mercutio, Benvolio, Romeo (until the Nurse enters)

   c. Act II, Scene V: Juliet and the Nurse

Setting a Purpose for Reading

Annotate the text for vocal and visual delivery.

- Note any physical interactions between the characters (for example, one character shoves another).
- Mark facial reactions of one character to the words or action of another character (for example, eye-rolling to express boredom or frustration).
- Circle unknown words and phrases. Try to determine the meaning of the words by using context clues, word parts, or a dictionary.

LEARNING STRATEGIES:
Role Playing, Oral Reading, Chunking the Text, Sketching

My Notes

Literary Terms
A **foil** is a character whose actions or thoughts are juxtaposed against those of a major character in order to highlight key attributes of the major character.

Friends and Foils

My Notes

Working from the Text

4. Rehearse the scene with an emphasis on the interactions between the protagonist and the foil and their reactions to each other. Perform your scene for at least one other group.

5. Choose one of the characters in your scene. On separate paper, create a visual representation of your character's motivation. See the following example for Tybalt. Sketch an outline and annotate it with your analysis on the corresponding body parts as follows:

   • Head: your character's thoughts
   • Heart: your character's desires
   • Arms: your character's actions
   • Legs: your character's obstacles

Thoughts: I can't believe Romeo had the gall to crash our party. I want to teach him a lesson. Stupid Montague dog!

Desires: I love my family and I would do anything to protect the Capulet honor. Risk my life? Get in trouble with the law? Bring it on!

Actions: I just sent a letter to Romeo challenging him to a duel. I'm waiting to hear if that coward is man enough to face the Prince of Cats.

Obstacles: My uncle told me to ignore Romeo and leave him alone. Also, the last time I started a fight the Prince threw a bit of a fit . . . something about "on pain of death" and my uncle's life. I wasn't really listening—it was a pretty long speech.

Check Your Understanding

Briefly explain the purpose of a foil.

Writing to Sources: Explanatory Text

Choose one of the friend/foil relationships you read in Act II: Scene III, Romeo and Friar Lawrence; Scene IV, Mercutio, Benvolio, and Romeo; or Scene V, Juliet and the Nurse. Write a paragraph that explains how the protagonist interacts with the foils. Explain the purpose that the foil(s) serve. Be sure to:

• Identify the scene, and name the protagonist and the foils.
• Include direct quotations and specific examples from the text to support your explanation.
• Use a coherent organization structure and make connections between specific words, images, and the ideas conveyed.

A Wedding and a Brawl

Learning Targets

- Analyze a scene for dramatic irony.
- Compare and contrast the representation of a scene in two different media.
- Analyze characters' interactions and evaluate how their conflicting motives advance the plot.

LEARNING STRATEGIES:
Oral Reading, Close Reading, Marking the Text, Sketching, Graphic Organizer, Chunking the Text, Discussion Groups

Act II, Scene VI: Identifying Irony

1. Act II, Scene VI ends just as Romeo and Juliet are heading to church to be married. Why does Shakespeare have the wedding take place off stage?

Preview

In this activity, you and your acting company will conduct an oral reading of Act II, Scene VI.

Setting a Purpose for Reading

- Underline examples of dramatic irony.
- Circle unknown words and phrases. Try to determine the meaning of the words by using context clues, word parts, or a dictionary.

Working from the Text

2. Read of the Friar's final words to Romeo before Juliet arrives. Highlight metaphors that reveal the Friar's true feelings about the wedding.

> "These violent delights have violent ends
> And in their triumph die, like fire and powder,
> Which, as they kiss, consume. The sweetest honey
> Is loathsome in its own deliciousness
> And in the taste confounds the appetite.
> Therefore love moderately. Long love doth so.
> Too swift arrives as tardy as too slow."

3. How does the Friar really feel about Romeo and Juliet's wedding? Why do the Friar and Nurse, adults who care deeply about the young lovers, allow Romeo and Juliet to act so quickly on their feelings?

4. Complete the following graphic organizer in a small group in which each group member takes a different character.

My Notes

A Wedding and a Brawl

Character (What are the main thoughts, desires, actions, and obstacles motivating him at the end of Act II?)	Textual Evidence (What are the lines that reveal his thoughts, desires, actions and obstacles in Act III, Scene I?)	Commentary (What do these lines tell you about conflicts or shifts in the character's motivation?)
Romeo:		
Mercutio:		
Tybalt:		
Benvolio:		

My Notes

_____

_____

_____

_____

_____

Preview

In this part of the activity, you and your acting company will conduct an oral reading of Act III, Scene I and discuss character motivation. Rehearse the scene several times.

Setting a Purpose for Reading

- Annotate the text for the character's vocal and visual delivery.
- Circle unknown words and phrases. Try to determine the meaning of the words by using context clues, word parts, or a dictionary.

Drama

from *Romeo* and *Juliet*

by William Shakespeare

ROMEO: I do protest, I never injured thee,

65 But love thee better than thou canst **devise**,

Till thou shalt know the reason of my love:

And so, good Capulet,—which name I **tender**

As dearly as my own,—be satisfied.

MERCUTIO: O calm, dishonourable, **vile** submission!

70 *Alla stoccata* carries it away   *Draws*

Tybalt, you rat-catcher, will you walk?

TYBALT: What wouldst thou have with me?

MERCUTIO: Good king of cats, nothing but one of your nine

lives; that I mean to make bold withal, and as you

75 shall use me hereafter, drybeat the rest of the

eight. Will you pluck your sword out of his pitcher

by the ears? Make haste, lest mine be about your

ears ere it be out.

TYBALT: I am for you.   *Drawing*

80 ROMEO: Gentle Mercutio, put thy rapier up.

MERCUTIO: Come, sir, your **passado**.   *They fight*

ROMEO: Draw, Benvolio; beat down their weapons.

Gentlemen, for shame, forbear this outrage!

Tybalt, Mercutio, the Prince expressly hath

85 Forbidden **bandying** in Verona streets:

Hold, Tybalt! good Mercutio!

TYBALT under ROMEO's arm stabs MERCUTIO, and flies with his followers

MERCUTIO: I am hurt.

A **plague** o' both your houses! I am sped.

90 Is he gone, and hath nothing?

devise: plan

tender: love

vile: disgusting

passado: Italian for "forward thrust"

bandying: fighting

plague: horrible illness

A Wedding and a Brawl

Second Read

- Reread the scene to answer these text-dependent questions.
- Write any additional questions you have about the text in your Reader/Writer Notebook.

5. **Key Ideas and Details:** What does Romeo mean when he says that he loves Tybalt?

6. **Key Ideas and Details:** How does this scene highlight the great conflict in Romeo's life?

7. **Key Ideas and Details:** How does Mercutio feel about the fight compared to Romeo?

Working from the Text

8. Revisit the textual evidence column of your graphic organizer, and add any textual evidence or commentary. Then, choose one key line for each character. Copy these lines into the first column of the following graphic organizer. Be sure to choose lines from different chunks of Act III, Scene I, so that you are not trying to evaluate several lines in quick succession.

9. As you view a film interpretation of Act III, Scene I, take notes on how the actor's delivery and blocking communicate a character's motivation.

Act III, Scene I—Director: _____

Character (Key line)	Vocal Delivery (Describe the tone, volume, pitch, rate, and/or pauses used.)	Visual Delivery (Describe the actor's movements, gestures, and facial expressions.)	Blocking (How and where is the actor positioned when delivering the line?)
Romeo:			
Mercutio:			
Tybalt:			
Benvolio:			

A Wedding and a Brawl

WORD
CONNECTIONS

Roots and Affixes

Motive, motivate, and *motivation* all come from the same Latin root, *mōtīvus,* which means "serving to move" or "causing movement." This would be what causes a person to commit a crime (*motive*), for example, or what prompts a teenage girl to marry her family's enemy (*motivation*). Whether emotional or physical, the words *motive, motivate,* and *motivation* all suggest movement.

Check Your Understanding: Collaborative Discussion

With your acting group, write brief responses to the following questions.

- How do the actors emphasize key lines, and how is their interpretation different from yours?

- How does the director use other theatrical elements, such as set design, sound, music, and lighting, to indicate a shift in the mood of the scene?

- What is added to or absent from the scene in this interpretation?

- How do the conflicting motives of the characters in this scene advance the plot of the drama?

My Notes

Writing to Sources: Argument Text

Write a critique of the film performance you have just watched. State your opinion about the effectiveness of the scene. Include the actors' vocal delivery, visual delivery, and blocking in your critique. Be sure to:

- Begin with a topic sentence that clearly states your opinion.
- Support your claim by including one or more specific quotes or examples, their effect, and other related evidence from the film.
- Incorporate appropriate terminology to discuss theatrical elements and film techniques.

Emotional Roller Coaster

Learning Targets

- Analyze the development of a theme over the course of the play through an illustrated timeline.
- Make connections between plot events and their effect on characters' emotions.

Emotional Ups and Downs

1. Coming-of-age stories involve characters who are learning how to deal with the intense emotions of young adulthood. Using the following graphic organizer, brainstorm some of the events that have caused the "ups" and "downs" of Juliet's emotions.

Juliet's Ups	Juliet's Downs

LEARNING STRATEGIES:
Oral Reading, Graphic Organizer, Chunking the Text, Rereading, Paraphrasing, Marking the Text

My Notes

Emotional Roller Coaster

2. Work with a partner or small group to create an illustrated timeline on poster paper that graphs the emotional roller coaster of the protagonists' emotions so far in the play.

- Place events in chronological order (Act I on the far left).
- Add images to illustrate each event.
- Use two different colors (or symbols) to distinguish Juliet's emotions from Romeo's regarding each event.
- Indicate whether the emotions they are feeling about each event are positive or negative by placing events with positive emotions at the top of the timeline and events with negative emotions at the bottom.
- Leave room at the end for events from the remainder of the play.

Preview

In this activity, you will read the remainder of Act III with your acting group.

Setting a Purpose for Reading

- Use strategies such as oral reading, chunking the text, paraphrasing, or marking the text to help you make meaning.
- Circle unknown words and phrases. Try to determine the meaning of the words by using context clues, word parts, or a dictionary.
- After each scene, add new events to your timeline.

Working from the Text

3. In one color, draw a line connecting all of Juliet's events. In another color, draw a line connecting Romeo's events. What do the ranges of emotions reveal about the characters and their situations?

Check Your Understanding

Work with your group to construct a thesis statement that answers the following question: What is Shakespeare's theme relating to coming of age in *Romeo and Juliet*?

Explanatory Writing Prompt

Write a paragraph explaining how *Romeo and Juliet* is a coming-of-age drama. Explain what it has in common with other coming-of-age texts that you have studied this year. Include issues that Romeo and Juliet face that teenagers today still deal with. Be sure to:

- Explain your ideas with reflective commentary.
- Use the best details from the text to clarify your explanation.
- Correctly state the names and authors of any texts you reference.

TWISTing Their Words

Learning Targets
- Analyze soliloquies for performance cues.
- Examine how complex characters develop a theme.

Monologue vs. Soliloquy

1. Review the literary term *monologue*. In your own words, explain the difference between a **soliloquy** and a monologue.

2. Work with a small group to skim and scan Acts II and III to find examples of soliloquies and monologues; add them to the following graphic organizer. Identify them by act, scene, speaker, and first line as in the examples. Try to find two more of each.

Monologues in Acts II and III	Soliloquies in Acts II and III
Act III, Scene II, Juliet: "Shall I speak ill of him that is my husband?"	Act II, Scene III, Friar Lawrence: "The grey-eyed morn smiles on the frowning night."

3. With your acting company, choose a soliloquy that is not part of the scene you are performing in Embedded Assessment 1.

4. Complete the following TWIST graphic organizer about your chosen soliloquy, citing textual evidence and making inferences about how Shakespeare intended the lines to be performed. Consider vocal and visual delivery.

LEARNING STRATEGIES:
Skimming/Scanning, Graphic Organizer, Chunking the Text, Quickwrite, TWIST

Literary Terms
A **soliloquy** is a long speech delivered by an actor alone on the stage, usually representing his or her internal thoughts.

WORD CONNECTIONS

Roots and Affixes
Soliloquy contains the root *sol* from the Latin word *soli*, meaning "one," "alone," or "lonely." This root also appears in *solo*, *solitary*, and *solitude*.

My Notes

TWISTing Their Words

Literary Element	Textual Evidence	Inferences
Tone:		
Word Choice (Diction):		
Imagery:		
Symbol:		
Theme:		

Performing a Soliloquy

5. Select a key segment of the soliloquy to deliver from memory. Try some of these strategies to help you memorize lines:

   a. Visualize the lines by creating word pictures in your head in response to the imagery and diction.

   b. Chunk the text into phrases and lines. Learn them one chunk at a time, building on what you have memorized.

   c. Say the lines out loud using the vocal and visual delivery that you would use in performance.

   d. Write down the lines several different times during the process of committing them to memory.

6. After you have rehearsed, perform your lines for your acting company. With your group, develop a rubric for effective performance, including vocal delivery, visual delivery, and other theatrical elements (including blocking). Use this rubric to evaluate your own and your peers' performance rehearsals. Refer to the performance section of the Scoring Guide for Embedded Assessment 1 for ideas.

7. **Quickwrite:** Choose at least one of the following prompts to respond to in writing.

   • What performance clues does Shakespeare provide within the language of his soliloquy?

   • What other purposes does a soliloquy serve? Why does Shakespeare include them?

   • What does the audience learn from watching characters struggle aloud with conflicting motives (thoughts, desires, actions, obstacles)?

Check Your Understanding

Identify several themes that Shakespeare develops in the soliloquies in Acts II and III.

My Notes

INDEPENDENT READING LINK

Read and Discuss

Create and complete a TWIST chart for a section of your independent reading selection. Summarize the information in your chart to a small group. Answer any questions group members may have.

A Desperate Plan

My Notes

Learning Targets

- Analyze the subtext of a passage to determine the true meaning and impact of a character's words.
- Plan, rehearse, and perform exaggerated visual delivery to communicate meaning to an audience.

The Cost of Advice

1. Part of the process of coming of age is learning and accepting that sometimes parents and other trusted adults make mistakes. Complete the following graphic organizer to identify how the adults in Juliet's life are making mistakes that contribute to her frustration by the end of Act III.

Adult Decision or Advice	Effect on Juliet
Juliet's father threatens to disown her if she refuses to marry Paris.	She has the impossible choice of breaking her wedding vows or losing her family and starving on the streets.
Juliet's mother. . .	
The Nurse. . .	

2. As Juliet becomes more alienated from her family and friends, she relies more frequently on the audience understanding the **subtext**. Revisit the passage in Act III, Scene V, in which Lady Capulet visits Juliet's bedroom immediately after Romeo has left.

Summarize her statements to her mother about Romeo.

Summarize the subtext of her statements (what she really means).

Preview

In this activity, you will read the beginning of Act IV. In this scene, Juliet seeks advice from Friar Lawrence.

Setting a Purpose for Reading

- Mark the text of the passage by putting Juliet's subtext in parentheses. The first line has been done for you as an example.
- Circle unknown words and phrases. Try to determine the meaning of the words by using context clues, word parts, or a dictionary.
- Use strategies such as oral reading, chunking the text, paraphrasing, or marking the text to help you make meaning.

Literary Terms
Subtext is the underlying or implied meaning in dialogue or the implied relationship between characters in a book, movie, play, or film. The subtext of a work is not explicitly stated.

Drama

from *Romeo and Juliet*

by William Shakespeare

PARIS: Happily met, my lady and my wife!

JULIET: That may be, sir, when I may be a wife. *(Which is never, because I'm already married.)*

PARIS: That may be must be, love, on Thursday next.

JULIET: What must be shall be.

20 FRIAR LAWRENCE: That's a certain text.

PARIS: Come you to make **confession** to this father?

JULIET: To answer that, I should confess to you.

PARIS: Do not deny to him that you love me.

JULIET: I will confess to you that I love him.

25 PARIS: So will ye, I am sure, that you love me.

JULIET: If I do so, it will be of more price,

Being spoke behind your back, than to your face.

PARIS: Poor soul, thy face is much abused with tears.

JULIET: The tears have got small victory by that;

30 For it was bad enough before their **spite**.

PARIS: Thou wrong'st it, more than tears, with that report.

JULIET: That is no **slander**, sir, which is a truth;

And what I spake, I spake it to my face.

PARIS: Thy face is mine, and thou hast slander'd it.

35 JULIET: It may be so, for it is not mine own.

My Notes

confession: admitting your sins to a priest

spite: hatred

slander: a maliciously false statement

A Desperate Plan

Second Read

- Reread the play to answer these text-dependent questions.
- Write any additional questions you have about the text in your Reader/Writer Notebook.

3. **Craft and Structure:** Why does Juliet refuse to give Paris a direct answer to any of his questions?

4. **Key Ideas and Details:** How does Paris feel about Juliet?

Working from the Text

5. In a small group, conduct an oral reading of the passage. In addition to Paris, Juliet, and Friar Lawrence, assign one group member the role of Juliet's subtext. After Juliet speaks, that group member will read aloud Juliet's true thoughts.

6. In an actual performance, subtext has to be expressed through visual delivery. Use the following graphic organizer to make a plan for visual delivery as you read the rest of Act IV, Scene I.

What Juliet Would Rather Do Than Marry Paris: Textual Evidence	Plan for Visual Delivery (movements, expressions, gestures)
The Friar's Plan for Juliet: Textual Evidence	Plan for Visual Delivery (movements, expressions, gestures)

7. Choose a section of lines (either Juliet's or the Friar's) to rehearse and perform with exaggerated visual delivery.

8. As you continue to read Act IV, look for other examples of subtext.

Check Your Understanding

- Why is it important to keep the subtext in mind when you are performing a scene?
- Why do stage actors usually use more exaggerated visual delivery than film actors, particularly when performing Shakespeare?

The Fault in Their Stars

Learning Targets

- Plan an interpretation that emphasizes the emotional impact and dramatic irony of Act V.
- Compare a personal plan to a film director's interpretation and evaluate the effectiveness of each.

LEARNING STRATEGIES:
Skimming/Scanning, Graphic Organizer, Sketching

Victims of Fate

1. In the Prologue to Act I, Shakespeare calls Romeo and Juliet "star-crossed lovers." In Act V, when Romeo thinks Juliet is dead, he declares, "Then I defy you, stars!" What accidental and unfortunate events in the play support the theme that Romeo and Juliet are the victims of fate, or "the stars"?

Act V of *Romeo and Juliet*

2. **Scenes I and II:** Gather more evidence that Romeo and Juliet are victims of fate. What key events, without which there could be no tragic ending, happen in these scenes?

3. Before you read Scene III, review the definition of *dramatic irony*. What key information does the audience have that Romeo is lacking?

4. **Scene III:** Think like a director and take notes in the first three columns of the following graphic organizer on how you would use vocal and visual delivery as well as other theatrical elements to intensify the emotional impact and emphasize the dramatic irony.

My Notes

The Fault in Their Stars

Theatrical Element/ My Choices as Director	How My Choices Would Intensify the Emotional Impact	How My Choices Would Emphasize the Dramatic Irony	Director's Choices	Intended Effect
Vocal Delivery:				
Visual Delivery:				
Other Theatrical Elements:				

Working from the Text

5. Work with a partner to visualize Act III Scene V. On separate paper, one of you should sketch the scene from the audience's perspective while the other sketches an aerial view. Use the "playbook" approach to block your scene for character placement and movement.

6. Observe how a film director interprets the scene. In the fourth column, take notes on choices the director makes concerning vocal delivery, visual delivery, and other theatrical elements. In the last column, make inferences about the effect you think the director intended to create.

Check Your Understanding

How effective are the director's choices in intensifying the emotional impact and emphasizing dramatic irony?

Explanatory Writing Prompt

In Activity 5.1, you thought about the Essential Question: How do actors and directors use theatrical elements to create a dramatic interpretation? Now that you have read and analyzed the play *Romeo and Juliet* and watched selections from various film versions, revisit your initial response. Write a paragraph explaining how your response has grown, changed, and developed throughout this unit. Be sure to:

- Include a summary of your initial response to the Essential Question.
- Give examples that clearly compare and contrast your earlier thoughts with your current thoughts.
- Include reflective commentary in your response.

Independent Reading Checkpoint

Review your independent reading. What have you learned about the ways a film director interprets scenes and actors deliver scenes? How might you apply this thinking about a dramatic interpretation to your independent reading text? How does studying the elements of film help you better understand and appreciate a play?

My Notes

Presenting a Dramatic Interpretation

ASSIGNMENT

Your assignment is to work collaboratively with your acting company to interpret, rehearse, and perform a scene from William Shakespeare's *Romeo and Juliet*. In preparation, each member of the acting company will create a staging notebook providing textual evidence and commentary on the planned interpretation. Finally, you will write a reflection evaluating your final performance.

Planning: Take time to make a performance plan.	▪ How will you prepare a staging notebook that reflects your primary role in the production? (See Activity 5.7 for guidelines.) ▪ How will your acting company effectively integrate theatrical elements such as vocal and visual delivery, blocking, props, costumes, lighting, music, sound, and set design into your final performance? ▪ As an actor, how will you learn your lines and prepare vocal and visual delivery? ▪ As a director, how will you guide the acting company and prepare theatrical elements? ▪ As a dramaturge, how will you research to provide background information?
Rehearsing: Collaborate with your acting company to polish your performance.	▪ When and where will you meet to rehearse your scene several times? ▪ How can the director's feedback and the dramaturge's research enhance the acting company's performance? ▪ How could you use a video recording of one of your rehearsals to help you improve the quality of the performance? ▪ How can another acting company help you rehearse by providing feedback on your performance?
Performing: Perform your scene for an audience of your peers.	▪ How will the director introduce the scene? ▪ Who will prompt actors who need assistance with their lines? ▪ After the performance, how will the dramaturge explain how the performance reflects his or her research?
Evaluating: Write an evaluation of your group's final performance.	▪ What were the strengths of your performance? What challenges did you face? ▪ How can you use the Scoring Guide to ensure your understanding of the criteria for this piece?

🛜 Technology Tip

As you collaborate on this project, find ways to create collaborative documents using wikis or online document sharing as a way of creating a rehearsal schedule, establishing a common document format, and sharing ideas with other members of your acting company.

Reflection

After completing this Embedded Assessment, think about how you went about accomplishing this task, and respond to the following questions:

- How did different acting companies use theatrical elements to enhance their performance in memorable ways?
- How did performing a scene help you understand or appreciate the play?

SCORING GUIDE

Scoring Criteria	Exemplary	Proficient	Emerging	Incomplete
Ideas	The performance • represents an insightful interpretation of the scene and clearly communicates the intended effect to the audience • includes a reflection that represents the creative thinking of the entire acting company, with insightful commentary on the challenges and the final performance.	The performance • represents a clear interpretation of the scene and communicates it effectively to the audience • includes a reflection on the process of preparing for and performing the scene, including commentary on challenges faced and an evaluation of the final performance.	The performance • shows an attempt to interpret the scene • may not clearly communicate the scene to the audience • includes a reflection that summarizes the process rather than the thinking behind the interpretation and the performance.	The performance • is not coherent and does not clearly communicate the scene to the audience • includes a reflection that is minimal and simply lists the steps in the process; it does not reflect the thinking of the group or the effect of the performance.
Structure	• The staging notebook is detailed and shows evidence of a high degree of collaboration • The interpretive performance shows a high degree of planning for visual and vocal delivery.	• The staging notebook contains all required entries in a clearly organized format • An effective performance communicates planning for visual elements and rehearsal for vocal delivery.	• The staging notebook does not contain all required entries and may be poorly organized • The performance shows some planning for visual elements and rehearsal for vocal delivery.	• The staging notebook contains few if any of the required entries • The performance shows a lack of planning for visual elements and rehearsal for vocal delivery.
Use of Language	The performance • demonstrates a creative use of diction to communicate the scene • includes a thorough script (in staging notebook) with annotations for effective delivery of lines.	The performance • includes appropriate and effective vocal and visual delivery of dialogue • includes a script (in staging notebook) annotated for appropriate delivery of lines.	The performance • attempts the use of appropriate dialogue to communicate the scene • includes some elements of a script (in staging notebook) annotated for delivery of lines.	The performance • includes little evidence of an attempt to craft appropriate dialogue for the scene • may not include a script (in staging notebook) or annotations for delivery of lines.

Previewing Embedded Assessment 2: Is Shakespeare Relevant?

My Notes

Learning Targets

- Analyze the skills and knowledge needed to complete Embedded Assessment 2 successfully.
- Analyze and evaluate reasons and evidence in an online debate.
- Identify and apply rhetorical appeals in a debate.

Making Connections

Describe one of the activities in the first half of the unit that helped prepare you to do well on Embedded Assessment 1. What did you do and learn in the activity, and how did it prepare you for success?

Essential Questions

How would you answer the questions now?

1. How do actors and directors use theatrical elements to create a dramatic interpretation?

2. Why do we study Shakespeare?

ACADEMIC VOCABULARY
Synthesis is the act of combining ideas from different sources to create, express, or support a new idea. In this usage, *synthesis* refers to combining ideas from different sources to create, express, or support a claim.

Developing Vocabulary

Return to the Table of Contents and note the Academic Vocabulary and Literary Terms you have studied so far in this unit. Which words/terms can you now move to a new category on a QHT chart? Which could you now teach to others that you were unfamiliar with at the beginning of the unit?

Unpacking Embedded Assessment 2

Read the assignment for Embedded Assessment 2: Writing a **Synthesis** Argument.

Your assignment is to compose an argument for or against the inclusion of William Shakespeare's *Romeo and Juliet* in the ninth-grade curriculum. You will evaluate research and gather evidence from a variety of sources about Shakespeare's relevance and influence in today's world. Finally, you will synthesize and cite your evidence in an argumentative essay that maintains a formal style and tone appropriate to your audience and purpose, uses rhetorical appeals including logical reasoning, and includes all the organizational elements of an argumentative essay.

In your own words, summarize what you will need to know to complete this assessment successfully. With your class, create a graphic organizer to represent the skills and knowledge you will need to complete the tasks identified in Embedded Assessment 2.

Choosing Sides

3. For each of the following sentences, circle your response, from 1 (Strongly Agree) to 5 (Strongly Disagree). If you are neutral or have no opinion, circle 3.

1 2 3 4 5: I believe in love at first sight.

1 2 3 4 5: Reading classical literature is important.

1 2 3 4 5: I like to perform onstage.

1 2 3 4 5: Teenagers often lie to their parents.

1 2 3 4 5: Friends are more important than boyfriends and girlfriends.

1 2 3 4 5: My parents know what's best for me.

1 2 3 4 5: The government should support theater and the arts.

1 2 3 4 5: Teenagers can experience true love.

1 2 3 4 5: *Romeo and Juliet* is too violent.

1 2 3 4 5: You should forgive your enemies.

1 2 3 4 5: Murderers do not deserve to be citizens of society.

1 2 3 4 5: I would risk my life for someone I loved.

1 2 3 4 5: I doubt that Shakespeare wrote all his plays himself.

1 2 3 4 5: I would try to get revenge if someone killed my friend.

1 2 3 4 5: Music is important to me.

1 2 3 4 5: Getting married very young is a mistake.

1 2 3 4 5: I believe in fate.

1 2 3 4 5: I like to argue.

4. Choose one of the statements that you strongly agree or disagree with. List three reasons to support your opinion.

5. Review the definitions of the rhetorical appeals that you studied previously in Unit 1. Consider the reasons you listed to support your opinion; label each with the type of rhetorical appeal your reason emphasized: pathos, logos, or ethos. Revise your support to include only valid or logical reasons.

My Notes

Previewing Embedded Assessment 2: Is Shakespeare Relevant?

6. Together with a group of your peers, you will explore an online debate website to gather reasons and evidence for one side of an issue related to Shakespeare and/or *Romeo and Juliet*. Write down your issue and the website address and take notes in the column for either PRO (in favor of) or CON (against) in the following graphic organizer.

Evaluate the validity of the arguments in the debate with the following questions:

- Is the reasoning valid? That is, is the reasoning sound and supported by evidence?
- Is the evidence relevant and sufficient?
- Are any of the statements false or illogical?

Choose the reasons that best support your assigned side. Try to emphasize reasons that are logical first, then reasons that appeal to ethos. Avoid support that depends on pathos.

Issue:_____

Website:_____

PRO	CON

7. Use your notes to stage an informal debate with the group that researched the opposing viewpoint. While you are listening to their side, take notes in the appropriate column so that you can respond to their points during rebuttal.

8. As you listen to your classmates debate another issue related to Shakespeare, take notes in the following graphic organizer to record the different rhetorical appeals used in the debate.

Issue:_____

Rhetorical Appeals	PRO	CON
Logos		
Ethos		
Pathos		

Check Your Understanding

What was the most convincing evidence that you heard or used today? Why? What kind of appeals were used?

My Notes

_____
_____
_____
_____
_____
_____
_____
_____
_____
_____
_____
_____
_____
_____
_____
_____
_____
_____
_____
_____
_____
_____
_____
_____

INDEPENDENT READING LINK

Read and Research

Research and find another play by William Shakespeare, or a novel that was inspired by his work. You may want to consult the Independent Reading list, conduct a web search, or ask your teacher, librarian, or peers for suggestions.

Shakespeare in the Modern Age

LEARNING STRATEGIES:
SOAPSTone, Drafting, Sharing
and Responding, Marking the
Text

My Notes

Learning Targets

- Analyze an article to evaluate whether the author's tone is appropriate to the audience and purpose.
- Identify reasons and gather evidence to support a claim.

Preview

In this activity, you will read an article that questions Shakespeare's relevance.

Setting a Purpose for Reading

- In one color, highlight the text evidence that supports the inclusion of *Romeo and Juliet* in ninth-grade curriculum. In another color, highlight the text that challenges the inclusion of *Romeo and Juliet*.
- Circle unknown words and phrases. Try to determine the meaning of the words by using context clues, word parts, or a dictionary.

Article

On the Bard's Birthday, Is Shakespeare Still Relevant?

by Alexandra Petri

1 Whenever I want to depress myself, I make a list of Shakespeare plays and cross out all the ones whose plots would be ruined if any of the characters had a smartphone. It's a depressingly short list.

2 Soon, if we want to do a modern staging of his work, we'll have to stipulate that "In fair Verona, where we lay our scene/The cell reception was spotty/From ancient grudge that brake the AT&T." Well, not that. Something better.

3 "Romeo and Juliet would obviously text each other about the poison," audiences would point out. "Why doesn't Hermia use her GPS?" "If he was so worried about the Ides, Caesar should have just telecommuted."

4 Misunderstandings and missed communications now come in entirely different flavors. We are all in touch all the time, and the confusions that blossom from that are not quite the ones the Bard guessed at. Autocorrect replaces **malapropism**. You don't leave your fiancée asleep in the woods unless you want to wind up on a "Dateline" special. When your coworker implies that Desdemona is cheating on you with Cassio, you don't go ballistic demanding handkerchiefs. You just log her keystrokes.

5 And the words. ("Words! Words! Words!" as Hamlet says.) What are we supposed to do with them?

6 To make it through his works, high school students are forced to consult books like "No Fear Shakespeare," which drains all the poetry out in the hopes of making him moderately **comprehensible**.

malapropism: misuse of words

comprehensible: understandable

7 Insert Hamlet's most famous soliloquy into the grinder of that book:

> "To be, or not to be? That is the question—
>
> Whether 'tis nobler in the mind to suffer
>
> The slings and arrows of outrageous fortune,
>
> Or to take arms against a sea of troubles,
>
> And, by opposing, end them? To die, to sleep—
>
> No more—and by a sleep to say we end
>
> The heartache and the thousand natural shocks
>
> That flesh is heir to—'tis a consummation
>
> Devoutly to be wished! To die, to sleep.
>
> To sleep, perchance to dream—ay, there's the rub"

and you get: "The question is: is it better to be alive or dead? Is it nobler to put up with all the nasty things that luck throws your way, or to fight against all those troubles by simply putting an end to them once and for all? Dying, sleeping—that's all dying is—a sleep that ends all the heartache and shocks that life on earth gives us—that's an achievement to wish for. To die, to sleep—to sleep, maybe to dream. Ah, but there's the catch!"

8 "But Shakespeare is beautiful! Shakespeare is life **glimpsed** through the cut glass of poetry!"

glimpsed: seen briefly

9 Ah, but there's the catch! What's the point, if the language is so far away that we have to do that to it?

10 Maybe Shakespeare has nothing to say to us. Nobody else from the early 1600s still sees himself so regularly adapted. When was the last time you watched a BBC version of Marlowe's *Tamburlaine*?

11 Bardolatry[1] seems **infinitely** old, but it is of comparatively recent vintage. First, Bowdler had his way with the works, removing all the naughty bits and notably tacking on a happy ending to *King Lear*. The **apotheosis** was not instant. The sonnets weren't **in vogue** for years. Shakespeare has only gradually clawed his way up to the **pinnacle** of English letters, shoving Chaucer and Tennyson and Melville and Dickens down whenever they got grabby and even elbowing Jane Austen from time to time.

infinitely: neverendingly

apotheosis: the elevation of someone to the highest status
in vogue: in fashion
pinnacle: peak

12 There's a certain level of celebrity occupied by people who are famous primarily because they are famous.

13 Is Shakespeare one of them? Do we only read him because we've seemingly always read him?

14 Why do we keep dragging class after class, kicking and screaming, through the wilds of *Romeo and Juliet*?

15 We don't even know who the guy was.

16 Perhaps Shakespeare was born today.

17 Possibly he died today.

---

[1] **Bardolatry:** unquestioning admiration for Shakespeare (the Bard)

Shakespeare in the Modern Age

skittish: quick to startle

hack: an artist who produces poor work simply to make money

prolific: producing a large amount of work

groundlings: audience members who sit in cheap seats

WORD CONNECTIONS

Etymology

For Pete's sake is a substitution for the blasphemous phrase "for Christ's sake." People who did not want to take the Lord's name in vain substituted Pete (potentially short for St. Peter) into the phrase. Shakespeare was famous for inventing and altering well-known phrases, making them his own. While he didn't invent this one, it remains a popular idiom.

My Notes

18 He's an awfully hard man to nail down. As a historical figure, he is proverbially **skittish**. He might have been Francis Bacon, for Pete's sake. You wouldn't get in the car of a man who said he might be Francis Bacon but was not sure. Why read one?

19 Besides, the man was obviously a **hack**. Jonathan Franzen clearly takes his craft more seriously. Nobody is as **prolific** as Shakespeare who thinks he's producing Great Lasting Works of Genius. He's more a P. G. Wodehouse or an Agatha Christie. Stephen King could learn a thing or two from Shakespeare when it comes to pleasing the **groundlings**.

20 Why give him this place of honor?

21 Look at his most famous play. *Hamlet*? A whiny college student, evidently overeducated and underemployed, comes home for break, sees a ghost and dithers. Eventually some pirates show up, but wouldn't you know, they remain offstage. Shakespeare is one of the few writers in history who, given the option of including pirates in a play, thinks, "Nah, you know what? I'd rather have this dithering hipster talk about mortality some more."

22 Come to think of it, maybe he's never been more relevant.

23 People complain about their Millennials moving home. Try having Hamlet in your basement for a semester. "Tis not alone my inky cloak, good mother, nor customary suits of solemn black . . ." That would get old at breakfast, I imagine.

24 His plays still tell the truth, boiled down to their essences.

25 *King Lear*: Your kids put you in a home? You should be so lucky!

26 *Titus Andronicus* (or, "Guess Who's Coming As Dinner"?): Cannibalism is never the answer.

27 *Romeo and Juliet*: Check your messages before ingesting poison.

28 *The Tempest*: Wizards pretty much get to do whatever they want.

29 And he's one of the few writers we still have in common. We're dragged through the thorns of his work so that we'll have something to talk about on the other side.

30 That is a definite part of his charm. He's a common vocabulary, a common set of heroes and villains and everyone in between.

31 These are not plays we read and see together as a generation or a country. They're works we enjoy as a species. Shakespeare offers a roadmap to the human. And he does it in verse—sometimes tightly knotted little **ornate** gardens of verse like *Midsummer Night's Dream*, other times vast prosy expanses like *Hamlet*. Before Sarah Palin was coining new words, the Bard was on it.

ornate: beautifully detailed

32 In their proper place, the bright lines that have since sunk into **cliche** still retain their power to dazzle.

cliche: trite or obvious

33 Write what you know? Shakespeare **adamantly** didn't. But in the process, he wrote what we all know.

adamantly: refusing to change opinion

34 And he didn't need a smartphone to do it.

Second Read

- Reread the article to answer these text-dependent questions.
- Write any additional questions you have about the text in your Reader/Writer Notebook.

1. **Key Ideas and Details:** What is the central purpose of this article?

2. **Craft and Structure:** What is the tone of this article?

3. **Key Ideas and Details:** According to the article, why does Shakespeare's work remain important today?

4. **Key Ideas and Details:** How has reading Shakespeare changed for modern students?

5. **Key Ideas and Details:** What reasons might critics give as to why Shakespeare is no longer relevant?

My Notes

Shakespeare in the Modern Age

Working from the Text

6. Consider the tone, purpose, and intended audience of the article. Conduct a SOAPSTone analysis of the article using the graphic organizer below.

SOAPSTone	Analysis	Textual Support
Speaker:		
Occasion:		
Audience:		
Purpose:		
Subject:		
Tone:		

7. Do you think that the writer or speaker uses an appropriate tone for the audience and purpose?

8. How might the style change if the author were rewriting it for a different medium (book, newspaper, magazine, speech, e-mail, Twitter post, letter ...)?

9. How might the style change if the author were rewriting it for a different audience (children, teenagers, lawmakers, college professors . . .)?

My Notes

Language and Writer's Craft: Rhetorical Questions

In an argument, writers use rhetorical questions to appeal to an audience. A rhetorical question is one for which no answer is expected or required. It may direct readers' thoughts to an implied answer, point out the absurdity of an opposing point of view, emphasize a point, or otherwise nudge readers in the direction the writer wants them to go. For example, in "On the Bard's Birthday, Is Shakespeare Still Relevant?" Petri asks the following rhetorical question:

"What's the point, if the language is so far away that we have to do that to it?"

Notice how the writer embeds the main question—that of Shakespeare's relevance today—into this question. In the next paragraph, notice how Petri continues to expand on this question of Shakespeare's relevance:

"When was the last time you watched a BBC version of Marlowe's *Tamburlaine*?"

PRACTICE Identify three other rhetorical questions in the essay, and explain how each one relates to the main point of the text. How do these rhetorical questions shape the argument?

Check Your Understanding

Write a thesis statement for or against the inclusion of *Romeo and Juliet* in the ninth-grade curriculum, citing specific text evidence from the essay for support.

Explain How an Argument Persuades

Explain how Petri structures her argument either for or against the relevancy of Shakespeare. Then write a paragraph evaluating the effectiveness of her argument. Be sure to:

- Identify the claim made by the writer and analyze how clear and direct it is.
- Explain what reasons and supporting evidence the writer uses and how counterclaims are addressed. Evaluate the effectiveness of the reasons, evidence, and refutations of counterclaims.
- Include full citations and attribution for quotations.

My Notes

Shakespeare's Globe

LEARNING STRATEGIES:
Marking the Text, Drafting,
Graphic Organizer

Learning Targets

- Gather and evaluate evidence from two articles as well as synthesize information to make inferences.
- Write a synthesis paragraph about Shakespeare's global influence.

Shakespeare's Global Influence

1. Before becoming the first black president of South Africa, Nelson Mandela spent 27 years in prison for his struggles against his country's racist policies of apartheid. While in prison, he signed his name next to his favorite quotation from a copy of *The Complete Works of William Shakespeare*:

> "Cowards die many times before their deaths, The valiant never taste of death but once."—from *Julius Caesar*

What does this quote mean to you? What significance might it have had for Nelson Mandela?

My Notes

Preview

In this activity, you will read two articles that examine Shakespeare's global influence.

Setting a Purpose for Reading

- Using your color codes, highlight evidence for or against the importance of Shakespeare.
- Circle unknown words and phrases. Try to determine the meaning of the words by using context clues, word parts, or a dictionary.
- Underline parts of the text that emphasize the connection between Shakespeare and the world.

Article

Britain Puts on a Shakespeare Marathon as World Arrives for the Olympic Games

by Jill Lawless, *The Washington Post/Associated Press* (2012)

1   LONDON — As the world comes to Britain for the Olympics, Britain is celebrating arguably its greatest gift to the world—the plays of William Shakespeare.

2   Anyone who doubts that accolade for the playwright dead almost 400 years might want to go to the new "Shakespeare: Staging the World" exhibition at the British Museum, and look at the final exhibit, a well-worn, one-volume collection of Shakespeare's plays.

3 The book is the property of Sonny Venkatrathnam, a former South African anti-apartheid prisoner. He secretly kept it in the notorious Robben Island prison but shared it with other inmates, who underlined and autographed the passages that meant the most to them.

4 The book lies open at lines from *Julius Caesar*—"Cowards die many times before their deaths/The valiant never taste of death but once"—signed "N. R. D. Mandela."

5 "In a way, Nelson was the Caesar of the ANC," said Venkatrathnam, who spent several years in the prison with African National Congress leader Mandela in the 1970s. "I think it resonated with his philosophy."

6 Mandela—now the revered 94-year-old former president of post-apartheid South Africa—is one of more than 30 inmates whom Venkatrathnam asked to sign the volume. It became known as the "Robben Island Bible," because Venkatrathnam told prison warders— who had banned nonreligious books—that it was "the Bible by William Shakespeare." He plastered its cover with cards celebrating the Hindu festival of Diwali in a successful bid to disguise the contents from guards.

7 "They would come and say, 'What's that?' I'd say, 'It's my Bible,'" said Venkatrathnam, a dapper 76-year-old who traveled to London for the opening of the exhibition. "For all the years on the island they wouldn't touch it."

8 British Museum director Neil MacGregor said the book is "a wonderful symbol of what Shakespeare means to all of us."

9 The exhibition, which opens Thursday, is part of an outpouring of Shakespearean activity in Britain that includes the opening ceremony of the July 27–Aug. 12 Olympic Games. Director Danny Boyle's ceremony, entitled "Isles of Wonder," is inspired by the strange and enchanted island of *The Tempest*.

10 Other helpings of the Bard include a cycle of history plays, currently being shown on Saturday night prime-time BBC television, and the Royal Shakespeare Company's epic World Shakespeare Festival. Since April, the RSC, based in Shakespeare's home town of Stratford-upon-Avon, has been bringing companies from around the world to stage his plays in Britain.

11 The productions, in more than 40 languages, have ranged from an Iraqi *Romeo and Juliet* to a Russian *Midsummer Night's Dream* and a Brazilian circus *Richard III*.

12 American director Peter Sellars, whose contribution to the festival is *Desdemona*—a **reimagining** of *Othello* by U.S. writer Toni Morrison and Malian singer Rokia Traore—said Shakespeare is truly a writer for the whole world.

reimagining: thinking about in a new, creative way

13 "He was a guy who—and not for reasons of branding—called his theater 'The Globe,'" Sellars said.

14 The British Museum show, which runs through Nov. 25, combines artifacts from Shakespeare's time—including the only surviving manuscript in the playwright's handwriting—with recorded readings by actors to **evoke** an era that seems both familiar and alien.

evoke: produce

15 In Shakespeare's day, London was just beginning to attract people from around the world, emerging as the center of a **nascent** empire.

nascent: beginning to develop

My Notes

_____

Shakespeare's Globe

co-curator: one of two or more people in charge

excavated: dug out of the earth

sorcery: witchcraft

exuberance: enthusiasm
resonance: deep meaning
predicaments: difficult situations

My Notes

_____

_____

_____

ideological: relating to someone's personal views and beliefs

_____

_____

_____

_____

_____

_____

_____

_____

_____

_____

_____

16   "As the world comes to London in 2012, this Olympic summer, we are going to look at how the world came to London and how London saw the world 400 years ago," said Jonathan Bate, **co-curator** of the exhibition.

17   The exhibition roams through Shakespeare's influences, from the rural English landscapes of his youth to the country's dynastic power struggles, the discoveries emerging from the New World, the arrival of visitors from abroad and the creation of Britain as a country with the union of the crowns of England and Scotland under James I.

18   Some items suggest a cold, violent world a long way from our own. There's King Henry V's jousting helmet, a bear skull **excavated** from the site of an Elizabethan theater—where bear-baiting went on alongside drama—and an iron "witch's collar" and metal gag used to punish women accused of **sorcery**.

19   But the parallels with our own era of migration, globalization and political uncertainty are ever-present.

20   It is hard to nail down the secret of Shakespeare's genius. It rests on some combination of the **exuberance** of his language and the **resonance** of the human **predicaments** he depicts, from lovers battling family disapproval to kings struggling to live up to the burdens of power.

21   Shakespeare set plays in Venice and Verona, Denmark and Egypt—places he had read about but never visited. His plays in turn helped create the world view of his audience, and have been influencing audiences around the world ever since.

22   "He was genuinely a global figure—perhaps the greatest global export this country has ever produced," Bate said.

23   His ability to speak to audiences around the world is undimmed.

24   "The great thing about Shakespeare is that he speaks to everyone," Venkatrathnam said. "Regardless of your political or **ideological** position, you can find something that speaks directly to you. To me, he is the universal philosopher."

Second Read

- Reread the article to answer these text-dependent questions.
- Write any additional questions you have about the text in your Reader/Writer Notebook.

2. **Craft and Structure:** What does the author mean when she says that Shakespeare was a "global figure"?

3. **Craft and Structure:** What is the significance of the name of Shakespeare's theater?

4. **Key Ideas and Details:** What is the scope of the exhibition Bate curated?

5. **Key Ideas and Details:** Why was 2012 a perfect time to create the exhibition about Shakespeare?

My Notes

_____
_____
_____
_____
_____
_____
_____
_____
_____
_____
_____
_____
_____

Article

On Love and War, Iraq Learns from Shakespeare

by Shelina Zahra Janmohamed, *Daily Star*

1   As part of the 2012 Summer Olympics hosted in London, the Royal Shakespeare Company challenged theater groups around the world to create **contemporary** re-imaginings of 16th century playwright William Shakespeare's classics. Of the many unique and creative performances, *Romeo and Juliet in Baghdad*, performed by the Iraqi Theatre Company, caught my eye. Could one of Europe's greatest romantic tragedies, written in the 16th century, tell us something about Iraq in the 21st century?

2   Adapted into **colloquial** Arabic and performed by an Iraqi cast with English subtitles above the stage, the story, while written in an Iraqi context, is a familiar one. It opens with two brothers, Montague and Capulet, who have feuded for nine years over who will steer their family's pearl-diving ship. This serves as an **apropos** metaphor for Iraq at the beginning of the war. Romeo and Juliet, who like all the play's characters retain their original Shakespearean names, have already met and fallen in love before the feud. They have been kept apart by the cycle of violence resulting from the feud between their fathers.

contemporary: modern; from the present time

colloquial: ordinary or familiar (language)

apropos: fitting

My Notes

3 The play focuses less on their romance and more on how families, communities and nations can easily and quickly be torn apart. The story prompts the audience to reflect on how pride, regret, a lack of mutual understanding and interference from the outside are obstacles to resolving conflicts peacefully. Once blood has been spilled, we are never sure if peace can be restored.

4 The play's director, Monadhil Daood, fled Iraq in his 20s after staging a play under Saddam Hussein about the Iran-Iraq war. In 2008, he founded the Iraqi Theatre Company to "bring a contemporary cultural voice of unity and inclusiveness into the civic discourse in Iraq." Monadhil says that "I think my [play] *Romeo and Juliet in Baghdad* will be a mirror. The audience will see themselves on the stage."

5 In the buzzing auditorium, I saw his prediction come true. The emotional effect the play had on its audience was clear. During the performance, many had eyes filled with tears. At joyous moments, audience members tapped along to the wedding songs and laughed at the inclusion of an old Iraqi folk story about a beetle looking for love.

imposter: a deceptive person
betrothed: engaged to marry

6 During the most emotional moment of all, I felt almost swept off my chair at the audience's roar of approval as the **imposter**, who was **betrothed** to Juliet against her will, and who had stoked the tension between the two families, was cast out by Juliet's father, Capulet. This character, a miserable hard-liner, represents the presence of Al-Qaeda in Iraq. Through Capulet's action, the betrothal is reversed and his presence is no longer accepted.

7 The real story of *Romeo and Juliet in Baghdad* is of the audience, who see their lives played out before their eyes. The drama was a chance to create enough distance from their own stories so that they could look at the effect of the last nine years on their homeland, with its **immense** loss, death, and suffering. It was an opportunity to move on, make sense, find **catharsis**, and even laugh.

immense: huge
catharsis: the release of built-up emotions

8 The play at its heart is a universal story of the birth and development of conflict, stoked by fear, misunderstanding, and pride. It shows how outside forces can stoke conflict and divide groups of people, and reflects on the need for unity.

9 In this case, a love story is a **portal** into a world that audiences might otherwise never be able to begin to understand. By connecting with the story of young lovers—a theme that **transcends** time and culture—we can learn about the **nuances** of today's Iraqi society. The play helps viewers understand tight-knit family structures and the once strong historic relationships between Sunni and Shiite Muslims that are now being broken down. In fact, people around the world might find a lot in common with the ordinary folk of Iraq and their aspirations to bring an end to violence and live better lives.

portal: gateway; entrance

transcends: rises above
nuances: slight variations

10 But more importantly, through such plays, we are confronted with universal truths: conflict persists across human societies and it must be addressed before it spirals out of control. But most of all, the aspiration to love and be loved is present in all times and places, whether in Baghdad or Verona, for lovers like Romeo and Juliet, or for brothers like Montague and Capulet.

Second Read

- Reread the article to answer these text-dependent questions.
- Write any additional questions you have about the text in your Reader/Writer Notebook.

6. **Key Ideas and Details:** What major changes did the director make in this version of the play compared to the original?

7. **Key Ideas and Details:** What universal truths and themes are present in the Iraqi version of this play?

8. **Key Ideas and Details:** Why did this version of the play resonate so strongly with its audience?

9. **Craft and Structure:** What was the central metaphor in this version of the play, and what did it represent?

My Notes

Shakespeare's Globe

My Notes

Working from the Text

10. Meet with a partner. Summarize the key points and share your textual evidence and commentary to complete the graphic organizer.

Article	Textual Evidence of Shakespeare's Influence on the Community	Commentary on his Relevance to the Community
"On Love and War . . ." (Janmohamed) Community:		
"Britain Puts on a Shakespeare Marathon . . ." (Lawless) Community:		

Language and Writer's Craft: Using and Citing Sources

Using quoted and paraphrased text from sources is an important way to support the main points of your argument or analysis. There are several ways to integrate quoted text smoothly into your own writing.

You can use a transitional word or phrase to introduce a quote that supports a point you are making:

> Shakespeare's plays have become irrelevant because they have lost their original context. The world of Shakespeare is not our world. As Petri points out, students today "don't even know who the guy was."

You can use a quote in a sentence that provides commentary or explanation of the quote:

> Although we are far removed from Shakespeare's time, and, as Petri says, "don't even know who the guy was," we can still apply the universal truths found in his writing to our own context.

You can also paraphrase another writer to support your point. If you do not need the exact words, this is a fine option, but you must still give credit to the source:

> As Petri notes in the essay, students today do not even know who Shakespeare was—neither his birthday nor the date on which he died.

PRACTICE Use each of these three methods to incorporate a quotation from one of the texts in this activity into your own writing. Choose from these methods to support the claim in your argument.

Check Your Understanding

What is the difference between relevance and influence?

Argument Writing Prompt

Write a draft of a paragraph to support the claim that Shakespeare has a significant global influence. Be sure to:

- Use a topic sentence that states your claim.
- Use parenthetical or in-text citations for at least one quote of support from each text.
- Integrate the evidence with commentary from both texts that explains how the evidence supports your claim.

INDEPENDENT READING LINK

Read and Discuss

Think about your independent reading selection. Discuss with a peer whether the text has a significant influence on the world, and whether or not it should. Explain the central ideas of your selection as you argue for or against its influence.

My Notes

Did Shakespeare Invent Teenagers?

LEARNING STRATEGIES:
Quickwrite, Chunking the
Text, Sharing and Responding,
Graphic Organizer

ACADEMIC VOCABULARY
A **counterclaim** is an alternate or
opposing claim with **concessions**
that the opposing side has
valid points and/or **refutations**
explaining why the writer's
position is more valid.

Learning Targets
- Analyze how an author's point of view is developed and supported by evidence.
- Write an argumentative paragraph that distinguishes claims and counterclaims.

Teenagers Today
1. **Quickwrite:** Compare and contrast the teenagers in *Romeo and Juliet* with teenagers today. What do you and your peers have in common with Romeo, Juliet, Mercutio, Benvolio, and Tybalt? How are you different?

Preview
In this activity, you will read an article that argues that Shakespeare "invented" teenagers as we know them today. Consider his claim, and then work with your class to develop a **counterclaim**.

Setting a Purpose for Reading
- Using your color codes, highlight evidence for or against the idea that Shakespeare invented teenagers.
- Circle unknown words and phrases. Try to determine the meaning of the words by using context clues, word parts, or a dictionary.

My Notes

ABOUT THE AUTHOR
Stephen Marche is a novelist who writes a monthly column about culture for *Esquire* magazine. Ten years ago he chose Shakespeare as the subject of his Ph.D. dissertation because he believed that Shakespeare would never bore him. He was correct. In the introduction to *How Shakespeare Changed Everything*, he writes: "I learned when I was a professor that teaching Shakespeare to undergraduates is one of the easiest gigs in the history of the world. If you can't make a room full of young people care about Shakespeare, then you probably shouldn't be around young people or Shakespeare."

Article

from How Shakespeare *Changed Everything*

by Stephen Marche

Chunk 1

1 Shakespeare described the terrifying beauty of the adolescent so early in its development, and so definitively and so thoroughly, that it is only a slight exaggeration to say that he invented teenagers as we know them today. *Romeo and Juliet*, his extended study of the humiliations and glories of adolescence, is the biggest hit of all

time; everybody knows the story even if they haven't seen the play. Just one year after its first performance in 1596, the Quarto publication proclaimed that "it hath been often (with great applause) plaid publiquely." Unlike most of Shakespeare's plays, it has never slipped out of fashion. *Hamlet*—Shakespeare's other great play about adolescence—is the only piece performed more regularly onstage, and when you consider how often and how successfully *Romeo and Juliet* has been adapted into other media, into operas and ballads and musicals, its popularity is even more staggering. The most popular brand of Cuban cigars? *Romeo y Julietta*. People just love to watch a couple of dumb kids make out and die. And they are awfully young, these dumb Veronese kids who make out for us and then die. Shakespeare doesn't ever tell us Romeo's exact age, but we know about Juliet. In the first act, her nurse discusses her age at length, and it's creepy. In two weeks she will be fourteen.

Chunk 2

2 *Romeo and Juliet* has to be fudged. In the eighteenth century, David Garrick understood that his audiences wanted a pure and innocent Romeo and Juliet, and he gave them a sentimentalized version of the play, which was so much to their liking that his version survived intact for over a century. To make the young lovers totally heroic, he had to make them less complicated—the first thing to go was Romeo's love for Rosaline at the beginning of the play. Romeo's mooning over another girl is embarrassing to everybody; he seems unreliable, and it's a bit insulting to Juliet. Garrick's audience wanted Romeo and Juliet to be proper first lovers. He gave the audience what it wanted. He also fiddled with several lines, in order to remove, in his words, "the Jingle and Quibble which were always thought a great objection to performing it." He cut the dirty jokes…. And he also cut down on the rhyming—it made the lovers seem too silly and too unrealistic. The biggest change, however, was the death scene. Garrick let Juliet wake up before Romeo is properly dead—a **flamboyant** effect that is not in the original.

3 Garrick created teenagers who were icons of **purity** in a corrupt adult world. But Shakespeare, unlike Garrick, never spares his adolescents their ridiculousness. The first snatch of dialogue between Romeo and Juliet is beautiful and absurd. Notice that the dialogue follows the rhyme pattern of a Shakespearean sonnet.

ROMEO: If I **profane** with my unworthiest hand

This holy shrine, the gentle sin is this,

My lips, two blushing pilgrims, ready stand

To smooth that rough touch with a tender kiss.

JULIET: Good pilgrim, you do wrong your hand too much,

Which mannerly devotion shows in this,

For saints have hands that pilgrims' hands do touch,

And palm to palm is holy palmers' kiss.

ROMEO: Have not saints lips, and holy palmers too?

JULIET: Ay, pilgrim, lips that they must use in prayer.

ROMEO: O, then, dear saint, let lips do what hands do;

They pray, grant thou, lest faith turn to despair.

JULIET: Saints do not move, though grant for prayers' sake.

ROMEO: Then move not, while my prayer's effect I take.   *They kiss.*

My Notes

flamboyant: bold; showy

purity: state of being free of anything that pollutes or dirties

profane: treat irreverently

Did Shakespeare Invent Teenagers?

purged: cleansed

Thus from my lips, by yours, my sin is **purged**.

JULIET: Then have my lips the sin that they have took.

ROMEO: Sin from thy lips? O trespass sweetly urged!

Give me my sin again.   *He kisses her.*

JULIET   You kiss by the book.

vague: unclear
palpable: obvious

4 The **vague** but **palpable** effect of this sudden advent of ABAB CDCD EFEF GG rhyme is inexplicable beauty. Only the sharpest members of the audience could conceivably be sharp enough to notice that the lovers have dipped into sonnet form, but Shakespeare leaves us with an inarticulate impression that the young lovers are somehow strange and magical. Garrick took the sonnet out of the scene exactly because it made their love seem too ridiculous and artificial. But Shakespeare wants them ridiculous. That's how kids are. And the last line is perfect: "You kiss by the book." It sounds to me exactly like what a thirteen-year-old girl says after a first kiss, like she's been kissing forever, like she knows all about kissing, like she's read the book.

My Notes

Chunk 3

5 Nothing could seem more natural to us than the rebellion of teenagers, which explains why *Romeo and Juliet* has fit easily into twentieth-century pop culture. Irving Berlin referred to the pair in a bunch of different songs, as have Bob Dylan, Bruce Springsteen, Madonna, Tom Waits, Dire Straits, Alanis Morissette, Aerosmith, Elvis Costello, and the Indigo Girls. Lou Reed's "Romeo Had Juliette" is a surprisingly conservative retelling of the story. On the street, the young crack dealers dream of automatic weapons, random murder, and the decline of Western civilization. Inside, Romeo clutches a cross and Juliet. The young in Lou Reed's song are the **harbingers** of **apocalyptic** social decay, and their only redemption is the love they preserve against the despair everywhere around them.

harbingers: foreshadowers
apocalyptic: predicting imminent disaster

6 In *The Wild One*, a woman at a bar asks Marlon Brando what he's rebelling against. "Whaddaya got?" he slurs back. The teenage rebel cannot say: "I believe that the incidental tax rate is too high for local corporations," or "our agribusiness policies are short-sighted." No. That would not be nearly stupid or grand enough. The most important feature of adolescent rebellion is that it's doomed. It must come to an end. In this, as well, Shakespeare was right at the beginning. He defined what it means to be "star-cross'd." The opposition between the adolescent and the mature orders of the world can have only two possible endings. One is comic: The teenager grows up, develops a sense of humor, gets married, has kids, moves to the suburbs, gets fat, and becomes boring. That's what happens to most Romeos and Juliets. The other is tragic: The teenager blows up in a blaze of glory. We much prefer to live in the comedy. We much prefer to watch the tragedy.

absurdity: foolishness

7 Shakespeare loves his teenagers as he paints them in all their **absurdity** and nastiness. That basic honesty, neither idealizing nor afraid, has kept Romeo and Juliet fresh. Leonardo DiCaprio and Claire Danes became the dominant young actors of their generation through their performances in Baz Luhrmann's *Romeo + Juliet*. Justin Bieber, with his swagger coach and overwhelming fame, comes appropriately from Stratford, the home of North America's biggest Shakespeare festival.

nostalgia: wistful desire for the past
loathing: strong dislike

8 Shakespeare created this category of humanity, which now seems as organic to us as the spring. In place of **nostalgia** and **loathing**, Shakespeare would have us look at teenagers in a spirit of wonder, even the spotty ones and the awkward ones and the wild ones. They're us before we fall into categories: not children, not adults, not monsters, not saints. They're beautiful because they do not fit. They're too much themselves and not enough.

Second Read

- Reread the nonfiction text to answer these text-dependent questions.
- Write any additional questions you have about the text in your Reader/Writer Notebook.

2. **Key Ideas and Details:** How does *Romeo and Juliet* help define adolescence?

3. **Craft and Structure:** How does the central purpose of the article influence its tone?

4. **Key Ideas and Details:** Why did David Garrick think he had to change the characterization of Romeo and Juliet?

5. **Craft and Structure:** Why is it significant that Romeo and Juliet's first dialogue is written in sonnet form?

6. **Key Ideas and Details:** How has *Romeo and Juliet* influenced modern culture?

My Notes

Did Shakespeare Invent Teenagers?

Working from the Text

7. In the graphic organizer, summarize the purpose of each chunk in developing Marche's argument. After taking notes on the reasons and evidence the author provides, generate your own reasons and evidence to support a counterclaim. Use rhetorical appeals emphasizing logos and ethos. Examples include the following:

- **Logos:** *Most teenagers know more about technology than their parents.*
- **Ethos:** *My friends and I are more level-headed than Romeo and Juliet.*
- **Pathos:** *It is unkind and unfair to call teenagers ignorant.*

Example Claim: Shakespeare invented teenagers as we know them today.

Example Counterclaim: Teenagers today are very different from the characters in Shakespeare's plays.

Objective Summary (Main idea of the text)	Claim (Reasons and textual evidence the author uses to support his argument)	Concessions and Refutations (Reasons and personal evidence why the argument is valid or not)
Chunk 1:		
Chunk 2:		
Chunk 3:		

Responding to Counterclaims

8. Review your graphic organizer with a partner or small group and identify the strongest reasons and evidence in support of both the claim and counterclaim.

9. The paragraph that follows supports Marche's claim by acknowledging and responding to counterclaims. Mark the text as follows:

- Underline sentences or clauses that support Marche's claim.
- Put brackets around sentences or clauses that acknowledge counterclaims.
- Circle transition words that clarify the relationship between claims and counterclaims.

Shakespeare presents teenagers who seem true to life and realistic even though they were portrayed 500 years ago. Even though today's teen is more likely to be carrying an iPhone than a broadsword, they act exactly the same. As Stephen Marche observes, "The opening scene of *Romeo and Juliet* shows young men terrorizing the streets of Verona with instantly recognizable teenage nastiness" (Marche). The modern teenager did not invent the practice of bullying, although that doesn't make it any less of a problem. Teenagers today continue to make rash decisions and struggle with the consequences. They also endure parental meddling that is less than helpful just as in *Romeo and Juliet*. Teenage accessories and fashion may have changed since Shakespeare's day, but adolescence itself is still the same ordeal.

Argument Writing Prompt

Write a paragraph against Stephen Marche's argument by stating your own claim and responding to his ideas with your own reasons and evidence. (The reasons and evidence in the counterclaim column of your graphic organizer will now become the reasons and evidence to support your claim.) Be sure to:

- Include a topic sentence that states your claim.
- Use transitions and properly cited textual evidence to introduce counterclaims.
- Respond to Marche's counterclaims, using transitions and rhetorical appeals of logos and ethos.

INDEPENDENT READING LINK

Read and Connect

Create a chart similar to the one used in this activity to document how the author of your independent reading selection treats characters of different ages. Include columns for main ideas about age groups, quotations that support the ideas, and how this might compare to Shakespeare's treatment of teenagers.

Shakespeare Behind Bars

LEARNING STRATEGIES:
Metacognitive Markers, Note-taking, Graphic Organizer, Discussion Groups

My Notes

Learning Targets
- Evaluate evidence and make inferences.
- Use the elements of an argument in writing.

Preview
In this activity, you will read an article about prisoners who perform Shakespeare.

Setting a Purpose for Reading
- Mark the text with metacognitive markers:
  - ? = Questions about the text
  - ! = Reactions related to the text
  - * = Comments about the text
- Circle unknown words and phrases. Try to determine the meaning of the words by using context clues, word parts, or a dictionary.

Article

Kentucky Inmates Turned Actors Explore Selves Through Shakespeare Play

by Sean Rose, *Courier Journal*

1 Gene Vaughn waited nervously behind two swinging doors in the prison chapel of the Luther Luckett Correctional Complex.

2 On any other day this would be just a chapel and Vaughn would be just one of the 1,072 inmates locked in the medium security Oldham County prison.

3 But on a recent June night, Vaughn and 23 other inmates became characters in Shakespeare's *Merchant of Venice*, reviewing their lines in the final moments before the curtain drew back on opening night.

foray: venture

4 For some, the nine months they spent preparing marked their first **foray** into acting. For others, it was a journey into self-exploration, a chance to review past mistakes and analyze an uncertain future.

5 "I used to think that acting was acting, that it was something I'd be good at, that all of us convicts would be good at," said cast member Jerry Guenther, who is serving 45 years for murder. "We live a lie. But in here, our acting is not acting: it's telling the truth."

converted: changed

6 Each year the Shakespeare Behind Bars program at Luther Luckett takes on a new play. Their stage is **converted** from a chapel within the razor wire-ringed state prison near La Grange.

7 "Shakespeare understood the human condition like nobody else," said Matt Wallace, now in his third year directing the program of inmate performances. "The themes that are in these plays resonate so deeply in these guys. Through these plays they're digging up some of the most painful and horrific parts of their lives."

8 Since October, the cast and crew has gathered three times a week to prepare for performances that began June 2 and will wrap up Thursday—eight shows put on to entertain other inmates, the cast members' families, and state correction officials.

9 The actors are a varied group, serving sentences from 4 years to life without parole for a host of crimes, including sex offenses, robbery, and murder.

10 And those backgrounds help them identify with Shakespeare's characters in a way many outside prison walls can't.

11 At the heart of the play is Shylock, a Jewish money lender played by Vaughn, a convicted murderer serving a 40-year sentence. **Ostracized** because of his religion, Shylock tries to exact revenge upon a hateful rival who comes to him for a loan, demanding that he wager his life against the loan.

12 "It deals with race. It deals with **discrimination**. It deals with gambling, debt, cutting people. It deals with it all," Tim Jett, an inmate serving as assistant director, said in an interview during early rehearsal. "And we were all living that some way, somehow. We were all living it."

Every man must play a part

13 Putting on a full-length Shakespeare production in a prison setting brings a host of unique challenges.

14 Rehearsals rarely last more than two hours because of the prison's daily schedule. Some men quit, and others are forced to drop out if they're sent to solitary confinement or shipped to another institution.

15 Some finish their sentences and are released.

16 Jett, after five years behind bars for sexual abuse, served out his term in April. To the rest of the crew, he was the luckiest man in Shakespeare Behind Bars.

17 But Jett thought otherwise, and decided to write a letter asking Secretary of Justice and Public Safety J. Michael Brown to **defer** his release for 60 days so he could stay until the end of the show. He received no response and was released in March.

18 Unlike other prison programs, Shakespeare Behind Bars offers no "good time" or credits for early release.

19 "The only thing they get for being in this is the satisfaction of completing something," said Josh Lewis, a classification and treatment officer who is the program's **sponsor**.

Do we not bleed?

20 Early rehearsals were rough. The prison radios drowned out the actors' lines. And the Elizabethan speech taxed some of the play's eight new members.

21 But the cast and crew eventually formed a bond that turned the gatherings into a mix of theater work and group therapy. Although many of them have trusted few people in their lives, they increasingly **confided** in each other.

22 Before opening night, with all on edge, Wallace sought to refocus their attention on what's important. He asked everyone to go around and explain why they joined the program. Up went the hand of Guenther, a 13-year member and one of the elder statesmen of Shakespeare Behind Bars.

23 "This is the safest place in the world," Guenther told the other inmates.

My Notes

ostracized: excluded from society

discrimination: treating someone differently from all others

defer: delay

sponsor: a person who is responsible for another person or event

confided: discussed private matters with a trusted person

Shakespeare Behind Bars

parole: release from prison before
the end of a sentence
botched: gone wrong

My Notes

24 Guenther is one of the more experienced actors in the group, having played Hamlet in a previous performance, but took a minor role this season because of a **parole** hearing in February. He hoped to be released after 25 years of a 45-year sentence for killing an undercover Shively police officer during a **botched** drug deal.

25 Instead the parole board ruled that he wouldn't be eligible for release for another 10 years.

26 The news hit Guenther and his fellow Shakespeare cast hard.

27 At 6-feet-5 and 330 pounds, the former star high school offensive lineman brings an enthusiasm to the play that is contagious.

28 "The thing I always flash back to is how fast a bad decision can lead to complete catastrophe," Guenther told the group. "The only thing I can say is I was a kid and I didn't mean for it to happen. You can't fix what's already broken. And God knows I wish I could."

29 Vaughn, a close friend of Guenther, spoke up.

30 "Regardless of what you do, you're always going to be reminded of what you did," he said.

31 Those in the circle nodded silently in agreement.

Quality of mercy is not strain'd

32 Within each man's sentence is a separate punishment, one that many of them see as inescapable even after leaving prison. For the rest of their lives they will be convicted felons.

33 It's a burden they recognize as unavoidable, as much a part of their lives as prison meals and daily dorm counts.

34 Months into rehearsal, the members are quick to connect with Shylock's status as a second-class citizen amid his Christian neighbors. When Shylock lashes out, a small debate stirs among the men as to whether he is victim or villain.

35 Judging a character outright is damaging, Wallace said. And the same applies to the Shakespeare Behind Bars members, he said.

36 "Society has already judged them," Wallace said. "It's going to do no good if I come in here and judge them for what they've done."

37 Reading over *The Merchant of Venice*, Vaughn said "it just reminds you of yourself, of the things you've done in your life."

instances: individual occurrences

38 As the season progressed, inmates dug deeper into their own lives through their characters, in some **instances** making peace with a past they'd rather forget.

39 That was the case for Vaughn, who saw his link to Shylock through abuse.

40 Vaughn said he was 6 years old when two neighbors sexually abused him. Until last year he never told anyone, though, and the burden of the secret bore on him.

recklessness: state of acting
unconcerned with consequences
critical mass: the amount needed
to produce a result

41 Vaughn doesn't blame his situation in life on that, but he's sure he's acted more recklessly because of it. The **recklessness** reached **critical mass** on March 22, 1989, when Vaughn was involved in the death of a Louisville woman he met at a night club. He was sentenced to 40 years.

42 "I didn't care," Vaughn said of his life then. "I didn't care what people thought about me. I didn't care what happened to me. At that point you feel like nothing is going to change for you anyway. But that's where I was totally wrong."

43 In prison and through Shakespeare, Vaughn said he has had time to **contemplate** mercy, and how it offers something to aspire toward.

contemplate: thoughtfully consider

44 "When you have done something in your life so bad, you try to go about the right way to tell people that you're sorry," he said. "But there's certain people you're not going to be able to say you're sorry to, like my victim, my victim's family. So I can only hope that somewhere in their life they can say I forgive you to a certain extent. To me that's some type of mercy."

Outside to behold

45 About 50 inmates turned out for opening night, and after the final scene they gave the performance a standing ovation.

46 "For those two hours, those three hours, you don't even feel like you're in prison," said inmate Kevin Hesson, a new Shakespeare member. "You feel like you're in a theater outside of here. You don't feel the razor wire."

47 After congratulations, the men hurried to change out of their costumes and get back to their dorms, first spreading their arms and legs at the chapel entrance to be frisked.

48 There would be more performances, but for now they were back on the prison schedule—and the 9 P.M. head count was just 10 minutes away.

Second Read

- Reread the article to answer these text-dependent questions.
- Write any additional questions you have about the text in your Reader/Writer Notebook.

1. **Key Ideas and Details:** What is the central purpose of this article?

2. **Craft and Structure:** What do you think Jerry Guenther meant when he said, "But in here our acting's not acting; it's telling the truth"?

3. **Key Ideas and Details:** Why are inmates the perfect cast for many of Shakespeare's plays?

My Notes

Shakespeare Behind Bars

My Notes

_____
_____
_____
_____
_____
_____
_____
_____
_____
_____
_____
_____
_____
_____
_____
_____
_____
_____
_____

4. **Key Ideas and Details:** Why did *The Merchant of Venice* in particular resonate with the inmates performing it?

5. **Key Ideas and Details:** What do inmates gain from partaking in projects like Shakespeare Behind Bars?

6. **Key Ideas and Details:** What challenges do the inmates at Luther Luckett have to overcome in order to stage their production?

Working from the Text

7. Consider the following quotations about prisons. Analyze what each one means and to what extent do you agree or disagree. Add your responses to the graphic organizer below.

Quote	Meaning	Agree or Disagree and Why
"The degree of civilization in a society can be judged by entering its prisons." —Fyodor Dostoyevsk		
"All in all, punishment hardens and renders people more insensible; it concentrates; it increases the feeling of estrangement; it strengthens the power of resistance." —Friedrich Nietzsche		
"One is absolutely sickened, not by the crimes that the wicked have committed, but by the punishments that the good have inflicted; and a community is infinitely more brutalized by the habitual employment of punishment than it is by the occasional occurrence of crime." —Oscar Wilde		
"And where the offence is, let the great axe fall." —William Shakespeare		

8. **Discuss:** Two of the primary purposes of our criminal justice system are punishment and rehabilitation. For prisoners, *rehabilitation* means to restore a person to a useful life, often through education. Which purpose do you think is more important? Why?

9. Prepare to write a letter to a representative from the state or federal government either in support of or against funding for programs like Shakespeare Behind Bars by completing the following graphic organizer.

Hook:

Claim:

Reasons and evidence to support the claim:	**Counterclaim:**	
	Reasons and evidence to support counterclaim:	**Concessions and refutations:**

Concluding statement/call to action:

Check Your Understanding

Present your letter to another group. If possible, find a group that disagrees with your claim. As you listen to their letter, add new reasons and evidence to the graphic organizer or write notes in the My Notes space.

Argument Writing Prompt

Find a partner or small group that agrees with your claim and work together to write a letter of argument. Be sure to:

• Include an introduction that uses a hook and states your claim.

• Defend your claim and respond to the counterclaims with support that depends primarily on logic and ethos.

• Use transitions and properly cited textual evidence.

ACADEMIC VOCABULARY
In an argument, the **hook** is an opening that grabs the reader's attention and establishes a connection between the reader and the writer.
The **concluding statement** should follow from and support the argument. It may include a **call to action** or plea for the reader to do something about the issue.

LEARNING STRATEGIES:
Graphic Organizer, Note-taking,
Marking the Text, Discussion
Groups

My Notes

_____

_____

_____

_____

_____

_____

_____

_____

_____

_____

_____

_____

_____

_____

_____

_____

_____

curriculum: regular classes
taught in a school or program
trappings: characteristic signs
pantheon: a place where heroes
congregate

putative: commonly regarded
as right
gobbets: fragments; pieces

acute: severe
uncanny: mysterious;
inexplicable

Learning Targets
- Identify the essential elements of an argument in an article.
- Create a graphic organizer and a writer's checklist, in preparation for writing a synthesis argument.

Preview
In this activity, you will read an article that argues for giving Shakespeare the "heave-ho."

Setting a Purpose for Reading
- Using your color codes, highlight evidence for or against the studying of Shakespeare.
- Circle unknown words and phrases. Try to determine the meaning of the words by using context clues, word parts, or a dictionary.

Article

Why It's Time to Give the Bard the Heave-ho!

by Brandon Robshaw, *The Independent*

1   As a tribute to Shakespeare this St George's day, isn't it time we dropped him from the National **Curriculum**? The Bard is a national monument. Nor is there anything wrong with that. Along with a flag, an anthem, and a football team, a national writer is part of the **trappings** of nationhood. The Italians have Dante, the Germans have Goethe, the French have a **pantheon** which includes Molière, Racine, Victor Hugo, and Proust.

2   And Shakespeare is peculiarly well-suited to be ours, for both literary and non-literary reasons. The date of his death and the **putative** date of his birth neatly fall on our patron saint's day; he belongs to the golden age of Elizabethan expansionism; his history plays chronicle our kings and queens and contain quotable patriotic **gobbets** ("This precious stone set in the silver sea," "We few, we happy few," etc.). His output is staggeringly prolific—38 dramatic works in all the genres, several long poems and over 150 sonnets—and his plays work well enough dramatically to be constantly performed today. He had, as George Orwell put it, an amazing skill at putting one word beside another; as well as **acute** psychological insight, the largeness of mind to give great lines even to minor or unfavored characters, an unmatched ear for rhythm, and an **uncanny** ability to coin memorable phrases which, in many cases, have passed into general usage.

3   One might even say that appreciation of Shakespeare is the touchstone of an educated literary taste. If you don't like him, you don't get it. Voltaire and Tolstoy famously didn't, but then English wasn't their mother tongue.

4 The trouble is that most schoolchildren today don't like him and don't get it. And this isn't their fault. Shakespeare wrote over 400 years ago. Few people realize how much English has changed in just the last generation. Grammar and vocabulary have altered to the extent that teenagers tend to dismiss anything written before about 1960 as "Old English."

5 Besides, the large and increasing number of second-language speakers are in the same boat as Voltaire and Tolstoy from the start. We don't have anything like the unified national culture we had when I first studied Shakespeare in the 1970s. Then, most schoolchildren had at least some exposure to the King James Bible, the Book of Common Prayer and Hymns Ancient and Modern. We still didn't find Shakespeare easy, but at least we didn't need to have "thee" and "thou" explained to us.

6 Even the key selling point that many Shakespearisms have entered common usage is gradually losing its force as the years go by. I was recently taken aback to discover that virtually none of a class of London teenagers had encountered the expression "one fell swoop." Well, you might say, here's your chance to teach them, then. But that cannot be the justification for making Shakespeare **compulsory**—to teach outdated idioms that no one under the age of 40 uses.

7 We need to think more clearly about the purpose of **enshrining** Shakespeare in this manner. If it's to preserve his national monument status, this is an unnecessary and counter-productive way of going about it. If it is to teach those things that literature is supposed to teach—**aesthetic** pleasure, understanding of character, moral sensitivity, liberal humanist values, an **inkling** of the techniques by which literary texts work their magic—then Shakespeare is simply not delivering. It's like handing pupils treasure in a locked chest. More contemporary texts may not offer quite such riches, but at least the kids could open the box.

8 Making today's school children read Shakespeare is about as sensible as compelling them to read Ulysses or Tristram Shandy. For all but a few—the brightest and best-read—it is a form of torture. Yet it's laid down in the National Curriculum that all British children of secondary school age must study not one but two Shakespeare plays. It is, as Will himself would say, a custom more honored in the breach than in the observance—and in practice, many teachers **circumvent** the difficulty by teaching a fragment of *Romeo and Juliet* and then showing the class *West Side Story*.

9 By the time students come to choose their AS-levels [preparation for college], those with a liking for literature should be ready to appreciate the riches Shakespeare has to offer. Let them wait until then. This isn't "dumbing down." Force-feeding children Shakespeare can only **induce** nausea and a lifelong **aversion**. If we want Shakespeare to be for all time as well of an age, we must let students come to him when they are willing and able to make the effort needed to enjoy him. Surely this is a tribute our national writer deserves?

Second Read

- Reread the article to answer these text-dependent questions.
- Write any additional questions you have about the text in your Reader/Writer Notebook.

1. **Key Ideas and Details:** Why do many schools continue to put Shakespeare in the curriculum?

My Notes

compulsory: required

enshrining: preserving with respect

aesthetic: concerned with notions of beauty
inkling: hint

circumvent: get around

induce: cause
aversion: strong feeling of dislike

Give Up the Bard

2. **Key Ideas and Details:** What does the author mean when he compares Shakespeare to a locked treasure chest?

3. **Key Ideas and Details:** According to the author, what is the best way for students to be exposed to Shakespeare?

Working from the Text

4. Consider the essential elements of an argument. On separate paper, create a graphic organizer that represents each of these elements and leaves sufficient room for notes as you plan a synthesis argument.

5. Using the Scoring Guide for Embedded Assessment 2, create a Writer's Checklist to evaluate a synthesis argument.

6. Work with a partner or small group to evaluate Robshaw's argument using your Writer's Checklist. What suggestions would you make to strengthen his writing through revision?

Essential Elements of an Argument

- **Hook:** an opening that grabs the reader's attention and establishes a connection between the reader and the writer.
- **Claim(s):** a clear and straightforward statement of the writer's belief and what is being argued.
- **Reasons and Evidence:** in support of a claim, reasons are developed through the use of evidence and rhetorical appeals (pathos, ethos, and logos).
- **Counterclaim(s):** alternative or opposing claims with concessions that the opposing side has valid points and/or refutations explaining why the writer's position is more valid.
- **Concluding Statement:** a summary or call to action that follows from and supports the argument.

Return to the essay and find text evidence for each element of an argument.

 Independent Reading Checkpoint

Review your independent reading. Analyze how reading the works of William Shakespeare, and/or novels that were based on his work, has influenced you as a reader. Reflect on the ways you might observe Shakespeare's themes in daily life.

Writing a Synthesis Argument

ASSIGNMENT

Your assignment is to compose an argument for or against the inclusion of William Shakespeare's *Romeo and Juliet* in the ninth-grade curriculum. You will evaluate research and gather evidence from a variety of sources about Shakespeare's relevance and influence in today's world. Finally, you will synthesize and cite your evidence in an argumentative essay that maintains a formal style and tone appropriate to your audience and purpose, uses rhetorical appeals including logical reasoning, and includes all the organizational elements of an argument.

Planning: Take time to make a plan for your essay.	▪ What is your position on the topic?
	▪ How can you state your claim as a preliminary thesis statement?
	▪ How can you use the print and nonprint texts in this unit as possible evidence for your claim?
	▪ How will you evaluate evidence to be sure that the reasoning is valid and the evidence relevant as support for both your claim and the opposing viewpoint?
	▪ How will you develop reasons for and against your claim and be sure that you are using a variety of rhetorical appeals (logos and ethos)?
	▪ How can you use an outline or other graphic organizer to plan your essay and be sure that you include all the elements of an effective argument: a hook, claim, reasons, evidence, counterclaim(s), and a concluding statement or call to action?
Drafting and Revising: Compose your synthesis argument.	▪ How can you be sure you're not plagiarizing? How will you use parenthetical or in-text citation to credit the sources of your evidence and quotes?
	▪ How will you develop and strengthen your draft through revision to produce clear and coherent writing?
	▪ How will you check that you have maintained a formal style and tone appropriate to your audience and purpose?
	▪ How can you use transitional words, phrases, and clauses to link ideas and clarify relationships?
Editing and Publishing: Prepare a final draft for publication.	▪ How will you proofread and edit your essay for proper conventions of standard English capitalization, punctuation, spelling, grammar, and usage?
	▪ What tools are available for you to further polish and refine your work, such as a dictionary, thesaurus, spell-check, or grammar check?
	▪ How can the Scoring Guide help you evaluate how well you have met the requirements of the assignment?

Reflection

After completing this Embedded Assessment, think about how you went about accomplishing this task, and respond to the following question: Which articles from this unit did you select to support your argument, and why? What made a source useful for your purpose?

Writing a Synthesis Argument

SCORING GUIDE

Scoring Criteria	Exemplary	Proficient	Emerging	Incomplete
Ideas	The argument • skillfully presents a claim and provides appropriate background for the issue • synthesizes evidence from a variety of sources that strongly support the claim • summarizes and refutes counterclaims with relevant reasoning and clear evidence • concludes by clearly summarizing the main points and reinforcing the claim.	The argument • supports a claim that is clearly presented with appropriate background details • synthesizes evidence from multiple sources to support the claim • develops claims and counterclaims fairly and uses valid reasoning, relevant and sufficient evidence, and a variety of rhetorical appeals • concludes by revisiting the main points and reinforcing the claim.	The argument • states a thesis but does not adequately explain the issue or provide background details • attempts to synthesize evidence from several sources to support the claim • develops some counterclaims, but reasoning may not be completely relevant or sufficient for the evidence cited • concludes by listing the main points of the thesis.	The argument • states a vague or unclear thesis and does not explain the issue or provide background details • contains no synthesis of evidence from different sources to support the claim • may not develop counterclaims, and reasoning may not be relevant or sufficient for the evidence cited • concludes without restating the main points of the thesis.
Structure	The argument • follows a clear structure with a logical progression of ideas that connect the essential elements of hook, claim, evidence, counterclaims, and conclusion • links main points with effective transitions that establish coherence.	The argument • establishes clear relationships between the essential elements of hook, claim, evidence, counterclaims, and conclusion/call to action • uses transitions to link the major sections of the essay and create coherence.	The argument • demonstrates an awkward progression of ideas, but the reader can understand them • uses some elements of hook, claim, evidence, and conclusion • spends too much time on some irrelevant details and uses few transitions.	The argument • does not follow a logical organization • includes some details and elements of an argument, but the writing lacks clear direction and uses no transitions to help readers follow the line of thought.
Use of Language	The argument • uses a formal style and tone appropriate to audience and purpose • smoothly integrates and cites textual evidence from multiple sources • shows excellent command of Standard English.	The argument • uses a formal style and tone appropriate to the audience and purpose • correctly cites textual evidence from at least three sources • follows conventions of Standard English.	The argument • mixes informal and formal writing styles • cites some textual evidence but citations may be missing or inaccurate • includes some incorrect capitalization, punctuation, spelling, grammar, or usage.	The argument • uses mostly informal writing style • uses some textual evidence but does not include citations • includes incorrect capitalization, punctuation, spelling, grammar, or usage that interfere with meaning.

Resources

Unit 1 Independent Reading List

Suggestions for Independent Reading

The Independent Reading Lists for each unit are divided into the categories of Literature and Nonfiction/Informational Text. Each list comprises titles related to the theme and content of the unit. For your independent reading, you can select from this wide array of titles, which have been chosen based on complexity and interest. You can also do your own research for other titles that captivate your interest and relate to the unit of study.

Unit 1: Coming of Age

Literature

Author	Title	Lexile
Anderson, Laurie Halse	*Speak*	690L
Chbosky, Stephen	*The Perks of Being a Wallflower*	720L
Crutcher, Chris	*Whale Talk*	1000L
Draper, Sharon	*Tears of a Tiger*	700L
Feinstein, John	*Foul Trouble*	770L
Forman, Gayle	*If I Stay*	830L
Garcia, Cristina	*Dreaming in Cuban*	940L
Gibbons, Kaye	*Ellen Foster*	870L
Green, John	*The Fault in Our Stars*	850L
Hinton, S.E	*The Outsiders*	750L
Jenkins, George, Sampson Davis, and Rameck Hunt	*We Beat the Street*	860L
Kluger, Steve	*Last Days of Summer*	900L
Knisley, Lucy	*Relish: My Life in the Kitchen*	970L
Martinez, Victor	*Parrot in the Oven: Mi Vida*	1000L
McCarthy, Cormac	*All the Pretty Horses*	940L
Murphy, Julie	*Dumplin'*	710L
Myers, Walter Dean	*Slam*	750L
Nelson, Jandy	*I'll Give You the Sun*	740L
Paolini, Christopher	*Eragon*	710L
Peltzer, David	*A Child Called It*	850L
Vlahos, Len	*The Scar Boys*	910L
Wesselhoeft, Conrad	*Dirt Bikes, Drones, and Other Ways to Fly*	590L
Zevin, Gabrielle	*Elsewhere*	720L

Nonfiction/Informational Text

Author	Title	Lexile
Álvarez, Julia	*Once Upon a Quincenera: Coming of Age in America*	N/A
Beyer, Ramsey	*Little Fish: A Memoir of a Different Kind of Year*	N/A
Bruchac, Joseph	*Jim Thorpe, Original All-American*	950L
Frank, Anne	*The Diary of a Young Girl*	1080L
Huebner, Mark	*Sports Bloopers: All-star Flubs and Fumbles*	N/A
Soto, Gary	*Living Up the Street*	1140L

Unit 2 Independent Reading List

Unit 2: Defining Style

Literature

Author	Title	Lexile
Black, Holly and Cecil Castellucci (Editors)	*Geektastic: Stories from the Nerd Herd*	N/A
Callanan, Liam	*The Cloud Atlas*	N/A
Capote, Truman	*Breakfast at Tiffany's*	N/A
Crutcher, Chris	*Athletic Shorts: Six Short Stories*	N/A
Dahl, Roald	*The Umbrella Man and Other Stories*	860L
Gaiman, Neil	*Coraline*	740L
Gaiman, Neil	*M Is for Magic*	880L
Gaiman, Neil	*Stardust*	970L
Goldman, William	*The Princess Bride*	870L
King, Stephen	*The Green Mile*	910L
Levithan, David	*The Realm of Possibility*	NP
Link, Kelly	*Pretty Monsters: Stories*	740L
Martel, Yann	*Life of Pi*	830L
Murdock, Catherine Gilbert	*Dairy Queen*	990L
Poe, Edgar Allen and Vincent Price (Editor)	*18 Best Stories by Edgar Allan Poe*	1220L
Salinger, J.D.	*The Catcher in the Rye*	790L
Soto, Gary	*Buried Onions*	850L
Stiefvater, Maggie, Tessa Gratton, and Brenna Yovanoff	*The Curiosities: A Collection of Stories*	N/A
Wallace, Daniel	*Big Fish: A Novel of Mythic Proportions*	N/A
Zusak, Markus	*The Book Thief*	730L

Nonfiction/Informational Text

Author	Title	Lexile
Burton, Tim	*Tim Burton*	N/A
Burton, Tim and Leah Gallo (Editor)	*The Art of Tim Burton*	N/A
Ferenczi, Aurélien	*Masters of Cinema: Tim Burton*	N/A
Lubar, David	*Extremities: Stories of Death, Murder, and Revenge*	570L

Unit 3 Independent Reading List

Unit 3: Coming of Age in Changing Times

Literature

Author	Title	Lexile
Baldwin, James	*Go Tell It on the Mountain*	1030L
Beah, Ishmael	*A Long Way Gone: Memoirs of a Boy Soldier*	920L
Blum, Jenna	*Those Who Save Us*	N/A
Bray, Libba	*A Great and Terrible Beauty*	760L
Burns, Olive Ann	*Cold Sassy Tree*	930L
Butler, Octavia E.	*Kindred*	580L
Cheva, Cherry	*She's So Money*	920L
Condie, Ally	*Matched*	680L
Cormier, Robert	*The Chocolate War*	820L
Danticat, Edwidge	*Behind the Mountains*	940L
Danticat, Edwidge (Editor)	*The Butterfly's Way: Voices from the Haitian Dyaspora in the United States*	N/A
Doyle, Roddy	*Paddy Clarke Ha Ha Ha*	410L
Ellison, Ralph	*Invisible Man*	950L
Erdrich, Louise	*Tracks*	780L
Nye, Naomi Shihab	*Habibi*	850L
Ryan, Pam Muñoz	*Esperanza Rising*	750L
Wright, Richard	*Black Boy*	950L

Nonfiction/Informational Text

Author	Title	Lexile
Baldwin, James	*The Fire Next Time*	1300L
Fisher, Antwone Quenton	*Finding Fish*	1080L
Griffin, John Howard	*Black Like Me*	990L
Litwack, Leon F.	*Trouble in Mind: Black Southerners in the Age of Jim Crow*	N/A
Margolick, David	*Elizabeth and Hazel: Two Women of Little Rock*	N/A
Partridge, Elizabeth	*Marching for Freedom: Walk Together, Children, and Don't You Grow Weary*	960L
Williams, Jay	*Life Is Not an Accident*	N/A
Wright, Simeon and Herb Boyd	*Simeon's Story: An Eyewitness Account of the Kidnapping of Emmett Till*	1050L

Unit 4 Independent Reading List

Unit 4: Exploring Poetic Voices		
Literature		
Author	**Title**	**Lexile**
Angelou, Maya	*I Know Why the Caged Bird Sings*	1330L
Bruchac, Joseph	*Code Talker: A Novel About the Navajo Marines of World War Two*	910L
Crane, Hart	*The Complete Poems*	NP
Cummings, E.E.	*Selected Poems*	NP
Dickinson, Emily	*The Complete Poems of Emily Dickinson*	NP
Eliot, T.S.	*Old Possum's Book of Practical Cats*	NP
Frost, Robert	*The Poetry of Robert Frost*	NP
Giovanni, Nikki	*Ego-Tripping and Other Poems for Young People*	NP
Grimes, Nikki	*Bronx Masquerade*	670L
Hart, Moss and George S. Kaufman	*You Can't Take It With You*	NP
Heppermann, Christine	*Poisoned Apples: Poems for You, My Pretty*	NP
Hughes, Langston	*Selected Poems of Langston Hughes*	NP
Lorde, Audre	*The Collected Poems of Audre Lorde*	NP
Masters, Edgar Lee	*Spoon River Anthology*	NP
Millay, Edna St. Vincent	*Renascence and Other Poems*	NP
Myers, Walter Dean	*Here in Harlem: Poems in Many Voices*	NP
Myers, Walter Dean	*Street Love*	NP
Neruda, Pablo	*The Essential Neruda: Selected Poems*	NP
Sexton, Anne	*The Complete Poems*	NP
Silko, Leslie Marmon	*Ceremony*	890L
Nonfiction/Informational Text		
Author	**Title**	**Lexile**
Anothony, David H. and Stephanie Kuligowski	*Langston Hughes: Harlem Renaissance Writer*	710L
Brown, Monica	*Pablo Neruda: Poet of the People*	970L
Jiménez, Francisco	*The Circuit: Stories from the Life of a Migrant Child*	N/A
Lau, Alan Chong	*Blues and Greens: A Produce Worker's Journal*	N/A
Myers, Walter Dean	*The Greatest: Muhammed Ali*	1030L
Rodriguez, Luis J.	*Always Running*	830L
Woodson, Jacqueline	*Brown Girl Dreaming*	990L

Unit 5 Independent Reading List

Unit 5: Coming of Age on Stage

Literature

Author	Title	Lexile
Haddon, Mark	*The Curious Incident of the Dog in the Night-Time*	1180L
Hansberry, Lorraine	*A Raisin in the Sun*	NP
Ibsen, Henrik	*A Doll's House*	NP
Levithan, David and Daniel Ehrenhaft (Editors)	*21 Proms*	820L
Miller, Arthur	*All My Sons*	NP
Miller, Arthur	*Death of a Salesman*	NP
Myers, Walter Dean	*What They Found: Love on 145th Street*	830L
Oliver, Lauren	*Delirium*	920L
Paterson, Katherine	*Jacob Have I Loved*	880L
Rostand, Edmond	*Cyrano de Bergerac*	NP
Rose, Reginald	*Twelve Angry Men*	NP
Simon, Neil	*The Odd Couple*	NP
Wilde, Oscar	*The Importance of Being Earnest*	NP
Wilder, Thornton	*Our Town*	NP
Williams, Tennessee	*A Streetcar Named Desire*	NP
Williams, Tennessee	*The Glass Menagerie*	NP
Wilson, August	*Fences*	NP
Wilson, August	*The Piano Lesson*	NP
Zindel, Paul	*The Effect of Gamma Rays on Man-in-the-Moon Marigolds*	NP

Nonfiction/Informational Text

Author	Title	Lexile
Bhutto, Benazir	*Daughter of Destiny: An Autobiography*	N/A
Bilas, Jay	*Toughness: Developing True Strength on and off the Court*	N/A
Cunxin, Li	*Mao's Last Dancer*	810L
Moody, Anne	*Coming of Age in Mississippi*	870L
Yep, Lawrence (Editor)	*American Dragons: Twenty-Five Asian American Voices*	990L

Independent Reading Log

NAME _____ DATE _____

Directions: This log is a place to record your progress and thinking about your independent reading during each unit. Add your log pages to your Reader/Writer Notebook or keep them as a separate place to record your reading insights.

Unit _____

Independent Reading Title _____

Author(s) _____ Text Type _____

Pages read: from _____ to _____

_____

_____

_____

_____

_____

Independent Reading Title _____

Author(s) _____ Text Type _____

Pages read: from _____ to _____

_____

_____

_____

_____

_____

_____

Independent Reading Title _____

Author(s) _____ Text Type _____

Pages read: from _____ to _____

_____

_____

_____

_____

_____

_____

Unit _____

Independent Reading Title _____

Author(s) _____ Text Type _____

Pages read: from _____ to _____

_____

_____

_____

_____

_____

Independent Reading Title _____

Author(s) _____ Text Type _____

Pages read: from _____ to _____

_____

_____

_____

_____

_____

Independent Reading Title _____

Author(s) _____ Text Type _____

Pages read: from _____ to _____

_____

_____

_____

_____

_____

_____

_____

Independent Reading Title _____

Author(s) _____ Text Type _____

Pages read: from _____ to _____

_____

_____

_____

_____

_____

_____

_____

SpringBoard Learning Strategies

READING STRATEGIES

STRATEGY	DEFINITION	PURPOSE
Chunking the Text	Breaking the text into smaller, manageable units of sense (e.g., words, sentences, paragraphs, whole text) by numbering, separating phrases, drawing boxes	To reduce the intimidation factor when encountering long words, sentences, or whole texts; to increase comprehension of difficult or challenging text
Close Reading	Accessing small chunks of text to read, reread, mark, and annotate key passages, word-for-word, sentence-by-sentence, and line-by-line	To develop comprehensive understanding by engaging in one or more focused readings of a text
Diffusing	Reading a passage; noting unfamiliar words; discovering meaning of unfamiliar words using context clues, dictionaries, and/or thesauruses; and replacing unfamiliar words with familiar ones	To facilitate a close reading of text, the use of resources, an understanding of synonyms, and increased comprehension of text
Double-Entry Journal	Creating a two-column journal (also called Dialectical Journal) with a student-selected passage in one column and the student's response in the second column (e.g., asking questions of the text, forming personal responses, interpreting the text, reflecting on the process of making meaning of the text)	To assist in note-taking and organizing key textual elements and responses noted during reading in order to generate textual support that can be incorporated into a piece of writing at a later time
Graphic Organizer	Using a visual representation for the organization of information from the text	To facilitate increased comprehension and discussion
KWHL Chart	Setting up discussion that allows students to activate prior knowledge by answering "What do I know?"; sets a purpose by answering "What do I want to know?"; helps preview a task by answering "How will I learn it?"; and reflects on new knowledge by answering "What have I learned?"	To organize thinking, access prior knowledge, and reflect on learning to increase comprehension and engagement
Marking the Text	Selecting text by highlighting, underlining, and/or annotating for specific components, such as main idea, imagery, literary devices, and so on	To focus reading for specific purposes, such as author's craft, and to organize information from selections; to facilitate reexamination of a text
Metacognitive Markers	Responding to text with a system of cueing marks where students use a ? for questions about the text; a ! for reactions related to the text; a * for comments about the text; and underline to signal key ideas	To track responses to texts and use those responses as a point of departure for talking or writing about texts
OPTIC	**O** (Overview): Write notes on what the visual appears to be about. **P** (Parts): Zoom in on the parts of the visual and describe any elements or details that seem important. **T** (Title): Highlight the words of the title of the visual (if one is available). **I** (Interrelationships): Use the title as the theory and the parts of the visual as clues to detect and specify how the elements of the graphic are related.	To analyze graphic and visual images as forms of text

STRATEGY	DEFINITION	PURPOSE
OPTIC (continued)	**C** (Conclusion); Draw a conclusion about the visual as a whole. What does the visual mean? Summarize the message of the visual in one or two sentences.	
Predicting	Making guesses about the text by using the title and pictures and/or thinking ahead about events which may occur based on evidence in the text	To help students become actively involved, interested, and mentally prepared to understand ideas
Previewing	Examining a text's structure, features, layout, format, questions, directions, prior to reading	To gain familiarity with the text, make connections to the text, and extend prior knowledge to set a purpose for reading
QHT	Expanding prior knowledge of vocabulary words by marking words with a Q, H, or T (Q signals words students do not know; H signals words students have heard and might be able to identify; T signals words students know well enough to teach to their peers)	To allow students to build on their prior knowledge of words, to provide a forum for peer teaching and learning of new words, and to serve as a prereading exercise to aid in comprehension
Questioning the Text* The AP Vertical Teams Guide for English (109–112)	Developing levels of questions about text; that is, literal, interpretive, and universal questions that prompt deeper thinking about a text	To engage more actively with texts, read with greater purpose and focus, and ultimately answer questions to gain greater insight into the text; helps students to comprehend and interpret
Paraphrasing	Restating in one's own words the essential information expressed in a text, whether it be narration, dialogue, or informational text	To encourage and facilitate comprehension of challenging text
RAFT	Primarily used to generate new text, this strategy can also be used to analyze a text by examining the role of the speaker (R), the intended audience (A), the format of the text (F), and the topic of the text (T).	To initiate reader response; to facilitate an analysis of a text to gain focus prior to creating a new text
Rereading	Encountering the same text with more than one reading	To identify additional details; to clarify meaning and/or reinforce comprehension of texts
SIFT* The AP Vertical Teams Guide for English (17–20)	Analyzing a fictional text by examining stylistic elements, especially symbol, images, and figures of speech in order to show how all work together to reveal tone and theme	To focus and facilitate an analysis of a fictional text by examining the title and text for symbolism, identifying images and sensory details, analyzing figurative language and identifying how all these elements reveal tone and theme
Skimming/Scanning	Skimming by rapid or superficial reading of a text to form an overall impression or to obtain a general understanding of the material; scanning focuses on key words, phrases, or specific details and provides speedy recognition of information	To quickly form an overall impression prior to an in-depth study of a text; to answer specific questions or quickly locate targeted information or detail in a text
SMELL* The AP Vertical Teams Guide for English (138–139)	Analyzing a persuasive speech or essay by asking five essential questions: • Sender-receiver relationship—What is the sender-receiver relationship? Who are the images and language meant to attract? Describe the speaker of the text. • Message—What is the message? Summarize the statement made in the text.	To analyze a persuasive speech or essay by focusing on five essential questions

STRATEGY	DEFINITION	PURPOSE
SMELL* (continued)	• Emotional Strategies—What is the desired effect? • Logical Strategies—What logic is operating? How does it (or its absence) affect the message? Consider the logic of the images as well as the words. • Language—What does the language of the text describe? How does it affect the meaning and effectiveness of the writing? Consider the language of the images as well as the words.	
SOAPSTone*	Analyzing text by discussing and identifying Speaker, Occasion, Audience, Purpose, Subject, and Tone	To facilitate the analysis of specific elements of nonfiction literary and informational texts and show the relationship among the elements to an understanding of the whole
Summarizing	Giving a brief statement of the main points or essential information expressed in a text, whether it be narration, dialogue, or informational text	To facilitate comprehension and recall of a text
Think Aloud	Talking through a difficult passage or task by using a form of metacognition whereby the reader expresses how he/she has made sense of the text	To reflect on how readers make meaning of challenging texts and to facilitate discussion
TP-CASTT* The AP Vertical Teams Guide for English (94–99)	Analyzing a poetic text by identifying and discussing Title, Paraphrase, Connotation, Attitude, Shift, Theme, and Title again	To facilitate the analysis of specific elements of a literary text, especially poetry. To show how the elements work together to create meaning
Visualizing	Forming a picture (mentally and/or literally) while reading a text	To increase reading comprehension and promote active engagement with text
Word Maps	Using a clearly defined graphic organizer such as concept circles or word webs to identify and reinforce word meanings	To provide a visual tool for identifying and remembering multiple aspects of words and word meanings

*Delineates AP strategy

WRITING STRATEGIES

STRATEGY	DEFINITION	PURPOSE
Adding	Making conscious choices to enhance a text by adding additional words, phrases, sentences, or ideas	To refine and clarify the writer's thoughts during revision and/or drafting
Brainstorming	Using a flexible but deliberate process of listing multiple ideas in a short period of time without excluding any idea from the preliminary list	To generate ideas, concepts, or key words that provide a focus and/or establish organization as part of the prewriting or revision process
Deleting	Providing clarity and cohesiveness for a text by eliminating words, phrases, sentences, or ideas	To refine and clarify the writer's thoughts during revision and/or drafting
Drafting	Composing a text in its initial form	To incorporate brainstormed or initial ideas into a written format

STRATEGY	DEFINITION	PURPOSE
Free writing	Writing freely without constraints in order to capture thinking and convey the writer's purpose	To refine and clarify the writer's thoughts, spark new ideas, and/or generate content during revision and/or drafting
Generating Questions	Clarifying and developing ideas by asking questions of the draft. May be part of self-editing or peer editing	To clarify and develop ideas in a draft; used during drafting and as part of writer response
Graphic Organizer	Organizing ideas and information visually (e.g., Venn diagrams, flowcharts, cluster maps)	To provide a visual system for organizing multiple ideas, details, and/or textual support to be included in a piece of writing
Looping	After free writing, one section of a text is circled to promote elaboration or the generation of new ideas for that section. This process is repeated to further develop ideas from the newly generated segments	To refine and clarify the writer's thoughts, spark new ideas, and/or generate new content during revision and/or drafting
Mapping	Creating a graphic organizer that serves as a visual representation of the organizational plan for a written text	To generate ideas, concepts, or key words that provide a focus and/or establish organization during the prewriting, drafting, or revision process
Marking the Draft	Interacting with the draft version of a piece of writing by highlighting, underlining, color-coding, and annotating to indicate revision ideas	To encourage focused, reflective thinking about revising drafts
Note-taking	Making notes about ideas in response to text or discussions; one form is the double-entry journal in which textual evidence is recorded on the left side and personal commentary about the meaning of the evidence on the other side.	To assist in organizing key textual elements and responses noted during reading in order to generate textual support that can be incorporated into a piece of writing at a later time. Note-taking is also a reading and listening strategy.
Outlining	Using a system of numerals and letters in order to identify topics and supporting details and ensure an appropriate balance of ideas	To generate ideas, concepts, or key words that provide a focus and/or establish organization prior to writing an initial draft and/or during the revision process
Quickwrite	Writing for a short, specific amount of time in response to a prompt provided	To generate multiple ideas in a quick fashion that could be turned into longer pieces of writing at a later time (may be considered as part of the drafting process)
RAFT	Generating a new text and/or transforming a text by identifying and manipulating its component parts of Role, Audience, Format, and Topic	To generate a new text by identifying the main elements of a text during the prewriting and drafting stages of the writing process
Rearranging	Selecting components of a text and moving them to another place within the text and/or modifying the order in which the author's ideas are presented	To refine and clarify the writer's thoughts during revision and/or drafting
Self-Editing/Peer Editing	Working individually or with a partner to examine a text closely in order to identify areas that might need to be corrected for grammar, punctuation, spelling	To provide a systematic process for editing a written text to ensure correctness of identified components such as conventions of Standard English

STRATEGY	DEFINITION	PURPOSE
Sharing and Responding	Communicating with another person or a small group of peers who respond to a piece of writing as focused readers (not necessarily as evaluators)	To make suggestions for improvement to the work of others and/or to receive appropriate and relevant feedback on the writer's own work, used during the drafting and revision process
Sketching	Drawing or sketching ideas or ordering ideas. Includes storyboarding, visualizing	To generate and/or clarify ideas by visualizing them. May be part of prewriting
Substituting/Replacing	Replacing original words or phrases in a text with new words or phrases that achieve the desired effect	To refine and clarify the writer's thoughts during revision and/or drafting
TWIST* The AP Vertical Teams Guide for English (167–174)	Arriving at a thesis statement that incorporates the following literary elements: tone, word choice (diction), imagery, style, and theme	To craft an interpretive thesis in response to a prompt about a text
Webbing	Developing a graphic organizer that consists of a series of circles connected with lines to indicate relationships among ideas	To generate ideas, concepts, or key words that provide a focus and/or establish organization prior to writing an initial draft and/or during the revision process
Writer's Checklist	Using a co-constructed checklist (that could be written on a bookmark and/or displayed on the wall) in order to look for specific features of a writing text and check for accuracy	To focus on key areas of the writing process so that the writer can effectively revise a draft and correct mistake
Writing Groups	A type of discussion group devoted to sharing and responding of student work	To facilitate a collaborative approach to generating ideas for and revising writing

SPEAKING AND LISTENING STRATEGIES

STRATEGY	DEFINITION	PURPOSE
Choral Reading	Reading text lines aloud in student groups and/or individually to present an interpretation	To develop fluency; differentiate between the reading of statements and questions; practice phrasing, pacing, and reading dialogue; show how a character's emotions are captured through vocal stress and intonation
Note-taking	Creating a record of information while listening to a speaker or reading a text	To facilitate active listening or close reading; to record and organize ideas that assist in processing information
Oral Reading	Reading aloud one's own text or the texts of others (e.g., echo reading, choral reading, paired readings)	To share one's own work or the work of others; build fluency and increase confidence in presenting to a group
Rehearsal	Encouraging multiple practices of a piece of text prior to a performance	To provide students with an opportunity to clarify the meaning of a text prior to a performance as they refine the use of dramatic conventions (e.g., gestures, vocal interpretations, facial expressions)
Role-Playing	Assuming the role or persona of a character	To develop the voice, emotions, and mannerisms of a character to facilitate improved comprehension of a text

COLLABORATIVE STRATEGIES

STRATEGY	DEFINITION	PURPOSE
Discussion Groups	Engaging in an interactive, small group discussion, often with an assigned role; to consider a topic, text, or question	To gain new understanding of or insight into a text from multiple perspectives
Think-Pair-Share	Pairing with a peer to share ideas; before sharing ideas and discussion with a larger group	To construct meaning about a topic or question; to test thinking in relation to the ideas of others; to prepare for a discussion with a larger group

Graphic Organizer Directory

English Language Arts Graphic Organizers

Audience Notes and Feedback

Definition and Reflection

Editor's/Writer's Checklist

Evaluating Online Sources

Fallacies 101

OPTIC

Presenting Scoring Guide

RAFT

SMELL

SOAPSTone

TP-CASTT Analysis

TP-CASTT

Verbal & Visual Word Association

Web Organizer

Word Map

English Language Development Graphic Organizers

Active Listening Feedback

Active Listening Notes

Cause and Effect

Character Map

Collaborative Dialogue

Conclusion Builder

Conflict Map

Conversation for Quickwrite

Idea and Argument Evaluator

Idea Connector

Key Idea and Details Chart

Narrative Analysis and Writing

Notes for Reading Independently

Opinion Builder

Paragraph Frame for Conclusions

Paragraph Frame for Sequencing

Paraphrasing and Summarizing Map

Peer Editing

Persuasive/Argument Writing Map

Roots and Affixes Brainstorm

Round Table Discussion

Sequence of Events Time Line

Text Structure Stairs

Unknown Word Solver

Venn Diagram for Writing a Comparison

Word Choice Analyzer

Audience Notes and Feedback

Scoring Criteria	Notes/Feedback
Introduction/Conclusion	
Timing	
Voice	
Eyes/Gestures	
Use of Media, Visuals, Props	
Audience Engagement	

Definition and Reflection

Academic Vocabulary Word

Definition in own words

Graphic Representation (literal or symbolic)

My experiences with this concept:

- I haven't really thought about this concept.

  _____

- I have only thought about this concept in Language Arts class.

  _____

- I have applied this concept in other classes.

  _____

- I have applied this concept outside of school.

  _____

My level of understanding:

- I am still trying to understand this concept.

  _____

- I am familiar with this concept, but I am not comfortable applying it.

  _____

- I am very comfortable with this concept and I know how to apply it.

  _____

- I could teach this concept to another classmate.

  _____

Editor's / Writer's Checklist

Organizational Elements

	Does your title express the topic and engage the reader?
	Do you have an engaging hook or lead to open your essay?
	Do you end your introductory paragraph with a thesis statement that states an opinion on a topic and suggests an organization?
	Do you have topic sentences that relate to the thesis statement?
	Do your body paragraphs contain detail and commentary to support your topic sentences?
	Do you include transitions to link ideas?
	Do your body paragraphs contain concluding sentences that also act as transitional statements to the next paragraph?
	Have you ended your essay with a strong conclusion that comments on the significance of your thesis ideas?

Sentence Elements

	Have you revised to make sure all sentences are complete sentences?
	Do your sentences contain vivid verbs and descriptive adjectives when appropriate?
	Is the verb tense of your writing consistent? Do the subject and verb agree?
	Is pronoun use appropriate and consistent?
	Is parallel structure used to advantage and when appropriate?
	Do you vary sentence beginnings? Have you started sentences with a subordinate clause?
	Are your sentence types (simple, compound, complex) and lengths varied for interest and emphasis?
	Have you tried to include figurative and sensory language for effect?
	Have you used appositives when appropriate?
	Have you checked punctuation use for correctness, especially for appositives, complex sentences, and parallel structure?
	Have you incorporated and punctuated quoted material correctly?

Evaluating Online Sources

The URL
- What is its domain?
  - .com = a for-profit organization
  - .gov, .mil, .us (or other country code) = a government site
  - .edu = affiliated with an educational institution
  - .org = a nonprofit organization

- Is this URL someone's personal page?
- Why might using information from a personal page be a problem?
- Do you recognize who is publishing this page?
- If not, you may need to investigate further to determine whether the publisher is an expert on the topic.

Sponsor:
- Does the website easily give information about the organization or group that sponsors it?
- Does it have a link (often called "About Us") that leads you to that information?
- What do you learn?

Timeliness:
- When was the page last updated (usually this is posted at the top or bottom of the page)?
- How current a page is may indicate how accurate or useful the information in it will be.

Purpose:
- What is the purpose of the page?
- What is its target audience?
- Does it present information or opinion?
- Is it primarily objective or subjective?
- How do you know?

Author:
- What credentials does the author have?
- Is this person or group considered an authority on the topic?

Links
- Does the page provide links?
- Do they work?
- Are they helpful?
- Are they objective or subjective?

Fallacies 101

Ad Hominem (Against the Man)/ Genetic Fallacy	"My opponent, a vicious and evil person, should absolutely never be elected to office." The Volkswagen Beetle is an evil car because it was originally designed by Hitler's army.
Straw Man	People say that Mark Twain was a good author, but I disagree. If he was such a good author, why didn't he write using his own name?
Appeal To Pity	"Jonathan couldn't have cheated! He's such a nice boy and he tries so hard."
Ad Baculum (Scare Tactics)	If you don't support the party's tax plan, you and your family will be reduced to poverty. Chairman of the Board: "All those opposed to my arguments for the opening of a new department, signify by saying, 'I resign.'"
Slippery Slope Fallacy	"If I don't study for the test, then I'm going to get a bad grade. If I get a bad grade on the test, I'll get a bad grade in the class, and I won't get into a good college. Getting into a good college is the most important part of getting a good job; so if I don't study for the test, I won't get a good job!"
Argument from Outrage	The airline cancelled my flight an hour before takeoff and wouldn't tell me why. This is an outrage! We should all boycott the company.
Red Herring	The new dress code banning slogan t-shirts isn't fair. Students have the right to free speech just like anyone else.
Hasty Generalization	They hit two home runs in the first inning of the season. This team is going all the way to the World Series!
Post Hoc	I ate a turkey sandwich and now I feel tired, so the turkey must have made me tired.
Ad Populum	You should turn to channel 6. It's the most watched channel this year. There is always a long line at that restaurant, so the food must be really good.
Either/Or	We can either stop using cars or destroy Earth. We must drill now or we'll remain dependent on foreign oil suppliers.

OPTIC

Title of Piece:	
Artist: _____	Type of artwork: _____

Overview	Look at the artwork for at least 10 seconds. Generate questions; e.g., What is the subject? What strikes you as interesting, odd, etc.? What is happening?
Parts	Look closely at the artwork, making note of important elements and details. Ask additional questions, such as: Who are the figures? What is the setting and time period? What symbols are present? What historical information would aid understanding of this piece?
Title	Consider what the title and any written elements of the text suggest about meaning. How does the title relate to what is portrayed?
Interrelationships	Look for connections between and among the title, caption, and the parts of the art. How are the different elements related?
Conclusion	Form a conclusion about the meaning/theme of the text. Remember the questions you asked when you first examined it. Be prepared to support your conclusions with evidence.

Presenting Scoring Guide

Scoring Criteria	Exemplary	Proficient	Emerging	Incomplete
Introduction / Conclusion	The presentation • provides a clear, engaging, and appropriate introduction to the topic or performance • provides a clear, engaging, and appropriate conclusion that closes, summarizes, draws connections to broader themes, or supports the ideas presented.	The presentation • provides a clear and appropriate introduction to the topic or performance • provides a clear and appropriate conclusion that closes, summarizes, draws connections to broader themes, or supports the ideas presented.	The presentation • provides an adequate introduction to the topic or performance • provides an adequate conclusion that closes, summarizes, draws connections to broader themes, or supports the ideas presented.	The presentation • does not provide an introduction to the topic or performance • does not provide a conclusion that closes, summarizes, draws connections to broader themes, or supports the ideas presented.
Timing	The presentation • thoroughly delivers its intended message within the allotted time • is thoughtfully and appropriately paced throughout.	The presentation • mostly delivers its intended message within the allotted time • is appropriately paced most of the time.	The presentation • delivers some of its intended message within the allotted time • is sometimes not paced appropriately.	The presentation • does not deliver its intended message within the allotted time • is not paced appropriately.
Voice (Volume, Pronunciation)	The presentation • is delivered with adequate volume enabling audience members to fully comprehend what is said • is delivered with clear pronunciation.	The presentation • is delivered with adequate volume enabling audience members to mostly comprehend what is said • is delivered with mostly clear pronunciation.	The presentation • is delivered with somewhat adequate volume enabling audience members to comprehend some of what is said • is delivered with somewhat clear pronunciation.	The presentation • is not delivered with adequate volume, so that audience members are unable to comprehend what is said • is delivered with unclear pronunciation.
Eyes/Gestures	The presentation • is delivered with appropriate eye contact that helps engage audience members • makes use of thoughtfully selected gestures and/or body language to convey meaning.	The presentation • is delivered with some appropriate eye contact that helps engage audience members • makes use of gestures and/or body language to convey meaning.	The presentation • is delivered with occasional eye contact that sometimes engages audience members • makes some use of gestures and/or body language to convey meaning.	The presentation • is not delivered with eye contact to engage audience members • makes little or no use of gestures and/or body language to convey meaning.
Use of Media, Visuals, Props	The presentation • makes use of highly engaging visuals, multimedia, and/or props that enhance delivery.	The presentation • makes use of visuals, multimedia, and/or props that enhance delivery.	The presentation • makes use of some visuals, multimedia, and/or props that somewhat enhance delivery.	The presentation • makes use of few or no visuals, multimedia, and/or props that enhance delivery.
Audience Engagement	The presentation • includes thoughtful and appropriate interactions with and responses to audience members.	The presentation • includes appropriate interactions with and responses to audience members.	The presentation • includes a few interactions with and responses to audience members.	The presentation • does not include interactions with and responses to audience members.

RAFT

Role	Who or what are you as a writer?
Audience	As a writer, to whom are you writing?
Format	As a writer, what format would be appropriate for your audience (essay, letter, speech, poem, etc.)?
Topic	As a writer, what is the subject of your writing? What points do you want to make?

SMELL

Sender-Receiver Relationship—Who are the senders and receivers of the message, and what is their relationship (consider what different audiences the text may be addressing)?

Message—What is a literal summary of the content? What is the meaning/significance of this information?

Emotional Strategies—What emotional appeals (*pathos*) are included? What seems to be their desired effect?

Logical Strategies—What logical arguments/appeals (*logos*) are included? What is their effect?

Language—What specific language is used to support the message? How does it affect the text's effectiveness? Consider both images and actual words.

SOAPSTone

SOAPSTone	Analysis	Textual Support
S What does the reader know about the writer?		
O What are the circumstances surrounding this text?		
A Who is the target audience?		
P Why did the author write this text?		
S What is the topic?		
Tone What is the author's tone, or attitude?		

TP-CASTT Analysis

Poem Title:

Author:

Title: Make a Prediction. What do you think the title means before you read the poem?

Paraphrase: Translate the poem in your own words. What is the poem about? Rephrase difficult sections word for word.

Connotation: Look beyond the literal meaning of key words and images to their associations.

Attitude: What is the speaker's attitude? What is the author's attitude? How does the author feel about the speaker, about other characters, about the subject?

Shifts: Where do the shifts in tone, setting, voice, etc., occur? Look for time and place, keywords, punctuation, stanza divisions, changes in length or rhyme, and sentence structure. What is the purpose of each shift? How do they contribute to effect and meaning?

Title: Reexamine the title. What do you think it means now in the context of the poem?

Theme: Think of the literal and metaphorical layers of the poem. Then determine the overall theme. The theme must be written in a complete sentence.

TP-CASTT

Poem Title:

Author:

T		
P		
C		
A		
S		
T		
T		

Verbal & Visual Word Association

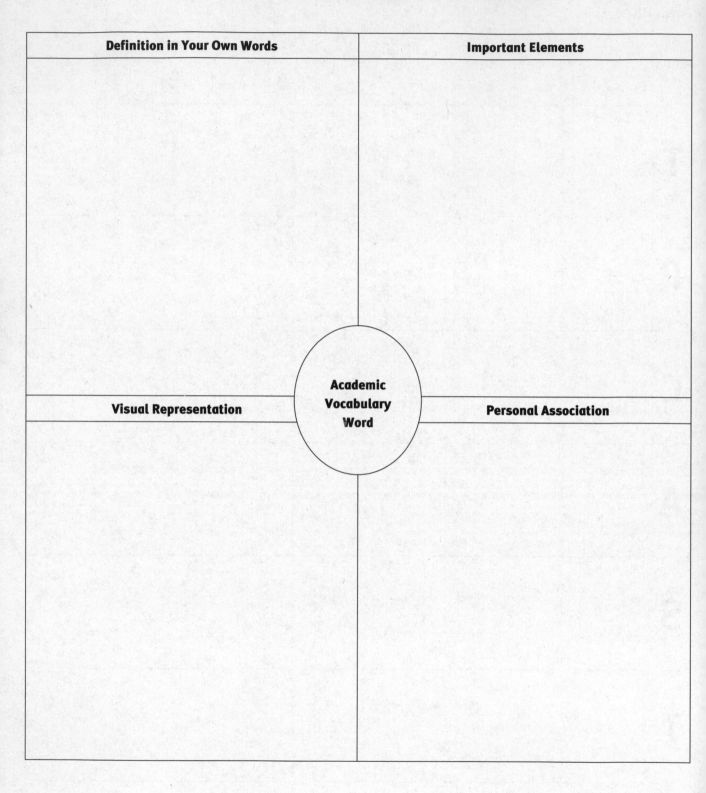

Definition in Your Own Words	Important Elements

Academic Vocabulary Word

Visual Representation	Personal Association

Web Organizer

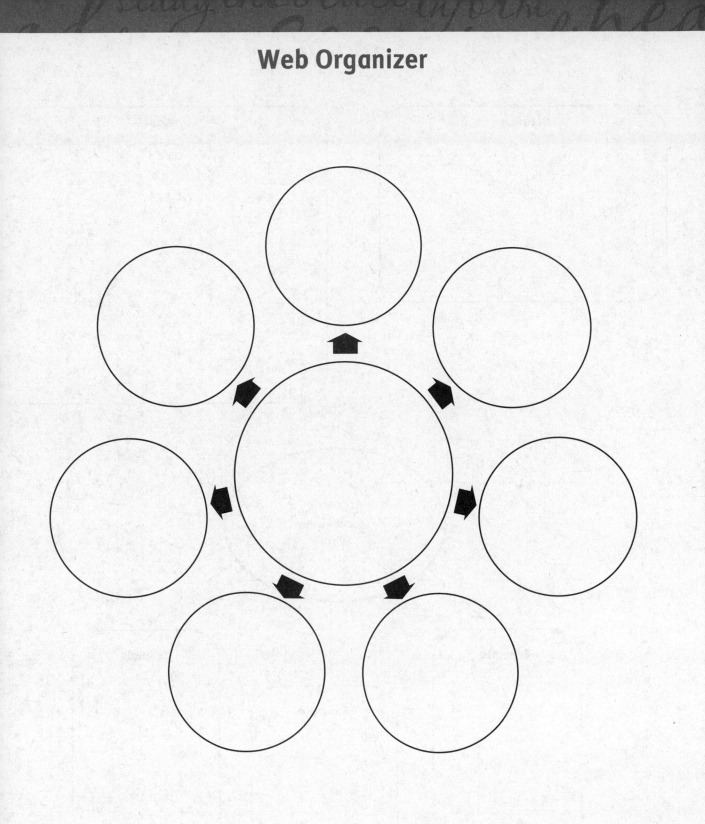

Word Map

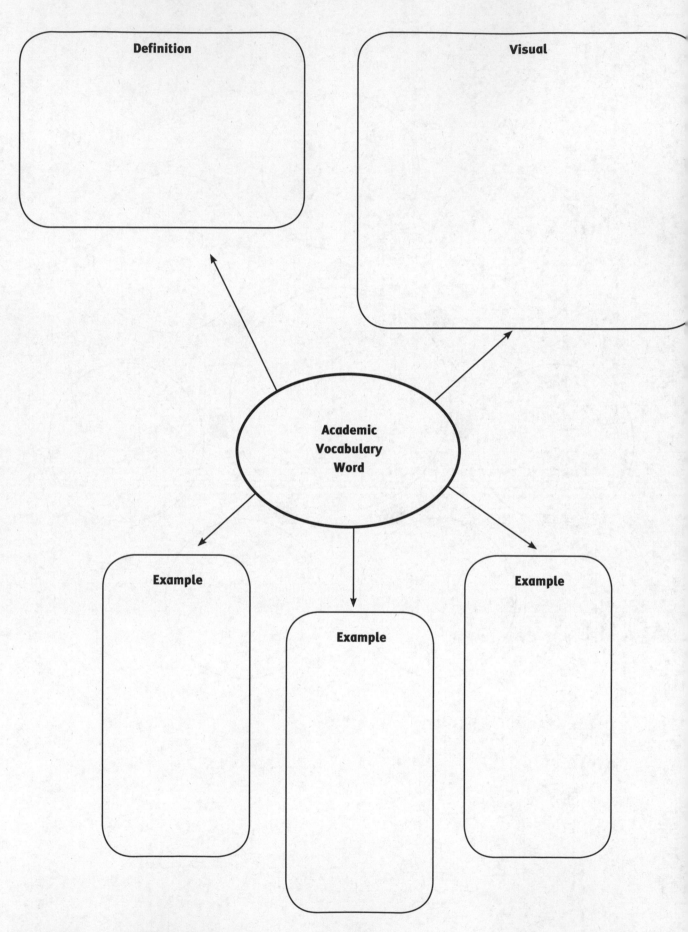

Definition

Visual

Academic
Vocabulary
Word

Example

Example

Example

Active Listening Feedback

senter's name: _____

ntent

at is the presenter's purpose? _____

at is the presenter's main point? _____

you agree with the presenter? Why or why not? _____

_____

_____

rm

the presenter use a clear, loud voice? ☐ yes ☐ no

the presenter make eye contact? ☐ yes ☐ no

ne thing I really liked about the presentation:

_____

_____

_____

ne question I still have:

_____

_____

_____

ther comments or notes:

Active Listening Notes

Title: _____

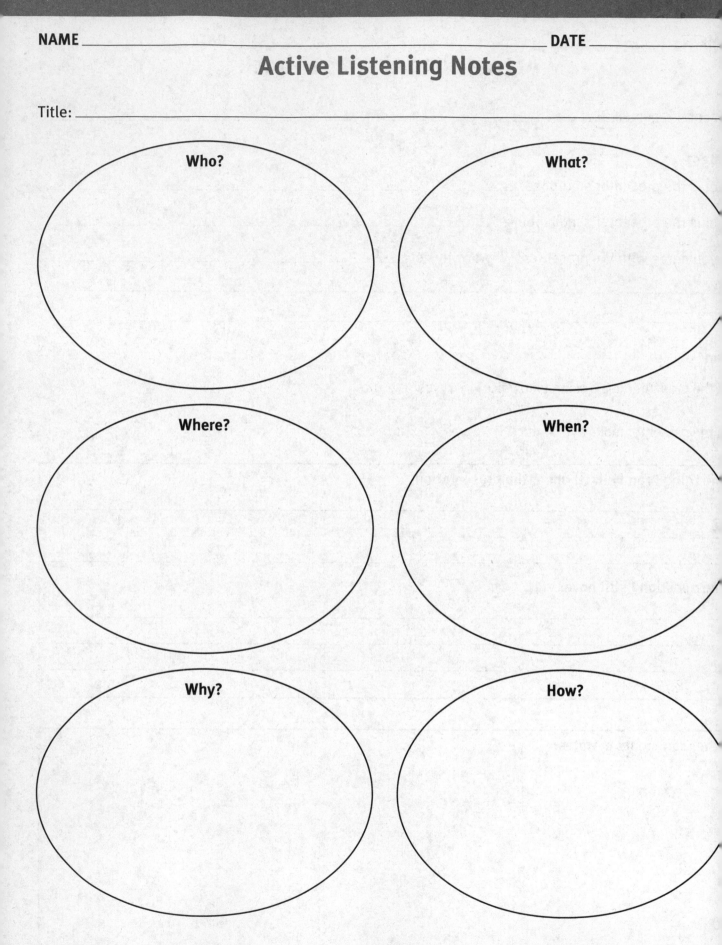

Who?

What?

Where?

When?

Why?

How?

Cause and Effect

e: _____

Cause: What happened?

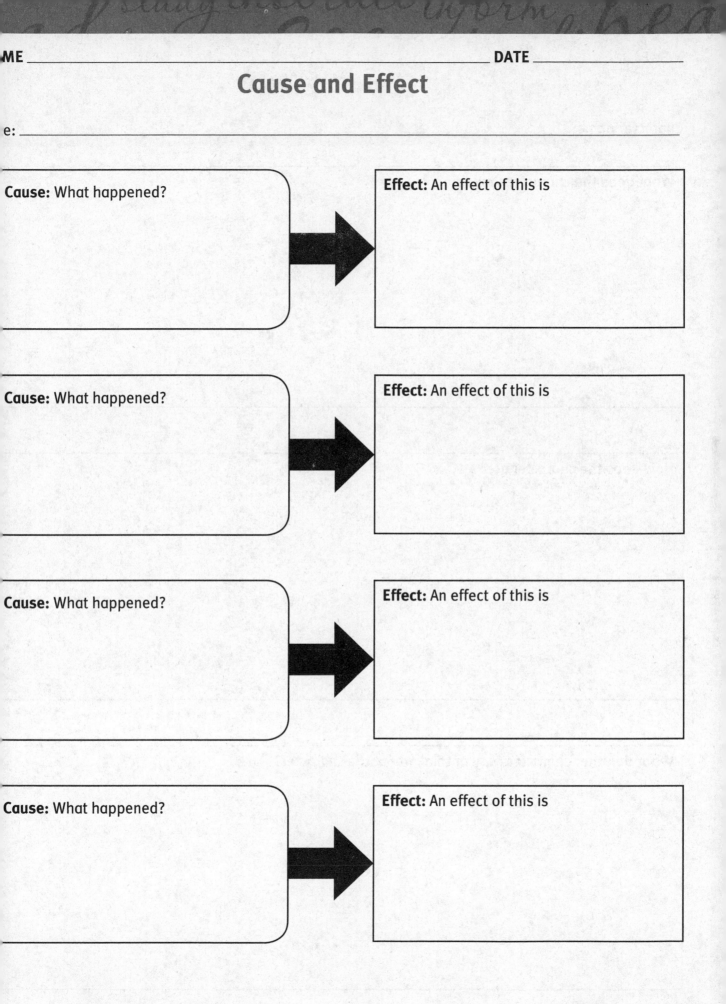

Effect: An effect of this is

Cause: What happened?

Effect: An effect of this is

Cause: What happened?

Effect: An effect of this is

Cause: What happened?

Effect: An effect of this is

Character Map

Character name: _____

What does the character look like?

How does the character act?

What do other characters say or think about the character?

Collaborative Dialogue

pic: _____

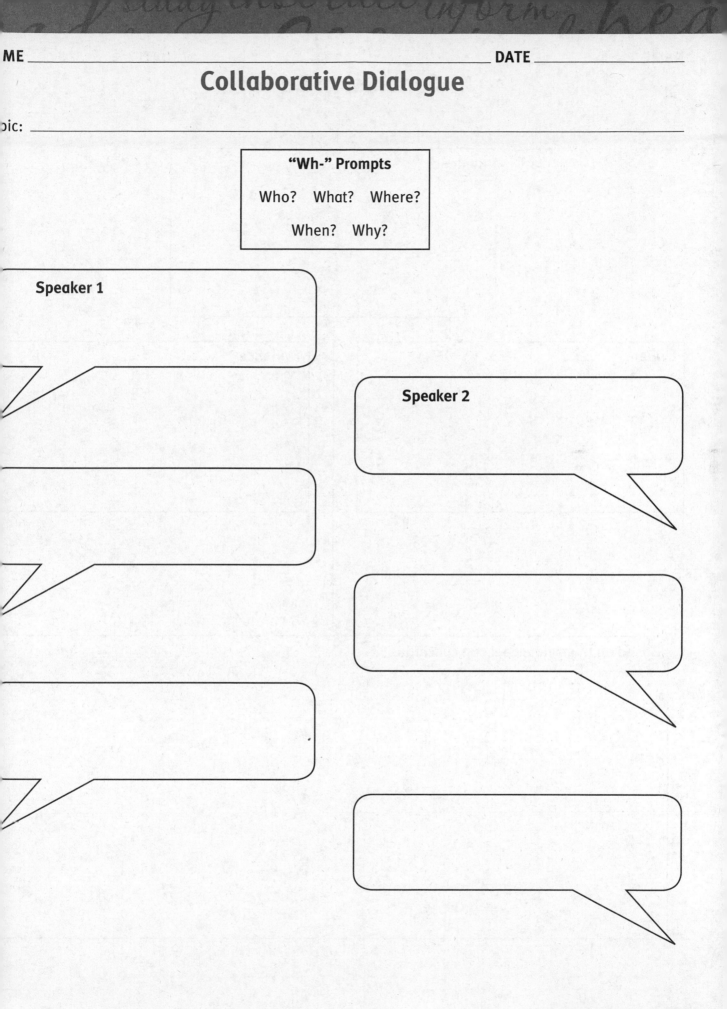

"Wh-" Prompts

Who?   What?   Where?

When?   Why?

Speaker 1

Speaker 2

Conclusion Builder

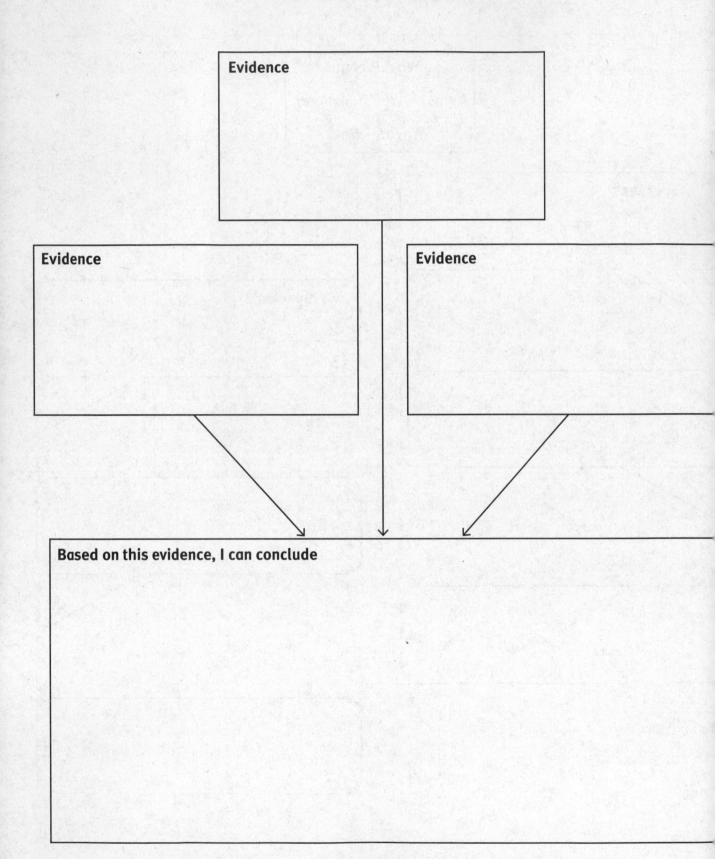

Evidence

Evidence

Evidence

Based on this evidence, I can conclude

Conflict Map

e: _____

hat is the main conflict in this story?

hat causes this conflict?

ow is the conflict resolved?

hat are some other ways the conflict could have been resolved?

Conversation for Quickwrite

1. Turn to a partner and restate the quickwrite in your own words.

2. Brainstorm key words to use in your quickwrite response.

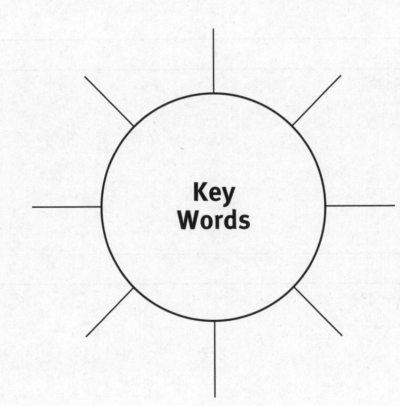

Key Words

3. Take turns explaining your quickwrite response to your partner. Try using some of the key wor

4. On your own, write a response to the quickwrite.

Idea and Argument Evaluator

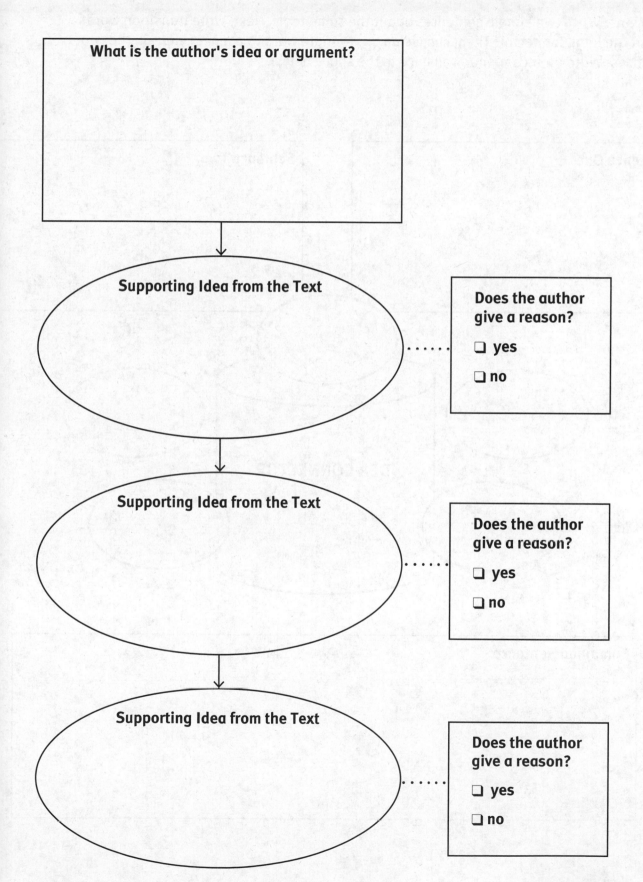

What is the author's idea or argument?

Supporting Idea from the Text

Does the author give a reason?

❑ yes

❑ no

Supporting Idea from the Text

Does the author give a reason?

❑ yes

❑ no

Supporting Idea from the Text

Does the author give a reason?

❑ yes

❑ no

Idea Connector

Directions: Write two simple sentences about the same topic. Next, write transition words around the Idea Connector. Then, choose an appropriate word to connect ideas in the two sentences. Write your combined sentence in the space below.

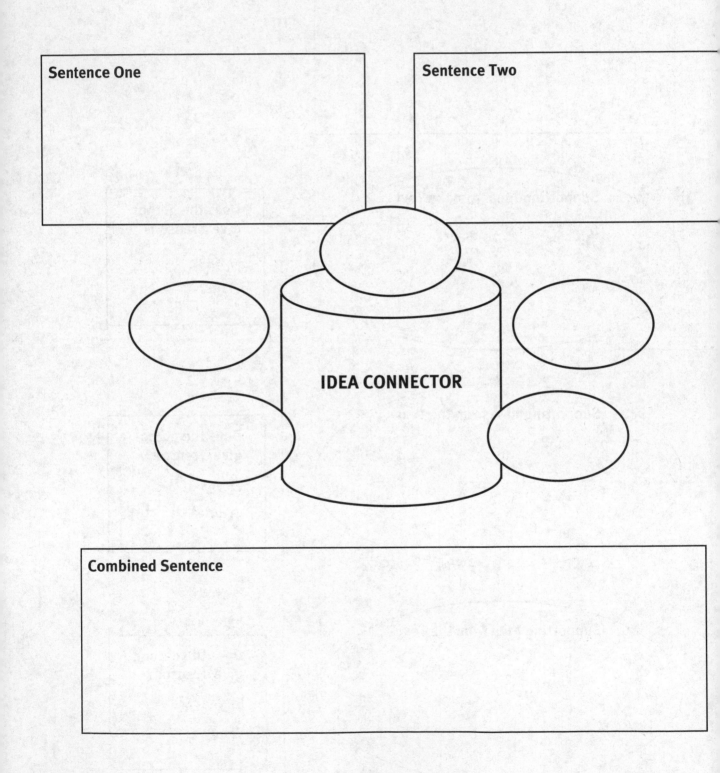

Sentence One

Sentence Two

IDEA CONNECTOR

Combined Sentence

Key Idea and Details Chart

Title/Topic _____

Key Idea _____
_____
_____

Supporting Detail 1 _____
_____
_____

Supporting Detail 2 _____
_____
_____

Supporting Detail 3 _____
_____
_____

Supporting Detail 4 _____
_____
_____

Restate topic sentence: _____
_____

Concluding sentence: _____
_____

Narrative Analysis and Writing

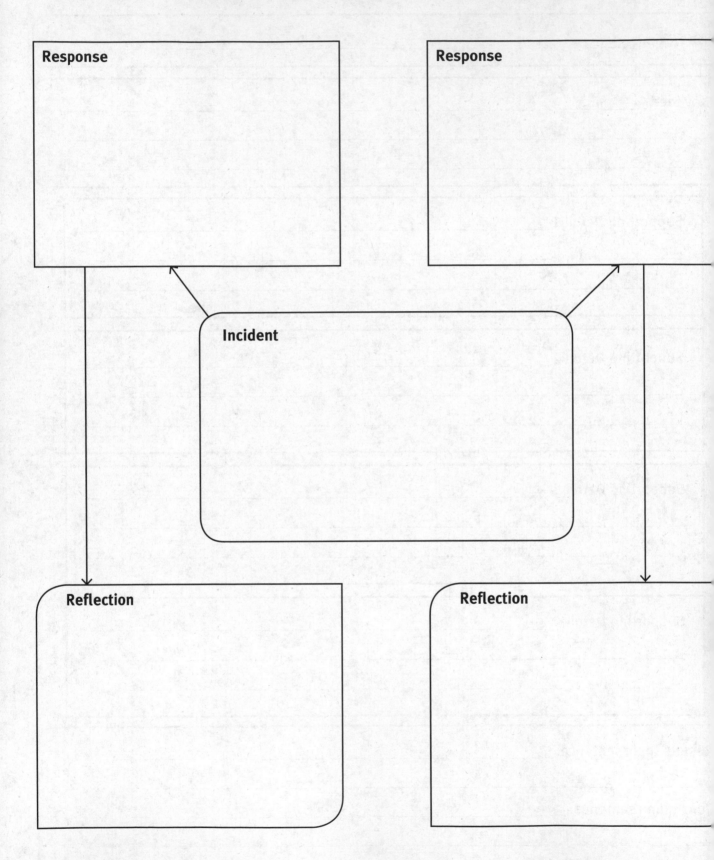

Response

Response

Incident

Reflection

Reflection

Notes for Reading Independently

e: _____

| he main characters are | The setting is | The main conflict is |

| The climax happens when | The conflict is resolved when |

brief summary of _____

Opinion Builder

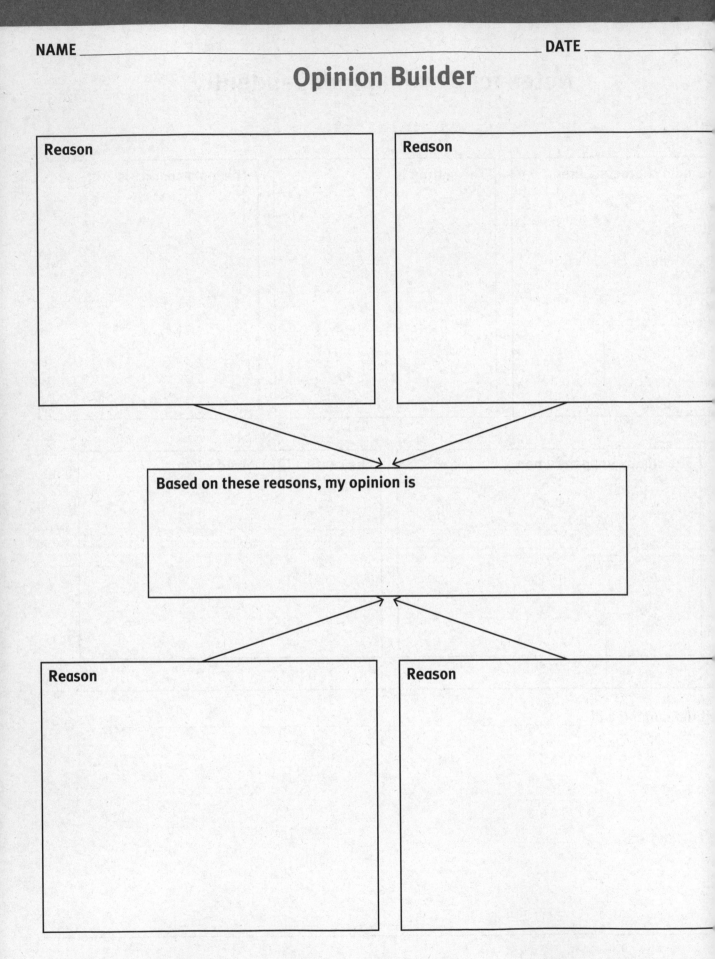

Reason

Reason

Based on these reasons, my opinion is

Reason

Reason

Paragraph Frame for Conclusions

onclusion
Vords and
hrases

hows that

ased on

uggests that

ads to

dicates that

fluences

The _____ (story, poem, play, passage, etc.)
shows that (helps us to conclude that) _____
_____
_____

There are several reasons why. First, _____
_____
_____
_____
_____

A second reason is _____
_____
_____
_____
_____

Finally, _____
_____
_____
_____
_____

In conclusion, _____
_____
_____
_____
_____

Paragraph Frame for Sequencing

Sequence Words and Phrases

at the beginning

in the first place

as a result

later

eventually

in the end

lastly

In the _____ (story, poem, play, passage, etc.)

there are three important _____

(events, steps, directions, etc.)

First, _____

_____

_____

_____

Second, _____

_____

_____

_____

Third, _____

_____

_____

_____

Finally, _____

_____

_____

_____

Paraphrasing and Summarizing Map

What does the text say?	How can I say it in my own words?

ow can I use my own words to summarize the text?

Peer Editing

Writer's name: _____

Did the writer answer the prompt? ☐ yes ☐ no

Did the writer provide evidence to support his or her reasons? ☐ yes ☐ no

Is the writing organized in a way that makes sense? ☐ yes ☐ no

Did the writer vary sentence structures to make the writing more interesting? ☐ yes ☐ no

Are there any spelling or punctuation mistakes? ☐ yes ☐ no

Are there any grammar errors? ☐ yes ☐ no

Two things I really liked about the writer's story:

1. _____

   _____

   _____

2. _____

   _____

   _____

One thing I think the writer could do to improve the writing:

1. _____

   _____

   _____

Other comments or notes:

Persuasive/Argument Writing Map

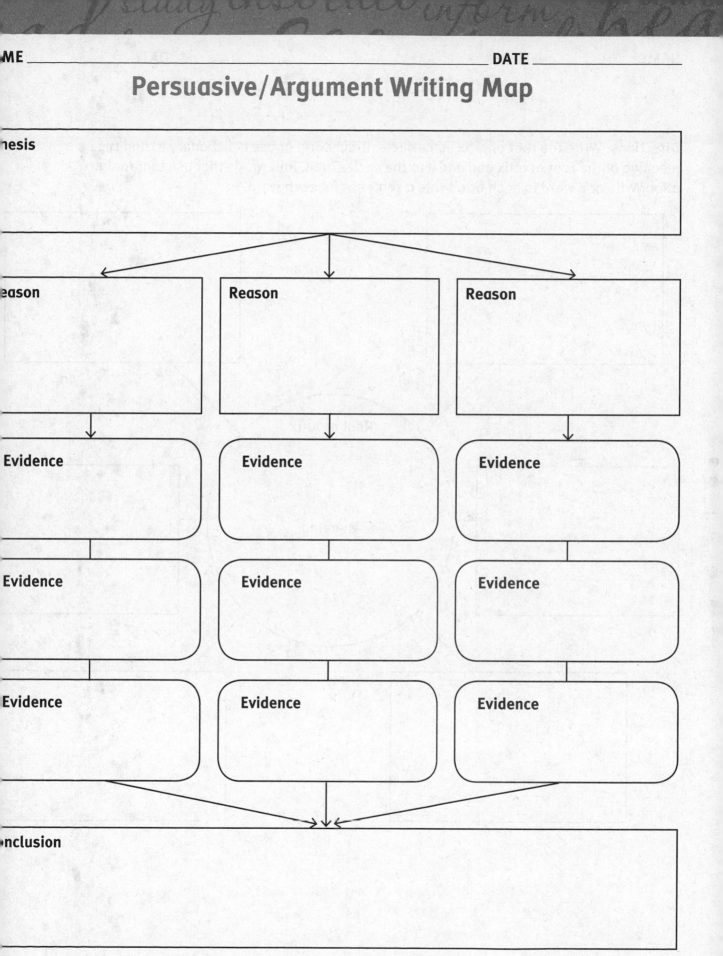

...hesis

...eason

Reason

Reason

Evidence

Evidence

Evidence

Evidence

Evidence

Evidence

Evidence

Evidence

Evidence

...nclusion

Roots and Affixes Brainstorm

Directions: Write the root or affix in the circle. Brainstorm or use a dictionary to find the meaning of the root or affix and add it to the circle. Then, find words that use that root or affix. Write one word in each box. Write a sentence for each word.

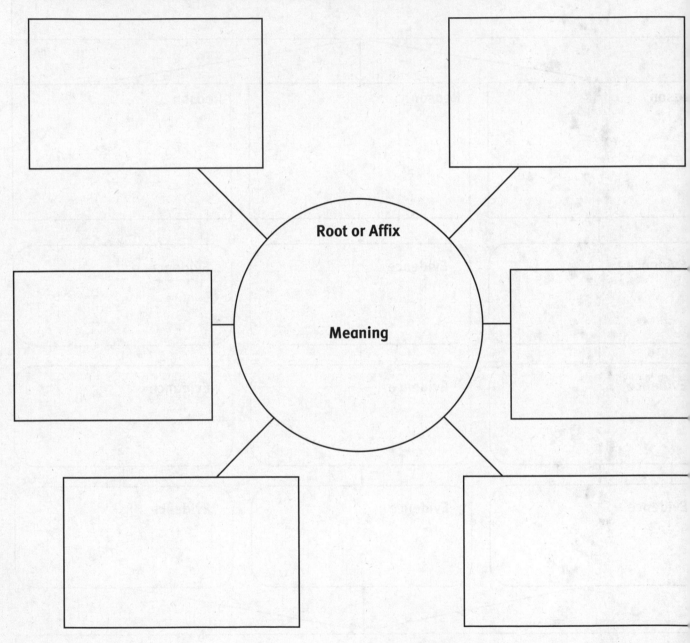

Root or Affix

Meaning

Round Table Discussion

rections: Write the topic in the center box. One student begins by stating his or her ideas
ile the student to the left takes notes. Then the next student speaks while the student to
or her left takes notes, and so on.

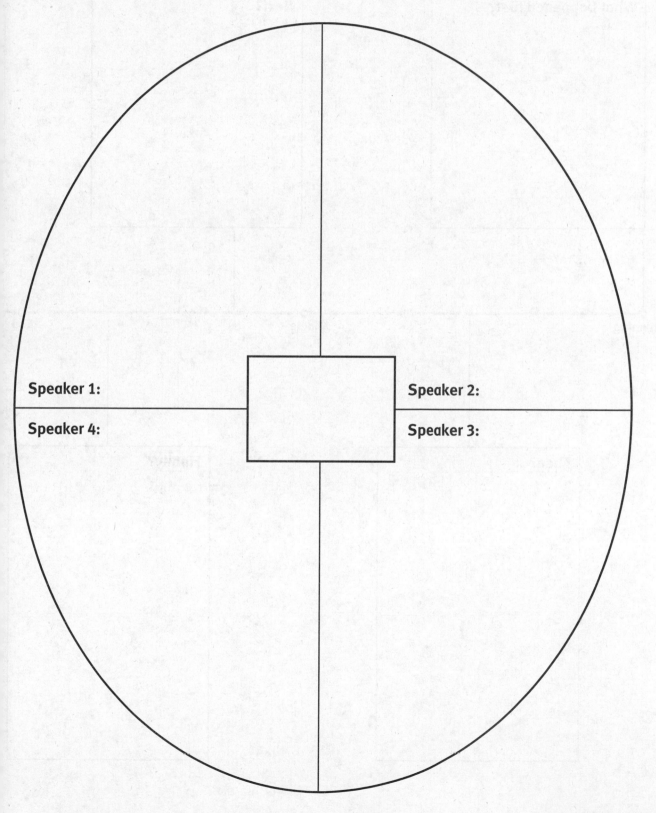

Speaker 1:

Speaker 2:

Speaker 4:

Speaker 3:

Sequence of Events Time Line

Title: _____

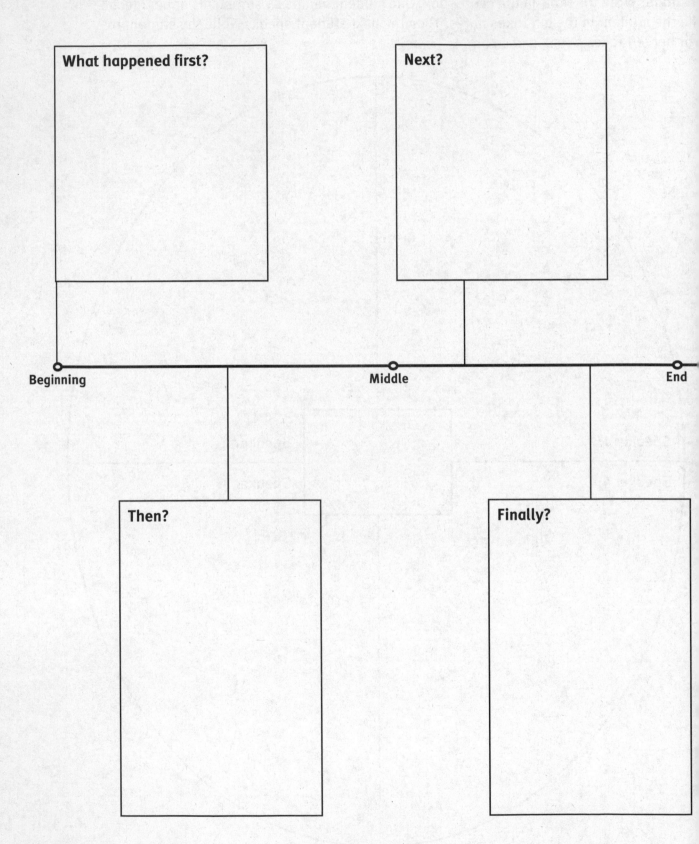

What happened first?

Next?

Beginning

Middle

End

Then?

Finally?

Text Structure Stairs

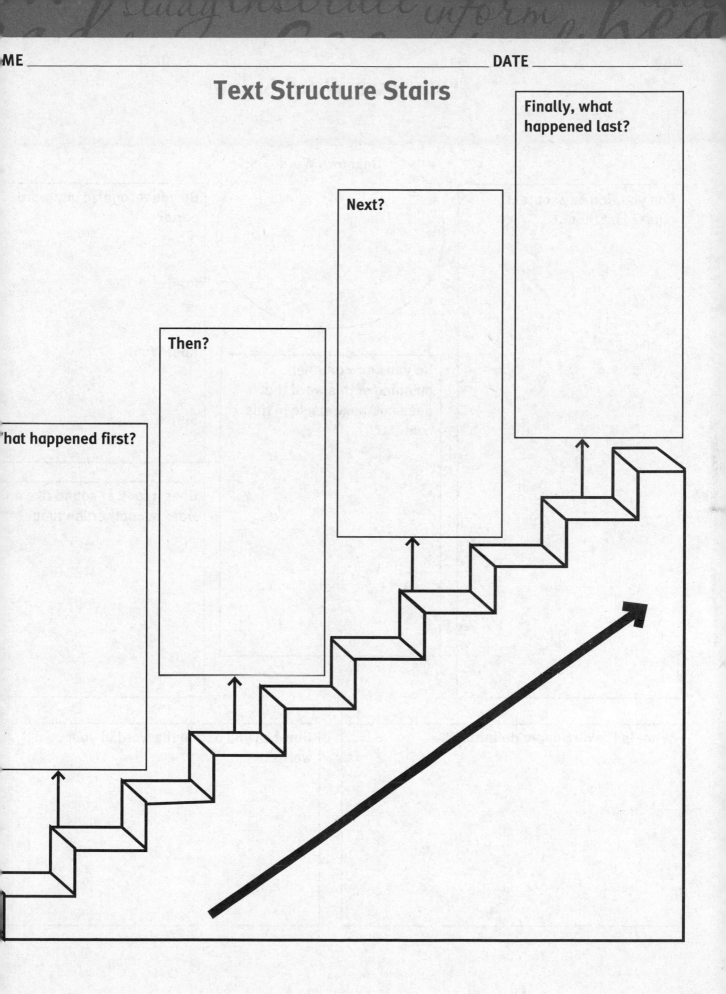

Finally, what
happened last?

Next?

Then?

hat happened first?

Unknown Word Solver

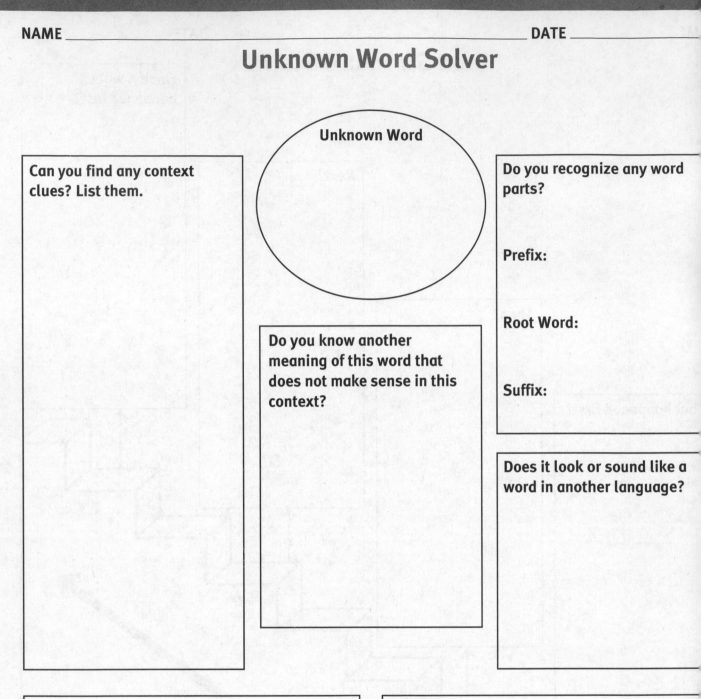

Unknown Word

Can you find any context clues? List them.

Do you recognize any word parts?

Prefix:

Root Word:

Suffix:

Do you know another meaning of this word that does not make sense in this context?

Does it look or sound like a word in another language?

What is the dictionary definition?

How can you define the word in your own words?

Venn Diagram for Writing a Comparison

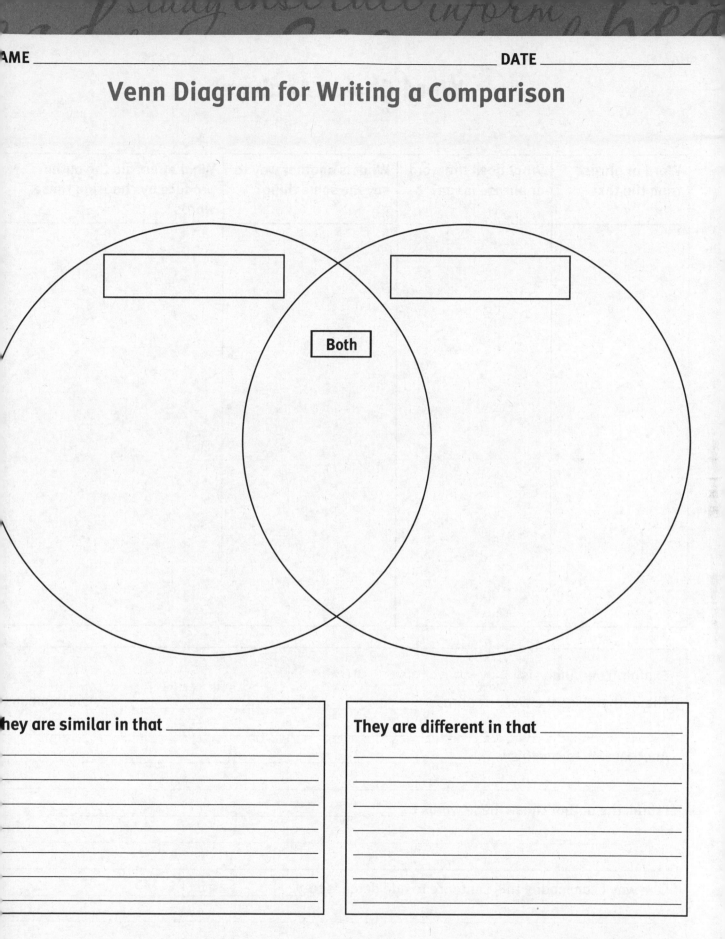

| | Both | |

hey are similar in that _____
_____
_____
_____
_____
_____

They are different in that _____
_____
_____
_____
_____
_____
_____

Word Choice Analyzer

Word or phrase from the text	What does the word or phrase mean?	What is another way to say the same thing?	What effect did the author produce by choosing these words?

Explain Your Analysis

The author uses the word or phrase _____ , which means

_____

Another way to say this is _____

_____

I think the author chose these words to _____

_____

_____

One way I can modify this sentence to add detail is to _____

_____

Glossary / Glosario

A

active-voice verbs: verbs for which the subject performs the action
verbos en voz activa: forma verbal que indica que el sujeto realiza la acción

advertising techniques: specific methods used in print, graphics, or videos to persuade people to buy a product or use a service
técnicas publicitarias: métodos específicos usados en impresos, gráfica o videos para persuadir a las personas a comprar un producto o usar un servicio

alliteration: the repetition of initial consonant sounds in words that are close together
aliteración: repetición de sonidos consonánticos iniciales en palabras cercanas

allusion: a reference made to a well-known person, event, or place from history, music, art, or another literary work
alusión: referencia a una persona, evento o lugar muy conocidos de la historia, música, arte u otra obra literaria

analogy: a comparison between two things for the purpose of drawing conclusions on one based on its similarities to the other
analogía: comparación entre dos cosas con el propósito de sacar conclusiones sobre las semejanzas que una cosa tiene a otra

anaphora: the repetition of the same word or group of words at the beginnings of two or more clauses or lines
anáfora: repetición de la misma palabra o grupo de palabras al comienzo de una o más cláusulas o versos

anecdotal evidence: evidence based on personal accounts of incidents
evidencia anecdótica: evidencia basada en relatos personales de los hechos

annotated bibliography: a list of sources used in research along with comments or summaries about each source
bibliografía anotada: lista de fuentes utilizadas en la investigación, junto con comentarios o resúmenes acerca de cada fuente

antagonist: the character who opposes or struggles against the main character
antagonista: personaje que se opone o lucha contra el personaje principal

aphorism: a short statement expressing an opinion or general truth
aforismo: afirmación corta que expresa una opinión o verdad general

Archetypal Criticism: criticism that deals with symbols and patterns that recur in the literature of widely diverse cultures
crítica de arquetipos: examinación de la literature basada en símbolos y diseño

archetypes: universal symbols—images, characters, motifs, or patterns—that recur in the myths, dreams, oral traditions, songs, literature, and other texts of peoples widely separated by time and place
arquetipos: símbolos universales—imágenes, personajes, motivos o patrones—reiterativos en los mitos, el arte y la literatura alrededor del mundo

archival footage: film footage taken from another, previously recorded, source
cortometraje de archivo: fragmento de película tomada de otra fuente grabada previamente

argument: a form of writing that presents a particular claim or idea and supports it with evidence
argumento: forma de redacción que presenta una opinión o idea particular y la apoya con evidencia

argumentation: the act or process of arguing that includes the *hook* (quotation, example, or idea that catches readers' attention), *claim* (the opinion or thesis statement), *support* (evidence in the form of facts, statistics, examples, anecdotes, or expert opinions), *concession* (the writer's admission that the other side of the argument has a valid point), *refutation* (a well-reasoned denial of an opponent's point, based on solid evidence), and *call to action* (a request of readers)
argumentación: la estructura de una argumentación incluye el *gancho* (cita, ejemplo o idea que capta la atención del lector), *afirmación* (declaración de opinión o tesis), *apoyo* (evidencia en forma de hechos, estadísticas, ejemplos, anécdotas u opiniones de expertos), *concesión* (admisión por parte del escritor de que la otra parte del debate tiene un punto válido), *refutación* (negación bien razonada de una opinión del oponente, basada en evidencia sólida) y *llamado a la acción* (petición inspirada de lectores)

argument by analogy: a comparison of two similar situations, implying that the outcome of one will resemble the outcome of the other
argumento por analogía: comparación de dos situaciones semejantes, infiriendo que el resultado de será parecido al resultado de la otra

artistic license: the practice of rewording of dialogue, alteration of language, or reordering of the plot of a text created by another artist
licencia artística: la costumbre de reformular un diálogo, aliteración de palabras, o arreglo de la trama de un texto creado por otro artista

aside: a short speech spoken by an actor directly to the audience and unheard by other actors on stage
aparte: alocución breve dicha por un actor directamente al público y que no escuchan los demás actores que están en el escenario

assonance: the repetition of similar vowel sounds in accented syllables, followed by different consonant sounds, in words that are close together
asonancia: repetición de sonidos vocálicos similares en sílabas acentuadas, seguida de diferentes sonidos consonánticos, en palabras que están cercanas

audience: the intended readers, listeners, or viewers of specific types of written, spoken, or visual texts
público: lectores objetivo, oyentes o espectadores de tipos específicos de textos escritos, hablados o visuales

audience analysis: determination of the characteristics and knowledge of the people who will read a work or hear a speech
análisis del público: determinar las características y conocimiento de las personas que leen una obra o escuchan un discurso

author's purpose: the specific reason or reasons for the writing; what the author hopes to accomplish
propósito del autor: razón específica para escribir; lo que el autor espera lograr

autobiography: an account written by a person about his or her own life
autobiografía: narración de una vida escrita por el propio sujeto del relato

B

balanced sentence: a sentence that presents ideas of equal weight in similar grammatical forms to emphasize the similarity or difference between the ideas
oración balanceada: oración que representa ideas de igual peso en formas gramaticales similares para enfatizar la semejanza o diferencia entre las ideas

bias: an inclination or mental leaning for or against something; prevents impartial judgment
sesgo: inclinación o tendencia mental a favor o en contra de algo, lo que impide una opinión imparcial

bibliography: a list of the sources used for research
bibliografía: lista de fuentes primarias en la preparación de un texto

biography: a description or account of events from a person's life, written by another person
biografía: descripción o narración de la vida de una persona o los sucesos importantes de su vida escritos por otra persona

blank verse: unrhymed verse
verso libre: verso que no tiene rima

blocking: in drama, the way actors position themselves in relation to one another, the audience, and the objects on the stage
bloqueo: en drama, el modo en que los actores se sitúan entre sí, con el público y los objetos en el escenario

book review: a formal assessment or examination of a book
reseña de libro: evaluación o examinación formal de un libro

C

cacophonous: harsh and unpleasant sounding
cacofónico: sonidos molestos y desagradables

call to action: a restatement of the claim and what the writer wants the reader to do
llamado a la acción: repetición de la afirmación y lo que el escritor quiere que el lector responda

caricature: a visual or verbal representation in which characteristics or traits are exaggerated or distorted for emphasis
caricatura: representación visual o verbal en la que las características o rasgos se exageran o se distorsionan para dar énfasis

catalog poem: a poem that uses repetition and variation in the creation of a list, or catalog, of objects or desires, plans, or memories
lista en poema: poema que usa repetición y variación en la creación de una lista o catálogo, de objetos o deseos o planes o memorias

cause: an action, event, or situation that brings about a particular result
causa: acción, suceso o situación que produce un resultado particular

censor: to examine materials for objectionable content
censurar: examinar materiales por contenido desagradable

censorship: the act of suppressing public speech or publication of materials deemed to be offensive by the censor
censura: acto de suprimir un discurso público o publicación de materiales considerados ofensivos por un censor

challenge: to oppose or refute a statement that has been made
poner en duda: oponerse a algo o refutar una declaración que alguien ha hecho

characterization: the methods a writer uses to develop characters
caracterización: métodos que usa un escritor para desarrollar personajes

characters: people, animals, or imaginary creatures that take part in the action of a story. A short story usually centers on a *main character* but may also contain one or more *minor characters*, who are not as complex, but whose thoughts, words, or actions move the plot along. A character who is *dynamic* changes in response to the events of the narrative; a character who is *static* remains the same throughout the narrative. A *round* character is fully developed—he or she shows a variety of traits; a *flat* character is one-dimensional, usually showing only one trait.

personajes: personas, animales o criaturas imaginarias que participan en la acción de un cuento. Un cuento corto normalmente se centra en un *personaje principal*, pero puede también contener uno o más *personajes secundarios*, que no son tan complejos, pero cuyos pensamientos, palabras o acciones hacen avanzar la trama. Un personaje que es *dinámico* cambia según los eventos del relato; un personaje que es *estático* permanece igual a lo largo del relato. Un personaje *complejo* está completamente desarrollado: muestra una diversidad de rasgos; un personaje *simple* es unidimensional, mostrando normalmente sólo un rasgo.

character sketch: a brief description of a literary character
reseña del personaje: breve descripción de un personaje literario

chorus: in traditional or classic drama, a group of performers who speak as one and comment on the action of the play
coro: en el drama tradicional o clásico, grupo de actores que hablan al unísono y comentan la acción de la obra teatral

cinematic elements: the features of cinema—movies, film, video—that contribute to its form and structure: *angle* (the view from which the image is shot), *framing* (how a scene is structured), *lighting* (the type of lighting used to light a scene), *mise en scène* (the composition, setting, or staging of an image, or a scene in a film), and *sound* (the sound effects and music accompanying each scene)
elementos cinematográficos: las características del cine—películas, filmaciones, video—que contribuyen a darle forma y estructura: *angulación* (vista desde la cual se toma la imagen), *encuadre* (cómo se estructura una escena), iluminación (tipo de *iluminación* que se usa para una escena), y *montaje* (composición, ambiente o escenificación de una imagen o escena en una película), y *sonido* (efectos sonoros y música que acompañan cada escena)

cinematic techniques: the methods a director uses to communicate meaning and to evoke particular emotional responses from viewers
técnicas cinematográficas: métodos que emplea un director para comunicar un significado y evocar cierta respuesta emocional de los videntes

claim: a thesis statement describing the position the writer is taking on an issue
afirmación: declaración de opinión (o tesis) que asevera una idea o establece un debate hacia una posición específica

cliché: an overused expression or idea
cliché: expresión o idea que se usa en exceso

climax: the point at which the action reaches its peak; the point of greatest interest or suspense in a story; the turning point at which the outcome of a conflict is decided
clímax: punto en el que la acción alcanza su punto culminante; punto de mayor interés en un cuento; punto de inflexión en el que se decide el resultado del conflicto

coherence: the quality of unity or logical connection among ideas; the clear and orderly presentation of ideas in a paragraph or essay
coherencia: calidad de unidad o relación lógica entre las ideas; presentación clara y ordenada de las ideas en un párrafo o ensayo

commentary: the expression of opinions or explanations about an event or situation
comentario: expresión oral o escrita de opiniones o explicaciones sobre una situación, tema o suceso

complementary: combined in a way that enhances all elements combined
complementario: combinar dos o más elementos de una manera que mejora los dos

complex character: a character that has multiple or conflicting motivations
personaje complejo: personaje que tiene motivaciones multiples o conflictivas

complex sentence: a sentence containing one independent clause and one or more subordinate clauses
oración compleja: oración que contiene una cláusula independiente y una o más cláusulas subordinadas

complications: the events in a plot that develop a conflict; the complications move the plot forward in its rising action
complicaciones: sucesos de una trama que desarrollan el conflicto; las complicaciones hacen avanzar la trama en su acción ascendente

compound sentence: a sentence containing two independent clauses
oración compuesta: oración que contiene dos cláusulas independientes

concession: an admission in an argument that the opposing side has valid points
concesión: admitir en un debate que el lado opositor tiene opiniones válidas

concluding statement: a statement that follows from and supports the claim made in an argument
declaración concluyente: declaración que sigue de la afirmación, o la apoya, en un argumento

conflict: a struggle or problem in a story. An *internal conflict* occurs when a character struggles between opposing needs or desires or emotions within his or her own mind. An *external conflict* occurs when a character struggles against an outside force. This force may be another character, a societal expectation, or something in the physical world.
conflicto: lucha o problema en un cuento. Un *conflicto interno* ocurre cuando un personaje lucha entre necesidades o deseos o emociones que se contraponen dentro de su mente. Un *conflicto externo* ocurre cuando un personaje lucha contra una fuerza externa. Esta fuerza puede ser otro personaje, una expectativa social o algo del mundo físico.

connotation: the associations and emotional overtones attached to a word beyond its literal definition, or denotation; a connotation may be positive, negative, or neutral
connotación: asociaciones y alusiones emocionales unidas a una palabra más allá de su definición literal o denotación; una connotación puede ser positiva, negativa, o neutra

consonance: the repetition of final consonant sounds in stressed syllables with different vowel sounds
consonancia: repetición de sonidos consonánticos finales en sílabas acentuadas con diferentes sonidos vocálicos

context: the circumstances or conditions in which something exists or takes place
contexto: circunstancias o condiciones en las que algo ocurre

conventions: standard features, practices, and forms associated with the way something is usually done
convenciones: prácticas y formas usuales asociadas con las costumbres de hacer algo

counterclaim: a position taken by someone with an opposing viewpoint
contrareclamación: posición que toma una persona con un punto de vista contrario

couplet: two consecutive lines of verse with end rhyme; a couplet usually expresses a complete unit of thought
copla: dos líneas de versos consecutivos con rima final; una copla normalmente expresa una unidad de pensamiento completa

credibility: the quality of being trusted or believed
credibilidad: calidad de ser confiable o creíble

critical lens: a particular identifiable perspective as in Reader Response Criticism, Cultural Criticism, etc., through which a text can be analyzed and interpreted
ojo crítico: punto de vista particular identificable como por ejemplo Teoría de la recepción, Crítica sociocultural, etc., por medio del que se puede analizar e interpretar un texto

cultural conflict: a struggle that occurs when people with different cultural expectations or attitudes interact
conflicto cultural: lucha que ocurre cuando interactúan personas con diferentes expectativas o actitudes culturales

Cultural Criticism: criticism that focuses on the elements of culture and how they affect one's perceptions and understanding of texts
crítica cultural: analizar un texto basándose en elementos culturales y como ellos afectan la percepción y lacomprensión de textos

culture: the shared set of arts, ideals, skills, institutions, customs, attitude, values, and achievements that characterize a group of people, and that are passed on or taught to succeeding generations
cultura: conjunto de artes, ideas, destrezas, instituciones, costumbres, actitud, valores y logros compartidos que caracterizan a un grupo de personas, y que se transfieren o enseñan a las generaciones siguientes

cumulative (or loose) sentence: a sentence in which the main clause comes first, followed by subordinate structures or clauses
oración acumulativa (o frases sueltas): oración cuya cláusula principal viene primero, seguida de estructuras o cláusulas subordinadas

D

deductive reasoning: a process of drawing a specific conclusion from general information
razonamiento deductivo: proceso en que se usa información general para sacar una conclusión específica

defend: to support a statement that has been made
defender: dar apoyo a una declaración que alguien ha hecho

denotation: the precise meaning of a word
denotación: significado literal de una palabra

detail: a specific fact, observation, or incident; any of the small pieces or parts that make up something else
detalle: hecho, observación o incidente específico; cualquiera de las pequeñas piezas o partes que constituyen otra cosa

dialect: the distinctive language—including the sounds, spelling, grammar, and diction—of a specific group or class of people
dialecto: lenguaje distintivo, incluyendo sonidos, ortografía, gramática y dicción, de un grupo o clase específico de personas

dialogue: the words spoken by characters in a narrative or film
diálogo: palabras que dicen los personajes en un relato o película

dialogue tags: the phrases that attribute a quotation to the speaker, for example, *she said* or *he bellowed*
marcas del diálogo: frases que atribuyen la cita de un hablante, por ejemplo, *dijo ella* o *bramó él.*

diction: a writer's word choices, which often convey voice and tone
dicción: selección de palabras por parte del escritor; elemento estilístico que ayuda a transmitir voz y tono

diegetic sound: any sound that can logically be heard by characters on screen
sonido diegético: sonidos lógicos que los personajes pueden oír en una escena en la pantalla

direct characterization: specific information about a character provided by the narrator or author
caracterización directa: información específica sobre un personaje creada por un narrador o autor

discourse: the language or speech used in a particular context or subject
discurso: lenguaje o habla usada en un contexto o tema en particular

documentary or nonfiction film: a genre of filmmaking that provides a visual record of actual events using photographs, video footage, and interviews
documental o película de no-ficción: género cinematográfico que realiza un registro visual de sucesos basados en hechos por medio del uso de fotografías, registro en videos y entrevistas

dominant group: a more powerful group that may perceive another group as marginalized or subordinate
grupo dominante: un grupo más poderoso que puede percibir a otro grupo como maginado o subordinado

drama: a play written for stage, radio, film, or television, usually about a serious topic or situation
drama: obra teatral escrita para representar en un escenario, radio, cine o televisión, normalmente sobre un tema o situación seria

dramatic irony: a form of irony in which the reader or audience knows more about the circumstances or future events than the characters within the scene
ironía dramática: una forma de la ironía en que los lectores o el público sabe más sobre las circunstancias o sucesos futuros que los personajes en la escena

dramaturge: a member of an acting company who helps the director and actors make informed decisions about the performance by researching information relevant to the play and its context
dramaturgo: socio de una compañía teatral que ayuda al director y a los actores tomar decisiones informadas sobre la interpretación investigando información relevante a la obra teatral y su contexto

dynamic (or round) character: evolves and grows in the story and has a complex personality
personaje dinámico: personaje complejo que evoluciona a lo largo de la trama literaria

E

editorial: an article in a newspaper or magazine expressing the opinion of its editor or publisher
editorial: artículo de periódico o revista, que expresa la opinión de su editor

effect: the result or influence of using a specific literary or cinematic device; a result produced by a cause
efecto: resultado o influencia de usar un recurso literario o cinematográfico específico; resultado o producto de una causa

elaborate: to expand on or add information or detail about a point and thus to develop the point more fully
elaborar: extender o agregar información o detalles sobre un asunto, y asi desarrollar el asunto de manera más completa

empirical evidence: evidence based on experiences and direct observation through research
evidencia empírica: evidencia basada en experiencias y en la observación directa por medio de la investigación

emulate: to imitate an original work or person
emular: imitar una obra original

enfranchisement: having the rights of citizenship, such as the right to vote
emancipación: tener los derechos de la ciudananía, tales como el derecho al voto

epigram: a short, witty saying
epigrama: dicho corto e ingenioso

epigraph: a phrase, quotation, or poem that is set at the beginning of a document or component
epígrafe: frase, cita, o poema que aparece al comienzo de un documento o componente

epithet: a descriptive word or phrase used in place of or along with a name
epíteto: palabra o frase descriptiva usada en lugar de o junto con un nombre

ethos: (ethical appeal) a rhetorical appeal that focuses on the character or qualifications of the speaker
ethos: (recurso ético) recurso retórico centrado en la ética o en el carácter o capacidades del orador

euphonious: a harmonious or pleasing sound
eufónico: un sonido armonioso y agradable

evaluate: to make a judgment based on an analysis about the value or worth of the information, idea, or object
evaluar: dar una opinión basándose en un análisis sobre el valor o mérito de la información, idea, u objeto

evidence: the information that supports a position in an argument; forms of evidence include facts, statistics (numerical facts), expert opinions, examples, and anecdotes; *see also* anecdotal, empirical, and logical evidence
evidencia: información que apoya o prueba una idea o afirmación; formas de evidencia incluyen hechos, estadística (datos numéricos), opiniones de expertos, ejemplos y anécdotas; *ver también* evidencia anecdótica, empírica y lógica

exaggeration: a statement that represents something as larger, better, or worse than it really is
exageración: representar algo como más grande, mejor o peor que lo que realmente es

exemplification: the act of defining by example by showing specific, relevant examples that fit a writer's definition of a topic or concept
ejemplificación: definir por ejemplo mostrando ejempos específicos y relevantes que se ajustan a la definición de un tema o concepto del escritor

explicit theme: a theme that is clearly stated by the writer
tema explícito: tema que está claramente establecido por el escritor

exposition: events that give a reader background information needed to understand a story (characters are introduced, the setting is described, and the conflict begins to unfold)

exposición: sucesos que dan al lector los antecedentes necesarios para comprender un cuento. Durante la exposición, se presentan los personajes, se describe el ambiente y se comienza a revelar el conflicto.

expository writing: a form of writing whose purpose is to explain, describe, or give information about a topic in order to inform a reader

escrito expositivo: forma de la escritura cuyo propósito es explicar, describir o dar información sobre un tema para informar al lector

extended metaphor: a comparison between two unlike things that continues throughout a series of sentences in a paragraph or lines in a poem

metáfora extendida: metáfora que se extiende por varios versos o a través de un poema completo

external coherence: unity or logical connection between paragraphs with effective transitions and transitional devices

coherencia externa: unidad o conexión lógica entre párrafos con transiciones efectivas y recursos transitionales

F

fallacy: a false or misleading argument

falacia: argumento o poema falso o engañoso

falling action: the events in a play, story, or novel that follow the climax, or moment of greatest suspense, and lead to the resolution

acción descendente: sucesos de una obra teatral, cuento o novela posteriores al clímax, o momento de mayor suspenso, y que conllevan a la resolución

Feminist Criticism: criticism that focuses on relationships between genders and examines a text based on the patterns of thought, behavior, values, enfranchisement, and power in relations between and within the sexes

crítica feminista: se enfoca en la relación entre los sexos y examina un texto basándose en el diseño de pensamiento, comportamiento, valores, emancipación, y poder en las relaciones entre los sexos

figurative language: the use of words to describe one thing in terms of another

lenguaje figurativo: lenguaje imaginativo o figuras retóricas que no pretenden ser tomados literalmente; el lenguaje figurativo usa figuras literarias

film techniques: the methods a director uses to communicate meaning and to evoke particular emotional responses in viewers

técnicas cinematográficas: metodos que usa un director en la comunicación del significado y evocar una respuesta emocional específica en los videntes

fixed form: a form of poetry in which the length and pattern are determined by established usage of tradition, such as a sonnet

forma fija: forma de poesía en la que la longitud y el patrón están determinados por el uso de la tradición, como un soneto

flashback: an interruption or transition to a time before the current events in a narrative

flashback: interrupción en la secuencia de los sucesos para relatar sucesos ocurridos en el pasado

flat (or static) character: a character who is uncomplicated and stays the same without changing or growing during the story

personaje estático: personaje no complicado que permanence del mismo caracter y que no cambia a lo largo de una historia

foil: a character whose actions or thoughts are juxtaposed against those of a major character in order to highlight key attributes of the major character

antagonista: personaje cuyas acciones o pensamientos se yuxtaponen a los de un personaje principal con el fin de destacar atributos clave del personaje principal

folktale: a story without a known author that has been preserved through oral retellings

cuento folclórico: cuento sin autor conocido que se ha conservado por medio de relatos orales

footage: literally, a length of film; the expression is still used to refer to digital video clips

metraje: literalmente, la longitud de una película; la expresión aún se usa para referirse a video clips digitales

foreshadowing: the use of hints or clues in a narrative to suggest future action

presagio: uso de claves o pistas en un relato para sugerir una acción futura

form: the particular structure or organization of a work

forma: estructura o organización particular de una obra

free verse: poetry without a fixed pattern of meter and rhyme

verso libre: poesía que no sigue ningún patrón, ritmo o rima regular

G

genre: a kind or style of literature or art, each with its own specific characteristics. For example, poetry, short story, and novel are literary genres. Painting and sculpture are artistic genres.

género: tipo o estilo de literatura o arte, cada uno con sus propias características específicas. Por ejemplo, la poesía, el cuento corto y la novela son géneros literarios. La pintura y la escultura son géneros artísticos.

genre conventions: the essential features and format that characterize a particular genre, or style of literature or art

convenciones genéricas: características básicas y el formato que caracterizan un género específico

graphic novel: a book-length narrative, or story, in the form of a comic strip rather than words

novela gráfica: narrativa o cuento del largo de un libro, en forma de tira cómica más que palabras

graphics: images or text used to provide information on screen
gráfica: imágenes o texto que se usa para dar información en pantalla

H

hamartia: a tragic hero's fatal flaw; an ingrained character trait that causes a hero to make decisions leading to his or her death or downfall
hamartia: error fatal de un héroe trágico; característica propia de un personaje que causa que un héroe tome decisiones que finalmente llevan a su muerte o caída

hero: the main character or protagonist of a play, with whom audiences become emotionally invested
héroe: personaje principal o protagonista de una obra teatral, con el que el público se involucra emocionalmente

historical context: the circumstances or conditions in which something takes place
contexto historico: circuntancias o condiciones en las cuales algo sucede o pasa

hook: an opening in an argument or a piece of writing that grabs the reader's attention
gancho: cita, anécdota o ejemplo interesante al comienzo de un escrito, que capta la atención del lector

Horatian satire: satire that pokes fun at human foibles and folly with a witty, gentle, even indulgent tone
sátira de Horacio: sátira en que se burla de las debilidades y locuras con un tono suave, ingenioso, hasta indulgente

humor: the quality of being amusing
humor: calidad de ser divertido

hyperbole: exaggeration used to suggest strong emotion or create a comic effect
hipérbole: exageración que se usa para sugerir una emoción fuerte o crear un efecto cómico

I

iamb: a metrical foot that consists of an unstressed syllable followed by a stressed syllable
yambo: pie métrico que consta de una sílaba átona seguida de una sílaba acentuada

iambic pentameter: a rhythmic pattern of five feet (or units), each consisting of one unstressed syllable followed by a stressed syllable
pentámetro yámbico: patrón rítmico de cinco pies (o unidades) de una sílaba átona seguida de una sílaba acentuada

image: a word or phrase that appeals to one of more of the five senses and creates a picture
imagen: palabra o frase que apela a uno o más de los cinco sentido y crea un cuadro

imagery: the verbal expression of sensory experience; descriptive or figurative language used to create word pictures; imagery is created by details that appeal to one or more of the five senses
imaginería: lenguaje descriptivo o figurativo utilizado para crear imágenes verbales; la imaginería es creada por detalles que apelan a uno o más de los cinco sentidos

imperialism: a policy of extending the rule or influence of a country over other countries or colonies; the political, military, or economic domination of one country by another
imperialismo: política de extender el dominio o la influencia de un país sobre otros países o colonias; dominio político; militar o económico de un país sobre otro(s)

implied theme: a theme that is understood through the writer's diction, language construction, and use of literary devices
tema implícito: tema que se entiende a través de la dicción del escritor, construcción lingüística y uso de recursos literarios

indirect characterization: a narrator's or author's development of a character through the character's interactions with others, thoughts about circumstances, or speaking his or her thoughts aloud
caracterización indirecta: el desarrollo de un personaje según un narrador o autor por las interacciones del personaje con otros, pensamientos sobre las circunstancias, o su habilidad de enunciar sus pensamientos en voz alta

inductive reasoning: a process of looking at individual facts to draw a general conclusion
razonamiento inductivo: proceso de observación de hechos individuales para sacar una conclusión general

inference: a conclusion about ideas or information not directly stated
inferencia: conclusion sobre las ideas o información no presentadas directamente

interior monologue: a literary device in which a character's internal emotions and thoughts are presented
monólogo interior: recurso literario en el que se presentan las emociones internas y pensamientos de un personaje

interpretation: the act of making meaning from something, such as a text
interpretación: acto de interpretar un significado de algo, tal como un texto

internal coherence: unity or logical connection within paragraphs
coherencia interna: unidad o conexión lógica entre párrafos

irony: a literary device that exploits readers' expectations; irony occurs when what happens turns out to be quite different from what was expected. *Dramatic irony* is a form of irony in which the reader or audience knows more about the circumstances or future events in a story than the characters within it; *verbal irony* occurs when a speaker or narrator says one thing while meaning the opposite; *situational irony* occurs when an event contradicts the expectations of the characters or the reader.

ironía: recurso literario que explota las expectativas de los lectores; la ironía ocurre cuando lo que se espera resulta ser bastante diferente de lo que realmente ocurre. La *ironía dramática* es una forma de ironía en la que el lector o la audiencia saben más acerca de las circunstancias o sucesos futuros de un cuento que los personajes del mismo; la *ironía verbal* ocurre cuando un orador o narrador dice una cosa queriendo decir lo contrario; la *ironía situacional* ocurre cuando un suceso contradice las expectativas de los personajes o del lector.

J

justice: the quality of being reasonable and fair in the administration of the law; the ideal of rightness or fairness

justicia: calidad de ser razonable e imparcial en la administración de la ley; ideal de rectitud o equidad

Juvenalian satire: satire that denounces, sometimes harshly, human vice and error in dignified and solemn tones

sátira de Juvenal: sátira de denuncia, a veces con aspereza, los vicios y errores humanos con tonos dignos y solemnes

juxtaposition: the arrangement of two or more things for the purpose of comparison

yuxtaposición: ordenamiento de dos o más cosas con el objeto de compararlas

L

lining out: the process of creating line breaks to add shape and meaning in free verse poetry

llamada y respuesta: proceso de crear rupturas de lineas para dar forma y significado en la poesía del verso libre

literal language: the exact meanings, or denotations, of words

lenguaje literal: los signficados y denotaciones exactos de las palabras

literary theory: a systematic study of literature using various methods to analyze texts

teoría literaria: intento de establecer principios para interpretar y evaluar textos literarios

logical evidence: evidence based on facts and a clear rationale

evidencia lógica: evidencia basada en hechos y una clara fundamentación

logos: (logical appeal) a rhetorical appeal to reason or logic

logos: (apelación lógica) apelación retórica que usa la evidencia factual y la lógica para apelar al sentido de la razón

M

main idea: a statement (often one sentence) that summarizes the key details of a text

idea principal: declaración (con frecuencia una oración) que resume los detalles claves de un texto

marginalize: to relegate or confine a person to a lower or outer limit

marginar: relegar o confinar a una persona a un límite bajo o ajeno

Marxist Criticism: criticism that asserts that economics provides the foundation for all social, political, and ideological reality

crítica marxista: ver un text a través de la perspectiva en que la economía proporciona la fundación de toda realidad social, política, e ideológica

media: collectively refers to the organizations that communicate information to the public

medios de comunicación: colectivamente refiere a las organizaciones que comunican información al público

media channel: a method an organization uses to communicate, such as radio, television, website, newspaper, or magazine

canales mediaticos: método que usa una organización en la comunicación como radio, televisión, sitios de web, periódico, o revista

metacognition: the ability to know and be aware of one's own thought processes; self-reflection

metacognición: capacidad de conocer y estar consciente de los propios procesos del pensamiento; introspección

metaphor: a comparison between two unlike things in which one thing is spoken of as if it were another, for example, the moon was a crisp white cracker

metáfora: comparación entre dos cosas diferentes en la que se habla de una cosa como si fuera otra, por ejemplo, la luna era una galletita blanca crujiente

meter: a pattern of stressed and unstressed syllables in poetry

métrica: patrón de sílabas acentuadas y átonas en poesía

mise en scène: the composition, or setting, of a stage

puesta en escena: la composición o el lugar de un escenario

monologue: a dramatic speech delivered by a single character in a play

monólogo: discurso dramático que hace un solo personaje en una obra teatral

montage: a composite picture that is created by bringing together a number of images and arranging them to create a connected whole

montaje: cuadro compuesto que se crea al reunir un número de imágenes y que al organizarlas se crea un todo relacionado

mood: the atmosphere or predominant emotion in a literary work, the effect of the words on the audience

carácter: atmósfera o sentimiento general en una obra literaria

motif: a recurrent image, symbol, theme, character type, subject, or narrative detail that becomes a unifying element in an artistic work or text

motivo: imagen, símbolo, tema, tipo de personaje, tema o detalle narrativo recurrente que se convierte en un elemento unificador en una obra artística

musical (or sound) device: the use of sound to convey and reinforce the meaning or experience of poetry
aparatos musicales: uso del sonido para transmitir y reforzar el significado o experiencia de la poesía

myth: a traditional story that explains the actions of gods or heroes or the origins of the elements of nature
mito: cuento tradicional que explica las acciones de dioses o héroes, o los orígenes de los elementos de la naturaleza

N

narration: the act of telling a story
narración: acto de contar un cuento

narrative: a story about a series of events that includes character development, plot structure, and theme; can be a work of fiction or nonfiction
narrativa: narración sobre una serie de sucesos que incluye el desarrollo de personajes, estructora del argumento, y el tema; puede ser una obra de ficción o no ficción

narrative pacing: the speed at which a narrative moves
compás de la narrativa: la rapidez en que una narrativa pasa

narrator: the person telling the story
narrador: persona que cuenta una historia

non-diegetic sound: sound that cannot logically be heard by the characters on screen; examples include mood music and voice-overs
sonido no diegético: voces y comentarios superpuestos; sonidos que no provienen de la acción en pantalla.

O

objective: based on factual information
objetivo: basado en información de hechos

objective tone: a tone that is more clinical and that is not influenced by emotion
tono objetivo: tono que es mas aséptico y que no se deja influir por la emoción

objectivity: the representation of facts or ideas without injecting personal feelings or biases
objetividad: representación de los hechos o ideas sin agregar sentimientos o prejuicios personales

ode: a lyric poem expressing feelings or thoughts of a speaker, often celebrating a person, event, or thing
oda: poema lírico que expresa sentimientos o pensamientos de un orador, que frecuentemente celebra a una persona, suceso o cosa

onomatopoeia: the occurrence of a word whose sound suggests its meaning
onomatopeya: palabras cuyo sonido sugiere su significado

oral interpretation: a planned oral reading that expresses the meaning of a written text
interpretación oral: lectura oral planeada que interpreta el signficado de un text escrito

oral tradition: the passing down of stories, tales, proverbs, and other culturally important ideas through oral retellings
tradición oral: traspaso de historias, cuentos, proverbios y otras historias de importancia cultural por medio de relatos orales

oxymoron: words that appear to contradict each other; for example, cold fire
oxímoron: palabras que parecen contradecirse mutuamente; por ejemplo, fuego frío

P

paradox: a statement that contains two seemingly incompatible points
paradoja: declaración que contiene dos asuntos aparentemente incompatibles

parallel structure (parallelism): refers to a grammatical or structural similarity between sentences or parts of a sentence, so that elements of equal importance are equally developed and similarly phrased for emphasis
estructura paralela (paralelismo): se refiere a una similitud gramatical o estructural entre oraciones o partes de una oración, de modo que los elementos de igual importancia se desarrollen por igual y se expresen de manera similar para dar énfasis

paraphrase: to briefly restate ideas from another source in one's own words
parafrasear: volver a presentar las ideas de otra fuente en nuestras propias palabras

parenthetical citations: used for citing sources directly in an essay
citas parentéticas: usadas en citas de fuentes primarias en un ensayo

parody: a literary or artistic work that imitates the characteristic style of an author or a work for comic effect or ridicule
parodia: obra literaria o artística que imita el estilo característico de un autor o una obra para dar un efecto cómico o ridículo

passive-voice verbs: verb form in which the subject receives the action; the passive voice consists of a form of the verb *be* plus a past participle of the verb
verbos en voz pasiva: forma verbal en la que el sujeto recibe la acción; la voz pasiva se forma con el verbo *ser* más el participio pasado de un verbo

pathos: (emotional appeal) a rhetorical appeal to the reader's or listener's senses or emotions
pathos: (apelación emocional) apelación retórica a los sentidos o emociones de los lectores u oyentes

patriarchal: having the male as head of the household and with authority over women and children
patriarcal: sociedad en que el varón es jefe del hogar en el cual mantiene autoridad sobre las mujeres y niños

perception: one person's interpretation of sensory or conceptual information
percepción: interpretación de una persona en cuanto a información sensorial o conceptual

periodic sentence: a sentence that makes sense only when the end of the sentence is reached, that is, when the main clause comes last
oración periódica: oración que tiene sentido sólo cuando se llega al final de la oración, es decir, cuando la cláusula principal viene al final

persona: the voice assumed by a writer to express ideas or beliefs that may not be his or her own
personaje: voz que asume un escritor para expresar ideas o creencias que pueden no ser las propias

personification: a figure of speech that gives human qualities to an animal, object, or idea
personificación: figura literaria que da características humanas a un animal, objeto o idea

perspective: a way of looking at the world or a mental concept about things or events, one that judges relationships within or among things or events
perspectiva: manera de visualizar el mundo o concepto mental de las cosas o sucesos, que juzga las relaciones dentro o entre cosas o sucesos

persuasive argument: an argument that convinces readers to accept or believe a writer's perspective on a topic
argumento persuasivo: argumento que convence a los lectores a aceptar o creer en la perspectiva de un escritor acerca de un tema

photo essay: a collection of photographic images that reveal the author's perspective on a subject
ensayo fotográfico: recolección de imágenes fotográficas que revelan la perspectiva del autor acerca de un tema

plagiarism: the unattributed use of another writer's words or ideas
plagio: usar como propias las palabras o ideas de otro escritor

plot: the sequence of related events that make up a story
trama: secuencia de sucesos relacionados que conforman un cuento o novela

poetic structure: the organization of words, lines, and images as well as ideas
estructura poética: organización de las palabras, versos e imágenes, así como también de las ideas

poetry: language written in lines and stanzas
poesía: género literario que se concreta en un poema y está sujeto a medida o cadencia

point of view: the perspective from which a narrative is told, that is, first person, third-person limited, or third-person omniscient
punto de vista: perspectiva desde la cual se cuenta un relato, es decir, primera persona, tercera persona limitada o tercera persona omnisciente

precept: a rule, instruction, or principle that guides a person's actions and/or moral behavior
precepto: regla, instrucción o principio que guía las acciones de una persona y/o conducta moral de alguien

primary footage: film footage shot by the filmmaker for the text at hand
metraje principal: filmación hecha por el cineasta para el texto que tiene a mano

primary source: an original document or image created by someone who experiences an event first hand
fuente primaria: documento original que contiene información de primera mano acerca de un tema

prologue: the introduction or preface to a literary work
prólogo: introducción o prefacio de una obra literaria

prose: ordinary written or spoken language, using sentences and paragraphs, without deliberate or regular meter or rhyme; not poetry or song
prosa: forma común del lenguaje escrito o hablado, usando oraciones y párrafos, sin métrica o rima deliberada o regular; ni poesía ni canción

protagonist: the central character in a work of literature, the one who is involved in the main conflict in the plot
protagonista: personaje central de una obra literaria, el que participa en el conflicto principal de la trama

proverb: a short saying about a general truth
proverbio: dicho corto sobre una verdad general

Q

qualify: to consider to what extent a statement is true or untrue (to what extent you agree or disagree)
calificar: consider hasta qué punto una declaración es verdadera o falsa

quatrain: a four-line stanza in a poem
cuarteta: en un poema, estrofa de cuatro versos

R

Reader Response Criticism: criticism that focuses on a reader's active engagement with a piece of print or nonprint text; shaped by the reader's own experiences, social ethics, moral values, and general views of the world
crítica de reacción del lector: análisis de un texto basado en las experiencias, ética social, valores, y percepciones generales del mundo

reasoning: the thinking or logic used to make a claim in an argument
razonamiento: pensamiento o lógica que se usa para hacer una afirmación en un argumento

refrain: a regularly repeated line or group of lines in a poem or song, usually at the end of a stanza
estribillo: verso o grupo de versos que se repiten con regularidad en un poema o canción, normalmente al final de una estrofa

refutation: the reasoning used to disprove an opposing point
refutación: razonamiento que se usa para rechazar una opinión contraria

reliability: the extent to which a source provides quality and trustworthy information
confiabilidad: grado en el que una fuente da información confiable y de buena calidad

renaissance: a rebirth or revival
renacimiento: un volver a nacer o una reanimación

repetition: the use of any element of language—a sound, a word, a phrase, a line, or a stanza—more than once
repetición: uso de cualquier elemento del lenguaje—un sonido, una palabra, una frase, un verso o una estrofa—más de una vez

resolution (denouement): the end of a text, in which the main conflict is finally resolved
resolución (desenlace): final de una obra teatral, cuento o novela, en el que el conflicto principal finalmente se resuelve

résumé: a document that outlines a person's skills, education, and work history
currículum vitae: documento que resume las destrezas, educación y experiencia laboral de una persona

rhetoric: the art of using words to persuade in writing or speaking
retórica: arte de usar las palabras para persuadir por escrito o de manera hablada

rhetorical appeals: emotional, ethical, and logical arguments used to persuade an audience to agree with the writer or speaker
recursos retóricos: uso de argumentos emocionales, éticos y lógicos para persuadir por escrito o de manera hablada

rhetorical context: the subject, purpose, audience, occasion, or situation in which writing or speaking occurs
contexto retórico: sujeto, propósito, audiencia, ocasión o situación en que ocurre el escrito

rhetorical devices: specific techniques used in writing or speaking to create a literary effect or enhance effectiveness
dispositivos retóricos: técnicas específicas que se usan al escribir o al hablar para crear un efecto literario o mejorar la efectividad

rhetorical question: a question that is asked for effect or one for which the answer is obvious
pregunta retórica: pregunta hecha para producir un efecto o cuya respuesta es obvia

rhyme: the repetition of sounds at the ends of words
rima: repetición de sonidos al final de las palabras

rhyme scheme: a consistent pattern of rhyme throughout a poem
esquema de la rima: patrón consistente de una rima a lo largo de un poema

rhythm: the pattern of stressed and unstressed syllables in spoken or written language, especially in poetry
ritmo: patrón de sílabas acentuadas y no acentuadas en lenguaje hablado o escrito, especialmente en poesía

rising action: the movement of a plot toward a climax or moment of greatest excitement; the rising action is fueled by the characters' responses to the conflict
acción ascendente: movimiento de una trama hacia el clímax o momento de mayor emoción; la acción ascendente es impulsada por las reacciones de los personajes ante el conflicto

round (or dynamic) character: a character who evolves and grows in the story and has a complex personality
personaje dinámico: personaje que evoluciona y crece en la historia y que tiene una personalidad compleja

S

satire: a manner of writing that mocks social conventions, actions, or attitudes with wit and humor
sátira: manera de escribir en que se burla de convenciones sociales, acciones, o actitudes con ingenio y humor

scenario: an outline, a brief account, a script, or a synopsis of a proposed series of events
escenario: bosquejo, relato breve, libreto o sinopsis de una serie de sucesos propuestos

secondary audience: a group that may receive a message intended for a target audience
audiencia secundaria: grupo que puede recibir un mensaje orientado a una audiencia específica

secondary source: a discussion about or commentary on a primary source; the key feature of a secondary source is that it offers an interpretation of information gathered from primary sources
fuente secundaria: discusión o comentario acerca de una fuente primaria; la característica clave de una fuente secundaria es que ofrece una interpretación de la información recopilada en las fuentes primarias

sensory details: details that appeal to or evoke one or more of the five senses—sight, sound, smell, taste, and touch
detalles sensoriales: detalles que apelan o evocan uno o más de los cinco sentidos—vista, oído, gusto, olfato, y tacto

sensory images: images that appeal to the reader's senses—sight, sound, smell, taste, and touch
imágenes sensoriales: imágenes que apelan a los sentidos del lector—vista, oído, olfato, gusto, y tacto

sequence of events: the order in which things happen in a story
secuencia de eventos: orden en que los sucesos de una historia pasan:

setting: the time and place in which a story happens
ambiente: tiempo y lugar en el que ocurre un relato

simile: a comparison of two different things or ideas using the words *like* or *as*, for example, the moon was as white as milk
símil: comparación entre dos o más cosas o ideas diferentes usando las palabras *como* o *tan*, por ejemplo, la luna estaba tan blanca como la leche

situational irony: a form of irony that occurs when an event contradicts the expectations of the characters or the reader
ironía situacional: ocurre cuando un evento contradice las espectativas de los personajes o el lector

slanters: rhetorical devices used to present the subject in a biased way
soslayo: recursos retóricos para presentar el tema de modo sesgado

slogan: a short, catchy phrase used for advertising by a business, club, or political party
eslogan: frase corta y tendenciosa que usa como publicidad para un negocio, club o partido político

social commentary: an expression of an opinion with the goal of promoting change by appealing to a sense of justice
comentario social: expresión de una opinión con el objeto de promover el cambio al apelar a un sentido de justicia

soliloquy: a long speech delivered by an actor alone on the stage; represents the character's internal thoughts
soliloquio: discurso largo realizado por un actor sobre el escenario que representa sus pensamientos internos

sonnet: a 14-line lyric poem, usually written in iambic pentameter and following a strict pattern of rhyme
soneto: poema lírico de catorce versos, normalmente escrito en un pentámetro yámbico y que sigue un patrón de rima estricto

speaker: the imaginary voice or persona of the writer or author
orador: voz o persona imaginaria del escritor o autor

stage directions: instructions written into the script of a play that indicate stage actions, movements of performers, or production requirements
direcciones escénicas: instrucciones escritas en un guión o drama que indican acción, movimiento de actors, o requisitos de la producción

stakeholder: a person motivated or affected by a course of action
participante: persona motivada o afectada por el curso de una acción

stanza: a group of lines, usually similar in length and pattern, that form a unit within a poem
estrofa: grupo de versos, normalmente similares en longitud y patrón, que forman una unidad dentro de un poema

static (or flat) character: a character who is uncomplicated and remains the same without changing or growing throughout a narrative
personaje estático: personaje que no cambia a lo largo de una narrativa

stereotype: an oversimplified, generalized conception, opinion, and/or image about particular groups of people
estereotipo: concepto generalizado, opinión y/o imagen demasiado simplificada acerca de grupos específicos de personas

stichomythia: in drama, the delivery of dialogue in a rapid, fast-paced manner, with actors speaking emotionally and leaving very little time between speakers
esticomitia: en el drama, es la rendición del diálogo de una manera rápida con actores que hablan con emoción, dejando espacio muy breve entre los hablantes

storyboard: a tool to show images and sequencing for the purpose of visualizing a film or a story
guión gráfico: método de mostrar imágenes y secuencias con el propósito de visualizar una película o historia

strategize: to plan the actions one will take to complete a task
estrategizar: planear las acciones de uno para complir una tarea

structure: the way a literary work is organized; the arrangement of the parts in a literary work
estructura: manera en que la obra literaria está organizada; disposición de las partes en una obra literaria

style: the distinctive way a writer uses language, characterized by elements of diction, syntax, imagery, organization, and so on
estilo: manera distintiva en que un escritor usa el lenguaje, caracterizada por elementos de dicción, sintaxis, lenguaje figurado, etc.

subculture: a smaller subsection of a culture, for example, within the culture of a high school may be many subcultures
subcultura: subsección más pequeña de una cultura, por ejemplo, dentro de la cultura de una escuela secundaria puede haber muchas subculturas

subjective tone: a tone that is obviously influenced by the author's feelings or emotions
tono subjetivo: tono obviamente influído por los sentimientos o emociones del autor

subjectivity: judgment based on one's personal point of view, opinion, or values
subjetividad: en base en nuestro punto de vista, opinión o valores personales

subordinate: a person or group that is perceived as having a lower social or economic status
subordinado: persona o grupo percibido de ser de rango social o estado económico bajo

subplot: a secondary or side story that develops from and supports the main plot and usually involves minor characters
argumento secundario: una historia secundaria o periférica que apoya el argumento principal y que suele involucrar a personajes secundarios o menores

subtext: the underlying or implicit meaning in dialogue or the implied relationship between characters in a book, movie, play, or film; the subtext of a work is not explicitly stated

subtexto: significado subyacente o implícito en el diálogo o la relación implícita entre los personajes de un libro, película, u obra teatral. El subtexto de una obra no se establece de manera explícita.

survey: a method of collecting data from a group of people; it can be written, such as a print or online questionnaire, or oral, such as an in-person interview

encuesta: método para recolectar datos de un grupo de personas; puede ser escrita, como un impreso o cuestionario en línea, u oral, como en una entrevista personal

symbol: anything (object, animal, event, person, or place) that represents itself but also stands for something else on a figurative level

símbolo: cualquier cosa (objeto, animal, evento, persona o lugar) que se representa a sí misma, pero también representa otra cosa a nivel figurativo

symbolic: serving as a symbol; involving the use of symbols or symbolism

simbólico: que sirve como símbolo; que implica el uso de símbolos o simbolismo

synecdoche: a figure of speech in which a part is used to represent the whole or vice versa

sinécdoque: figura retórica en que una parte se usa para representar el todo, o vice-versa

syntax: the arrangement of words and the order of grammatical elements in a sentence; the way in which words are put together to make meaningful elements, such as phrases, clauses, and sentences

sintaxis: disposición de las palabras y orden de los elementos gramaticales en una oración; manera en que las palabras se juntan para formar elementos significativos como frases, cláusulas y oraciones

synthesis: the act of combining ideas from different sources to create, express, or support a new idea

síntesis: acto de combinar ideas de diferentes fuentes para crear, expresar o apoyar una nueva idea

T

target audience: the intended group for which a work is designed to appeal or reach

público objetivo: grupo al que se pretende apelar o llegar con una obra

textual commentary: explanations about the significance or importance of supporting details or examples in an analysis

comentario textual: explicaciones acerca de la importancia de los detalles que tienen apoyo o ejemplos en un análisis

textual evidence: the details, quotations, and examples from a text that support the analysis or argument presented

evidencia textual: detalles, citas, y ejemplos de un texto que apoyan el análisis o la argumentación presentada

theatrical elements: elements used by dramatists and directors to tell a story on stage. Elements include *costumes* (the clothing worn by actors to express their characters), *makeup* (cosmetics used to change actors' appearances and express their characters), *props* (objects used to help set the scene, advance a plot, and make a story realistic), *set* (the place where the action takes place, as suggested by objects, such as furniture, placed on a stage), and *acting choices* (gestures, movements, staging, and vocal techniques actors use to convey their characters and tell a story).

elementos teatrales: elementos utilizados por los dramaturgos y directores para contar una historia en el escenario. Los elementos incluyen *vestuario* (ropa que usan los actores para expresar sus personajes), *maquillaje* (cosméticos que se usan para cambiar la apariencia de los actores y expresar sus personajes), *elementos* (objetos que se usan para ayudar a montar la escena, avanzar la trama y crear una historia realista), *plató* (lugar donde tiene lugar la acción, según lo sugieren los objetos, como muebles, colocados sobre un escenario), y *opciones de actuación* (gestos, movimientos, representación y técnicas vocales que se usan para transmitir sus personajes y narrar una historia).

thematic statement: an interpretive statement articulating the central meaning or message of a text

oración temática: afirmación interpretativa que articula el significado o mensaje central de un texto

theme: a writer's central idea or main message; *see also* explicit theme, implied theme

tema: idea central o mensaje principal acerca de la vida de un escritor; *véase también* tema explícito, tema implícito

thesis: the main idea or point of an essay or article; in an argumentative essay the thesis is the writer's position on an issue

tesis: idea o punto principal de un ensayo o artículo; en un ensayo argumentativo, la tesis es la opinión del autor acerca de un tema

tone: a writer's (or speaker's) attitude toward a subject, character, or audience

tono: actitud de un escritor u orador acerca de un tema

topic sentence: a sentence that states the main idea of a paragraph; in an essay, the topic sentence also makes a point that supports the thesis statement

oración principal: oración que establece la idea principal de un párrafo; en un ensayo, la oración principal también establece una proposición que apoya el enunciado de la tesis

tragedy: a dramatic play that tells the story of a character, usually of a noble class, who meets an untimely and unhappy death or downfall, often because of a specific character flaw or twist of fate

tragedia: obra teatral dramática que cuenta la historia de un personaje, normalmente de origen noble, que encuentra una muerte o caída imprevista o infeliz, con frecuencia debido a un defecto específico del personaje o una vuelta del destino

tragic hero: an archetypal hero based on the Greek concept of tragedy; the tragic hero has a flaw that makes him or her vulnerable to downfall or death

héroe trágico: héroe arquetípico basado en el concepto griego de la tragedia; el héroe trágico tiene un defecto que lo hace vulnerable a la caída o a la muerte

transcript: a written copy or record of a conversation that takes place between two or more people

transcripción: copia escrita de una conversación que sucede entre dos o más personas

U

understatement: the representation of something as smaller or less significant than it really is; the opposite of exaggeration or hyperbole

subestimación: representación de algo como más pequeño o menos importante de lo que realmente es; lo opuesto a la exageración o hipérbole

V

valid: believable or truthful
válido: creíble o verídico

validity: the quality of truth or accuracy in a source
validez: calidad de verdad o precisión en una fuente

verbal irony: a form of irony that occurs when a speaker or narrator says one thing while meaning the opposite

ironía verbal: ocurre cuando un hablante o narrador dice una cosa mientras quiere decir lo opuesto

verify: to prove or confirm that something is true
verificar: probar o confirmar que algo es verdadero

vignette: a picture or visual or a brief descriptive literary piece

viñeta: ilustración o representación visual o pieza literaria descriptiva breve

visual delivery: the way a performer on stage interprets plot, character, and conflict through movement, gestures, and facial expressions

presentación visual: manera en que un actor en un escenario interpreta trama, carácter, y conflicto a través de movimiento, gestos, y expresiones de la cara

visual rhetoric: an argument or points made by visuals such as photographs or by other visual features of a text

retórica visual: argumentos o asuntos representados en visuales como fotos u otros rasgos visuales de un texto

vocal delivery: the way a performer on stage expresses the meaning of a text through volume, pitch, rate or speed of speech, pauses, pronunciation, and articulation

presentación vocal: manera en que se expresan las palabras en el escenario, por medio del volumen, tono, rapidez o velocidad del discurso, pausas, pronunciación y articulación

voice: a writer's (or speaker's) distinctive use of language to express ideas as well as his or her persona

voz: manera en que el escritor u orador usa las palabras y el tono para expresar ideas, así como también su personaje o personalidad

Index of Skills

Literary Skills

Alliteration, 315
Allusions, 104
Analogies, 144
Anaphora, 15, 284
Argument, 62
Assonance, 292
Attitude, 330
Audience, 42, 73, 357, 410, 411, 417
Author's purpose, 104, 110, 113, 161, 166, 181, 251
Autobiography, 146
Biography, 147
Cacophony, 290
Characterization, 150, 153, 164, 232, 240, 427
Characters, 12, 46, 96, 98, 100, 104, 112, 113, 121, 125, 134, 153, 158, 159, 164, 168, 171, 174, 222, 229, 230, 231, 239, 241, 242, 246, 248, 250, 255, 262, 266, 361, 393, 424
  analysis, 373
  flat, 265
  motivation, 381, 382, 384, 386, 388
  primary, 265
  secondary, 265
  static, 269
Claims, 62, 65, 66
Conflict, 46, 95, 96, 98, 112, 226, 230, 231, 232, 241, 242, 246, 248, 249, 286, 388
  external, 96, 98, 231
  internal, 96, 98, 231
Context, 191, 195, 372
Counterclaims, 62, 420, 424, 425
Description, 6, 8, 39, 46, 56, 98, 112, 146, 161, 197, 230, 252, 289
Details, 39, 40, 42, 48, 102, 110, 112, 113, 121, 125, 142, 145, 148, 150, 157, 158, 161, 164, 166, 168, 171, 174, 190, 212, 230, 237, 254, 264, 289, 343, 362, 380, 390
Dialogue, 112, 116, 121, 164, 168, 171, 174, 230
Diction (word choice), 6, 25, 27, 42, 99, 104, 151, 154, 155, 207, 230, 278, 299, 301, 302, 327, 330, 343, 393
  formal, 18
Drama, 353, 356
Dramaturge, 369, 371, 372, 373
Essential Questions, 4, 61, 94, 141, 186, 221, 278, 323, 352, 402
Ethos, 67, 74, 424, 425
Euphony, 290

Figurative language, 101, 103, 111, 125, 138, 313, 315, 317, 320, 363
Flashbacks, 16, 23, 27
Foil, 381, 382
Foreshadowing, 23, 39, 113, 246
Form, 280
Hyperbole, 308, 309
Images/imagery, 6, 25, 27, 42, 99, 100, 101, 103, 104, 110, 120, 121, 125, 133, 135, 138, 144, 151, 154, 155, 158, 187, 215, 226, 230, 237, 278, 282, 289, 295, 298, 299, 301, 302, 305, 309, 317, 320, 327, 358, 371, 373, 382, 390. 393
Inferences, 6, 7, 99, 113, 118, 153, 161, 166, 198, 209, 210, 226, 234, 252, 271, 358, 363, 364, 391, 399
Interview narratives, 31, 32, 34, 43, 46, 57, 62
Irony, 104, 383
  dramatic, 126, 134, 383, 397, 399
  situational, 104, 112, 126, 134
  verbal, 126, 134, 135
Juxtaposition, 16, 23, 24, 27
Literary present, 241
Literary Terms, 2, 6, 9, 15, 16, 25, 35, 67, 92, 99, 101, 104, 126, 141, 144, 146, 148, 149, 184, 237, 265, 276, 280, 282, 285, 290, 293, 296, 303, 313, 318, 350, 353, 356, 357, 366, 367, 381, 391, 394
Logos, 67, 74, 424, 425
Memoirs, 35
Metaphors, 313, 317, 355, 363, 417
  extended, 303, 309
Monologue, 354, 355, 356, 363, 364, 369, 391
Mood, 125, 149, 151, 154
Moral message, 314
Motif, 237
Narratives, 9, 95, 98, 100, 112, 121, 125, 139, 158, 230
Narrators, 9, 11, 23, 32, 126, 132, 295, 307, 308, 316, 329
Pathos, 67, 74
Personification, 281
Perspective, 110, 112, 167, 249, 265, 281, 325, 272, 399
Plot, 46, 95, 96, 135, 159, 164, 168, 174, 237, 266, 357, 388
  diagram, 95
  elements of, 95, 96
  subplot, 233, 237, 241
Poetry, 35
  anthologies, 278, 289, 321

catalog poems, 293
central idea, 102
couplets, 301, 318, 319, 320
frame poems, 282
free verse, 279, 280, 293, 302, 308, 317, 329
iambic pentameter, 318, 357
musical (sound) devices, 290
odes, 313, 316, 317
persona, 325
poetic devices, 339
quatrains, 318, 319, 320
rhyme scheme, 285, 320
sonnets, 318, 320, 357, 372, 423
stanzas, 282
structure of, 137, 329, 330, 341, 343
Point of view, 27, 43, 46, 56, 97–98, 99, 110, 121, 155, 227, 230
  first person, 97
  third-person limited, 97
  third-person omniscient, 97
Prologue, 356, 357, 358, 372
Prose, 35
Refrain, 317
Repetition, 15, 40, 72, 76, 282, 289, 295, 317, 379
Rhetoric, 67
Rhetorical appeals, 61, 67, 72, 74, 76, 80, 207, 255, 260, 403, 405, 424, 425
Rhythm, 296, 357
Setting, 46, 100, 109, 112, 125, 159, 164, 187, 190, 213, 221, 228, 230, 246, 248, 249, 252, 279
Shifts, 69, 330
Similes, 313, 317
Soliloquys, 391, 393
Style, 99–100, 154–155, 159, 342, 343, 410
Subtext, 394, 396
Symbol(ism), 101, 111, 120, 137, 237, 326
Synesthesia, 346
Syntax, 6, 13, 42, 99, 143
Tableau, 358
Theatrical elements, 366, 367
Theme, 46, 111, 112, 121, 148, 239, 247, 262, 295, 308, 330, 354, 357, 393
Title, 316, 327, 330
Tone, 6, 54, 104, 111, 149, 154, 299, 304, 316, 324, 327, 338, 354
Tragedy, 356, 357, 358
Transcripts, 49
Voice, 4, 6, 12, 24, 31, 40, 42, 48, 54, 338

Reading Skills

Analyzing, 76, 80, 303, 310
Annotating the text, 7, 8, 52, 53, 88, 99, 101, 103, 272, 312, 359, 361, 362, 372, 381, 382
Chunking the text, 90, 239–240, 241, 361, 362, 390, 393, 394, 424
Close reading, 103, 110, 120, 148, 155, 159, 162–163, 164, 168, 171, 174, 176, 192, 196, 205, 209, 224, 227, 229, 230, 236, 237, 249, 252, 258, 295, 312, 329, 339, 363, 374
Compare and contrast, 87, 229, 243, 365, 379, 380
Discussion groups, 4, 8, 42, 61, 164, 166, 168, 171, 174, 175, 190, 197, 207, 213, 217, 221, 225, 237, 239, 240, 242, 252, 253, 264, 272, 279, 290, 312, 317, 319, 329, 352, 361, 362, 364, 365, 383, 390, 391, 396, 402, 404, 431
Double-entry journals, 9, 12, 176
Graphic organizers, 4, 7, 8, 9, 12, 26, 32, 40, 41, 48, 53, 61, 63, 74, 87, 95, 141, 144, 151, 154, 156, 158, 159, 161, 162, 163, 164, 165, 174, 177, 178, 186, 187, 199, 200, 206, 221, 226, 231, 232, 233, 237, 238, 243, 247, 252, 253, 260, 262, 265, 271, 290, 301, 302, 308, 323, 324, 329, 342, 344, 352, 358, 359, 363, 364, 365, 364, 380, 384, 386, 387, 389, 391, 394, 396, 402, 404, 410, 418, 424, 425, 430, 431, 434
Imagery, 101, 120, 298, 305, 324
Independent Reading Checkpoint, 54, 88, 138, 180, 218, 272, 320, 344, 399, 434
Independent Reading Link, 5, 9, 32, 49, 61, 67, 94, 100, 112, 121, 135, 141, 147, 158, 162, 173, 186, 210, 221, 231, 241, 248, 259, 278, 290, 302, 312, 324, 330, 343, 352, 362, 380, 393, 402, 419, 425
Inferring, 6, 7, 12, 24, 25, 39, 46, 52, 226, 228, 234, 262, 271, 358, 363, 364, 391, 399
Interpretation, 161, 163, 279, 371, 372, 388
Levels of questions, 113, 131, 161, 217, 239, 295, 312
Marking the text, 9, 14, 15, 16, 23, 27, 30, 35, 41, 44, 55, 64, 68, 76, 78, 81, 97, 99, 101, 103, 104, 113, 123, 136, 142, 149, 151, 191, 192, 202, 207, 208, 221, 222, 226, 228, 234, 237, 241, 242, 245, 246, 247, 249, 255, 266, 267, 272, 278, 280, 282,

293, 296, 299, 303, 305, 306, 310, 313, 315, 318, 325, 328, 331, 339, 353, 359, 362, 369, 375, 381, 383, 384, 390, 394, 406, 412, 420, 425, 426, 432, 445
Metacognitive markers, 196, 356, 426
Note-taking, 5, 9, 11, 15, 23, 29, 39, 46, 52, 61, 63, 65, 72, 85, 102, 109, 118, 124, 132, 137, 142, 144, 145, 147, 150, 153, 158, 159, 160, 161, 162, 164, 166, 168, 170, 171, 174, 175, 176, 186, 187, 192, 196, 205, 209, 214, 215, 216, 217, 221, 224, 226, 227, 229, 236, 237, 243, 258, 265, 266, 269, 281, 288, 289, 290, 295, 297, 301, 304, 307, 311, 314, 316, 317, 319, 326, 329, 340, 342, 344, 354, 357, 360, 361, 366, 379, 386, 396, 397, 404, 409, 414, 417, 423, 424, 429, 433
Oral reading, 103, 361, 381, 383, 384, 390, 393, 394, 396
Paraphrasing, 319, 330, 361, 362, 390, 394
Poetry, 279, 293, 310, 324, 327, 328, 329, 330, 331, 339, 340, 342
Predicting, 162, 163, 225, 226, 237, 330
Reflecting, 219, 361
Rereading, 11, 23, 39, 46, 52, 65, 72, 80, 85, 88, 102, 109, 118, 120, 124, 132, 137, 147, 150, 153, 192, 196, 205, 209, 224, 227, 229, 236, 258, 269, 281, 288, 295, 297, 301, 304, 307, 311, 314, 316, 319, 326, 329, 340, 342, 354, 357, 360, 363, 379, 386, 394, 396, 409, 414, 417, 423, 429, 433
Reviewing notes, 30, 138, 145, 148, 178, 215, 218, 226, 249, 323, 404
Role playing, 43, 158, 361
Second read, 11, 23, 39, 46, 52, 65, 72, 80, 85, 102, 109, 118, 124, 132, 137, 147, 150, 153, 192, 196, 205, 209, 224, 227, 229, 236, 258, 269, 281, 288, 227, 229, 236, 258, 269, 281, 288, 295, 297, 301, 304, 307, 311, 314, 316, 319, 326, 329, 340, 342, 354, 357, 360, 379, 386, 396, 409, 414, 417, 423, 429, 433
Sharing and responding, 5, 12, 27, 164, 166, 167, 168, 174, 217, 225, 237, 239, 279, 290, 418
SIFT, 110, 137, 312, 364
Sketching, 230, 254, 358, 367, 371, 372, 373, 382, 390, 399
Skimming/scanning, 110, 133, 359, 363, 391
SMELL, 74, 75, 258–259
SOAPSTone analysis, 47, 48, 49, 206, 410

Socratic Seminar, 261
Summarizing, 4, 9, 61, 112, 186, 187, 221, 225, 230, 238, 289, 297, 323, 352, 394, 402, 418, 424
Synthesizing, 261
T-chart, 309
Textual evidence, 7, 23, 90, 125, 137, 157, 161, 205, 206, 231, 232, 233, 237, 243, 246, 247, 249, 252, 262, 271, 327, 364, 391, 418
Theme, 298, 312, 354
Think-pair-share, 5, 7, 12, 27, 43, 95, 101, 103, 135, 144, 161, 187, 200, 213, 225, 231, 266, 290, 359, 390, 418, 419, 425
Title, 326, 330
Tone, 298, 312, 316, 319, 327, 354, 409, 410
TP-CASTT, 329, 330, 338
TWIST, 301, 302, 308, 312, 343, 391, 392
Visualizing, 40, 254, 361, 391, 399
Visuals, 207, 297
Web graphic organizer, 187

Writing Skills

Analogies, 144
Analytical text, 166–167, 169, 173, 174, 175, 179, 298, 338
Annotated bibliography, 373
Annotating the text, 31, 34, 99, 373
Argument, 62, 66, 76, 77, 167, 173, 207, 260, 434
Audience, 77, 80, 217, 368, 393, 410
Bibliography, 212
Brainstorming, 42, 58, 95, 96, 144, 213, 231, 249, 272, 342, 344, 351, 389
Call to action, 62, 88, 255, 431, 434, 435
Chicago Manual of Style, 201, 214
Claims, 62, 63, 66, 76, 85, 103, 138, 161, 163, 167, 170, 171, 173, 177, 179, 180, 207, 210, 218, 260, 266, 270, 312, 388, 402, 411, 419, 425, 431, 434
Collaborative documents, 400
Commentary, 110, 135, 169, 170, 171, 173, 175, 179, 190, 201, 210, 211, 219, 231, 237, 248, 254, 260, 271, 272, 362, 364, 373, 380, 386, 390, 399, 419
Compare and contrast, 244, 255, 343, 380, 399, 420
Concessions, 62
Concluding statements, 27, 138, 334, 343, 431, 434
Conclusions, 30, 31, 62, 66, 88, 103, 145, 148, 157, 161, 171, 173, 175, 210, 218, 237, 241, 250, 251, 266, 272, 298, 345, 355
Counterclaims, 66, 86, 88, 207, 420, 424, 425, 431, 434

Media Skills

Cinematic style, 159, 160, 166
Cinematic techniques, 144, 154–155, 156, 158, 166, 168, 171, 253
   camera angles, 144, 164, 165
   camera movements, 144, 162, 163, 165
   editing, 144, 165
   flashbacks, 144, 159, 161
   lighting, 144, 159, 164, 165
   shots/framing, 144, 159, 162, 165
   sound, 144, 159, 163, 164, 165
Frame story, 162–163
Images, 162
Mood, 154–155, 156, 162, 163
Music, 317, 388
Oral presentations, 355
Poster creation, 197, 247, 266, 390
Staging, 352, 362, 366
Style, 144, 147, 181
T-chart, 305
Tone, 156, 162

Speaking and Listening Skills

Acting companies, 369, 371, 372, 381, 388, 391
Actor's Notebook, 373
Audience, 217, 367, 399
Audience engagement, 375
Debating, 404, 405
Director, 369, 371, 372, 375, 379
Director's Notebook, 372
Dramaturge, 369, 371, 372, 373
Dramaturge's Notebook, 373
Emphasis, 361
Evaluating, 216, 393, 400
Eye contact, 8, 200
Facial expression, 381
Graphic organizers, 369, 370, 371, 374, 397, 398
Group discussions, 369, 373, 382, 393
Meeting log, 372
Memorizing, 31, 372, 373, 393
Nonverbal communication, 8
Note-taking, 366, 386, 396, 397, 405
Oral interpretation, 334, 371
Oral presentations, 30, 63, 200, 216, 217, 364
Oral reading, 103, 361, 381, 383, 384, 390, 393, 394, 396
Performance contract, 371
Pitch, 361
Poetry, 279, 293, 310, 324, 327, 328, 329, 330, 331, 339, 300, 342
Rehearsing, 31, 88, 219, 334, 347, 361, 362, 364, 382, 393, 396, 400
Role play, 381

Rubrics, 393
Staging Notebooks, 369, 370, 371, 372
Tableau, 358
Technology Tips, 89, 400
Theatrical elements, 366, 367, 368, 374, 388, 383
   acting choices, 364
   blocking, 367, 368, 372, 375, 380, 386, 388, 393, 399
   costumes, 366, 373
   lighting, 372, 388
   makeup, 366
   music, 317, 388
   props, 366, 372
   set, 366, 372, 375, 380, 388
   sound, 372, 388
Visual delivery, 361, 362, 364, 372, 373, 381, 388, 391, 393, 396, 397, 399
Visuals, 372
Vocal delivery, 361, 362, 364, 372, 381, 386, 388, 391, 393, 397, 399

Language Skills

Adjectives, 13
Clauses, 120, 230
   dependent, 120, 172, 230, 311
   independent, 99, 120, 157, 245, 311
   nonrestrictive, 230
   parallel, 13
   relative, 230
   restrictive, 230
   transitional, 172
Conditional mood, 24
Conjunctions
   coordinating, 120, 157, 245
   correlative, 13
   subordinating, 120
Conjunctive adverbs, 181
Gerunds, 132, 305
Homonyms, 283, 289
Imperative mood, 24
Indicative mood, 24
Infinitives, 132, 305
Parallel structure, 13, 14, 15, 31, 41, 52, 76, 131, 135, 172, 256
Participles, 132, 305
Passive voice, 69, 269
Phrases
   noun, 13
   parallel, 13
   prepositional, 41, 191, 198, 311
Precise language, 301
Prepositions, 191
Present tense, 241
Pronouns
   reciprocal, 37, 114
   relative, 230

Punctuation
   comma, 157
   as cues for vocal delivery, 361
   dashes, 10, 11
   dialogue, 116
   in poetry, 310, 330
   question marks, 310, 356
   quotation marks, 28, 29, 201, 248
   semicolons, 11, 99, 157
Questions
   follow-up, 53, 58
   open-ended, 28, 29, 32, 33, 43, 52
Quotations
   direct, 28, 29, 43, 56, 88, 103, 210, 218
   indirect, 28
Sentences
   combining, 157, 245
   complex, 157
   compound, 11, 157, 245
   fragments, 40, 99
   structure, 99
   TAG sentence system, 298
   variety in, 338
Subjunctive mood, 18
Synonyms, 289
Syntax, 99
Transitions, 27, 38, 48, 103, 138, 172, 248, 262, 312, 419, 425, 431
Verbals, 132, 305, 309
Verbs
   mood of, 18, 24
   subjunctive, 18
   tenses, 241, 269, 302
Voice
   active, 69, 269
   inappropriate shifts in, 69
   passive, 69, 269

Vocabulary Skills

Academic Vocabulary, 2, 4, 6, 49, 62, 110, 184, 186, 187, 197, 201, 207, 211, 214, 221, 267, 276, 278, 309, 331, 342, 350, 361, 402, 420, 431
Analogies, 144
Connotation, 23, 25, 27, 86, 153, 330
Content connections, 192, 296, 306, 310
Denotation, 25, 101
Diffusing, 126, 131, 137, 359
Etymology, 11, 17, 123, 132, 313, 408
Graphic representations, 290
Multiple-meaning words, 116, 195, 222, 283, 306
Personal Poetry Glossary, 290, 291–292
Personal thesaurus, 289
QHT chart, 4, 141, 186, 221, 278, 290, 352, 402
Roots and affixes, 6, 97, 127, 194, 203, 257, 265, 268, 353, 388, 393
Word connections, 281, 356

Index of Authors and Titles

Credits

"Spotlight" from *Speak* by Laurie Halse Anderson. Copyright © 1999 by Laurie Halse Anderson. Reprinted by permission of Farrar, Straus and Giroux, LLC.

"Marigolds" by Eugenia Collier. Originally published in *Negro Digest*, November 1969. Reappeared in *Breeder and Other Stories* by Eugenia Collier, Black Classic Press, 1994. Used by permission of the author.

From *Always Running—La Vida Loca, Gang Days in L.A.* by Luis J. Rodriguez. (Curbstone Press, 1993) Reprinted with permission of Curbstone Press. Distributed by Consortium.

"'Race' Politics" from *Poems Across the Pavement* by Luis J. Rodriguez. Copyright © 1998 by Luis J. Rodriguez. Published by Tia Chucha Press. By permission of Susan Bergholz Literary Services, New York, NY and Lamy, NM. All rights reserved.

"WMDs" by Brian O'Connor *Men's Fitness*. Copyright © Weider Publications, LLC, a subsidiary of American Media, Inc. All rights reserved.

"Chuck Liddell" by Steve Yaccino *U.S. News & World Report* (August 21, 2008). Copyright © 2008 U. S. News & World Report LP.

"An Early Start on College" from *Minneapolis Star Tribune* (January 14, 2012). Copyright © 2012 StarTribune.

"Why College Isn't (And Shouldn't Have to Be) For Everyone" by Robert Reich, *Huffington Post* (April 9, 2012). Copyright © 2012 Bloomberg L.P.

"Actually, College Is Very Much Worth It" by Andrew J. Rotherham *TIME* (May 19, 2011). Copyright © 2011 Time Inc.

"The Stolen Party" by Liliana Heker © 1982, which appeared in *Other Fires: Short Fiction by Latin American Women*, edited and translated by Alberto Manguel © 1985. Reprinted by permission of Westwood Creative Artists Ltd.

From *Charlie and the Chocolate Factory* by Roald Dahl, copyright © 1964, renewed 1992 by Roald Dahl Nominee Limited. Used by permission of Alfred A. Knopf, an imprint of Random House Children's Books, a division of Random House, Inc.

"Jim Crow: Shorthand for Separation" by Rick Edmonds. Reproduced from *Forum*, the magazine of the Florida Humanities Council, an affiliate of the National Endowment for the Humanities.

"Letter from Birmingham Jail" by Martin Luther King, Jr. Reprinted by arrangement with The Heirs to the Estate of Martin Luther King, Jr. c/o Writers House as agent for the proprietor New York, NY. Copyright 1963 Dr. Martin Luther King, Jr.; copyright renewed 1991 Coretta Scott King.

"Civil Rights Timeline" from CNN.com. Copyright © 2007 Cable News Network.

From *Scout, Atticus & Boo: A Celebration of* To Kill a Mockingbird by Mary McDonagh Murphy. Copyright © 2010 by Mary McDonagh Murphy. HarperCollins Publishers.

From *To Kill a Mockingbird* by Harper Lee. Copyright © 1960 by Harper Lee. Foreword copyright © 1993 by Harper Lee. Reprinted by permission of HarperCollins Publishers.

From "In Defense of *To Kill a Mockingbird*" by Nicholas J. Karolides, Lee Burress, and John M. Keam, 1993, Scarecrow Press. Used by permission.

"Poetry" from *Selected Poems of Pablo Neruda*, translated by Alastair Reid, edited by Nathaniel Tarn and published by Jonathan Cape. Reprinted by permission of The Random House Group Ltd.

From *poemcrazy* by Susan G. Wooldridge, copyright © 1996 Susan G. Wooldridge. Used by permission of Crown Publishers, a division of Random House, Inc.

"Nikki-Rosa" from *Black Feeling, Black Talk, Black Judgment* by Nikki Giovanni. Copyright © 1968, 1970 by Nikki Giovanni. Reproduced by permission of HarperCollins Publishers.

"We Real Cool" by Gwendolyn Brooks. Reprinted by consent of Brooks Permissions.

"Fast Break" from *Wild Gratitude* by Edward Hirsch, copyright © 1985 by Edward Hirsch. Used by permission of Alfred A. Knopf, a division of Random House, Inc.

"Identity" by Julio Noboa Polanco. Used by permission of the author.

"Ego Tripping" from The Selected Poems of Nikki Giovanni by Nikki Giovanni. Compilation copyright © 1996 by Nikki Giovanni. Reproduced by permission of HarperCollins Publishers.

"Hanging Fire" from *The Collected Poems of Audre Lorde* by Audre Lorde. Copyright © 1978 by Audre Lorde. Used by permission of W. W. Norton & Company, Inc.

"Ode to My Socks" from *Full Woman, Fleshly Apple, Hot Moon: Selected Poetry of Pablo Neruda* by Pablo Neruda, translated by Robert Bly. Translation copyright © 1997 by Stephen Mitchell. Reproduced by permission of HarperCollins Publishers.

"Abuelito Who" from *My Wicked Wicked Ways* by Sandra Cisneros. Copyright © 1987 by Sandra Cisneros. Published by Third Woman Press and in hardcover by Alfred A. Knopf. By permission of Susan Bergholz Literary Services, New York, NY and Lamy, NM. All rights reserved.

"In Response to Executive Order 9066" by Dwight Okita. Used by permission.

"Young" by Anne Sexton from *All My Pretty Ones*. Copyright © 1962 by Anne Sexton. Reproduced by permission of SSL/Sterling Lord Literistic, Inc.

"Combing" by Gladys Cardiff from *Puget Soundings*, March 1971. Used by permission of Gladys Cardiff.

"Harlem" from *The Collected Poems of Langston Hughes* by Langston Hughes, edited by Arnold Rampersad with David Roessel, Associate Editor, copyright © 1994 by the Estate of Langston Hughes. Used by permission of Alfred A. Knopf, a division of Random House, Inc.

"'Hope' Is the Thing with Feathers" by Emily Dickinson from *The Poems of Emily Dickinson*, edited by R. W. Franklin. Copyright © 1999 Harvard University Press.

"Scars" from *Selected Poems by Daniel Halpern*, copyright © 1994 by Daniel Halpern. Used by permission of Alfred A. Knopf, a division of Random House, Inc.

"American Hero," copyright © 1992 Essex Hemphill from *Ceremonies*. Reprinted by permission of The Frances Goldin Literary Agency.

"Prayer to the Pacific" from *Storyteller* by Leslie Marmon Silko. 2d ed. New York: Penguin, 2012.

"In Cold Storm Light" from *Storyteller* by Leslie Marmon Silko. 2d ed. New York: Penguin, 2012.

From *West Side Story* by Arthur Laurents, Leonard Bernstein, Stephen Sondheim, and Jerome Robbins. Copyright © 1956. Reprinted by permission of Random House, Inc.

"On the Bard's Birthday, Is Shakespeare Still Relevant?" by Alexandra Petri *The Washington Post* (April 23, 2012). Copyright © 2012 The Washington Post.

"Britain Puts on a Shakespeare Marathon as World Arrives for the Olympic Games" by Jill Lawless *The Washington Post* (July 19, 2012). Reprinted from the Associated Press copyright © 2012.

"On Love and War, Iraq Learns from Shakespeare" by Shelina Zahra Janmohamed *The Daily Star* (July 24, 2012). Copyright © The Daily Star.

From *How Shakespeare Changed Eveything* by Stephen Marche. Copyright © 2011 by Stephen Marche. HarperCollins Publishers.

"Kentucky Inmates Turned Actors Explore Selves Through Shakespeare Play" by Sean Rose The Courier-Journal (June 15, 2012). Copyright © 2012 Courier-Journal.

"Why it's time to give the Bard the heave ho!" by Brandon Robshaw *The Independent* (April 24, 2008). Copyright © 2008 independent.co.uk.

Image Credits

Cover: Jill Ferry/Getty Images

1 © Aurora/Aurora Photo/Corbis; 17 CHAIWATPHOTOS/ Shutterstock; 34 TSpider/ Shutterstock; 85 Wyatt Rivard/Shutterstock; 103 Zvonimir Atletic/ Shutterstock; 111 dslaven/ Shutterstock; 122 Junede/Shutterstock; 122 Carnival at the Theatre of S. Gallo and S. Benedetto, 1856 (coloured litho) / Museo Correr, Venice, Italy / Bridgeman Images; 169 Bettmann/Corbis; 251 Inga Dudkina/ Shutterstock; 256 Lipskiy/ Shutterstock; 260 Microstock Man/Shutterstock; 262 NataLT/Shutterstock; 271 Samuel Borges Photography/Shutterstock; 275 The Sum of Recollections, 2002 (oil on panel), Riches, Lizzie (b.1950) / Private Collection / © Portal Painters / Bridgeman Images; 276 Luis Louro/Shutterstock; 282 Milkovasa/Shutterstock; 297 Emily L. Ainsley Fund © Gwendolyn Knight Lawrence, courtesy of the Jacob and Gwendolyn Lawrence Foundation; 298 swissmacky/ Shutterstock; 299 Jill Battaglia/Shutterstock; 301 lzf/ Shutterstock; 302 Vlue/Shutterstock; 306 Bill McKelvie/ Shutterstock; 310 Eugene Ivanov/Shutterstock; 317 Natalia Bratslavsky/Shutterstock; 325 imageZebra/ Shutterstock; 334 Ivelin Radkov/Shutterstock; 344 Shkvarko/Shutterstock; 347 Andre Adams/ Shutterstock; 373 Stocksnapper/Shutterstock; 377 Jon Naustdalslid/Shutterstock; 378 WEST SIDE STORY de JeromeRobbins et RobertWise avec Richard Beymer et Natalie Wood 1961 / Bridgeman Images; 379 GERSHBERG Yuri/Shutterstock; 379 Jon Naustdalslid/ Shuttershock; 395 s_bukley/Shutterstock; 398 Ljupco Smokovski/Shutterstock; 382 (c) lineartestpilot;